TERRITORIAL STATUS IN INTERNATIONAL LAW

This book develops a new theory of territorialism and international legal status of territories. It (i) defines the concept of territory, explaining how territories are created; (ii) redefines the concept of statehood, illustrating that statehood (rather than the statehood criteria) is territorial legal status established in the formal sources of international law; and (iii) grounds non-state territorial entities in the sources of international law to explain their international legal status. This fresh new theoretical perspective has both scholarly and practical importance, providing a tool to help decision-makers and judges in the practical application of international law both internationally and domestically.

Volume 91 in the series Studies in International Law

Studies in International Law

Recent titles in this series

Human Rights Commitments of Islamic States: Sharia, Treaties and Consensus
Paul McDonough

Intervention in Civil Wars: Effectiveness, Legitimacy, and Human Rights
Chiara Redaelli

General Principles as a Source of International Law: Art 38(1)(c) of the Statute of the International Court of Justice
Imogen Saunders

The Law of Humanity Project: A Story of International Law Reform and State-making
Ukri Soirila

Extraterritoriality and Climate Change Jurisdiction: Exploring EU Climate Protection under International Law
Natalie L Dobson

International Law and the War with Islamic State: Challenges for Jus ad Bellum and Jus in Bello
Saeed Bagheri

Private Actors as Participants in International Law: A Critical Analysis of Membership under the Law of the Sea
Armando Rocha

Truth and Transitional Justice: Localising the International Legal Framework in Muslim Majority Legal Systems
Alice Panepinto

State Responsibility for Non-State Actors: Past, Present and Prospects for the Future
Richard Mackenzie-Gray Scott

International Agreements between Non-State Actors as a Source of International Law
Melissa Loja

Judicial Decisions in International Law Argumentation: Between Entrapment and Creativity
Letizia Lo Giacco

South-South Migrations and the Law from Below: Case Studies on China and Nigeria
Oreva Olakpe

Territorial Status in International Law
Jure Vidmar

For a complete list of titles in this series
see www.bloomsbury.com/uk/series/studies-in-international-law/

Territorial Status in International Law

Jure Vidmar

•HART•
OXFORD • LONDON • NEW YORK • NEW DELHI • SYDNEY

HART PUBLISHING

Bloomsbury Publishing Plc

Kemp House, Chawley Park, Cumnor Hill, Oxford, OX2 9PH, UK

1385 Broadway, New York, NY 10018, USA

29 Earlsfort Terrace, Dublin 2, Ireland

First published in Great Britain 2024

A catalogue record for this book is available from the British Library.

A catalogue record for this book is available from the Library of Congress.

Library of Congress Control Number: 2023947946

ISBN: HB: 978-1-50995-948-8
ePDF: 978-1-50995-950-1
ePub: 978-1-50995-949-5

Typeset by Compuscript Ltd, Shannon

To find out more about our authors and books visit www.hartpublishing.co.uk. Here you will find extracts, author information, details of forthcoming events and the option to sign up for our newsletters.

Preface

OVER THE PAST years at Maastricht University, I have had the immense privilege of supervising several excellent emerging scholars and doctoral projects in international law. Discussions with doctoral students also helped me clarify my own thoughts on certain difficult conceptual questions of our discipline, and strengthen several arguments presented in this book. I am particularly indebted to Dr Leoni Ayoub, Dr Craig Eggett, Dr Lucia Leontiev, Dr Sarah McGibbon, Dr Remy Jorritsma, Dr Sarah Thin, Dr Laura Visser and Dr Liang Yu for giving me many excellent ideas, and showing me new ways of thinking about international law. I am grateful to Andrés H. Cáceres-Solari for his excellent research assistance, complemented by his ability to work to very strict deadlines. I also benefited greatly from the participants of the International Law Discussion Group at Maastricht, and from my present and former colleagues, in particular Dr Lea Raible, Dr Wim Muller and Dr Jennifer Sellin, with whom I frequently discussed territoriality in international law. My wife, Dr Rebekah Ahrendt, helped me shape my initial ideas on the topic and gave me very valuable feedback on several arguments articulated in this book. I also greatly benefitted from Rebekah's superb skills in navigating the library catalogues and databases. And she sympathetically supported me through the many late evenings I spent behind the computer finalising this book.

As far as possible, the book is accurate as of 1 June 2023.

Jure Vidmar
Maastricht, 31 August 2023

Contents

Acronyms

ARIO	Articles on Responsibility of International Organizations
ARSIWA	Articles on the Responsibility of States for Internationally Wrongful Acts
CJEU	Court of Justice of the European Union
ECHR	European Convention on Human Rights
ECtHR	European Court of Human Rights
EU	European Union
FRY	Federal Republic of Yugoslavia
GCIV	Fourth Geneva Convention
GCEU	General Court of the European Union
IAC	International armed conflict
ICC	International Criminal Court
ICCPR	International Covenant on Civil and Political Rights
ICESCR	International Covenant on Economic, Social and Cultural Rights
ICJ	International Court of Justice
ICTY	International Criminal Tribunal for the former Yugoslavia
IHL	International Humanitarian Law
ILC	International Law Commission
ISIL	Islamic State of Iraq and the Levant
ISIS	Islamic State of Iraq and Syria
NATO	North Atlantic Treaty Organization
NIAC	Non-international armed conflict
PCIJ	Permanent Court of International Justice
SADR	Sahrawi Arab Democratic Republic
SFRY	Socialist Federal Republic of Yugoslavia

TEU	Treaty on European Union
TFEU	Treaty on the Functioning of the European Union
TRNC	Turkish Republic of Northern Cyprus
UN	United Nations
UNESCO	United Nations Educational, Scientific and Cultural Organization
VCDR	Vienna Convention on Diplomatic Relations
VCLT	Vienna Convention on the Law of Treaties
WTO	World Trade Organization

Table of Cases

International Court of Justice

European Court of Human Rights

Other International Courts

Table of Treaties and Statutes

United Nations Treaty Series

League of Nations Treaty Series

Other Treaties

National Statutes

EU Regulation

Table of UN Documents

UN General Assembly Resolutions

UN Security Council Resolutions

Other UN Documents

1

Introduction

I. INTRODUCTION

THE SYSTEM OF international law is inherently territorial in nature.[1] This is because international law predominantly regulates relations between states, and states are presumed to have a territory.[2] The presumption also works in the other direction: contemporary rules of international law presume – or are at least commonly interpreted as if they presumed – that an inhabited territory needs to have a state.[3] Because of the close-knit territory–state relationship,[4] the whole structure of the international legal system falls apart when the legal status of a territory is ambiguous.[5] It is unclear which rules of international law are applicable – how and to whom should they apply – when it is impossible to objectively determine whether a territory forms a separate state or is a part of another state,[6] or if it is not entirely clear whether a territory has a state,[7] or when a territory's special status is acknowledged in practice though not necessarily in law.[8]

[1] Dino Kritsiotis, 'Public International Law and Its Territorial Imperative' (2009) 30 *Michigan Journal of International Law* 547.

[2] Chandran Kukathas, 'A Definition of the State' (2014) 33(2) *University of Queensland Law Journal* 357; Frederick Tse-shyang Chen, 'The Meaning of "States" in the Membership Provisions of the United Nations Charter' (2001) 12 *Indiana International Comparative Law Review* 25.

[3] Mark A Smith, 'Sovereignty over Unoccupied Territories – The Western Sahara Decision' (1977) 9 *Case Western Reserve Journal of International Law* 135.

[4] Malcolm Shaw, 'Peoples, Territorialism and Boundaries' (1997) 8(3) *European Journal of International Law* 478; Saskia Sassen, *Territory, Authority, Rights: From Medieval to Global Assemblages* (Princeton 2006); Stuart Elden, *The Birth of a Territory* (Chicago 2013).

[5] Anthony d'Amato, 'Purposeful Ambiguity as International Legal Strategy: The Two China Problem' in Jerzy Makarczyk (ed), *Theory of International Law at the Threshold of the 21st Century* (Brill 1997).

[6] Milena Sterio, 'The Case of Kosovo: Self-Determination, Secession, and Statehood Under International Law' (2010) 104 *Proceedings of the Annual Meeting (American Society of International Law* 361.

[7] Winston P Nagan, and Alitza M Haddad, 'Recognition of Palestinian Statehood: A Clarification of the Interests of the Concerned Parties' (2012) 40 *Georgia Journal of International & Comparative Law* 343.

[8] Lung-chu Chen, 'Taiwan's Current International Legal Status' (1998) 689 *Articles & Chapters*, 675–83.

To illustrate: while most scholars and governments would agree that Taiwan is not a state,[9] it does have some kind of international legal status.[10] But what exactly is this status, from where does it derive, and do the international legal rules prohibiting the use of force between states apply in relations between mainland China and Taiwan?[11] More than half of all states recognise Kosovo as a state.[12] But is it a state?[13] Does it have statehood for some states but not others?[14] Do Serbia, China and Russia, for example, need to treat Kosovo as a state? Palestine has acceded to certain international treaties as the *State* of Palestine.[15] It is thus a state for the purposes of these treaties.[16] But does this also mean that the State of Palestine actually has statehood? Does the State of Palestine have a territory in the sense of international law; and does the Palestinian territory have a state?[17] These are some difficult contemporary questions that vex international and domestic courts, governments and scholars.[18]

According to one well-known scholarly observation, 'the international legal status of most States most of the time is not in dispute'.[19] It appears that scholarship has too easily learned to live with this situation. As accurate as the observation may be, it also reveals a gap in the existing theories of statehood, territory and legal status – a gap that has never been adequately addressed. Why is it possible that ambiguous territorial situations exist under international law? Why is it possible that the legal status of a territory is not always clear? This book argues that the reason such ambiguities to exist and persist is that international legal doctrine has misconceived the concept of statehood, failed to properly theorise the notion of territory, and failed to define the legal status of non-state territories.[20]

The overall aim of this book is to develop a new theory of international legal status of territories: a theory that does not fail in difficult or marginal examples and explains ambiguities.

[9] James Crawford, *The Creation of States in International Law* (OUP 2006); PCW Chan, 'The Legal Status of Taiwan and the Legality of the Use of Force in a Cross-Taiwan Strait Conflict' (2010) 8 *Chinese Journal of International Law* 455; D'Amato (n 5) 109–21.

[10] Chen (n 8) 675–83.

[11] Quoc Tan Trung Nguyen, 'Does International Law Protect Taiwan?' (2022) 2(14) *United States Asia Law Institute Perspectives* 2.

[12] Sterio (n 6) 361–65.

[13] ibid, 361–65.

[14] Edward Newman and Gëzim Visoka, 'The Foreign Policy of State Recognition: Kosovo's Diplomatic Strategy' (2018) 14 *Foreign Policy Analysis* 367.

[15] Situation in the State of Palestine (2020) ICC, Pre-Trial Chamber I, ICC-01/18.

[16] Nagan and Haddad (n 7) 343–421.

[17] Steven Kay and Joshua Kern, 'The Statehood of Palestine and Its Effect on the Exercise of ICC Jurisdiction' (*Opinio Juris*, 5 July 2019), opiniojuris.org/2019/07/05/the-statehood-of-palestine-and-its-effect-on-the-exercise-of-icc-jurisdiction%EF%BB%BF, accessed 15 December 2022.

[18] ibid.

[19] Crawford (n 9) 98.

[20] ibid.

The book argues that the concepts of territory, statehood and non-state territories have been misconceptualised in contemporary international law because: (i) existing theories are too focused on the statehood criteria rather than statehood itself; (ii) it remains unclear what kind of legal persons states are; (iii) territorialism in international law has been too influenced by dated pre-United Nations (UN) Charter concepts; (iv) scholars have tried to explain the creation and alteration of legal status of territories by either overtly legalising or overtly politicising the process; (v) legal status is sometimes only explained retroactively through the methodologically questionable approach of reading history backwards; (vi) the recent focus on the legal capacity of non-state actors has blurred the picture and established an incorrect state/non-state dichotomy; and (vii) scholars have created several non-legal terms of art to explain the existence and functioning of non-state territorial entities which create more problems than they solve.

II. STATE OF THE ART

A. Mistaken Focus on the Statehood Criteria

Contemporary theories are predicated on the concept of the statehood criteria, which stem from the 1933 Montevideo Convention on the Rights and Duties of States. Article 1 of the Convention provides that: 'A State as a person of international law shall possess the following characteristics: a) a permanent population; b) a defined territory; c) government; and d) capacity to enter into relations with the other states.'[21] It is the predominant view that these criteria form a part of customary international law.

The statehood criteria draw heavily on late nineteenth-century Austro-German legal positivism. In his seminal work *Allgemeine Staatslehre*, which preceded the Montevideo Convention by three decades, Georg Jellinek conceptualised the state as *Land, Volk und Herrscher*, ie Land, People and Ruler.[22] Jellinek presumes that once these criteria have been met, a state exists virtually as a natural person.[23] This is a reflection of what Stephen Neff calls the nineteenth-century positivist perception of 'the real personality of the state'.[24] Statehood rests on the notion of effectiveness of a government over a certain territory and the population inhabiting that territory. As such, the Jellinek/Montevideo understanding reflects Max Weber's sociological definition of a

[21] Montevideo Convention on the Rights and Duties of States of 1933 (adopted 26 December 1933, entered into force 26 December 1934) 165 LNTS 19 (Montevideo Convention), art 1.

[22] Georg Jellinek, *Allgemeine Staatslehre* (O Häring 1905).

[23] ibid.

[24] Stephen Neff, 'The Dormancy, Rise and Decline of Fundamental Liberties of States' (2016) 4 *Cambridge Journal of International and Comparative Law* 482.

state as a 'human community that (successfully) claims the monopoly of the legitimate use of physical force within a given territory'.[25] But does this definition normatively define statehood or merely describe the consequences of it?

It is certainly the case that most states meet the statehood criteria most of the time. But the more important question is whether they are states because they meet the statehood criteria or whether they meet the statehood criteria because they are states. It appears that contemporary theories of statehood adopt the former view, while this book develops an argument that it is actually the latter. This book seeks to show that the erroneous causal link between the Montevideo criteria and statehood has led to several misconceptions about the nature of statehood, the notion of legal status, and the concept of territory under international law. The so-called statehood criteria are in fact not criteria for statehood; the fact that most states meet them is a consequence of their statehood. Statehood is created outside of the Montevideo formula.

To be sure, the Montevideo statehood criteria have already been subject to much criticism. But criticism has either diagnosed some problems without fixing them or prescribed misguided cures. It is commonly said that the statehood criteria are at the same time too inclusive and too exclusive.[26] In practice, that means that sometimes non-states meet them and sometimes states do not meet them. In response, some theorists have tried to reconcile the statehood criteria and the fact that states are in reality created outside of the Montevideo formula. For instance, Hersch Lauterpacht proposed that once the Montevideo criteria are met, foreign states have a duty to grant recognition to the territorial entity and thus create its statehood.[27] This view is problematic as such a duty has never been established through the formal sources of law. Recognition remains at discretion of states. In some circumstances, states may be under an obligation to withhold it, but they never are under an obligation to grant recognition. Another attempt to solve the inadequacy of Montevideo is James Crawford's expansion of the list of the statehood criteria with additional ones.[28] This proposition is based on the particular experience of Southern Rhodesia and still assumes that states emerge upon meeting the statehood criteria, except that the list of criteria may be longer than the classical 'Montevideo Four'. This Montevideo-plus theory still cannot explain why Somaliland[29] is not a state and what might be the legal statuses of Kosovo[30] and Palestine.[31]

[25] Max Weber, *Basic Concepts in Sociology* (Citadel 1964).

[26] Patrick Dumberry, 'Remarks by Patrick Dumberry' (2013) 107 *Proceedings of Annual Meeting of the American Society of International Law* 213.

[27] Hersch Lauterpacht, *Recognition in International Law* (first published 1947, CUP 2013).

[28] Crawford (n 9) 109–21.

[29] Temesgen Sisay Beyene, 'Declaration of Statehood by Somaliland and the Effects of Non-Recognition under International Law' (2019) 10(1) *Beijing Law Review* 196.

[30] Sterio (n 6) 361–65.

[31] Nagan and Haddad (n 7) 343–421.

The statehood criteria have attracted much focus in international legal scholarship, sometimes as Montevideo pure, sometimes as Montevideo-plus and sometimes in combination with an external act of recognition. Yet, surprisingly little has been said in international legal theory about what statehood *is*, ie statehood independent of a (check)list of criteria, or statehood as a theoretical concept of international law. The lack of such theoretical clarity has wider consequences. It is not only the concept of statehood that remains unexplained theoretically, but also the status of contested territorial entities. In other words, the lack of clarity on what a state is also results in a lack of clarity on what a state *is not*, and what other forms of territorial legal status contemporary international law may support.

The fact that sometimes the legal status of certain territories is unclear leads to several difficult conceptual problems in contemporary international law, often with severe practical consequences. If a treaty provides that it is 'open to states', can entities with an ambiguous legal status become parties to that treaty, and what does it mean for their legal status if they do? Can entities with an ambiguous legal status incur international responsibility under the law of state responsibility? If the use of force in the sense of UN Charter is predicated on force being used by one state against another state, is the 'use of force' by or against an entity with ambiguous legal status even a use of force in the sense of international law?[32] Finally, if a certain territorial unit is not itself a state and does not formally belong to another state, what actually is its legal status under international law? Apart from Antarctica, does contemporary international law allow the existence of non-state territories or does it actually require that all land on Earth needs to be divided between state territories (consider the complicated status of Palestine)?[33] This book develops theoretical tools to solve these practical questions.

B. Natural or Legal Personality?

The conceptual and terminological confusion pertaining to states and statehood has its roots in the nature and structure of international law, and the theoretical constructions of international legal personality, legal status and territorialism. In other words, the confusion in the law of statehood is a symptom of a larger problem that goes back to a lack of understanding of what a person of international law is, and what its relationships are with the concepts of territory and legal status.

Indeed, it remains unsettled in international legal theory whether states are natural or legal persons. It is therefore unsurprising that theorists and

[32] Nguyen (n 11) 2–4.
[33] Nagan and Haddad (n 7) 343–421.

practitioners continue to have fundamentally divergent views on what a state is and how it comes into being. The natural person school, often followed by German positivist scholars, sees states as analogous to humans in a domestic setting.[34] They claim that states are born the way children are born, and birth happens on meeting the formal statehood criteria. Recognition by other states, however, issues a birth certificate.[35] Following this analogy, lacking a birth certificate may cause significant problems for a human being in their social life, but a human being exists naturally regardless of whether the birth certificate has been properly issued. According to the natural personality theory in international law, the same happens with states. States start to exist naturally once they meet the statehood criteria. A state that remains non-recognised may have significant problems with functioning in the international community, but it still is a state.[36]

Even in positivist scholarship, the natural personality theory has not been unanimously accepted and the counterargument is that states are not themselves natural persons but rather 'associations of natural persons'.[37] Lauterpacht furthermore argued that the adherents of natural personality theory presuppose that fulfilment of the Montevideo criteria is 'self-evident'. We are then forced to accept the rather awkward proposition that 'a State exists in international law as soon as it exists'.[38] This represents the prevailing, albeit not the only, view in contemporary scholarship that states are legal persons. The legal persons theory may indeed be the more sustainable perspective, but it still does not solve the puzzle entirely.

While the predominant understanding may now be that states are legal rather than natural persons,[39] the consequences of this determination have not been systemically accommodated within the sources of international law. Since states are not naturally born creatures but international legal constructs, it needs to be asked and answered *where* states are grounded in international law. If one rejects the natural or even metaphysical theories according to which states are treated as creatures of nature rather than law, this also has certain consequences for the law that governs the emergence and existence of states. It appears that most scholars have rejected the natural statehood theory, but remain attached to some of its underlying postulates, such as the so-called statehood criteria.[40] If statehood is not naturally created, it needs to be grounded as a legal status in the sources of international law, as enumerated in Article 38(1)

[34] Lassa Oppenheim, *International Law* (Longmans 1905); Stefan Talmon, *Kollektive Nichtanerkennung illegaler Staaten* (Mohr 2006).
[35] Talmon (n 34).
[36] ibid.
[37] Lauterpacht (n 27).
[38] ibid.
[39] Jean d'Aspremont, 'The Doctrine of Fundamental Rights of States and Anthropomorphic Thinking in International Law' (2015) 4 *Cambridge Journal of International and Comparative Law* 501.
[40] Shaw (n 4); Rowan Nicholson, *Statehood and the State-Like in International Law* (OUP 2019).

of the International Court of Justice (ICJ) Statute.[41] This has not been properly clarified in international legal theory. Scholarship has failed to explain where states and international legal status more broadly come from if they are not naturally born but legally created.

Looking at international practice, it can be said that sometimes states are created by international treaties.[42] In other examples, the existence of a state is accepted by other states in a less explicit way, but in practice states clearly indicate that they accept a certain entity as a separate state. The approach is evidently the same as that of the formation of the rules of customary international law, which requires a uniform – although not universal – state practice and *opinio juris*. Statehood is thus quite simply customary status under international law. While the prevailing doctrinal view is that the statehood criteria form a part of customary international law, it is rather that statehood itself is a legal status under customary international law.

This book conceptualises statehood anew, normatively defining the legal status of a territory under customary international law. This book thus seeks to develop a new theory of statehood as legal status of a territory. This new normative concept is the missing link that will allow a sustainable theoretical explanation not only of what states are and how they emerge, but also why sometimes they do not emerge. It will also eliminate ambiguity regarding the legal status of contested territorial entities.[43] The new theory of statehood offered by this book would also be the final nail in the coffin of the untenable natural statehood theory. Although predominantly rejected in contemporary scholarship and practice, the natural statehood theory has remained subtly present through the exaggerated focus on the statehood criteria rather than statehood as legal status.

C. The Notion of Territorialism is Influenced by Dated Historic Concepts

As noted above, the so-called Montevideo criteria draw from late nineteenth-century theoretical writings according to which a state simply needed a territory, a population and a ruler. This was also a time when international law still accepted colonialism and conquest as valid modes of territorial acquisition, while statehood was with some exceptions limited to the political entities in Europe and those created by European settlers elsewhere.[44] Self-determination is today a collective human right. While the exact normative scope of the right

[41] Statute of the International Court of Justice of 1945 (ICJ Statute), art 38.1.

[42] The Lateran Treaty of 1929 (entered into force 7 June 1929) 130 BFSP 791; State Treaty for the Re-establishment of an Independent and Democratic Austria (adopted 15 May 1955, entered into force 27 July 1955) 217 UNTS 223 (Austrian State Treaty).

[43] Sterio (n 6) 361–65; Nagan and Haddad (n 7).

[44] Antony Anghie, 'The Evolution of International Law: Colonial and Postcolonial Realities' (2006) 27 *Third World Quarterly* 739.

of self-determination remains somewhat controversial, it is settled that colonialism is prohibited and most colonial territories have been given an opportunity to choose independence.[45] While some colonial territories still exist against the wishes of their people,[46] these territorial situations are considered to be illegal under international law. New territorial conquest is prohibited and forceful change of territorial control considered to be illegal, even if in principle supported by local population.[47]

Existing legal doctrines and theories governing territorialism and legal status do not reflect these changes. Doctrinal writings discussing the concept of territory in international law still refer to the notions of discovery, conquest and cession. These notions are no longer compatible with the modern rules of international law. Conquest is prohibited by the UN Charter rules, while so-called discovery and cession are incompatible with the right of self-determination.[48] Yet, the theory of territorialism and legal status of a territory has never been systemically updated according to post-World War II rules of international law.

International law has been grappling with the decades – if not centuries – long great debate on whether recognition of states is a constitutive or a declaratory legal act.[49] While it recently appeared that the declaratory theory of recognition had won the great debate,[50] the international legal reactions to Kosovo's declaration of independence revived some constitutive voices.[51] However, it may well be that recognition in contemporary international law is neither declaratory nor constitutive. This is because in a world without *terrae nullius* and outside of the process of decolonisation, the legal status of a territory can be altered only at the expense of an existing state's territory and its territorial integrity. Modern practice instead suggests that the effects of recognition crucially depend on the underlying territorial situation and the legal status of the spatial area in which a new state is emerging. The great constitutive versus declaratory debate is therefore yet another anachronism in international law, developed in the times when territorialism and legal status were subjected to quite different rules than those in existence today. The legal effects of recognition need to be reconceptualised

[45] Robert McCorquodale, 'Self-Determination: A Human Rights Approach' (1994) 43 *International and Comparative Law Quarterly* 857.

[46] *Legal Consequences of the Separation of the Chagos Archipelago from Mauritius in 1965* (Advisory Opinion) General List No 169 (2019) ICJ.

[47] Jure Vidmar, 'The Annexation of Crimea and the Boundaries of the Will of the People' (2014) 16 *German Law Journal* 365.

[48] Anne Peters, 'Statehood after 1989: "Effectivites" between Legality and Virtuality' (2010) 3 *Proceedings of the European Society of International Law*.

[49] Stefan Talmon, 'The Constitutive Versus the Declaratory Theory of Recognition: Tertium non Datur?' (2005) 75(1) *British Yearbook of International Law* 101.

[50] Joshua Downer, 'Towards a Declaratory School of Government Recognition' (2021) 46 *Vanderbilt Law Review* 581.

[51] Colin Warbrick, 'Kosovo: The Declaration of Independence' (2008) 57(3) *International and Comparative Law Quarterly* 675.

in light of fundamental changes in the post-World War II international law. This book will thus argue that the whole concept of recognition theories has been misplaced. If statehood is defined as customary status under international law, recognition may well be nothing other than expression of *opinio juris*.

D. Over-legalised and Over-politicised Approaches

The confusion regarding the limits of international law in the process of creation and alteration of territorial status has led to two extreme approaches. Scholars and governments often try to either over-legalise or over-politicise the concept of territorial status. The over-legalised extreme is the attempt to explain the whole process by legal rules alone, discussed above. Such an argument would be that Kosovo is not a state because it does not completely fulfil the statehood criteria.[52] In the other extreme, it is often claimed that altering territorial status is all about power politics and that international law does not even matter.[53] In this view, Kosovo and Crimea are similar situations, except that the actors that exercised their political (super)powers were different. While power politics may well have been at work in both instances, Kosovo and Crimea are quite different situations in law. The relationship between law and politics needs to be rethought in this context. Keeping in mind that one is not dealing with natural persons here, but with inherently legal constructs; it thus needs to be asked how legal status is realised under international law.

By domestic law analogy, a corporation does not mysteriously incorporate itself and start to exist as soon as it exists, to paraphrase Lauterpacht.[54] If one rejects the theory of natural personality of states in international law, it also needs to be acknowledged that international legal status is not created by virtue of self-executing legal procedures under the law of statehood. It is rather a political development that creates a new legal status. The creation and alteration of legal status in international law is an extra-legal decision with legal consequences, much like establishing a corporation under domestic corporate law is a social or business decision to create a new legal person with a particular legal status. It is thus important that the relationship between law and politics regulating this subject matter is both properly acknowledged and properly delimited. This book thus defines statehood as a politically created legal status under customary international law.

[52] Alexander Orakhelashvili, 'Statehood, Recognition and the United Nations System: A Unilateral Declaration of Independence in Kosovo' (2008) 12 *Max Planck Yearbook of United Nations Law* 1.

[53] Bridget Coggins, *Power Politics and State Formation in the Twentieth Century: The Dynamics of Recognition* (CUP 2014); Daniel Millar, 'The Kosovan Precedent for the Annexation of Crimea' (*E-International Relations*, 18 March 2019), www.e-ir.info/pdf/77881, accessed 15 October 2022.

[54] Lauterpacht (n 27).

E. History Read Backwards

International legal doctrine has managed to downplay the problems of territorial ambiguity by reading history backwards. It is today common to say that the territorial status of, for example, Bangladesh only had to be clarified between 1971 and 1974.[55] Yet this is only possible because we now know that Bangladesh is a state, which was unclear in 1973.[56] If one were asked of Bangladesh's territorial status then, the answer would be as complicated as it is with respect to Kosovo today.[57] Furthermore, in some cases it is also possible to say that territorial status was clarified in the other direction. Between 1967 and 1970, Biafra exhibited a great degree of state-like legal capacities in the sense of Article 1 Montevideo, yet was subsequently reintegrated with Nigeria.[58] Most international legal scholars would argue that Biafra was not a state,[59] but this is again the advantage of being able to read history backwards. It may well be that, over time, international lawyers will likewise say that Kosovo's legal status merely had to be clarified, but this does not explain what its legal status is today. The book thus proposes a theory that is not based on the methodologically questionable approach of backwards reading of history, but which enables us to explain normatively the territorial status of a territory in a particular moment.

F. A Wrong Focus on Non-state Actors

Recent years have seen a great deal of scholarship discussing the legal nature and responsibility of non-state actors under international law.[60] In general, some inquiries into non-state actors try to hold such actors directly responsible for breaches of international law while others try to find ways to attribute their conduct to states. The problem with the label 'non-state actors' is that it is too broad and establishes a false dichotomy between states and all other actors capable of acting on the international plane. This means that very diverse actors, territorial and non-territorial, fall within the same category of non-state

[55] Crawford (n 9) 109–21.

[56] Joshua Castellino, 'The Secession of Bangladesh in International Law: Setting New Standards?' (1997) 7 *Asian Yearbook of International Law* 83.

[57] Sterio (n 6) 361–65.

[58] Ike Okonta and Kate Meagher, 'Legacies of Biafra: violence, identity and citizenship in Nigeria – introduction' (2009) 34(1) *Africa Development* 1.

[59] David Ijalaye, 'Was "Biafra" at Any Time a State in International Law?' (1971) 65 *American Journal of International Law* 551.

[60] d'Aspremont (n 39) 501–20; William T Worster, 'Functional Statehood in Contemporary International Law' (2020) 46(1) *Brooklyn Journal of International Law* 39; Cedric Ryngaert, 'Non-State Actors in International Law: A Rejoinder to Professor Thirlway' (2017) 64 *Netherlands International Law Review* 155.

actors, even though their capacities to act on the international plane and even incur responsibility under international law may be quite different.[61]

This book argues against the false dichotomy between states and non-state actors and instead considers how legal status is created under the sources of international law. International legal status indeed needs to be established in the sources of international law. It cannot be transposed from domestic law to the international level. For example, if a corporation is incorporated in the Netherlands and has a branch in a foreign state, this does not make it a person under international law.

It is well-established that international organisations have a degree of international legal capacity[62] and their legal status is created by states through their treaty-making powers.[63] But the international legal obligations of international organisations are very limited as they generally are *not* parties to very many international treaties and their capacity to be bound by customary international law remains controversial. In some largely historic situations other forms of international legal status have also been created, such as the Holy See and the Sovereign Order of Malta.[64] In most circumstances, however, legal status under international law is territorial in nature. The most common legal status is statehood, but it is not the only one. This book thus explores other such forms. It may well be that in reality certain non-state territorial entities have more legal obligations on the international plane than most international organisations do, but the legal status and legal capacity of such entities have never been conceptualised and theoretically grounded. What might be their treaty-making capacity? Are they bound by customary international law, for example? What implications would such capacities have for their legal status?

Most non-state actors discussed in contemporary scholarship do not have their status grounded in the formal sources of international law, so they do not have the capacity to be bound by the rules of this legal system. They were indeed not created by those who do have the law-making capacity on the international plane. In this sense, one needs to distinguish between legal persons under domestic law and those under international law. A legal status under domestic law does not imply a legal status under international law. Scholarly writings on non-state actors commonly make this mistake: they assume that an actor which is a legal person in domestic law must or should also possess an international legal status. But that is not the case where this actor's legal status has not been established under the formal sources of international law. This book thus rejects the

[61] José Alvarez, 'Are Corporations "Subjects" of International Law?' (2011) 11 *Santa Clara Journal of International Law* 1.

[62] *Reparation for Injuries Suffered in the Service of the United Nations* (Advisory Opinion) General List No 4 (1949) ICJ.

[63] Vienna Convention on the Law of Treaties between States and International Organizations or between International Organizations, UN Doc A/CONF.129/15 (VCLTIO), art 2.

[64] Cedric Ryngaert, 'The Legal Status of the Holy See' (2011) 3 *Goettingen Journal of International Law* 829.

commonly adopted dichotomy between states and non-state actors and clarifies what non-state forms of international (territorial) legal status have developed under treaty and customary international law; and what the international legal capacities of such entities are.

G. The Inadequate Category of 'States with Adjectives'

Scholarship has partially covered certain special non-state forms of territorial status. Much attention has been paid to the concept of international territorial administration, trusteeships, mandates and similar forms of internationalised territorial governance. Such arrangements have been ordinarily established by international treaties. In recent practice, they have also been set up by legally binding resolutions of the UN Security Council, which however also draw the authority from an international treaty – the UN Charter.[65] Significantly less attention has been paid to the legal status of those territorial entities that do not have their special territorial regimes derived from international treaty law. If a special territorial status falling short of statehood can be established by an international treaty, it is at least arguable that it could also develop under customary international law. After all, the doctrine of sources teaches that customary international law is no less authoritative than treaty law.[66]

When dealing with some territorial entities that have in practice developed a degree of territorial independence, some scholars have invented 'states with adjectives'. Terms such as *non-recognised states*,[67] *de facto states*,[68] *illegal states*,[69] *puppet states*[70] and *de facto regimes*[71] have commonly been used. Such terms are problematic. If 'state' is understood as a legal person and a term of art under international law, it cannot be qualified with adjectives that at the same time call a territorial entity a state and acknowledge that their legal status nevertheless is somewhat different. Some of these terms are also yet another untenable reminiscence of natural statehood theory which separates the so-called natural birth of a state from its 'birth certificate' that may not have been issued either on political ('unrecognised states') or legal ('illegal states') grounds.

[65] Marc Weller, *Contested Statehood* (OUP 2009).

[66] *Case Concerning Military and Paramilitary Activities in and against Nicaragua* (Judgment) General List No 70 (1986) ICJ, para 109.

[67] Nina Caspersen, *Unrecognized States: The Struggle for Sovereignty in the Modern International System* (CUP 2012).

[68] Adrian Florea, 'De Facto States in International Politics (1945–2011): A New Data Set' (2014) 40 *International Interactions* 788; Thomas De Waal, *Uncertain Ground: Engaging with Europe's De Facto States and Breakaway Territories* (Carnegie 2018).

[69] Talmon (n 34).

[70] Ryan Mitchell, 'Manchukuo's Contested Sovereignty: Legal Activism, Rights Consciousness, and Civil Resistance in a Puppet State' (2016) 3 *Asian Journal of Law and Society* 351.

[71] Jonte Van Essen, 'De Facto Regimes in International Law' (2012) 28 *Utrecht Journal of International and European Law* 31.

Moreover, the proposed adjectives to 'states' still do not fully explain every ambiguous territorial situation. With approximately 115 recognitions,[72] is Kosovo a recognised or a non-recognised state, and is it a state at all? Palestine generally would not qualify as a *de facto* regime according to the proponents of this term, but neither would Palestine neatly fall within any existing definition of statehood.[73] Northern Cyprus is often referred to either as an illegal state or a puppet state, yet its legal situation suggests rather that it is a part of Cyprus occupied by Turkey.[74]

Scholarly writings on 'states with adjectives' and 'de facto regimes' nevertheless identify the problem that certain non-state territorial entities have acquired a level of international legal capacity *de facto* (ie through state practice), although such practice has not necessarily been accepted as law (ie practice has not become coupled by *opinio juris*). This book argues that in dealing with the discrepancy between law and fact when it comes to the effective situation of a territory and its legal status, scholars have overlooked the classical customary international law dichotomy: state practice and *opinio juris*. While a rule of customary international law requires both, especially in its formative period it often happens that one is present, but not the other. If one accepts that territorial status is a legal status established under customary international law, it should not be surprising if an effective situation suggests one thing, but the law quite another. This is in fact a typical situation of state practice not being supplemented with *opinio juris*. This book thus elucidates the forms of territorial status that have either been developed under customary international law or are developed only partially through practice, yet with a lacking *opinio juris*. This book argues that special non-state territorial statuses can develop for different functional purposes, either under treaty law or in a less formalised way under customary international law.

H. Summary of Knowledge Gaps

In sum, a great deal of literature exists today that discusses self-determination, statehood criteria and recognition theories, while there is a paucity of doctrinal work that theorises the legal nature of statehood. Writers have focused on territory as a statehood criterion, but scholarship has failed to define the concept of territorial status. Doctrinal texts still discuss the modes of territorial acquisition, but those discussions are largely of historic interest and do not explain

[72] Jieun Choi, 'The Costs of Not Being Recognized as a Country: The Case of Kosovo' (*Brookings*, 16 November 2017), www.brookings.edu/blog/future-development/2017/11/16/the-costs-of-not-being-recognized-as-a-country-the-case-of-kosovo, accessed 3 December 2022.

[73] Nagan and Haddad (n 7) 343–421.

[74] Mira Lulic and Davor Muhvic, 'International Law and Cyprus Problem' (2009) 2 *Contemporary Legal and Economic Issues* 65.

how territorial status is altered in a world without *terrae nullius* and in which the general legal framework prohibits cession or shift in territorial status by occupation.[75] And while a great deal of doctrinal work has examined the role of non-state actors in international law, thus assuming a stark difference in international legal personality of states as opposed to non-states, the nature of international legal personality has remained undertheorised and inadequately defined. Scholarship also recognises that special non-state territorial statuses can be created by treaty law,[76] but has failed to acknowledge that the same can happen under customary international law. As a result, non-state territorial entities have been labelled with non-terms-of-art under international law, adding to conceptual ambiguity. If states have the right to self-defence, does that also apply to the so-called illegal, *de facto* and unrecognised states? If states enjoy immunity before the courts of foreign states, is such immunity also enjoyed by 'states with adjectives'? If only states can take part in the proceedings before the International Court of Justice (ICJ),[77] does that include or exclude so-called puppet states? There are no clear answers to these questions. This book argues that sweeping descriptive terms should be abandoned and international legal doctrine needs to develop adequate terms of art to appropriately categorise the instances of ambiguity pertaining to territorial status.

III. OBJECTIVES OF THE BOOK

The overall aim of this book is to develop a new theory of international legal status of territories. A new theory is needed because existing theories misconceive the concept of territory and the legal nature of statehood, and do not adequately ground, in international law, the legal status of non-state territorial entities. In order to develop such a new theory, this book pursues three main objectives that address the issues underlying the present doctrinal misconceptions:

(1) The concept of territory in international law needs to be re-theorised. Presently, international legal doctrine understands territory as a natural component of a state. A territory is not a natural element, however; it is a politically-created legal status established over a certain spatial area.
(2) The concept of statehood in international law needs to be re-defined. This book proposes a complete break with the so-called statehood criteria and asks what statehood is, ie statehood itself and independent of the statehood criteria. This also includes the question of whether the term state always needs to overlap with statehood as territorial status. Some evidence

[75] Gerry Simpson, 'MABO, International Law, Terra Nullius and the Stories of Settlement: An Unresolved Jurisprudence' (1993) 19 *Melbourne Law Review* 195.
[76] Crawford (n 9) 109–21.
[77] ICJ Statute, art 34.1.

indeed shows that this may not always be the case (eg Palestine's capacity to enter into treaties open to states is not necessarily the same as statehood as territorial status).

(3) The concept of non-state territorial entities needs to be grounded in the formal sources of international law. This book determines the legal status and capacities of non-state territorial entities on the international plane. It is clear that such territorial entities have a form of international legal status, but what is it and where is it derived from (eg Taiwan in many respects acts like a state, but what gives it the legal authority to do so and where are the limits to this)?

This book departs from four working propositions:

(1) All spatial areas on Earth have their respective legal statuses established in the formal sources of international law, in particular in treaty and customary international law. While spatial areas exist physically and naturally, their legal status is a question of law and created in the formal sources of international law.
(2) Statehood is legal status under customary international law and, as such, subject to all theoretical and practical difficulties significant for international custom, its formation and identification. Hence, legal status may not be objectively clear in every situation and at all times. Statehood can thus also be relative, depending on the other actors involved.
(3) A special non-state legal status of a territory can also be established under customary international law. Statehood may be the most common contemporary form of territorial legal status under international law, but it is not the only one. It is accepted in international legal doctrine that treaties can create special territorial regimes (eg international territorial administration, internationalised territories, etc), but it has not been properly acknowledged that such status can also be created in a less formalised way under customary international law.
(4) The word 'state' in international law does not always denote statehood. One needs to distinguish between territorial status on the one hand, and functional definitions of the state for the purposes of participation in international fora and treaty regimes on the other.

This book is not concerned with boundary disputes. While a boundary dispute could also be seen as an instance of territorial ambiguity, this book focuses on those territorial situations where ambiguity pertains to a territory as a whole; where the ambiguity is conceptual in nature and originates in the nature and structure of international law. In this sense, the legal statuses of Kosovo or Palestine are structural ambiguities, while boundary disputes between Belgium and the Netherlands are not. In the latter case it is clear that the disputed area belongs to one state or another; this is not a question of whether the disputed land is a state or has some other legal status in its own right under international law.

IV. METHODOLOGY: DOCTRINAL RESEARCH WITH INTERDISCIPLINARY AND COMPARATIVE ELEMENTS

This book is primarily doctrinal in nature in that it designs a new theory of legal status pertaining to territories, but it does so on the basis of an analysis of the law as it is. It does not seek to rewrite the law or speculate how the law should be. The approach is *de lege lata*, not *de lege ferenda*. This book argues, rather, that the existing theories governing the questions of territory, statehood and non-state territorial entities have not been properly constructed, and proposes a new normative theory of legal status grounded in the formal sources of public international law as enumerated in Article 38(1) ICJ Statute.[78] This book is predominantly grounded in public international law, but also draws on comparative law and government, political science, international relations, legal theory and comparative law. It thus combines doctrinal and interdisciplinary research.

This book employs elements of interdisciplinarity and comparative law analysis to make a doctrinal argument and design a new normative theory of legal status grounded in the formal sources of law. This is necessary because, as argued above, existing theories try to explain statehood by resorting to legal rules alone, thus ignoring the socio-political processes that create statehood. The existing theories are deficient precisely because they presume statehood is realised only as a matter of law, and because the consequences of statehood are interpreted as criteria for it. By way of comparison, football is played within certain rules. But looking at the rules alone does not tell us which team is going to win. A match needs to be played within these rules in order to get the winning team. Likewise, statehood is regulated by the rules of international law, but we need to study the political game played within these rules to understand how statehood is created, or not. This book thus seeks to go beyond the disciplinary boundaries and study the rules that regulate the political game.

The work of political scientists and international relations scholars will be used to identity the international practice of creating statehood and of relations between states with non-state territorial entities. One of the central claims this book makes is that international legal doctrine has wrongly labelled and miscategorised such practice. The relevant developments have often been more accurately investigated in international relations and political science scholarship, as scholars in these disciplines have not explained developments through the international lawyer's customary prism of the Montevideo statehood criteria. At the same time, international relations and political science scholarship has not synthesised analysed practice in a new legal theory, which is what this book will do.

[78] ICJ Statute, art 38.1.

V. STRUCTURE

The book is divided in four substantive chapters. Chapter two considers how a spatial area becomes a territory in international law. It argues that this is a social and political process which creates legal status. Discussing the concept of territory, geographers have observed that 'social science had long been filled with geographical terms and assumptions', while it remains unclear 'what do we mean when we talk of territory'.[79] Scholars in geography speak of *the territorial trap* into which we fall when we perceive territory as a natural feature rather than political and legal construct. As Stuart Elden further argues: '[W]hat we do when we accept the territorial trap is to buy into a state-centred narrative that naturalises and normalises this way of thinking.'[80]

This book shows that international law is an eminent example of a discipline that falls into the territorial trap. The Montevideo statehood criterion of a defined territory is but one example. A defined territory is generally seen in international legal scholarship as the natural component of a state. However, a territory is not a natural feature. Land and water are natural features, while territory is a socially and legally created construct. Misconstruing the concept of territory has led international legal scholars to ask how states are created without adequately explaining how territories are created. This book takes on this fundamental question and seeks to explain the process of creation of a territory (rather than state) in international law.

Chapter three turns to the law of statehood and seeks to define statehood as legal status of territories. Theoretical writings commonly define statehood through a descriptive set of criteria stemming from Article 1 of the 1933 Montevideo Convention which are usually said to have the status of customary rules of international law.[81] Most states more or less meet these criteria most of the time. But the question is whether states are states because they meet these criteria or whether they meet these criteria because they are states. Current statehood theories presume it is the former.[82] Chapter three argues it is actually the latter. The so-called statehood criteria are thus not criteria for statehood; rather, states meet them as a consequence of their statehood.

Chapter three breaks with the statehood criteria and asks what statehood is. It thus switches the focus to statehood itself rather than the statehood criteria. In chapter three, the normative argument that statehood is the legal status of a territory established in the formal sources of international law is developed. Sometimes states are created by international treaties. Most of the time, however, states emerge in a less formalised way under customary international law. Scholarship has thus far overlooked that the process of state creation is

[79] Elden (n 4).
[80] ibid.
[81] Montevideo Convention, art 1.
[82] Nicholson (n 40).

strikingly similar to the process of formation of customary international law. States are also created through state practice and *opinio juris*, and the process is thus prone to the conceptual and methodological problems of formation and identification of international custom.[83] Recognition in this model can be seen as an expression of *opinio juris*. It is thus not the statehood criteria that have the status of customary international law, but statehood itself.

Chapter three, therefore, redefines the concept of statehood in international law. It looks beyond the statehood criteria and grounds statehood in the formal sources of law as territorial legal status under customary international law.

Chapter four argues that all territorial entities in international law are *legal* persons. There is no place for natural personhood theory where territories rather than living creatures are concerned. Nevertheless, in no legal system do all persons, legal or natural, have exactly the same legal status vis-à-vis one another. This was already acknowledged by the ICJ in the 1949 *Reparations* Advisory Opinion where the Court reasoned: 'The subjects of law in any legal system are not necessarily identical in their nature or in the extent of their rights, and their nature depends upon the needs of the community.'[84] While the *Reparations* Advisory Opinion deals with standing of international organisations on the international plane, it has broader implications in that it acknowledges what some scholars have termed a sliding scale of international personality which may be applied beyond the distinction between the legal capacities of states and international organisations.[85] How this sliding scale operates and to whom it applies has never been thoroughly explained. Two legal problems are particularly exposed in this context: self-defence against non-state actors and legal capacity of non-state territorial entities.

In the current structure of international law, non-state actors are by definition also non-territorial actors. But the rules of the use of force are predicated on certain territorial assumptions and pursue to protect territorial integrity of states.[86] What happens when a non-state actor without a territory (eg a terrorist group) is involved? Moreover, what happens when a non-state actor is involved that may be deemed to actually have a territory?

Chapter four argues that these problems that manifest itself in the law on the use of force are symptoms of a larger conceptual problem in international

[83] Stefan Talmon, 'Determining Customary International Law: The ICJ's Methodology between Induction, Deduction and Assertion' (2015) 26 *European Journal of International Law* 417.

[84] Jure Vidmar, 'Palestine v United States: Why the ICJ Does not Need to Decide Whether Palestine is a State' (*EJIL:Talk!*, 22 November 2018), www.ejiltalk.org/palestine-v-united-states-why-the-icj-does-not-need-to-decide-whether-palestine-is-a-state, accessed 13 September 2022.

[85] Vincent Chetail, 'The Legal Personality of Multinational Corporations, State Responsibility and Due Diligence: The Way Forward Unity and Diversity of International Law' in Denis Alland, Vincent Chetail, Olivier de Frouville and Jorge E Viñuales (eds), *Essays in Honour of Prof. Pierre-Marie Dupuy* (Nijhoff 2014).

[86] United Nations Charter (adopted 26 June 1945, entered into force 24 October 1945) 1 UNTS 16 (UN Charter), art 2.4.

law: the ambiguity of legal status of certain non-state territories. While it is accepted in international legal doctrine that treaties can create special non-state territorial statuses, it has not been properly acknowledged that such statuses can also be created in a less formalised way under customary international law. Certain descriptive labels used in scholarship represent identification of relevant international practice, however. But such practice has not been synthesised in a comprehensive theory that would explain the legal status and international legal capacities of such entities under customary international law. This is what chapter four will do.

Chapter five turns to the normative meanings of 'the State'. The case of *Palestine v United States* is currently (as at May 2023) pending before the ICJ.[87] The ICJ Statute, however, only allows states to be parties in disputes before the Court.[88] Opinions are now divided whether the ICJ needs to decide on the substantive question of Palestine's legal status in order to rule on its jurisdiction, or whether it can avoid the statehood question and functionally rather than substantively treat Palestine as a state for the purposes of participation in certain procedures created by an international treaty (in this case the ICJ Statute).[89] This raises the question of the meaning of the term 'state' as a term of art under international law. Does the term 'state' necessarily denote the territorial legal status of statehood? If so, within which territory?

Moreover, Palestine also made a reference to the International Criminal Court (ICC) as a state party to the ICC Statute to start an investigation of the alleged international crimes in its *territory*.[90] Palestine may even be functionally considered as a state for the purposes of participation in certain treaty mechanisms, but when the ICC's territorial scope of jurisdiction is concerned, the question arises of whether Palestine as a *state party* to the ICC Statute has a territory and where.[91]

The legal ambiguities pertaining to international judicial proceedings involving Palestine are a consequence of an inadequate theoretical grounding of territorial status and legal personality in international law, whereby a great deal of attention is paid to the word 'state' used in certain treaties and treaty mechanisms. But this ambiguity cannot be resolved by recourse to the statehood criteria, the way some have suggested in the context of the ICJ and ICC

[87] *Relocation of the United States Embassy to Jerusalem (Palestine v United States of America)* (Application) General List No 176 (2018) ICJ.

[88] ICJ Statute, art 35.1.

[89] Marko Milanovic, 'Palestine Sues the United States in the ICJ re Jerusalem Embassy' (*EJIL:Talk!*, 30 September 2018), www.ejiltalk.org/palestine-sues-the-united-states-in-the-icj-re-jerusalem-embassy, accessed 23 November 2022; Alina Miron, 'Palestine's Application the ICJ, neither Groundless nor Hopeless. A Reply to Marko Milanovic' (*EJIL:Talk!*, 8 October 2018), www.ejiltalk.org/palestines-application-the-icj-neither-groundless-nor-hopeless-a-reply-to-marko-milanovic, accessed 19 October 2022; Vidmar (n 84).

[90] *Situation in the State of Palestine* (*Decision on the 'Prosecution request pursuant to article 19(3) for a ruling on the Court's territorial jurisdiction in Palestine'*) ICC-01/18 (5 February 2021).

[91] ibid.

proceedings involving Palestine. The answer is not in the statehood criteria, but in the underlying legal concepts – the fundaments to which this book seeks to go. The example points to a deeper conceptual problem of whether the procedural category of a 'state' in the context of international legal procedures necessarily overlaps with statehood as substantive legal status of territory. Chapter five therefore explores the difference between the substantive legal status of statehood in international law and procedural status of a state for the functional purpose of participation in certain treaty regimes and treaty-created mechanisms. The chapter sketches the difference between thc substantive and procedural rules pertaining to the matter, defines the state normatively, and explains what the term 'state' can mean in different legal contexts. In other words, the term 'state' may have more than one meaning in international law.

The concluding chapter six represents a synthesis of the book. It seeks to (i) redefine and re-theorise the concept of territory in international law; (ii) conceptualise statehood as territorial legal status; and (ii) ground the non-state territorial entities in the sources of international law and explain what their international legal status is. The newly synthesised theory on this basis will be able to explain the legal status of territories without accepting any structural ambiguity as is presently the case. It defines territory as an inherently legal concept and explain what forms of territorial status exist in contemporary international law.

In sum, this book seeks to address the challenges of the existing international legal theories which lead to ambiguity pertaining to international legal status of territories, and fail in difficult or marginal cases. Territorial ambiguity leads to structural regulatory ambiguity where the application of the rules of international law becomes unclear and uncertain. The change in legal doctrine proposed is relatively formalistic, but with notable consequences for the application of international law. International legal doctrine has accepted and acknowledged that statehood and special non-state territorial regimes can be created by international treaties. But it has been overlooked that this also happens, and more often so, under customary international law which is an equally authoritative source of international law as international treaties. Instead of conceptualising international legal status of territories as a matter of custom formation, scholarship has tried to invent new non-term-of-art labels which do not sit easily within the international legal system. But international legal rules and their effects can only be clear and properly defined where a certain factual situation is labelled with an appropriate normative term of art under international law. This has not been the case in many instances where legal status of territories is concerned. This book thus seeks to go back to the drawing board and ask what states and non-state territorial entities are in a formal sense. On this determination it also depends what substantive and procedural rights and duties they possess in the international legal system. This book thus designs a new normative theory of international legal status of territories that does not leave any instances of territorial status ambiguous or unclear.

2

The Concept of Territory in International Law

I. INTRODUCTION

ARTICLE 1 OF the Montevideo Convention refers to territory as a characteristic for statehood.[1] Scholars have taken this reference further and argued that a territory also needs to be defined, and called it a criterion for statehood.[2] It would appear, however, that the concept of territory presupposes a *defined spatial area*. In order words, a spatial area becomes a territory precisely because it is geographically defined and delimited. The question is then who defined a spatial area and created a territory, and for what purposes. When does a spatial area become a territory in the sense of international law?

Geographers have cautioned that social science – which for these purposes also includes legal science – often falls into the so-called 'territorial trap' whereby a territory is seen as a natural given rather than social construct.[3] But territory is an inherently social and legal concept. Land and sea are natural givens, while defining a legal entity's territory and territorial waters is a socio-political exercise. As Hans Kelsen argued, one often hears that a territory is defined by a river or mountain range.[4] This may well often, albeit not always, be the case, but which river and which mountain range will define a certain territory is a social decision with legal consequences, it is not a natural fact.[5]

While some geographers and social scientists have rejected such natural understandings of territory,[6] their critical voices have had little echo in international law where the territory remains to be taken as a physical or natural element. Alexis Galan has aptly observed that 'international legal scholarship

[1] Montevideo Convention on the Rights and Duties of States of 1933 (adopted 26 December 1933, entered into force 26 December 1934) 165 LNTS 19 (Montevideo Convention).

[2] Rosalyn Cohen, 'The Concept of Statehood in United Nations Practice' (1961) 109 *University of Pennsylvania Law Review* 1127. David B. Knight, 'The Middle East and the Emerging New World Order' (1992) 28(3) *GeoJournal* 311.

[3] Stuart Elden, 'Thinking Territory Historically' (2010) 15 *Geopolitics* 757.

[4] Hans Kelsen, *General Theory of Law and State* (Routledge 1961) 213.

[5] ibid.

[6] Robert McCorquodale and Raul Pangalangan, 'Pushing Back the Limitations of Territorial Boundaries' (2001) 12(5) *European Journal of International Law* 867.

has, for the most part, neglected the importance of geography. Territory, space, and boundaries have been largely taken for granted, while their relation to international law has been left unproblematised.'[7]

This chapter thus seeks to reconceptualise the notion of territory in international law. It defines the territory as the legal status of a certain spatial area. As such, territory is not a natural element; rather, it is a legal concept established in social relations. When the concept of territory is 'denaturalised', this has certain consequences for the structure and application of international law, which are highly dependent on territorial logic. A new theory of territorialism has doctrinal and practical consequences for, *inter alia*, the concept of the state and statehood, the legal status of non-state entities and the exercise of jurisdiction. It will be argued in this section that the misconception of the territory has led international legal doctrine to conflate the concept of statehood with that of jurisdictional authority. The notions of territory, statehood and jurisdiction need to be untangled in turn.

Subsequently, the chapter turns to the questions of territorial title and acquisition. It argues that the classical modes of creating territorial title are based on effective possession. This is not compatible with the United Nations (UN) Charter era rules of international law governing the use of force, self-determination and territorial integrity. As a consequence, the old modes of territorial acquisition, such as occupation, conquest and cession, are anachronistic and no longer applicable. Yet, the concept of territory in contemporary international law remains influenced by these anachronistic concepts. In a world without *terrae nullius*, territorial status is a zero-sum game, while other rules of international law prevent a shift in territorial title on the basis of effective possession alone. Hence, international law needs a complete break with the Montevideo criteria and similar assumptions of effectiveness-based territorial status.

II. TERRITORY AS A SOCIALLY AND LEGALLY BOUNDED SPATIAL AREA

A certain spatial area becomes a territory exclusively by human activity. As Jean Gottmann observes:

> [I]t would be illusory to consider territory as a purely physical phenomenon. The natural components of any given territory have been delimited by human action, and they are used by a certain number of people for specific purposes, all such uses and purposes being determined by and belonging to a political process. Territory is a concept generated by people organizing space for their own aims.[8]

[7] Alexis Galan, 'New Wine, Old Wineskins: On the Geographical Assumptions of International Constitutional Law' (2016) 19(2) *Journal of International Relations and Development* 222.

[8] Jean Gottmann, *The Significance of Territory* (University of Virginia Press 1975) 29.

In international legal doctrine, a similar observation was made by Hans Kelsen who argued that the proponents of the natural statehood theory[9] frequently refer to rivers and mountain ranges as natural delimitations of states.[10] According to Kelsen, this view is flawed, as a certain river or mountain range did not become a boundary as a result of natural forces. It was, rather, humans who decided that a certain river or mountain would be given the status of a boundary.[11] Moreover, many boundaries exist even in the absence of any natural barriers.

International law has nevertheless uncritically accepted the false assumption of the social sciences that territory is something natural, and has never properly acknowledged that certain political and legal procedures and meanings are grafted onto this concept. As Stuart Elden argues:

> [T]erritory is often assumed to be self-evident in meaning, allowing the study of its particular manifestations – territorial disputes, the territory of specific countries, etc – without theoretical reflection on 'territory' itself. Where it is defined, territory is either assumed to be a relation that can be understood as an outcome of territoriality, or simply as a bounded space … the state [has been described] as a 'bordered power container'.[12]

Theorising the concept of the territory as a social rather than natural concept, Elden concludes that '[t]erritory can be understood as political technology: it comprises techniques for measuring land and controlling terrain'.[13] Indeed, defining a territory under international law is a political exercise with legal consequences. A territory is thus not a naturally given fact, it is a socially created and delimited spatial area. Where a spatial area is bounded under the rules and for the purposes of international law, the area becomes territory in the international legal sense. Such a territory may have the status of statehood, but not always.[14] A territory may also be created under domestic private and public law,[15] but domestic legal regulation to this effect will not automatically result in international territorial status.

The concept of territory as a social spatial organisation is also intrinsically linked to the concept of possession, at least in Western tradition, and it is the concept of possession from which the international law's territorial attachment is derived. Elden argues that the use of the word territory presumes possession of land: '[T]he interest is in those that take a political-economic approach to the question of territory, stressing the linkage between territory and land,

[9] Hans Kelsen, 'Recognition in International Law: Theoretical Observations' (1941) 35(4) *American Journal of International Law* 605.

[10] Albert Perry Brigham, 'Principles in the Determination of Boundaries' (1919) 7(4) *Geographical Review* 201.

[11] ibid.

[12] Stuart Elden, *The Birth of a Territory* (University of Chicago Press 2013) 800.

[13] ibid, 811.

[14] Cf ch 4.

[15] Rocío del Pilar Peña-Huertas and others, 'Land Tenure Systems and Property Rights: Socio-legal Studies in the Colombian Case' (2018) 23(1–2) *Tilburg Law Review* 43.

seeing territory as a form of property.'[16] Elden then refers to Soja who argues: 'Conventional Western perspectives on spatial organisation are powerfully shaped by the concept of property, in which pieces of territory are viewed as "commodities" capable of being bought, sold, or exchanged at the market place.'[17] The attachment of territorialism and property has been explained with the sixteenth-century developments in cartography which made the making of bounded spatial units technically possible, and rediscovery of the concept of property in Roman private law which was applied to the concept of territorial sovereignty.[18]

Historically, territorialism was indeed not linked to statehood, but to the ruler as a physical person.[19] This had changed with the Treaty of Westphalia. As aptly observed by Nisha Shah: '[B]y the time of the Peace of Westphalia, the idea of discretely defined and relatively autonomous jurisdictions as the constituent units of political order, if not inscribed in political theory, was at least well-established practice … territory connoted the idea of spatially distinct forms of political jurisdiction and rule.'[20]

In the nascent period of modern international order, the concept of territory was associated with the exercise of jurisdictional authority which emanates from political power over a certain spatial area.[21] While in present-day political organisation such a political power often emanates from statehood, this has not always been the case and is not necessarily the case now. Indeed, '[t]erritory … did not have determinative power to shape the state. The relationship between the two was mutually constitutive: as much as territory informed the modern state's spatial arrangement, the consolidation of political power in state sovereignty increased the territory's political significance.'[22]

Territory is thus a political, legal and economic concept. Public international law builds on the notions of possession and ownership in property law, except that the possessor here is not an individual but a socio-political community. The relationship between the state and the territory is thus much more complex than contemporary theories of international law tend to acknowledge. It is too simplistic to conceptualise territory as a *criterion* for statehood.[23]

[16] Elden (n 3) 757–58, quoting Edward Soja, 'The Political Organization of Space' (1971) 8 Commission on College Geography Resource Paper, Washington DC, Association of American Geographers.

[17] ibid.

[18] Cedric Ryngaert and Duco W Hora Siccama, 'Ascertaining Customary International Law: An Inquiry into the Methods Used by Domestic Courts' (2018) 65 *Netherlands International Law Review* 1.

[19] John Breuilly, 'Modern Territoriality, the Nation-State, and Nationalism' in Matthias Middell and Steffi Marung (eds), *Spatial Formats under the Global Condition* (De Gruyter Oldenbourg 2019) 4.

[20] Nisha Shah, 'The Territorial Trap of the Territorial Trap: Global Transformation and the Problem of the State's Two Territories' (2012) 6(1) *International Political Sociology* 57.

[21] Asha Kaushal, 'The Politics of Jurisdiction' (2015) 78(5) *Modern Law Review* 759.

[22] Shah (n 20) 57–76.

[23] Dermott J Devine, 'The Requirements of Statehood Re-Examined' (1971) 34(4) *Modern Law Review* 410.

It could also be the other way around: a certain spatial area has the status of a territory precisely because it is backed by the factual and legal power of a political community. As such, it represents a separate 'bordered power container'.[24]

In modern times such a community would often be a state, but sometimes other forms of socio-political organisation may also create a territory. This will be further discussed below. It now needs to be considered how the state and the territory have become so closely intertwined and whether the two common assumptions of international legal doctrine are correct: (i) a state needs to have a territory in order to be a state;[25] and (ii) a territory needs to belong to a state.[26]

III. THE ENTANGLEMENT OF TERRITORY, JURISDICTION AND STATEHOOD

This section demonstrates that territory in contemporary international law lies at the intersection of jurisdiction and statehood. The two concepts have indeed become entangled and conflated in legal doctrine through their shared territorial pedigree. It will be argued that Article 1 of the Montevideo Convention more accurately describes (territorial) jurisdiction rather than statehood. Moreover, some writers have resorted to terms such as 'de facto states',[27] 'unrecognised states',[28] 'illegal states',[29] and similar. These are not states but instances of non-state authority capable of exercising jurisdiction in a certain spatial area. They are 'bordered power containers',[30] yet without statehood. International law indeed allows in some instances that jurisdiction may be exercised by non-states.[31] But such competence should not be conflated with statehood.

Scholars have acknowledged that jurisdiction is not an exclusive prerogative of states, and it should not always be equated with territorialism.[32] This book takes a step further and argues that the factual ability to exercise jurisdiction has been wrongly conflated with attributes of statehood. This is also a consequence of the undue conflation and entanglement of statehood, jurisdiction and territorialism. Lea Raible has observed that 'the relationship between a state's title to territory and its jurisdiction is frequently invoked, but rarely expressly

[24] Stuart Elden, 'Land, Terrain, Territory' (2010) 34(6) *Progress in Human Geography* 799.

[25] David Storey, 'States, Territory and Sovereignty' (2017) 102(3) *Geography* 116.

[26] Anna Stilz, 'Why Do States Have Territorial Rights?' (2009) 1(2) *International Theory* 185.

[27] Vildan Meydan, 'A Paradox of International (Non)Recognition: The Relationship Between De Facto States and Patron States' (2018) 1(1) *International Journal of Economics Politics Humanities and Social Sciences* 1.

[28] Anastasia Tataryn, Erdem Ertürk, 'Unrecognised States: The Necessary Affirmation of the Event of International Law' (2021) 32 *Law Critique* 331.

[29] Paweł Czubik, 'Sovereignty in International Law' in Anikó Raisz (ed), *International Law from a Central European Perspective. Legal Studies on Central Europe* (Central European Academic 2022).

[30] Elden (n 24) 799–817.

[31] Paul Schiff Berman, 'The Globalization of Jurisdiction' (2002) 151 *University of Pennsylvania Law Review* 311, 472–90.

[32] Cedric Ryngaert, *Jurisdiction in International Law* (OUP 2008) 50–76.

addressed'.[33] This chapter takes the view that although this was historically not always the case, it is now at least silently presumed that it is states that exercise jurisdiction, either territorially or extraterritorially. This has led to two main problems in contemporary international legal doctrine: (i) evidences of jurisdictional powers are conflated with (attributes of) statehood; and (ii) contemporary international legal doctrine has not adequately accommodated the fact that certain non-state authorities can exercise jurisdiction within a certain spatial area, and even outside of it.

A. The Conflation of Jurisdiction and Statehood via Territory

In international law, jurisdiction can have a range of meanings.[34] This is not the place to revisit them all. Cedric Ryngaert aptly defines the core premise of the concept of jurisdiction under general international law: '[J]urisdiction is commonly understood to refer to the legal authority of States to set and enforce rules with respect to acts that may, or may not, take place on their territory.'[35] Lea Raible further observes that 'all accounts of jurisdiction analysed suggest that it is connected to a notion of power. Sometimes this is referred to as power, sometimes as control, and sometimes as authority. This means that it is not yet clear what power in this context means.'[36]

While the terminology is not always clear, the term jurisdiction for the purposes of international law relates to the authority to prescribe and enforce the rules in a certain spatial area and over its inhabitants, and under some circumstances beyond that area.[37] Importantly, the concept of jurisdiction is closely linked to the concepts of power and authority, and defined with the territorial/extraterritorial dichotomy. As Ryngaert observes, '[t]he binary code territorial/extraterritorial has over the years come to be viewed as natural, reflecting the cartographic carving up of the world in distinct territorial entities (States) which are constitutionally autonomous vis-à-vis their peers'.[38]

The association of jurisdiction with a territorial base and power or authority to prescribe and enforce the law has blurred the line between evidence of effective exercise of jurisdiction with attributes of statehood. As Shah notes:

> Both shaping and shaped by the emergence of the modern sovereign state, territory becomes more than a 'portion of the earth's surface' – a physical space onto which meaning is inscribed – but a normative convention about distinct jurisdictions as the basis of legitimate political authority. Through this, territory and state become

[33] Lea Raible, *Human Rights Unbound: A Theory of Extraterritoriality* (OUP 2020) 160.

[34] Ryngaert (n 32) 1.

[35] Cedric Ryngaert, 'Jurisdiction' in Jean d'Aspremont and Sahib Singh (eds), *Concepts for International Law* (Edward Elgar 2019) 577.

[36] Raible (n 33) 100.

[37] Cf Shah (n 20) 62.

[38] Ryngaert (n 32) 56.

> inseparable not because the state occupies a (pre-given) territory, but because the state 'is a territory' … Made explicitly evident in Weber's … definition of the state.[39]

Indeed, Max Weber defines the state as: 'human community that (successfully) claims the *monopoly of the legitimate use of physical force within a given territory*'.[40] Weber's sociological definition falls very close to Georg Jellinek's legal definition of the state as '*Land, Volk und Herrscher*'.[41] A contemporary theorist has argued: 'To qualify as a "state," on my minimal definition, an institution must feature (i) binding collective rule setting by a territorial public authority and (ii) the ability to enforce its determinations in case of disputes.'[42] These descriptive definitions of the state resonate in the so-called Montevideo criteria.[43] What is in the background of all these *descriptions* of the state is that there should exist an organised political authority that exercises power over a certain spatial area and its population: 'a bordered power container'.[44] Yet, such legal and socio-political definitions of the state may much more accurately describe *jurisdiction* rather than statehood.[45]

While the power or the authority to prescribe and enforce the rules in contemporary international law generally lies with the state, this has not always been the case and it is not exclusively the case now. As Simon Reid-Henry notes: '[T]he state was not always territorially bound and when it was this was as the result of concerted effort rather than because of any natural tendency in the way societies come to be ordered. There is thus no ontological basis for societies to be organised into territorially discreet parcels of land.'[46] Saskia Sassen similarly argues:

> Today we think of the question of exclusive state authority as imbricated with territory and of nation-states as constituting equal jurisdictions. For both of these issues the question of territorial boundaries becomes critical. None of these was a significant factor in the political geometry of feudal lords, church, and empire. Even the Roman Empire's borders were not what we would consider borders today, particularly with regard to equal jurisdictions.[47]

Indeed, the association of jurisdiction, territory and statehood is a relatively modern phenomenon closely associated with the historic developments in cartography. As Ryngaert argues: '[The] cartographic practices gradually led to

[39] Shah (n 20) 64–65.

[40] Max Weber, 'Politics as a Vocation' in Tony Waters, and Dagmar Waters (eds), *Weber's Rationalism and Modern Society* (Springer 2015) 129–98 (emphasis added).

[41] Georg Jellinek, *Allgemeine Staatslehre* (Springer 1914) 144.

[42] Anna Stilz, *Territorial Sovereignty: A Philosophical Exploration* (OUP 2019) 14.

[43] ibid, 1.

[44] Elden (n 24) 799–817.

[45] Satvinder S Juss, 'Nationality Law, Sovereignty, and the Doctrine of Exclusive Domestic Jurisdiction' (1994) 9(2) *Florida Journal of International Law* 219.

[46] Simon Reid-Henry, 'The Territorial Trap: Fifteen Years On' (2011) 15 *Geopolitics* 752, 753.

[47] Saskia Sassen, *Territory, Authority, Rights: From Medieval to Global Assemblages* (Princeton 2006) 40.

changing ideas about appropriate and legitimate governance, finally ushering in novel political practices that presented territorially bounded political space and the attendant exclusive territorial jurisdiction of the State as logical and natural phenomena.'[48] In other words, the modern notion of the state has been conceptualised as a bounded jurisdictional unit. Jurisdiction and statehood have thus become either conflated or at least seen as two sides of the same coin.

While Ryngaert makes a claim for non-territorial variants of jurisdiction,[49] this chapter does not reject the territorial underpinnings of the concept of jurisdiction. It rather argues that it is precisely the legal authority in a certain spatial area which turns that area into a territory under international law.[50] Moreover, the close-knit relationship between jurisdiction, territory and the state has also led to a number of misconceptions whereby certain attributes of (territorial) jurisdiction have been misinterpreted as attributes of statehood. This book argues that the concepts of jurisdiction and statehood need to be separated. It is indeed common that statehood would normally come in pair with jurisdictional authority in a certain spatial area. But the causality does not necessarily or automatically work in the other direction: evidence of jurisdictional authority should not be taken as evidence of statehood.

B. Jurisdiction of Non-state Territories

In contemporary international law, it is presumed that states have the legal authority to prescribe and enforce rules territorially and, under some circumstances, also extraterritorially.[51] However, it is wrong to presume that international law gives such an authority *only* to states. Some non-state territorial entities indeed also have a degree of jurisdictional authority established under international law. For example, entities such as Hong Kong, Macao, Taiwan and even the European Union (EU) may have the authority under international law to prescribe and enforce rules within their territories and to an extent even extraterritorially.[52]

[48] Ryngaert (n 32) 56–57.

[49] ibid.

[50] Margaret Moore, 'Territorial Rights and Territorial Justice' (*The Stanford Encyclopedia of Philosophy*, 2020), plato.stanford.edu/archives/sum2020/entries/territorial-rights, accessed 22 August 2022.

[51] Cedric Ryngaert, 'The concept of jurisdiction in international law' in Alexander Orakhelashvili (ed), *Research Handbook on Jurisdiction and Immunities in International Law* (Edward Elgar 2015).

[52] Macau: The Basic Law of the Macao Special Administrative Regions of the People's Republic of China, 20 December 1999; Lung-chu Chen, 'Taiwan's Current International Legal Status' (1998) 689 *Articles & Chapters* 675; Dimitry Kochenov, 'Monitoring and Enforcement of the Rule of Law in the EU: Rhetoric and Reality' (2015) 11(3) *European Constitutional Law Review* 512.

These four entities most prominently hold an international legal status as parties to the World Trade Organization (WTO) Marrakesh Agreement.[53] Article XII(1) of the WTO Marrakesh Agreement provides:

> Any State or separate customs territory possessing full autonomy in the conduct of its external commercial relations and of the other matters provided for in this Agreement and the Multilateral Trade Agreements may accede to this Agreement, on terms to be agreed between it and the WTO.[54]

The non-states are thus members under the clause of 'separate customs *territory*' that enjoys a full autonomy within the functional scope of this agreement. This clause allows for participation in this specific treaty regime to territorially defined non-state units with own jurisdictional powers in the subject matter covered by the treaty.

Notably, Taiwan does not participate in the WTO treaty regime under this name, but as Chinese Taipei and Separate Customs Territory of Taiwan, Penghu, Kinmen, and Matsu.[55] The name is obviously a political compromise.[56] Taiwan is indeed a descriptive name used as a shorthand for Chinese Taipei and the authority calling itself the Republic of China, depending on the context.[57] However termed, it is clear that Chinese Taipei can only be able to participate in the WTO regime and comply with its obligations if it is assumed that it is able to exercise jurisdiction over the territory of the islands of Taipei, Penghu, Kinmen and Matsu. The WTO Marrakesh Agreement thus grants legal authority to the territory descriptively referred to as Taiwan to exercise jurisdiction, prescribe and enforce laws, for the functional purposes of the WTO treaty regime.

The situation with Hong Kong and Macao is different but also quite complex. Besides their respective WTO statuses under international treaty law,[58] they also have the international legal statuses established through international treaties concluded between China and Portugal (with respect to Macao),[59] and China and the United Kingdom (with respect to Hong Kong).[60] The EU's territory is

[53] Agreement Establishing the World Trade Organization (adopted 15 April 1994, entered into force 1 January 1995) 1867 UNTS 154 (Marrakesh Agreement).

[54] Marrakesh Agreement, art 12.1.

[55] 'Separate Customs Territory of Taiwan, Penghu, Kinmen and Matsu (Chinese Taipei) and the WTO' (*WTO*), www.wto.org/english/thewto_e/countries_e/chinese_taipei_e.htm, accessed 5 March 2022.

[56] Sigrid Winkler, 'Mainland China and Taiwan Face to Face in the WTO: A 10-Year Rollercoaster Ride' (2013) 41(3–4) *Asian Journal of Social Science* 287.

[57] Paul MA Linebarger, 'The Republic of China on Taiwan: A Descriptive Appraisal' (1963) 126(1) *World Affairs* 5.

[58] Lingliang Zeng, *Contemporary International Law and China's Peaceful Development* (Springer 2021) 493–506.

[59] Joint Declaration on the question of Macao (adopted 13 April 1987, entered into force 1 March 1999) 1498 UNTS 229 (Macao Declaration).

[60] Joint Declaration on the question of Hong Kong (adopted 19 December 1984, entered into force 27 May 1985) 1399 UNTS 33 (Hong Kong Declaration).

a concept derived from the territories of EU member states.[61] Nevertheless, the EU does have the legal authority to prescribe and enforce its rules in this spatial area, and in some respects outside of it. Such a legal authority derives from the Treaty on European Union (TEU)[62] and the Treaty on the Functioning of the European Union (TFEU)[63] as well as treaties the EU has concluded with numerous third countries,[64] including the WTO Agreement and bilateral trade agreements.[65]

The WTO regime cannot be generalised and applied across the board in public international law. It is nevertheless a good example of how an international treaty can for certain functional purposes create a special legal status of a certain territory. This territory has certain jurisdictional powers established under international law. But the exercise of jurisdiction does not occur on the flipside of statehood.

Historically, certain territories have been put under special territorial regimes with a degree of authority to prescribe and enforce jurisdiction. Examples are numerous, including the free cities,[66] international territories,[67] mandates[68] and Austria under the allied occupation.[69] The Svalbard (Spitsbergen) Treaty creates a special legal status of this territory within Norway,[70] and the Antarctic Treaty creates a special status of the non-state territory of Antarctica.[71] Finally, UN Security Council Resolution 1244 created a special territorial legal status of Kosovo within the Federal Republic of Yugoslavia,[72] and UN Security Council Resolution 1272 created a special territorial legal status of East Timor within Indonesia.[73]

[61] Eduardo Medeiros, 'Territorial Cohesion: An EU concept' (2016) 60 *European Journal of Spatial Development* 1.

[62] Consolidated Version of the Treaty on European Union of 2012 (adopted 13 December 2007, entered into force 1 December 2009) OJ C 115/01.

[63] Consolidated Version of the Treaty on the Functioning of the European Union of 2012 (adopted 25 March 1957, entered into force 1 December 2009) (2012) OJ L 326/47.

[64] 'Negotiations and agreements' (*European Commission*), policy.trade.ec.europa.eu/eu-trade-relationships-country-and-region/negotiations-and-agreements_en, accessed 7 November 2022.

[65] 'The EU and the WTO' (*European Commission*), policy.trade.ec.europa.eu/eu-trade-relationships-country-and-region/eu-and-wto_en, accessed 3 September 2022.

[66] Andrew Bodiford, 'Cities in International Law: Reclaiming Rights as Global Custom' (2020) 23(1) *City University of New York Law Review* 1.

[67] Ralph Wilde, *International Territorial Administration. How Trusteeship and the Civilizing Mission Never Went Away* (OUP 2008) 640.

[68] Friedrich Honig, 'International Law and the Transfer of Mandated Territories' (1936) 18(4) *Journal of Comparative Legislation and International Law* 204.

[69] Klaus Eisterer, 'Austria Under Allied Occupation' in Rolf Steininger, Gunter Bischof and Michael Gehler (eds), *Austria in the Twentieth Century* (Routledge 2002).

[70] The Spitsbergen Treaty of 1920 (adopted 9 February 1920, entered into force 14 August 1925) 2 LNTS 7.

[71] Antarctic Treaty System (adopted 1 December 1959, entered into force 23 June 1961) UNTS 402 (Antarctic Treaty).

[72] UNSC Res 1244 (10 June 1999) UN Doc S/RES/1244.

[73] UNSC Res 1272 (25 October 1999) UN Doc S/RES/1272.

It is thus not uncommon that special non-state legal statuses are created in certain territories under international law. Such legal statuses can create a degree of jurisdictional authority in a certain bounded spatial area, yet without creating statehood. This is how a non-state territory can become its own jurisdictional unit, a 'bordered power container',[74] under international law.

Such non-state jurisdictional units with an international legal status need to be distinguished from those that exist purely under domestic law. A state in the constitutional system of the United States may be its own jurisdictional unit for the purposes of United States' law, but not for the purposes of international law. The same would apply to various extents in other federal states, for example to *Länder* in Germany,[75] and to some non-federal states where certain competencies have been transferred to sub-state territories. A good example of the latter is devolution in the United Kingdom.[76] Even within the United Kingdom, there is a difference between Scotland and Wales on the one hand and Northern Ireland on the other. Scotland and Wales have their special legal statuses established exclusively as a matter of United Kingdom's constitutional law, but not under international law, although it may well be arguable that the right of self-determination applies to the people of Scotland and Wales. The status of Northern Ireland is established under the Good Friday Agreement, an international treaty, to which the Republic of Ireland also is a party.[77] Northern Ireland thus belongs to the territories over which a special jurisdictional regime was established under international law.

Separate non-state jurisdictional regimes in a certain territory can thus be established within an existing state or in the absence of a statehood status over that territory. The Antarctic Treaty is an example of a legal authority which created a separate legal status which indefinitely prevents that spatial area from forming a part of any state. On the other hand, territories in the absence of statehood can be created temporarily, as a transitional period before a permanent solution is found. This often happens in the context of post-conflict settlement, for example the Free Territory of Trieste and Austria under the allied occupation.

In sum, a legal authority can create a special jurisdictional regime in a certain territory. Such a legal authority can be either domestic or international. Where a special jurisdictional regime in a certain territory is created by a source of international law, this territory is granted an international legal status. It is common that such status is created by an international treaty. It will be argued in chapter four of this book that this status also exists in customary international law.

[74] Elden (n 24) 799–817.

[75] Stefan Talmon, 'State Jurisdiction and Immunities' in Stefan Talmon (ed), *German Practice in International Law: 2019* (CUP 2019).

[76] 'Universal Jurisdiction Law and Practice in England and Wales' (*Redress*, May 2022) redress.org/wp-content/uploads/2022/05/UJ-Law-and-Practice-in-England-and-Wales.pdf, accessed 8 December 2022.

[77] Good Friday Agreement of 1998 (entered into force 2 December 1999) 37 ILM 751.

C. Factual Exercise of Jurisdiction

Some non-states may have factual capacity to prescribe and enforce rules within a certain spatial area while no legal authority, international or domestic, gives them the power to do so. For example, Transnistria,[78] Somaliland[79] and historically Southern Rhodesia[80] are or were neither states, nor do or did they have a legal authority derived from international or domestic law of the parent state to prescribe and enforce rules in their territories.[81] In other words, they are or were 'bordered power containers',[82] yet without either international or constitutional legal authority to this effect. These are examples of *de facto* ability to exercise jurisdiction, but they are often wrongly labelled as *de facto* states or entities with *de facto* statehood.[83]

Somaliland can prescribe and enforce its own rules within the bounded spatial area.[84] It can do so on the basis of domestic *factual* developments, but no international legal instrument gives it the authority to do so.[85] Such a capacity is purely factual and not based in a legal authority. By way of comparison, the 1984 Joint Sino-British Declaration, an international treaty, spells out the status of Hong Kong and thus the extent of this territory's jurisdictional powers. Article 3 of the Sino-British Declaration *inter alia* provides:

> The Government of the People's Republic of China declares that the basic policies of the People's Republic of China regarding Hong Kong are as follows:
>
> (1) Upholding national unity and territorial integrity and taking account of the history of Hong Kong and its realities, the People's Republic of China has decided to establish, in accordance with the provisions of Article 31 of the Constitution of the People's Republic of China, a Hong Kong Special Administrative Region upon resuming the exercise of sovereignty over Hong Kong.
>
> (2) The Hong Kong Special Administrative Region will be directly under the authority of the Central People's Government of the People's Republic of China. The Hong Kong Special Administrative Region will enjoy a high degree of autonomy, except in foreign and defense affairs which are the responsibilities of the Central People's Government.[86]

[78] Bruno Coppieters, 'Abkhazia, Transnistria and North Cyprus: Recognition and Non-Recognition in Ceasefire and Trade Agreements' (2021) 226 *Post-Soviet Secessionism: Nation Building and State-Failure after Communism* 15.

[79] Mohamed Farah Hersi, 'Research Guide to the Somaliland Legal System' (*NYU Law*, Feb 2009) www.nyulawglobal.org/globalex/Somaliland.html, accessed 18 November 2022.

[80] M Aaron Benjamin Mutiti, 'Rhodesia and Her Four Discriminatory Constitutions' (1974) 4(2) *The African Review: A Journal of African Politics, Development and International Affairs* 259.

[81] Coppieters (n 78) 15–57.

[82] Elden (n 24) 799–817.

[83] Jonte van Essen, 'De Facto Regimes in International Law' (2012) 28(74) *Merkourios* 31.

[84] Hersi (n 79).

[85] Di Markus Virgil Hoehne, 'Somaliland: 30 Years of De Facto Statehood, and No End In Sight' (*ISPI*, 7 May 2021) www.ispionline.it/en/publication/somaliland-30-years-de-facto-statehood-and-no-end-sight-30363, accessed 17 November 2022.

[86] Hong Kong Declaration, art 3.

Notably, the Joint Declaration refers to territorial integrity of Hong Kong and creates a special jurisdictional regime in this territory. The territorial status of Hong Kong is thus created under international law. But this cannot be said of Somaliland where the ability to exercise jurisdiction is fact rather than law-based.[87] Taiwan is a more complex example and will be dealt with later in this book.[88]

Certain instances of effective exercise of jurisdiction have been looked at from the prism of statehood and interpreted as *de facto* states, non-recognised states and similar. These are, however, instances of effective exercise of jurisdiction, not of 'de facto statehood'.[89] An influential proponent of factual emergence of states and the concept of 'illegal states', Stefan Talmon, argues:

> Even if the illegal State is declared null and void by international law, it will still have a Parliament that passes laws, an administration that implements those laws, and courts that apply them. It will still exercise sovereign authority over all people (both local and foreign) and objects on its territory; marriages will be performed in accordance with its laws by its officials, as will divorces; claims for debts will be brought before its courts and the judgments will be enforced by its agents; internationally active trading companies will be set up under its laws; it will grant citizenship, issue passports and grant concessions; it will issue its own currency, government bonds and stamps, have a national airline, armed forces and a merchant fleet, have a register for ships and aircraft, and grant them the right to fly its flag.[90]

Talmon then concludes that it would be absurd to deny the existence of a state that has met the formal criteria for statehood.[91] The examples given by Talmon are, however, the consequences of a territorial entity's ability to exercise jurisdiction in a certain spatial area, they are not necessarily consequences of statehood and neither can such *de facto* jurisdictional powers create statehood.

Moreover, Talmon's argument focuses only on those situations of territorial illegality where the effective authority seeks to create a state. But the problem is broader and brings into question also other instances of territorial illegality. With respect to Namibia, South Africa did not seek to create a state, but continued to administer the territory.[92] With respect to Crimea[93] and subsequently the

[87] Virgil (n 85).

[88] Tay-sheng Wang, 'The Legal Development of Taiwan in the 20th Century: Toward a Liberal and Democratic Country' (2002) 11 *Pacific Rim Law & Policy Journal* 531.

[89] Hans-Joachim Heintze, 'Are De Facto Regimes Bound by Human Rights?' (2009) *Organization for Security and Co-operation in Europe Yearbook* 267.

[90] Stefan Talmon, 'The Constitutive Versus the Declaratory Theory of Recognition: Tertium non Datur?' (2005) 75(1) *British Yearbook of International Law* 101.

[91] ibid.

[92] John Seiler, 'South Africa in Namibia: Persistence, Misperception, and Ultimate Failure' (1982) 20(4) *Journal of Modern African Studies* 689.

[93] Steven Pifer, 'Crimea: Six years after illegal annexation' (*Brookings*, 17 March 2020), www.brookings.edu/blog/order-from-chaos/2020/03/17/crimea-six-years-after-illegal-annexation, accessed 17 March 2022.

Donetsk and Luhansk regions,[94] Russia annexed these Ukrainian territories, although the process did initially run through declarations of independence.[95] One can now say that Russia has the effective power to exercise jurisdiction within these territories, but this effective power does not change the legal statuses of the territories. The same logic needs to be applied to those instances where independence is sought. Factual power to exercise jurisdiction in a certain spatial area does not create territorial title and status.

The question of territorial title is indeed of central importance for distinguishing between the factual ability to exercise territorial jurisdiction on the one hand and statehood or lawful territorial acquisition on the other. Where territorial title is not created, there can be no statehood or territorial acquisition under international law. But there can still be effective territorial control and exercise of jurisdiction.

Northern Cyprus and Crimea are governed by the same international legal framework,[96] although the former formally claims it is an independent state and the latter has been annexed by another state. Both situations are marked by territorial illegality stemming from external use of force.[97] Yet, if Northern Cyprus were considered to be a state under international law, albeit an illegal one, this status would be determined exclusively by the wrongdoer's claim to this effect. Crimea in this model would not be a state, albeit an illegal one, simply because the wrongdoer decided to claim annexation rather than statehood with respect of this territory. Northern Cyprus, conversely, would be an illegal *state* because the wrongdoer chose to formally claim statehood rather than annexation. The question of territorial title is in the background of both Northern Cyprus and Crimea. In the former situation, territorial title is claimed by the authority calling itself 'Turkish Republic of Northern Cyprus' (TRNC) and in the latter it is claimed by Russia, an existing state. In both situations, the creation of legal title is prevented by territorial illegality caused by aggression.[98]

[94] Yasmeen Serhan, 'Russia's Annexation of Ukrainian Territory Is a Sign of Military Weakness' (*Time*, 29 September 2022), time.com/6217710/russia-annexation-ukraine-donetsk-luhansk-kherson-aporizhzhia, accessed 19 December 2022.

[95] 'Ukraine separatists declare independence' (*AlJazeera*, 12 May 2014), www.aljazeera.com/news/2014/5/12/ukraine-separatists-declare-independence, accessed 23 October 2022.

[96] Jure Vidmar, 'Crimea's Referendum and Secession: Why it Resembles Northern Cyprus More than Kosovo' (*EJIL:Talk!*, 20 March 2014), www.ejiltalk.org/crimeas-referendum-and-secession-why-it-resembles-northern-cyprus-more-than-kosovo, accessed 16 April 2022.

[97] Robin Geiß, 'Russia's Annexation of Crimea: The Mills of International Law Grind Slowly but They Do Grind' (2015) 9 *International Law Studies* 425.

[98] Annie Charalambous, 'Political controversy in northern Cyprus over proposed name change of breakaway state' (*InCyprus*, 23 February 2023), in-cyprus.philenews.com/news/local/political-controversy-in-northern-cyprus-over-proposed-name-change-of-breakaway-state, accessed 2 January 2022.

In the *Wall* Advisory Opinion, the International Court of Justice (ICJ) extended the concept of territorial illegality and the obligation to withhold recognition beyond the context of state creation:

> [T]he Court is of the view that all States are under an obligation not to recognize the illegal situation resulting from the construction of the wall in the Occupied Palestinian Territory, including in and around East Jerusalem. They are also under an obligation not to render aid or assistance in maintaining the situation created by such construction.[99]

This confirms that territorial illegality not only prevents state creation, but more generally prevents any change in territorial status under international law.

It is in practice indeed difficult to navigate between the *pro forma* claims of the wrongdoer in such situations. Russia initially backed declarations of independence of Crimea, Donetsk and Luhansk, and subsequently took action under domestic law to annex the territories, which it had previously recognised as states.[100] Conversely, the 'TRNC' declared independence, but Turkey did not formally annex it as a matter of domestic law. Yet, given its dependence on Turkey,[101] the 'TRNC' in many respects functions as if it were an annexed territory. The effect is the same or at least very similar, and international law cannot let legal regulation of territorial status be determined by the wrongdoer's *pro forma* claim. The line between territorial conquest and 'illegal statehood' is thus fuzzy and dependent on the claim the wrongdoer chooses to make at a particular moment.

It is better to focus on the underlying question of territorial title and status. The 'TRNC' has no legal authority to create statehood over the spatial area of northern Cyprus and Russia has no legal authority to acquire the spatial areas that form the territory of Ukraine. This makes both effective territorial situations illegal under international law. It is of little help, however, to introduce the concept of 'illegal statehood' if 'statehood' ought to have a legal meaning. One could descriptively use terminology such as *de facto* or illegal states to refer to 'bordered power containers' capable of exercising territorial jurisdiction, but not in the sense of statehood as a form of territorial status.[102]

The concept of illegal states has flaws of theoretical and practical nature, and ultimately conflates jurisdiction with statehood. A degree of effectiveness of such entities stems from the fact that they are able to exercise jurisdiction over a certain spatial area. But the ability to exercise jurisdiction does not imply

[99] *Legal Consequences of the Construction of a Wall* (Advisory Opinion) General List No 131 (2004) ICJ, para 159.

[100] Serhan (n 94).

[101] Feride Asli Ergul Jorgensen and Dilek Latif, 'Different than us? Reciprocal perceptions of the societies in Turkey and North Cyprus' (2022) 27(3) *Mediterranean Politics* 369.

[102] Elden (n 24) 799–817.

or even create a state or other form of territorial title (for example, territorial expansion).

This section has argued that the concept of statehood and other forms of legal status need to be detached from the concept of jurisdiction. It may well be true that it is primarily states which exercise jurisdiction in contemporary international law. But an exercise of jurisdiction is not an exclusive prerogative of states. International practice has indeed seen a great number of non-state territories with jurisdictional authority.

Therefore, evidence of effective exercise of jurisdiction should not be taken as evidence of statehood, albeit 'merely' *de facto*, illegal or unrecognised statehood.[103] Article 1 of the Montevideo Convention has become known as an elaboration of the statehood criteria, while it should, rather, be seen as a description of jurisdictional authority.[104] A state can only emerge in contemporary international law if the authority declaring independence has territorial title to spatial area in which it seeks to establish the legal status of statehood. Likewise, an existing state can only acquire new territory if it has territorial title to the spatial area concerned. In both circumstances, the territorial status of the spatial area will need to be altered and territorial title transferred. In contemporary international law this does not occur on the basis of effective possession. It is a legally regulated process which will be addressed in subsequent chapters of this book.

IV. REGULATING CONSEQUENCES OF EXERCISING FACTUAL JURISDICTION WITHOUT LEGAL TITLE

International legal doctrine has also accommodated certain other instances where the effective authority may bear a certain level of responsibility for its factual exercise of jurisdictional powers in a certain spatial area, but such responsibility would not interfere with territorial title. Examples are the law of occupation, the so-called Namibia exception and the extraterritorial jurisdictional model developed particularly in the case law of the European Court of Human Rights (ECtHR).

A. The Law of Occupation

The law of occupation is a good example of international law regulating certain consequences of the factual situation, however illegal it may be, yet without shifting the territorial title *de jure*. Eyal Benvenisti fundamentally

[103] Van Essen (n 83) 3149.
[104] Montevideo Convention, art 1.

defines occupation as 'effective control of a power … over a territory to which that power has no sovereign title, without the volition of the sovereign of that territory'.[105] Benvenisti further notes that 'the occupant's authority does not derive from a right to control but from the fact of control'.[106] The law of occupation thus shares the underlying idea of international humanitarian law: *jus in bello* is not contingent on legality or illegality under *jus ad bellum*. Likewise, the law of occupation applies even where the factual occupying power has no legal authority to govern a certain spatial area. While Benvenisti and some other authors refer to 'sovereign title',[107] this book uses the term 'territorial title'. This term is used to avoid another loaded term – sovereignty – which is used to describe multiple things in contemporary legal and political theory.[108] The term 'territorial title' refers to the legal authority of a public power to govern a certain spatial area. In the context of the law of occupation, the occupying power does not gain territorial title, but assumes certain obligations pertaining to the administration of the occupied territory.

The rules of the law of occupation may be said to have two basic components: spatial and personal.[109] The spatial component is primarily reflected in Article 42 of the 1907 Hague Regulations which, *inter alia*, provides: 'Territory is considered occupied when it is actually placed under the authority of the hostile army. The occupation applies only to the territory where such authority is established, and in a position to assert itself.'[110] The territorial status of occupation is thus a question of effective control and factual determination of when and where such a control has been established. As the ICJ noted in the *Congo v Uganda* case: 'The Court observes that, under customary international law, as reflected in Article 42 of the Hague Regulations of 1907, territory is considered to be occupied when it is actually placed under the authority of the hostile army, and the occupation extends only to the territory where such authority has been established and can be exercised.'[111]

The rules on the personal component of occupation are set out in the Fourth Geneva Convention (GCIV).[112] There is some debate, however, whether effective territorial control is in itself enough for the law of occupation to apply or

[105] Eyal Benvenisti, *The International Law of Occupation* (OUP 1993) 43.
[106] ibid.
[107] ibid, 348.
[108] John DB Miller, 'Sovereignty as a Source of Vitality for the State' (1986) 12(2) *Review of International Studies* 79; Martin Loughlin, 'The Erosion of Sovereignty' (2016) 45(2) *Netherlands Journal of Legal Philosophy* 57. See also Antonia Waltermann, *Reconstructing Sovereignty* (Springer 2019).
[109] Marko Milanovic, 'Al-Skeini and Al-Jedda in Strasbourg' (2012) 23(1) *European Journal of International Law* 121.
[110] Laws and Customs of War on Land (Hague IV) (adopted 18 October 1907, entered into force 26 January 1910) 205 CTS 277, art 42.
[111] *Case Concerning Armed Activities on the Territory of the Congo (Democratic Republic of the Congo v Uganda)* (Judgment) ICJ, General List No 116 (2005) ICJ, para 172.
[112] Geneva Convention Relative to the Protection of Civilian Persons in Time of War (adopted 12 August 1949, entered into force 21 October 1950) 75 UNTS 287 (Geneva Convention IV).

whether control over the population also needs to be established.[113] It is not necessary for the purposes of this book to thoroughly consider this question. It should suffice to recall Benvenisti's observation:

> The better interpretation of the test for occupation ... stipulates that occupation begins when the foreign army is in actual control over enemy territory, and is in a position to establish, if it so wishes, an authority of its own over the population. It is irrelevant whether the army actually does so. By assuming control over the land the occupant assumes responsibility over the population situated on that land.[114]

It is of particular significance for this book that the status of an occupied territory is accorded on the basis of factual determination and without regard to legal title or legal process. This is much different in the law of statehood, for example, where effective control does not create a legal status.[115]

Another important question in the law of occupation is whether these rules could potentially apply in any spatial area on Earth. While the 1907 Hague Regulations and the GCIV are generally applicable as customary international law, they appeared to be focused on states. It is thus questionable whether they can apply also in spatial areas that do not constitute (a part) of territory of any state.

In this regards, Article 2(2) of the GCIV, *inter alia*, provides: 'The Convention shall also apply to all cases of partial or total occupation of the territory of a High Contracting Party, even if the said occupation meets with no armed resistance.'[116] In the *Wall* Advisory Opinion, the ICJ stated:

> The object of the second paragraph of Article 2 [GC IV] is not to restrict the scope of application of the Convention, as defined by the first paragraph, by excluding therefrom territories not falling under the sovereignty of one of the contracting parties. It is directed simply to making it clear that, even if occupation effected during the conflict met no armed resistance, the Convention is still applicable. This interpretation reflects the intention of the drafters of the Fourth Geneva Convention to protect civilians who find themselves, in whatever way, in the hands of the occupying Power. Whilst the drafters of the Hague Regulations of 1907 were as much concerned with protecting the rights of a State whose territory is occupied, as with protecting the inhabitants of that territory, the drafters of the Fourth Geneva Convention sought to guarantee the protection of civilians in time of war, regardless of the status of the occupied territories, as is shown by Article 47 of the Convention.[117]

The Court thereby decided that the law of occupation applies even where an occupying power is not necessarily occupying a territory of another party to

[113] Tristan Ferraro, 'Determining the Beginning and End of an Occupation under International Humanitarian Law' (2012) 94(885) *International Review of the Red Cross* 133.

[114] Benvenisti (n 105) 50.

[115] Janis Grzybowski, 'To Be or Not to Be: The Ontological Predicament of State Creation in International Law' (2017) 28(2) *European Journal of International Law* 409.

[116] Geneva Convention IV, art 2.2.

[117] *Wall* Advisory Opinion, para 95.

the GCIV or indeed of another state. As long as a territory is occupied by a state, the law of occupation applies. This position may well prevent a gap or a legal black hole in ambiguous territorial situations where the territory in question may not even be a state, such as Palestine. But is the position doctrinally persuasive in terms of treaty law and in light of the fact that Palestine is not a party to the GCIV?

With regard to the effects of treaty law, the Court decided that the GCIV was applicable because of the situation prior to 1967 when Israel was in conflict with Jordan. Both Israel and Jordan were party to this particular treaty.[118] The present-day legal situation is thus still piggybacking on Jordan and it being party to the relevant treaty, and does not depend on the legal status of Palestine. While this view may be doctrinally defensible, the more problematic issue is the Court's interpretation of the scope of Article 2(2) GCIV.

It may well be that the object and purpose of Article 2(2) GCIV was to reiterate the applicability of the Convention to those situations where occupation is met by no armed resistance. But it is also clear that Article 2(2) textually refers to 'occupation of the territory of a high contracting party'.[119] It does not refer to occupation of *any* territory, which is how the ICJ obviously read it.

Arguably, the customary rule regulating the matter could be broader than Article 2(2) GCIV. By analogy, Article 2(4) UN Charter also refers to members of the UN while its customary reflection applies to all states, not only to UN members. This was even more important historically than it is today when nearly all states in the world are UN members.[120] There is thus no doubt that the customary reflection of Article 2(4) UN Charter would apply to and between all states in the world. It is a separate, and indeed much more controversial question, however, whether the customary reflection of Article 2(4) UN Charter would also apply to non-state territories and which ones (for example, Taiwan). These issues will be dealt with at a later stage of this book.[121]

Returning to the law of occupation, it appears that the law of occupation could indeed apply to any *populated* spatial area in the world, regardless of whether it constitutes a state territory. Following the ICJ's reasoning the *Wall* Advisory Opinion, this is the case because of the intentions of the drafters of the GCIV: they primarily sought to protect the inhabitants, not states.[122] Hence, it appears that Benvenisti is right in defining occupation as 'effective control of a

[118] Geneva Convention IV.

[119] Geneva Convention IV, art 2.2.

[120] 'Member States' (*United Nations*), www.un.org/en/about-us/member-states, accessed 30 October 2022.

[121] Ryan Fisher, 'Defending Taiwan: Collective Self-Defense of a Contested State' (2020) 32(1) *Journal of International Law* 101.

[122] 'Summary of the Geneva Conventions of 1949 and Their Additional Protocols' (*Red Cross*), www.redcross.org/content/dam/redcross/atg/PDF_s/International_Services/International_Humanitarian_Law/IHL_SummaryGenevaConv.pdf, accessed 5 January 2022.

power … over a territory to which that power has no sovereign title',[123] yet without a requirement of there being another *state's* territorial title to this spatial area. In order for the legal status of an occupied territory to be accorded, it only matters that the power in effective territorial control has no sovereign title to the spatial area in question, while the general legal status of that spatial area under general international law does not matter.

B. The Namibia Exception

Another example of international law accepting certain consequences of an effective territorial situation, yet without accepting a change in territorial status, is the so-called 'Namibia exception'.

In the *Namibia* Advisory Opinion, the ICJ reasoned:

> [T]he non-recognition of South Africa's administration of the Territory should not result in depriving the people of Namibia of any advantages derived from international co-operation. In particular, while official acts performed by the Government of South Africa on behalf of or concerning Namibia after the termination of the Mandate are illegal and invalid, this invalidity cannot be extended to those acts, such as, for instance, the registration of births, deaths and marriages, the effects of which can be ignored only to the detriment of the inhabitants of the Territory.[124]

The Namibia exception is explicitly mentioned in the International Law Commission's (ILC) Commentary to Article 41 of the Articles on the Responsibility of States for Internationally Wrongful Acts (ARSIWA)[125] which refers to the obligation of non-recognition 'as lawful a situation created by a serious breach within the meaning of article 40 [*jus cogens*]'.[126] Although territorial illegality, which will be further discussed later in this book,[127] precludes a change in legal status of a territory, international law allows for certain exceptions where private acts are concerned. In other words, certain sovereign acts of an illegal authority are accepted for the benefit of the population, regardless of the status of that authority and of the territory in question.

The *Namibia* exception has been applied by the European Court of Human Rights (ECtHR). In *Loizidou*, the Court held 'that international law recognises the legitimacy of certain legal arrangements and transactions in such a situation',

[123] Benvenisti (n 105) 43.

[124] *Legal Consequences for States of the Continued Presence of South Africa in Namibia (South West Africa) Notwithstanding Security Council Resolution 276 Namibia* (Advisory Opinion) General List No 53 (1971) ICJ, para 125.

[125] Articles on the Responsibility of States for Internationally Wrongful Acts (entered into force 8 January 2008) A/RES/62/61 (ARSIWA), Commentary to art 41, para 10.

[126] ARSIWA, art 41.2.

[127] Enrico Milano, *Unlawful Territorial Situations in International Law, Reconciling Effectiveness, Legality and Legitimacy* (Brill/Nijhoff 2005) 234–65.

for instance as regards the registration of births, deaths and marriages [quoting the ICJ *Namibia* Advisory Opinion] 'the effects of which can be ignored only to the detriment of the inhabitants of the [t]erritory'.[128] In *Cyprus v Turkey*, the ECtHR reasoned:

> As it [the Court] observed in its Loizidou judgment (*merits*) with reference to the Advisory Opinion of the International Court of Justice in the Namibia case, international law recognises the legitimacy of certain legal arrangements and transactions in situations such as the one obtaining in the 'TRNC,' for instance as regards the registration of births, deaths, and marriages, 'the effects of which can only be ignored to the detriment of the inhabitants of the [t]erritory.'[129]

The Court then went on to conclude that 'despite having been invited to do so by the Secretary-General of the UN, the ICJ resolutely rejected the approach refusing any effect to unlawful *de facto* regimes'.[130] Express references to the Namibia exception have been made by the ECtHR for example in *Mozer*[131] and *Güzelyurtlu*.[132] The effect of the Namibia exception was aptly summarised by Judge Pinto de Albuquerque in his dissent in *Chiragov:*

> [The] 'Namibia exception' has been enshrined in the Court's case-law, since the cases on the Turkish invasion of Cyprus, with the practical consequence that, when confronted with violations of Article 8 of the Convention and Article 1 of Protocol No. 1, the current and former inhabitants of a territory must exhaust the local remedies even in the case of a judicial system established by an unrecognised political regime, and even where they did not choose voluntarily to place themselves under its jurisdiction.[133]

It is of particular relevance to recall that the Court used the term 'unlawful *de facto* regimes' which are not without any effect and Judge Pinto de Albuquerque to 'judicial system established by an unrecognised political regime' under whose (involuntary) jurisdiction the inhabitants of the territory find themselves. These pronouncements go to the core of the situation at stake: the Namibia exception acknowledges that an illegal authority may still have the factual capacity to exercise jurisdiction over a territory and its population, and that certain aspects of this *de facto* jurisdictional power need to be accepted.

While Talmon argues that it would be absurd not to accept that an effective territorial authority is a state,[134] it is rather that it would be absurd not to accept

[128] *Loizidou v Turkey* App No 15318/89 (ECtHR, 23 March 1995), para 45.

[129] *Cyprus v Turkey* App No 25781/94 (ECtHR, 10 May 2001), para 90.

[130] ibid, para 94.

[131] *Mozer v the Republic of Moldova and Russia* App no 11138/10 (ECtHR, 23 February 2016), para 137.

[132] *Güzelyurtlu and Others v Cyprus and Turkey* App No 36925/07 (ECtHR, 29 January 2019), para 158.

[133] *Chiragov and Others v Armenia* App No 13216/05 (ECtHR, 16 June 2015), Dissenting Opinion of Judge Pinto de Albuquerque, para 4.

[134] Stefan Talmon, 'The Responsibility of Outside Powers for Acts of Secessionist Entities' (2009) 58(3) *International and Comparative Law Quarterly* 493.

certain aspects of jurisdictional power exercised by non-state effective territorial authorities. In contemporary international law, territorial title cannot change simply by evidence of effective exercise of territorial jurisdiction.[135] Territorial conquest is not compatible with the fundamental rules on territorial integrity and self-determination, as enshrined in UN Charter[136] and in the Declaration on Principles of International Law.[137] While international territorial status cannot be altered by effective power, rejections of birth, death, marriage and divorce certificates issued by effective public authorities, whatever their international legal status may be, would lead to absurd situations. Yet, it is one thing to accept a birth certificate issued by the so-called Turkish Republic of Northern Cyprus and quite another to claim that this entity is a state because it has the capacity to *inter alia* issue birth certificates. The factual capacity to issue birth certificates is a matter of effective exercise of jurisdiction which may well have effects under private international law even where the issuing authority is illegal and a non-state, while statehood is a matter of legal status under public international law. The concepts of jurisdiction and statehood need to be analysed separately.

What the Namibia exception did in effect was to detach certain aspects of South Africa's effective jurisdictional authority in Namibia (South-West Africa) from the question of legal status of territory under international law. Likewise, the acceptance of certain jurisdictional powers of the illegal Turkey-backed and Russia-backed jurisdiction in Northern Cyprus and Transnistria, respectively, should not be conflated with the question of their legal statuses, or even seen as *de facto* recognition of their statehood. It only means that these authorities have the ability to exercise *de facto* jurisdiction in respective spatial areas and that certain expects of such jurisdictional power need to be accommodated internationally, particularly under private international law, for the benefit of the inhabitants.

C. The Extraterritorial Jurisdictional Model and Effective Control

This chapter now turns to the entanglement of extraterritorial exercise of jurisdiction and effective control over a certain spatial area. Particularly relevant in this context is the case law of the ECtHR which has also developed a somewhat complicated relationship between these two concepts. While the Court's case law confirms the basic premise of this book – that territorial status is not created and altered by effective exercise of jurisdiction in a certain spatial area – the case law also points to the close-knit yet difficult relationship between territory and

[135] cf n 126 and accompanying text.

[136] Eugene Kontorovich, 'International Responses to Territorial Conquest' (2008) 102 *Proceedings of the Annual Meeting (American Society of International Law)* 437.

[137] UNGA Res 2625 (24 October 1970) UN Doc A/RES/2625 (XXV).

jurisdiction. The fundamental question at stake is whether and in which circumstances states parties to the European Convention on Human Rights (ECHR or the Convention) can violate the Convention when acting outside of their own territory. The problem is amplified by the wording of Article 1 ECHR: 'The High Contracting Parties shall secure to everyone within their jurisdiction the rights and freedoms defined in Section I of this Convention.'[138] When is somebody under jurisdiction of a state party to the Convention and what role does the spatial dimension play in this determination?

i. Effective Territorial Control in and Outside of the Law of Occupation

In *Banković*, the ECtHR argued that 'the desirability of avoiding a gap or vacuum in human rights' protection has so far been relied on by the Court in favour of establishing jurisdiction only when the territory in question was one that, but for the specific circumstances, would normally be covered by the Convention'.[139] In this particular case, the Court distinguished the situation in Northern Cyprus from that in the Federal Republic of Yugoslavia (FRY) as the Convention was applicable in the territory of Cyprus as a whole. In the territory of the 'TRNC', however, Turkey could be made responsible for its violations due to this state being in effective control of the spatial area concerned.[140] Conversely, the FRY was not a party to the Convention at the time of the factual occurrence that led to the *Banković* case, while states parties acting within the territory of the FRY did not bring the Convention along into the non-covered territory.

This doctrine has been modified in subsequent case law and the Convention has clearly been applied even with respect to the conduct of states parties in non-covered territories. In *Al-Skeini*, for example, the Court reasoned that 'the importance of establishing the occupying State's jurisdiction in … does not imply, *a contrario*, that jurisdiction under Article 1 of the Convention can never exist outside the territory covered by the Council of Europe member States'.[141] It is now settled that states parties to the ECHR can violate their obligations under the Convention even outside their own territories and regardless of whether the spatial area in question forms a part of the territory of another state party. At the same time, even the territorial state may retain its obligations in the spatial area over which it exercises no control as a result of another state's actions. In *Ilaşcu*, the Court declared that 'even in the absence of effective control over the Transdniestrian region, Moldova still has a positive obligation under Article 1 of the Convention to take the diplomatic, economic, judicial or other measures that it is in its power to take and are in accordance with international law to

[138] European Convention on Human Rights of 1953 (adopted 4 November 1950, entry into force 3 September 1953) ETS 5, art 1.

[139] *Banković and Others v Belgium* App No 52207/99 (ECtHR, 12 December 2001), para 80.

[140] ibid.

[141] *Al-Skeini and Others v the United Kingdom* App No 55721/07 (ECtHR, 7 July 2011), para 142.

secure to the applicants the rights guaranteed by the Convention'.[142] This issue has been criticised by some commentators,[143] but is not of central importance to this chapter. The focus will be on extraterritoriality and the examination of a discrepancy between effective territorial situation and the legal status of territory.

How is it determined when a state can violate or has violated the Convention extraterritorially? Remy Jorritsma argues: 'Looking at the Court's case law in retrospect, it is possible to discern that the extraterritorial application of the Convention has crystalised along the lines of two models: the personal model and the territorial model.'[144] The former model means that a state party to the ECHR exercises outside of its own territory effective control over an individual or group of individuals, while the latter model is spatial in nature. As the ECtHR reasoned in *Jaloud*, an 'exception to the principle that jurisdiction under Article 1 is limited to a State's own territory occurs when, as a consequence of lawful or unlawful military action, a Contracting State exercises effective control of an area outside that national territory'.[145]

The question then arises how much control is needed for the effective control threshold to be met and how does one geographically define such a spatial area where effective control is exercised. In this regard, one can in principle distinguish between two versions of the spatial model: (i) occupation;[146] and (ii) where a state party to the ECHR effectively controls a part of the territory of another state in a manner not falling within the ambit of the law of occupation. As Jorritsma further argues: 'The classical example of occupation is where a State's armed forces exercise territorial control so as to constitute an occupying power. Less straightforward, however, are situations that are not "classical" occupations in the sense of continued presence of a State's own armed forces.'[147]

In determining extraterritorial application of the Convention, the Court focuses on effective control over a spatial area and acknowledges that this can happen even outside of the framework of occupation under international humanitarian law. In *Georgia v Russia*, the Court reasoned:

> Generally speaking, international humanitarian law applies in a situation of 'occupation'. In the Court's view, the concept of 'occupation' for the purposes of international humanitarian law includes a requirement of 'effective control.' If there is 'occupation' for the purposes of international humanitarian law there will also

[142] *Ilaşcu and Others v Moldova and Russia* App No 48787/99 (ECtHR, 8 July 2004), para 331.
[143] Anthony Cullen and Steven Wheatley, 'The Human Rights of Individuals in De Facto Regimes under the European Convention on Human Rights' (2013) 13(4) *Human Rights Law Review* 691.
[144] Remy Jorritsma, *International Responsibility and Attribution of Conduct: An Analysis of Case Law on Human Rights and Humanitarian Law* (PhD thesis, University of Maastricht, 2021) 172.
[145] *Jaloud v the Netherlands* App No 47708/08 (ECtHR, 20 November 2014), para 138.
[146] *Al-Skeini* (n 141) paras 130–42.
[147] Jorritsma (n 144) 177. See also Remy Jorritsma, 'Unravelling Attribution, Control and Jurisdiction: Some Reflections on the Case Law of the European Court of Human Rights' in Helene Ruiz Fabri (ed), *International Law and Litigation: A Look into Procedure* (Baden Baden 2019) 659.

> be 'effective control' within the meaning of the Court's case-law, although the term 'effective control' is broader and covers situations that do not necessarily amount to a situation of 'occupation' for the purposes of international humanitarian law.[148]

The Court thereby assumed that whenever there is a situation of occupation in the sense of international humanitarian law,[149] the effective control test would be met and the occupied territory brought under the jurisdictional scope of the Convention. At the same time, a state party to the Convention may have effective control over a certain territory even outside of the framework of occupation. In other words, every occupation also implies effective control over the territory in question, but not every exercise of effective control implies an occupation of that territory in the technical sense of international humanitarian law.

The Court's pronouncement in *Georgia v Russia* is not entirely unproblematic, and it is debatable whether the doctrines outlined above work in every situation and without any further qualification. Marko Milanovic has called this approach of the Court 'overly simplistic',[150] and perhaps also inspired by the factual circumstances in *Georgia v Russia*. As Milanovic further argues, assuming that occupation always brings the occupied territory within the jurisdictional scope of the ECHR 'presupposes a clear line in IHL terms between an invasion and an occupation … neglects the … issue of subsequent insurgency within an occupied territory [and] … [the] idea of occupation necessarily requiring effective control has been very contested in recent years'.[151]

In other words, even where we are in principle dealing with occupation, it may be a bit too simplistic to presuppose that the effective control test would be met automatically and/or at all times. Nevertheless, the ECtHR's approach indicates at least a conceptual attempt to separate occupations from other territorial situations where a state party to the ECHR may be, lawfully or unlawfully, exercising effective control over a spatial area outside of its own territory.

The result of the effective control doctrine is that the spatial area under control of a state party to the ECHR becomes an extension of the territory of that state for the purposes of its obligations under the Convention. In the *Netherlands v Russia* case, the Court argued that the Convention applies 'where there is effective control over an area, whether exercised directly by the Contracting State's own armed forces or via the local subordinate administration, there is *ratione loci* jurisdiction … For Article 1 purposes, therefore, the area in question is treated as being indistinguishable from areas within the controlling State's sovereign borders.'[152]

[148] *Georgia v Russia* App No 38263/08 (ECtHR, 21 January 2021), para 196.
[149] ibid, 138–42.
[150] Marko Milanovic, 'Georgia v. Russia No. 2: The European Court's Resurrection of Bankovic in the Contexts of Chaos' (*EJIL:Talk!*, 25 January 2021), www.ejiltalk.org/georgia-v-russia-no-2-the-european-courts-resurrection-of-bankovic-in-the-contexts-of-chaos, accessed 6 October 2022.
[151] Milanovic (n 150).
[152] *The Netherlands v Russia* App No 28525/20 (ECtHR, 25 January 2023), para 561.

The applicability of the ECHR is thus a good example of how a legal regime can regulate the consequences of an effective territorial situation, regardless of how illegally it may have been realised, yet without changing the territorial title of the spatial area concerned. The question of territorial title was indirectly argued in *Ukraine v Russia* (re Crimea) before the ECtHR where one of the questions posed to the Court was whether Russia exercised its jurisdiction in Crimea territorially or extraterritorially. Implicit in this question was the legal status of Crimea and title to this territory. Perhaps somewhat surprisingly, the Court did not avoid this question, and argued that 'for the purposes of this admissibility decision, the Court will proceed on the basis of the assumption that the jurisdiction of the respondent State over Crimea is in the form or nature of "effective control over an area" rather than in the form or nature of territorial jurisdiction.'[153]

The Court's pronouncement on this matter is even more surprising because 'the form or nature' of jurisdiction should not really matter in the light of the position that the spatial area under effective control of a state is 'indistinguishable from areas within the controlling State's sovereign borders'.[154] It may well be that the ECtHR here overstepped the boundaries of the Convention and made a pronouncement on territorial status and territorial title under general public international law. This position is nevertheless consistent with established doctrines of public international law where territorial status does not change with effective control. This will be further discussed in subsequent sections.

ii. Determining the Spatial Area of an Effective Control

Another conceptual problem the ECtHR has faced, or in fact created, is the issue of an *ad hoc* definition of a spatial area in which a state party to the Convention extraterritorially exercises effective control. The spatial area for these purposes may not be an entire state or an administrative unit within the state, but a rather narrowly defined area in which agents of the state party to the Convention operate extraterritorially.

In *Jaloud*, the ECtHR reasoned:

> Although Netherlands troops were stationed in an area in south-eastern Iraq where SFIR [Stabilisation Force in Iraq] forces were under the command of an officer from the United Kingdom, the Netherlands assumed responsibility for providing security in that area, to the exclusion of other participating States, and retained full command over its contingent there.[155]
>
> …
>
> The Court is satisfied that the respondent Party exercised its 'jurisdiction' within the limits of its SFIR mission and for the purpose of asserting authority and control

[153] *Ukraine v Russia (re Crimea)* App No 20958/14 (ECtHR, 16 December 2020), para 349.
[154] *The Netherlands v Russia* (n 152) para 561.
[155] *Jaloud* (n 145) para 149.

> over persons passing through the checkpoint. That being the case, the Court finds that the death of Mr Azhar Sabah Jaloud occurred within the 'jurisdiction' of the Netherlands, as that expression is to be construed within the meaning of Article 1 of the Convention.[156]

Notably, the Court here established that the Netherlands assumed effective control and thus responsibility over a checkpoint. It did not matter what the status was of the Iraqi territory as a whole or of a larger area within Iraq (ie south-eastern Iraq). The ECtHR treated the checkpoint as the *territory* controlled by the Netherlands and thus within the jurisdictional scope of the ECHR.

The fundamental question that arises here is whether the Court is reinventing the wheel and creating several theoretical and practical problems in doing so. The question of extraterritorial application of the Convention could be conceptually covered by the rules of attribution under the law of state responsibility.[157] While the ECtHR often makes general references to these rules, as elaborated under ARSIWA, it fails to base its argumentation in the attribution rules.[158] The effective-control-based spatial model followed by the Court has become especially problematic.

It was argued above that in situations of occupation effective territorial control cannot be automatically presumed in all situations and at all times. The non-occupation spatial model creates the problem of *ad hoc* micro-territories where the state party to the Convention is presumed to be in effective control. An effectively controlled territory for these purposes can be a fairly small spatial area in which agents of a state party to the Convention operate. It does appear to be excessively arbitrary to define such micro-territories. The question of whether a state would have effective control over a certain spatial area outside of its own territory can quite crucially depend on the size of that area. In principle, the smaller the area, the higher the likelihood of there being effective control. To use an example, consider the French border control at St Pancras Station in London. If the territory were defined as the French passport control booth, France would likely have effective control in that spatial area. If the territory were defined as the whole of St Pancras Station, France probably would not be in effective control over the so-defined territory. And France most certainly would not have effective control if the territory were defined even more broadly, for example London or even the United Kingdom as a whole.

The logic is reminiscent of the logic of market dominance in competition law: the smaller the market, the greater the likelihood of market dominance of

[156] ibid, para 152.

[157] Cedric Ryngaert, 'Attributing Conduct in the Law of State Responsibility: Lessons from Dutch Courts Applying the Control Standard in the Context of International Military Operations' (2021) 36 *Utrecht Journal of International and European Law* 170.

[158] 'Report of the Steering Committee for Human Rights (CDDH) adopted at its 92nd meeting' (*ECHR*, 26 November 2019), www.echr.coe.int/LibraryDocs/COE-2020-The_place_of_the_ECHR_in_the_European_and_international_legal_order.pdf, accessed 13 December 2022.

a certain firm.[159] While competition law has developed very meticulous rules on market definition, the non-occupation spatial model for determining effective control lacks theoretical coherence, and the ECtHR's case law on the matter appears to be inconclusive and even contradictory.[160]

iii. Jurisdiction or Attribution?

The questions of jurisdiction and effective control are even more complicated where a state party to the Convention acts outside of own territory by proxy. Jorritsma argues:

> [A] State may, without ever having had its own 'boots on the ground,' control or otherwise support a non-State actor, which in turn can be said to exercise territorial control on the State's behalf. These situations have proven to pose difficulties, in particular because the question of occupation (or other forms of territorial control) and consequently the extraterritorial application of the Convention, is often intrinsically tied to the question of attribution.[161]

Indeed, the ECtHR has conflated on several occasions the questions of jurisdiction and state responsibility. As Milanovic argues:

> The key difference between Article 1 [ECHR] jurisdiction and attribution of conduct is that jurisdiction is the threshold criterion for the existence of legal obligations, that is, a prerequisite for the existence of a breach of the ECHR under Article 2(b) ASR [Articles on State Responsibility], and not a criterion of attribution under Article 2(a) ASR. The focus of the control tests under Article 1, which superficially resemble the language of control tests for attribution purposes, is on control over the victim of the human rights violation or the place where they are located, not on control over the actor that committed the violation.[162]

Nevertheless, the Court has in its case law blurred the distinction. This has become particularly obvious where a state party to the Convention has been deemed responsible for breaches of the Convention on the basis of a non-state actor involvement. The paramount examples are Northern Cyprus[163] and Transnistria.[164] Turkey and Russia, respectively, have been persistently found to be in violation of the Convention in these spatial areas. Clearly in the background of the Court's reasoning is attribution to Turkey and Russia of the

[159] Cf Ariel Ezrachi, *EU Competition Law: An Analytical Guide to the Leading Cases* (Hart 2014) 31–52.
[160] Marko Milanovic, 'Foreign Surveillance and Human Rights, Part 3: Models of Extraterritorial Application' (*EJIL:Talk!*, 27 November 2013), www.ejiltalk.org/foreign-surveillance-and-human-rights-part-3-models-of-extraterritorial-application, accessed 16 December 2022.
[161] Jorritsma (n 144) 659–94.
[162] Marko Milanovic, 'Special Rules of Attribution of Conduct in International Law' (2020) 96 *International Law Studies* 295.
[163] *Cyprus v Turkey* (n 129) para 80.
[164] *Ilaşcu* (n 142) para 442.

conduct of the 'TRNC' and Transnistrian authorities, although the Court persistently avoids using this language.[165] Indeed, in *Jaloud* the Court explicitly stated: 'The Court reiterates that the test for establishing the existence of "jurisdiction" under Article 1 of the Convention has never been equated with the test for establishing a State's responsibility for an internationally wrongful act under general international law.'[166]

This pronouncement of the Court is not persuasive. It is one thing to deviate from the attribution rules under general international law and quite another to claim that the whole exercise is not a matter of attribution at all. While some specialised legal regimes may have developed certain *lex specialis* attribution rules that depart from the generally applicable ones developed in the ICJ's *Nicaragua* test[167] and are further elaborated on in ARSIWA,[168] these are still rules of attribution.

Article 2 ARSIWA provides: 'There is an internationally wrongful act of a State when conduct consisting of an action or omission: (a) is attributable to the State under international law; and (b) constitutes a breach of an international obligation of the State.'[169] This provision encompasses the structure of an international legal obligation. There can be no internationally wrongful act if the state in question did not have the relevant legal obligation, and the conduct cannot be attributed to that state. To use the ECHR as an example, Australia cannot breach the ECHR because as a non-party it does not have any obligations under it. Turkey can breach the Convention, however, but only if the conduct in question is attributable to it. What the Court has actually done in its case law, such as *Loizidou*, is that without an explicit pronouncement it attributed the conduct of the 'TRNC' authorities to Turkey. This indeed means that Turkey can incur international responsibility for violations of the ECHR even if the relevant conduct occurred outside of Turkey and was formally not authored by a state organ of Turkey. But the Court can reach such a conclusion because it attributed to Turkey the conduct of the 'TRNC', a non-state actor for the purposes of international law. Even if the Court refuses to put a label on this process, this (silently) is still attribution.

It appears that the Court has become increasingly aware of the confusion. In *The Netherlands v Russia*, the Court reasoned:

> while the test for establishing the existence of jurisdiction under Article 1 of the Convention is not the same as the test for establishing a State's responsibility for an internationally wrongful act under international law, now codified in ARSIWA … there may be some areas of overlap in so far as the Court is invited to examine

[165] Milanovic (n 162) 295–393.
[166] *Jaloud* (n 145) para 154.
[167] *Case Concerning Military and Paramilitary Activities in and Against Nicaragua* (Judgment) General List No 70 (1986) ICJ, para 109.
[168] ARSIWA, art 8.
[169] ARSIWA, art 2.

> whether any acts of the perpetrators are to be attributed to the State in the context of its jurisdiction assessment. In determining whether an individual or entity may be considered a State agent, the rules set out in the ARSIWA as applied by international courts and tribunals are clearly relevant and the Court's case-law shows that they are taken into account.[170]

While the Court may be acknowledging the importance of attribution and ARSIWA, it maintains the artificial distinction between jurisdiction and attribution. As Milanovic has noted, 'the state must exercise jurisdiction through its own organs or agents … [in order] to establish whether certain individuals are … [state agents] the Court needs to apply the attribution standards of the law of state responsibility (which are *binding law*, not just something *relevant* and *to be taken into account*).[171] Indeed, the question here is whether a certain conduct can be classified as an act of a state party to the ECHR. This determination depends on the rules of attribution. And where the conduct in question can be attributed to a state party to the ECHR, the Convention applies.

It appears that in *The Netherlands v Russia*, the Court later in fact acknowledged that the Court's construction of jurisdiction is nothing other than attribution:

> [E]ven where allegations concern an area within the respondent State's *ratione loci* jurisdiction, that State will ultimately only be held responsible for breaches of the Convention if the impugned acts or omissions are attributable to it. In purely territorial cases, it is uncontroversial that the territorial State is responsible for the policies and actions of local administrations. Their acts and omissions are automatically attributable to the territorial State. It follows that in cases where a State's *ratione loci* jurisdiction is established outside its sovereign borders, the acts and omissions of the local administrations in the areas concerned will similarly be automatically attributable to the State which has Article 1 jurisdiction.[172]

Indeed, it is effective control over a spatial area outside of the state territory that makes the conduct of local authorities attributable to the controlling state. And here again the Court equated responsibility of the state for its territorial conduct with the conduct in a spatial area under the state's effective control. But why does the Court continue to conflate the matter with jurisdiction and does not more prominently and directly subscribe to the attribution tests under ARSIWA?

In sum, the concept of extraterritorial jurisdiction and the Court's dealings with the spatial model or jurisdiction are rather problematic. There is no problem with the presumption that a state party to the ECHR can violate its obligations

[170] *The Netherlands v Russia* (n 152) para 551.
[171] Marko Milanovic, 'The European Court's Admissibility Decision in Ukraine and the Netherlands v Russia: The Good, the Bad and the Ugly – Part I' (*EJIL:Talk!*, 26 January 2023), www.ejiltalk.org/the-european-courts-admissibility-decision-in-ukraine-and-the-netherlands-v-russia-the-good-the-bad-and-the-ugly-part-i, accessed 29 January 2023.
[172] *The Netherlands v Russia* (n 152) para 564.

under the Convention even with conduct that is geographically located outside of the state's own territory, regardless of whether that territory is otherwise covered by the Convention. It would be much more plausible, however, if the Court abandoned its doctrinally confusing approaches to jurisdiction and asked whether a certain extraterritorial conduct is attributable to the state party in question and whether that conduct potentially violates that state's obligations of the Convention. In other words, the Court should begin with the logic of Article 2 ARSIWA. And from there, it could develop certain *lex specialis* rules that could depart from Article 8 ARSIWA, for example. Effective control over a spatial area or persons could still be the threshold test for *attribution*, rather than jurisdiction. The concept of effective control of territory outside of the framework of occupation is also problematic. The smaller the territory the more likely it is that a certain state conducting extraterritorial operations with its agents would be in effective control of it. The Court has not developed a persuasive method to define a spatial area for these purposes.

The ECtHR's dealings with extraterritorial jurisdiction is not unproblematic and has been criticised by a number of academic commentators. Although not always entirely persuasive in its reasoning, the Court had to develop the doctrine of extraterritorial jurisdiction because territorial title and status under public international law are not created or altered by effective (territorial) control and *de facto* exercise of jurisdiction. In other words, the Court had to develop certain tools to prevent the legal vacuum that could arise due to the discrepancy between *de jure* territorial status and *de facto* territorial control. Despite some doctrinal deficiencies in the Court's case law, the ECtHR's judicial practice confirms that an effective exercise of jurisdictional powers within a certain spatial area does not create territorial title or alter territorial status.

V. THE ANACHRONISTIC CONCEPTS OF TERRITORIAL ACQUISITION

Territorial title was historically created by effective control in a certain spatial area. It has been demonstrated thus far in this chapter that this is no longer the case. Effective territorial control may lead to some obligations pertaining to territorial administration on the basis of effective exercise of jurisdiction, but does not create legal title.[173] Since territorial title nowadays is not created or altered by factual possession, territories cannot be acquired and territorial status cannot be changed on the basis of effective exercise of jurisdiction. This can only occur on the basis of a law-governed process. The whole extent of this process will be discussed in subsequent chapters in this book.[174] This chapter now turns to the historic modes of territorial acquisition and creation

[173] Grzybowski (n 115) 409–32.
[174] See chs 3 and 4.

of territorial status: occupation of *terrae nullius*, cession and conquest. It will be shown that these historic concepts are anachronistic and incompatible with the contemporary rules of international law. Yet, they still influence modern conceptualisations of territory, such as those that subscribe to the idea of there being statehood criteria,[175] and illegal and/or *de facto* states.[176]

A. The Obsolete Concept of *Terra Nullius*

An occupation of *terra nullius* was historically a valid mode of territorial acquisition.[177] The term occupation should not be conflated with the present-day term of art under international humanitarian law. When used historically, occupation is a descriptive term which indicates the factual creation of title to a territory deemed to be *terra nullius*. The status of *terra nullius* over a certain spatial area could only be established where this area was uninhabited. In *Western Sahara* Advisory Opinion, the ICJ reasoned:

> Whatever differences of opinion there may have been among jurists, the State practice of the relevant period indicates that territories inhabited by tribes or peoples having a social and political organization were not regarded as terrae nullius. It shows that in the case of such territories the acquisition of sovereignty was not generally considered as effected unilaterally through 'occupation' of terra nullius by original title but through agreements concluded with local rulers. On occasion, it is true, the word 'occupation' was used in a non-technical sense denoting simply acquisition of sovereignty; but that did not signify that the acquisition of sovereignty through such agreements with authorities of the country was regarded as an 'occupation' of a 'terra nullius' in the proper sense of these terms. On the contrary, such agreements with local rulers, whether or not considered as an actual 'cession' of the territory, were regarded as derivative roots of title, and not original titles obtained by occupation of terrae nullius.[178]

Even in the age of *terrae nullius*, the rules of international law had to determine the spatial scope of such a territory and delineate it from those territories with respect of which territorial title had already existed. In *Eastern Greenland* before the Permanent Court of International Justice (PCIJ), Norway claimed possession of the eastern part of Greenland in which Denmark had no colonies

[175] Adhiraj Lath and Abhinav Jena, 'The Lauterpacht Doctrine: An Objective Attempt Towards State Recognition?' (*Berkeley Journal of International Law*, 31 January 2021), www.berkeleyjournalofinternationallaw.com/post/the-lauterpacht-doctrine-an-objective-attempt-towards-state-recognition, accessed 7 October 2022.

[176] Grzybowski (n 115) 409–32.

[177] Joseph Ooko Nyangaga, 'The Doctrine of Occupation through "Terra Nullius" as a Right of Self-Determination of Peoples and the Legal Status of "Liberland" Territory under International Law' (2022) 13(1) *Beijing Law Review* 119.

[178] *Western Sahara* (Advisory Opinion) General List No 61 (1975) ICJ, para 80.

at the time. Norway's claim was that the eastern part of Greenland had been *terra nullius*.[179] The PCIJ did not subscribe to this view and referred to certain legal documents in which Greenland as a whole was referred to as being a territory.[180] Crucial for the Court's decision in this case was the definition of a spatial area which was considered to have the legal status of territory. Since Greenland as a whole constituted a territory, its non-colonised spatial areas could not be *terrae nullius*. Denmark had established territorial title to the entire spatial area of Greenland, not only a part of it.

Nowadays, the concept of *terra nullius* is obsolete. Even in *Island of Palmas*, Arbitrator Huber noted that already in the nineteenth-century international law had regard for 'the fact that most parts of the globe were under the sovereignty of States members of the community of nations, and that territories without a master had become relatively few'.[181] Territorial entitlement in contemporary international law has become a zero-sum game: it is not possible to create a new state or expand the territory of an existing state without breaking the territorial integrity of an existing state or of a non-state territory with an international legal status.[182] This is why it is untenable in contemporary international law to presume that a state emerges on meeting the Montevideo criteria which presume territorial effectiveness. Territorial title is nowadays not created by effective occupation or control over a spatial area. Certain other rules of international law are now in existence that protect territorial integrity of states and self-determination of peoples.

B. The Obsolete Modes of Effectiveness-based Territorial Acquisition

Just under nine years before the conclusion of the Montevideo Convention, Arbitrator Max Humber reasoned in *Island of Palmas*:

> Territorial sovereignty is, in general, a situation recognized and delimited in space, either by so-called natural frontiers as recognised by international law or by outward signs of delimitation that are undisputed, or else by legal engagements entered into between interested neighbours, such as frontier conventions, or by acts of recognition of States within fixed boundaries. If a dispute arises as to the sovereignty over a portion of territory, it is customary to examine which of the States claiming sovereignty possesses a title – cession conquest, occupation, etc. – superior to that which the other State might possibly bring forward against it.[183]

[179] *Legal Status of Eastern Greenland* (Judgment) PCIJ Series A/B. No 53 (5 April 1933), para 44.

[180] ibid, para 48.

[181] *Report of International Arbitral Awards, Island of Palmas case*, UN Rep Intl Arb Awards 829 (4 April 1928) (*Palmas* case), paras 845–46.

[182] Charles S Spencer, 'Territorial Expansion and Primary State Formation' (2010) 107(16) *Proceedings of the National Academy of Sciences* 119.

[183] *Palmas* case, paras 838–39.

Notably, Arbitrator Huber referred to 'natural frontiers', but added that they must be recognised by international law. This reinforces the position that it is quite untenable to speak of natural borders as a legal concept. While it may be in many respects practical to draw a boundary along a river or mountain range, the boundary is not a result of natural forces, but of a political decision. Moreover, on many occasions boundaries do not follow rivers and mountains, or follow them only partially.

Arbitrator Huber also equated sovereign title to territory with evidence of state power and its effective apparatus in a spatial area. In present-day terminology, one could say 'effective control'. It has been argued above that in contemporary international law effective control over a certain spatial area does not create territorial title.[184] But that was not the case in international law in force in the nineteenth and early twentieth centuries. As Arbitrator Huber further argued: 'Titles of acquisition of territorial sovereignty in present-day international law are either based on an act of effective apprehension, such as occupation or conquest, or, like cession, presuppose that the ceding and the cessionary Powers or at least one of them, have the faculty of effectively disposing of the ceded territory.'[185]

Moreover, the legal rules governing territorial title at the time were heavily focused on the question of whether a certain state actually took position over a territory or was merely entitled to do so. In *Clipperton Island*, the Arbitrator argued: 'It is beyond doubt that by immemorial usage having the force of law, besides the *animus occupandi*, the actual, and not the nominal, taking of possession is a necessary condition of occupation.'[186] This is because discovery only created 'right, as a state, to incorporate the island in her possessions' but in order to claim territorial title it had to be proved that the state 'also had effectively exercised the right'.[187]

If these rules were still applicable today, Russia's current administration of Crimea would probably create territorial title to this territory, but the rules of contemporary international law prevent that.[188] Indeed, where the legal status of territory is sought to be changed in violations of 'norms of general international law, in particular those of a peremptory character',[189] all states need to withhold recognition under Article 41 ARSIWA.[190] This is an obligation owed *erga omnes*, that is, toward everyone in the international community.

Foreign states are under the obligation to withhold recognition of the attempted shift of territorial title over Crimea. This territory may well be

[184] Charalambous (n 98).
[185] *Palmas* case, para 839.
[186] *Clipperton Island Arbitration (France v Mexico)* 2 RIAA 1105 (28 January 1931), para 393.
[187] ibid.
[188] Charalambous (n 98).
[189] *Accordance with International Law of the Unilateral Declaration of Independence in Respect of Kosovo* (Advisory Opinion) General List No 141 (2010) ICJ, para 81.
[190] ARSIWA, art 41.

incorporated into Russia in fact, but not in law. In the past, states could alter the legal status of a territory simply by exhibiting effective control over that spatial area. It was argued in preceding sections that contemporary international law still knows the concepts of occupation and effective control over a spatial area. But these concepts do not interfere with or even create territorial entitlement. They may create some obligations stemming from effective control exercised in a certain spatial area, but without altering the territorial title and the legal status under general international law.

Another historic mode of territory acquisition is cession. In theory, a state can cede a part of its territory to another state.[191] It can also cede its entire territory to another state and extinguish itself.[192] In practice, states very rarely cede their territories at free will but only because they are forced or coerced to do so. A good example is Gibraltar. Spain ceded this territory to Great Britain in the Treaty of Utrecht, after it had lost the War of the Spanish Succession.[193] Most instances of cession would be difficult to square with the rules of contemporary international law. It would appear that the right of self-determination would prevent any shift in territorial status without an approval of the will of the people.[194] Moreover, the rules of the use of force under Article 2(4)[195] and the prohibition of aggression as endorsed by the UN General Assembly resolution 3314,[196] would also appear to outlaw cession resulting from the use of force.

To take the contemporary (writing in April 2023) situation in Ukraine as an example, the rules on the use of force, the prohibition of aggression and the right of self-determination would prohibit any cession of Ukraine's territory to Russia, even if this were done in a peace treaty. Cession would in this situation result from Russia's aggression on Ukraine and it may well be that a treaty that would try to formalise such cession could be null and void as a result of Article 53 of the Vienna Convention on the Law of Treaties (VCLT), ie violation of *jus cogens*.[197] In addition, states would also be under the obligation *erga omnes* to withhold recognition under Article 41 ARSIWA. Even the hypothetical consent of Ukraine to cession would not change the legal situation as consent cannot be given for *jus cogens* violations.[198]

It would be possible to envisage a legally realised cession of territory in exceptional circumstances where the transfer of territorial title would result from genuine consent of the states concerned and clear support of the will of

[191] Robert Y Jennings and Arthur Watts, *Oppenheim's International Law* (OUP 1992) 244.
[192] ibid.
[193] Treaty of Utrecht of 1714, art 10.
[194] *Western Sahara* Advisory Opinion, para 59.
[195] United Nations Charter (adopted 26 June 1945, entered into force 24 October 1945) 1 UNTS 16 (UN Charter), art 2.4.
[196] UNGA Res 3314 (14 Dec 1974) UN Doc A/RES/3314 (XXIX).
[197] Vienna Convention on the Law of Treaties of 1969 (adopted 23 May 1969, entered into force 27 January 1980) 1155 UNTS 332 (VCLT), art 53.
[198] ARSIWA, art 26.

the people. One example could be a hypothetical transfer of the territory of Northern Ireland to the Republic of Ireland on the basis of the requirements stipulated for by the Good Friday Agreement.[199] But this possibility remains merely a hypothetical one.

Conquest also was a historically acknowledged method of creating territorial title. In *Eastern Greenland* case, the PCIJ observed:

> Conquest only operates as a cause of loss of sovereignty when there is war between two States and by reason of the defeat of one of them sovereignty over territory passes from the loser to the victorious State. The principle does not apply in a case where a settlement has been established in a distant country and its inhabitants are massacred by the aboriginal population.[200]

There is some debate in international legal doctrine whether conquest required formalisation in a peace treaty and when did it become illegal under international law.[201] If there was a peace treaty requirement, it would be difficult to distinguish between conquest and cession. It could be argued that treaty formalisation indeed turned conquest into cession.[202] There is no doubt that conquest is incompatible with the UN Charter era rules on the use of force, territorial integrity and self-determination.[203] Conquest would lead to a serious breach of *jus cogens* norms, at least the prohibitions of aggression and the right of self-determination, and the obligation to withhold recognition would apply *erga omnes*, as reflected in Article 41 ARSIWA.[204] While there are situations in which conquest was condemned by UN Security Council resolutions,[205] the prohibition of conquest applies under general international law and even without a specific resolution.

This position is reinforced by the Security Council's own pronouncement in Resolution 497 which states in the preamble: 'Reaffirming that the acquisition of territory by force is inadmissible, in accordance with the Charter of the UN, the principles of international law …'[206] The Security Council thus based its decision in the generally applicable sources of international law and not (only) in the *lex specialis* regimes applicable specifically to this particular context. The prohibition of conquest in international law went hand in hand with the developments in the international law on the use of force. The origins of the prohibition thus pre-date the Charter.[207] Yet, international legal doctrine has

[199] Good Friday Agreement (n 77).
[200] *Eastern Greenland* (n 179) para 47.
[201] Marcelo Kohen, 'Conquest' (*Max Planck Encyclopedia*), opil.ouplaw.com/display/10.1093/law:epil/9780199231690/law-9780199231690-e275, accessed 3 January 2023.
[202] ibid.
[203] UN Charter, arts 1.2 and 2.4.
[204] ARSIWA, art 41.
[205] UNSC Res 497 (17 December 1981) UN Doc S/RES/497; and UNSC Res 678 (29 November 1990) UN Doc S/RES/497.
[206] UNSC Res 678 (29 November 1990) UN Doc S/RES/497, preamble.
[207] Kohen (n 201).

never properly accommodated the fact that territorial title is a zero-sum game, while most of the old methods of moving the territorial title from one side of the equation to the other is no longer allowed.

C. The Territorial Zero-sum-game in the Age of the UN Charter

Historically, states acquired (new) territories by discovery and effective occupation of *terrae nullius*, and by cession from and conquest of territories previously belonging to other states. Nowadays, no spatial area on Earth is considered to be *terra nullius*. Cession and conquest are prohibited at least from the inception of the UN Charter.

Occupation and effective control are terms of art in contemporary international law, but they have different meanings than they did historically. They do not pertain to territorial title, but rather to certain level of responsibility when administering a spatial area, 'without the volition of the sovereign of that territory'.[208] A state cannot expand its territory by occupying the territory of another state. Even if such an occupation is sustained in fact, it is not recognised in law. At the same time, it is difficult to imagine how cession and conquest could be squared with the contemporary rules on self-determination, the use of force and prohibition of aggression. The concept of territorialism remains influenced by these obsolete nineteenth and early twentieth century concepts. The Montevideo Convention was concluded less than a decade after the *Island of Palmas* case. Article 1 of the Montevideo Convention and the *Island of Palmas* decision are both underpinned by the requirement of an effective control of a governing authority over a certain spatial area and its inhabitants. Yet, the Montevideo Convention remains influential today,[209] although effective control over a spatial area no longer creates legal title or status. Hence, not even statehood can be created in this way.

International law in fact always conceptualised territory as legal status, although historically status could be created or shifted simply by effective possession. This could result from an occupation of *terra nullius*, conquest or cession. But the rules of international law have evolved. A legal system cannot base legal entitlement on factual power.[210] Consider the situation under domestic law: the rightful owner of a bicycle is not the one who can prove that they are effectively using it. Of course, a bicycle can be stolen and the thief may effectively benefit from its possession. The thief may even be responsible for compliance with traffic rules when using a stolen bicycle. But the bicycle still will not become the thief's possession.

[208] Benvenisti (n 105) 43.
[209] Montevideo Convention.
[210] Lon Fuller, *The Morality of Law* (YUP 1969).

Contemporary international law adopts a similar position with respect of territories. This is probably no coincidence as territorialism has, at least in Western tradition, always been equated with property and possession.[211] A territory can be occupied or otherwise put under effective control of another state. That state may then become responsible for certain aspects of administration of that territory, but it will not establish legal possession of it. The legal status of territories nowadays is created in a legal process, in the sources of law, and no longer by factual power.[212] In international law this means that a territory needs to have a certain status established in treaty and/or customary law. And it will not always be the case that the factual situation will match the one in established in law.

In a world without *terrae nullius*, territorial acquisition has become a zero-sum game. In the UN Charter area, a state cannot acquire new territories without either diminishing the territory of another state or incorporating a territory that enjoys a certain other status under international law. In most circumstances, territorial acquisition would be prohibited. It is thus only possible in special and carefully defined circumstances on the basis of genuine consent of the states involved, supported by the will of the people. A new state can also only emerge in contemporary international law where the territory of another state is either diminished or the state is dissolved. But not every attempt at secession necessarily leads to territorial illegality. This issue will be further discussed in the following chapters of the book.

VI. CONCLUSION

The notion of territory is central for determining where, when and how the rules of international law are applied. But international legal doctrine has wrongly theorised territory as a natural feature rather than a legal construct. This chapter has demonstrated that territory is not naturally given; instead, territory is created under international law. Territory is legal status created in a certain spatial area. Contemporary international law distinguishes between several types of territorial status. These will be further explored in subsequent chapters. A new state can emerge or an existing state can acquire new territory only where there is a lawful transfer of territorial title. The applicable legal framework in the UN Charter era no longer allows creations of legal title on the basis of effective possession. Certain consequences and legal obligations may nevertheless follow from effective territorial control, however illegal it may be. The law

[211] Nicholas Blomley, 'The Territorialization of Property in Land: Space, Power and Practice' (2019) 7(2) *Territory, Politics, Governance* 233.

[212] Bernhard Knoll, *The Legal Status of Territories Subject to Administration by International Organisations* (CUP 2008) 18–52.

of occupation, for example, creates certain legal obligations for the occupying power, yet without creating legal title.

Where an authority is factually able to govern a spatial area, yet has no territorial title to that area, one can speak of an effective exercise of territorial jurisdiction, but not of statehood or territorial acquisition. The authority calling itself 'TRNC' may well be able to exercise jurisdiction over the spatial area of Northern Cyprus, but is not a state, not even an illegal one.[213] This is an example of an effective exercise of jurisdiction. Likewise, Russia may be able to enforce its jurisdiction in Crimea, but such factual capacity does not give it territorial title over this spatial area.

In order to have legal status established under international law, such a status needs to exist in the formal sources of international law. Sometimes special territorial statuses and even statehood status are established by international treaties. For non-states, some examples of such treaties include the Antarctic Treaty, the Svalbard Treaty and the Sino-British Joint Declaration on Hong Kong. Even states can sometimes be created by international treaties. Examples include the Lateran Treaty and the Austrian State Treaty. Most of the time, legal status of territories is established under and regulated by customary international law. These issues will be further elaborated on in subsequent chapters.

Nowadays, territorial title under international law is a zero-sum game. Most historic modes of territorial acquisition are prohibited in the UN Charter area due to developments of the rules on the use of force, territorial integrity and self-determination.[214] Nevertheless, altering legal status of a territory will not always be illegal under international law. It will be considered in subsequent chapters how statehood and certain non-state variants of legal status can be created in compliance with the UN Charter era rules on territorial title.

International legal status of a territory is created by territorial title. In order to create territorial status, an authority first needs to have legal title to do so. Territorial title is no longer created by effective control. States are not created or territorially expanded by effective possession. Effective control can, however, result in effective exercise of jurisdiction. International law does accommodate and regulate some consequences of such effective jurisdictional reality, but effective exercise of jurisdiction should not be conflated with statehood.

[213] Geiß (n 97) 425–49.
[214] UN Charter, arts 1.2 and 2.4.

3

Statehood as Legal Status

I. INTRODUCTION

DISCUSSIONS ON THE law of statehood usually start with the statehood criteria. These are elaborated in the Montevideo Convention on the Rights and Duties of States and are said to have acquired the status of customary international law: (i) a permanent population; (ii) a defined territory; (iii) government; and (iv) the capacity to enter into relations with other states.[1] While these criteria describe a state, or most states, they are often interpreted as being a legal definition of a state.[2]

International practice shows, however, that states do not emerge automatically and self-evidently when these criteria are met. The criteria are too inclusive and too exclusive at the same time. Certain entities, such as Somaliland,[3] meet them, but are not states; and certain states did not meet them, but have nevertheless emerged as states, such as Croatia and Bosnia-Herzegovina in 1992.[4] While most states meet the Montevideo criteria, it is probably more accurate to say that they meet them because they are states and not that they are states because they meet the criteria. The Montevideo criteria alone cannot answer these questions. The answer needs to lie elsewhere.

Some writers advance the argument that the Montevideo criteria have been supplemented by an additional set of legality-based statehood criteria.[5] However, the additional statehood criteria are not doctrinally accepted by all authors; some, rather, see these criteria as recognition requirements.[6] In any case, the concept of additional statehood criteria could, *perhaps*, explain why certain effective entities are not states *only* in situations of territorial illegality.[7]

[1] Montevideo Convention on the Rights and Duties of States of 1933 (adopted 26 December 1933, entered into force 26 December 1934) 165 LNTS 19 (Montevideo Convention), art 1.

[2] Rowan Nicholson, *Statehood and the State-Like in International Law* (OUP 2019) 127.

[3] James Crawford, *The Creation of States in International Law* (OUP 2006) 415–17.

[4] ibid, 398.

[5] ibid, 107; Robert McCorquodale, 'The Creation and Recognition of States' in S Blay, R Piotrowicz and BM Tsamenyi (eds), *Public International Law: An Australian Perspective* (OUP Australia 2005) 191.

[6] Stefan Talmon, 'The Constitutive Versus the Declaratory Theory of Recognition: Tertium non Datur?' (2005) 75(1) *British Yearbook of International Law* 101.

[7] Dermott J Devine, 'The Requirements of Statehood Re-Examined' (1971) 34(4) *Modern Law Review* 410.

If one does not accept the view that all attempts at unilateral secession are illegal,[8] one must acknowledge that even where no territorial illegality is attached to the situation, effective territorial jurisdictional units are not always states.[9] In other words, not even the concept of the additional statehood criteria adequately explains how new states emerge in contemporary international law.

The answer could lie in international recognition;[10] but why should it matter if recognition is declaratory?[11] Indeed, Macedonia was a state in 1992, despite being virtually universally non-recognised;[12] but why then is Somaliland not a state, albeit a non-recognised one?[13] One part of scholarship assumes that a state emerges automatically upon meeting the Montevideo criteria.[14] Another part disagrees with this assumption and argues that additional statehood criteria exist that, likewise automatically, bar entities from becoming states in situations of territorial illegality.[15] Both explanations thus assume that the statehood criteria have direct and automatic implications for the legal status of an entity, except that one school of thought suggests a supplement to Montevideo.

This chapter argues that the international law of statehood remains influenced by the nineteenth-century perception of 'state as effectiveness'[16] as well as by practice of decolonisation, where colonial powers were not seen to be entitled to a claim to territorial integrity in respect of oversees possessions.[17] In contemporary international law, states emerge differently and also need to be conceptualised differently. As demonstrated in the previous chapter, in present-day situations virtually all spatial areas on Earth are state territories and, in turn, are protected by the principle of territorial integrity of states.[18] The applicability

[8] Alexander Orakhelashvili, 'Statehood, Recognition and the United Nations System: A Unilateral Declaration of Independence in Kosovo' (2008) 12 *Max Planck Yearbook of United Nations Law* 1.

[9] Crawford (n 3) 403.

[10] *Reference Re Secession of Quebec* (Judgment) CAN SC 2 SCR 217 (20 August 1998) (*Quebec* case), para 155, where the Court argued that the ultimate success of unilateral secession would depend on international recognition.

[11] David J Harris, *Cases and Materials on International Law* (Sweet & Maxwell 2010) 145.

[12] Matthew CR Craven, 'What's in a Name? The Former Yugoslav Republic of Macedonia and Issues of Statehood' (1995) 16 *Australian Yearbook of International Law* 199.

[13] Markus Virgil Hoehne, 'Somaliland: 30 Years of De Facto Statehood, and No End In Sight' (*ISPI*, 7 May 2021) www.ispionline.it/en/publication/somaliland-30-years-de-facto-statehood-and-no-end-sight-30363, accessed 17 November 2022.

[14] Georg Jellinek, *Allgemeine Staatslehre* (Springer 1914) 137; Stefan Talmon, *Kollektive Nichtanerkennung illegaler Staaten* (Mohr 2006) 218–20.

[15] Devine (n 7) 410–17.

[16] Crawford (n 3) 37–95.

[17] Gregory H Fox, 'Self-Determination in the Post-Cold War Era: A New Internal Focus' (1995) 16(3) *Michigan Journal of International Law* 733.

[18] Malcom N Shaw, *International Law* (CUP 2018) 198; Anne Peters, 'Statehood after 1989: "Effectivites" between Legality and Virtuality' (2010) 3 *Proceedings of the European Society of International Law*.

of this principle does not, however, make the emergence of new states illegal.[19] The consequence of its operation is that new states do not emerge automatically but in the process of overcoming the competing claim to territorial integrity. The so-called 'statehood criteria' are not criteria for statehood, but, rather, certain consequences of effective jurisdictional power in a spatial area. Statehood needs to be grounded outside of the statehood criteria framework.

This chapter argues that statehood is legal status established under customary international law. The argument draws on the previous section and recalls that states are not objective natural facts and, therefore, their emergence cannot be seen as being analogical to such facts. States do not emerge automatically and self-evidently by meeting the statehood criteria. An argument is made that the principle of territorial integrity creates a zone of international legal neutrality in which foreign states may or may not accept the emergence of new states. The chapter further considers the limitations on the freedom of foreign states to accept the emergence of a new state. Such limitations are imposed by the norms of international law that determine territorial illegality. This chapter asks what the legal effects are of territorial illegality and how this interferes with the legal status of the entity. An argument is made that illegally created effective entities cannot be considered 'illegal states'[20] but neither can it be assumed that territorial integrity *automatically* results in an entity not being a state.[21]

In sum, the international law of statehood is marked by two fundamental problems: the conceptualisation of statehood through the statehood criteria and the perception that recognition is always a declaratory legal act. This chapter provides for an alternative view on the concept of statehood and its creation. It defines the state and the process of state creation outside of the so-called Montevideo formula, and argues that the emergence of a new state is a nexus of law and politics. Statehood is a legal status of a territory and it is a political process that creates it.

II. RETHINKING THE STATEHOOD CRITERIA

Writing in 1900, Georg Jellinek argued that in order to find a state, one needs to look for three elements: a territory, a population and public authority.[22] These three elements of the state fall close to the subsequently codified Montevideo criteria.[23] Jellinek's three elements of the state remain influential in positivist scholarship. In this view, whether an entity is a state depends on meeting these

[19] Abdelhamid El Ouali, *Territorial Integrity in a Globalizing World* (Springer 2012) 52–60.
[20] Talmon (n 6) 101–81.
[21] Crawford (n 3) 129.
[22] Jellinek (n 14) 137; Talmon (n 14) 218–20.
[23] Montevideo Convention, art 1.

criteria only.[24] A state comes into existence as an objective fact upon meeting the statehood criteria and its emergence is merely acknowledged by international law.[25] An analogy is drawn to the birth of a child: the applicable law does not create the fact of the birth of a child, but merely registers it.[26]

This explanation may work well where physical persons or tangible natural subjects or objects are concerned. But is a state an objective natural fact or can it, at least, be compared to natural facts by analogy? James Crawford argues that '[a] State is not a fact in the sense that a chair is a fact; it is a fact in the sense in which it may be said a treaty is a fact: that is, a legal status attaching to a certain state of affairs by virtue of certain rules or practices'.[27] In this view, the emergence of a new state is not a simple matter of a physical fact, but rather a matter of legal status. This section will now consider the problems of the perception that states emerge self-evidently and as something physical or natural.

A. The Place of Territorialism in the Law of Statehood

The Montevideo Convention, *inter alia*, invokes a defined territory.[28] It was argued in the previous chapter that a territory is not a natural element.[29] A territory is a social construct and legal status established in a certain spatial area. This was recognised for example by Hans Kelsen, who argued against the perception of there being natural state boundaries: '[T]raditional theory distinguishes between "natural" and "artificial," i.e., legal, boundaries; but the boundaries of a State always have a legal character, whether or not they coincide with such "natural" frontiers as, for instance, a river or a mountain range.'[30]

For example, where the territory of a new state is confined by the international legal principle of *uti possidetis*,[31] the state territory is defined in a political and legal process, and not as a result of natural forces. Indeed, the continents and the oceans are physical facts while delimitation on these physical facts can only be matters of social organisation law.[32] The Earth surface comes without any boundaries between states and, indeed, without any states. Boundaries are thus confined, territories defined, and states created for social purposes.

[24] Talmon (n 14) 218–20.

[25] Joshua Downer, 'Towards a Declaratory School of Government Recognition' (2021) 46 *Vanderbilt Law Review* 581, 581–611.

[26] Talmon (n 14) 218; Lassa Oppenheim, *International Law* (Longmans 1905) 264.

[27] Crawford (n 3) 5.

[28] Montevideo Convention, art 1.

[29] Robert McCorquodale and Raul Pangalangan, 'Pushing Back the Limitations of Territorial Boundaries' (2001) 12(5) *European Journal of International Law* 867.

[30] Hans Kelsen, *General Theory of Law and State* (Routledge 1961) 213.

[31] Steven Ratner, 'Drawing a Better Line: Uti Possidetis and the Borders of New States' (1996) 90 *American Journal of International Law* 590.

[32] Kelsen (n 30) 213.

Even if one took the existence of 'a defined territory' as a physical fact, the concept of the state could still not be seen as such. While Kosovo does have its territory, it is ambiguous whether it is a state under international law.[33] Building on Crawford's metaphor, looking at a chair, one can in principle objectively establish that this is a chair. One does not need to analyse the law to know that. The law may determine whether or not the chair was acquired legally and who its rightful owner is, but it is not a question of law whether the chair exists. This is different with states. Looking at a spatial area with a permanent population, such as Kosovo, does not tell us whether that particular area represents a state territory. This is a question of legal status rather than natural fact. It will be argued below that while Crawford appears to reject that natural statehood theory and accepts that statehood is legal status,[34] his concept of the additional statehood criteria nevertheless remains premised on some underlying principles of so-called natural statehood.

B. Does a State Exist as Soon as it Exists?

Another problem with the perception of factual statehood is, as Hersch Lauterpacht argued, its presumption that 'fulfilment of the Montevideo criteria is self-evident'.[35] This leads to the conceptual problem of identifying an 'objective fact' in the decentralised legal system of international law. It is true that this is a problem of international law in general, not only in the context of statehood specifically.[36] But it is also true what Lauterpacht observed: namely, if we accept that a state comes into existence objectively and automatically upon meeting the Montevideo criteria, we need to accept the rather awkward proposition that 'a State exists in international law as soon as it exists'.[37]

In response to such a circular explanation, Lauterpacht argued that recognition was constitutive.[38] In the absence of a central authority for determining whether or not a certain entity is a state, this duty needs to be performed by (existing) states. Once the statehood criteria are met, other states objectively confirm this fact by granting recognition, and then no doubt exists that a new state has emerged[39] – at least if recognition is universally granted. If it is not, the old problem of the constitutive theory arises: how many and whose recognitions

[33] Jure Vidmar, 'Kosovo: Unilateral Secession and Multilateral State-Making' in James Summers (ed), *Kosovo: A Precedent? The Declaration of Independence, the Advisory Opinion and Implications for Statehood, Self-Determination and Minority Rights* (Nijhoff 2011) 143–78.

[34] Crawford (n 3) 21.

[35] Hersch Lauterpacht, *Recognition in International Law* (first published 1947, CUP 2013) 41.

[36] Talmon (n 14) 218; Oppenheim (n 26) 218–19.

[37] Lauterpacht (n 35) 66.

[38] ibid, 58.

[39] ibid, 65–66.

are necessary to create an objective legal fact of the existence of a new state?[40] Lauterpacht tried to solve this problem by arguing that once the statehood criteria are met, foreign states have a *duty* to grant recognition. Other states thus objectively confirm the existence of a new state by granting recognition and, in so doing, end any doubt pertaining to the entity's legal status.[41]

A *duty* to grant recognition is the main problem of Lauterpacht's proposition: such a duty is not supported by state practice. Moreover, although under some circumstances states may be under an obligation to withhold recognition, the decision whether to grant recognition always remains in their political discretion.[42] In the absence of an obligation to grant recognition, Lauterpacht's approach does not work. Indeed, if recognition is constitutive and no *duty* exists to grant it, there may be entities that are recognised as states by some states but not by others. As a consequence, one still will not objectively know whether or not they are states.

What can be nevertheless said of Lauterpacht's proposition is that it very accurately diagnoses the problem: the explanation that 'a State exists as soon as it exists' is inadequate. Fulfilment of the statehood criteria is not self-evident and states do not emerge as a matter of (virtually) physical fact. The problem of Lauterpacht's proposition is thus not in the diagnosis; the problem is, rather, in the cure prescribed. This book accepts the diagnosis but argues that the solution is not compulsory recognition with constitutive effects but, rather, in conceptualisation of statehood as a legal status and its detachment from the idea of there being statehood criteria.

III. THE EMERGENCE AND EXISTENCE OF STATES

The question of how a new state emerges is closely related to the concept of the state in international law. Commenting on the *Kosovo* Advisory Opinion, Marc Weller exposes the question of whether a state emerges as a matter of fact or 'upon a grant of legal authority'.[43] He then continues that 'a grant of legal authority may be given either by the predecessor state through their *consent* to secession or, perhaps, exceptionally, by *collective international action* of the United Nations (UN) Security Council or *widespread recognition* triggered by the opposed, but effective, unilateral creation of statehood'.[44] Weller thus subscribes to the view that a state is not a fact in a natural sense; statehood

[40] James Leslie Brierly, *The Law of Nations* (OUP 1963) 138.
[41] Lauterpacht (n 35) 65–66.
[42] Kelsen (n 30) 223; Krystyna Marek, *Identity and Continuity of States in Public International Law* (Droz 1968) 137; Talmon (n 14) 103.
[43] Marc Weller, 'Modesty Can Be a Virtue: Judicial Economy in the ICJ *Kosovo* Opinion' (2011) 24(1) *Leiden Journal of International Law* 127.
[44] ibid (emphasis added).

is a question of legal status which is created in a political process with legal consequences. James Crawford, although in principle subscribing to the statehood criteria, also observed that 'it could be that the territories to be regarded as "sovereign" were determined by political rather than legal processes, yet the consequences of the principle in its application to such territories could be legal'.[45]

If states emerge upon a 'grant of legal authority' rather than 'factually', it needs to be asked what constitutes such a grant. The modes identified by Weller suggest that this is essentially a matter of overcoming the parent state's claim to territorial integrity.[46] And if 'sovereign territories' are created politically rather than as a matter of political automaticity, what does this tell us about the statehood criteria? This chapter argues that the principle of territorial integrity creates a zone of international legal neutrality. Since independence is not an international legal entitlement, new states cannot emerge automatically and self-evidently. The legal status of statehood is created in the political process of overcoming the counterclaim to territorial integrity.

A. The Principle of Territorial Integrity and the Sphere of International Legal Neutrality

The land surface of Earth is nowadays nearly entirely divided between states. Save for a few exceptions, it is for the most part impossible for a new state to emerge without breaking territorial integrity of an existing state. Some scholars and governments have argued that territorial integrity of states is an absolute norm, even *jus cogens*.[47] This would mean that a new state could almost never emerge, unless the predecessor state ceased to exist. Notably, had territorial integrity been a *jus cogens* norm, not even consent of the affected state would change the legal situation, as states cannot give consent to violation of *jus cogens* norms.[48] Others have been more cautious and have argued that the principle of territorial integrity prevents *unilateral* secession, while the affected state may waive its claim for territorial integrity.[49] Secession is thus said to be legal where consent is given by the affected state, but illegal where it is unilateral, ie where

[45] Crawford (n 3) 21.

[46] Weller (n 43) 127–47.

[47] *Accordance with International Law of the Unilateral Declaration of Independence in Respect of Kosovo* (Advisory Opinion) General List No 141 [2010] ICJ (*Kosovo* Advisory Opinion), para 5.

[48] Articles on the Responsibility of States for Internationally Wrongful Acts (entered into force 8 January 2008) A/RES/62/61 (ARSIWA), art 26.

[49] Orakhelashvili (n 8) 1–44, arguing: 'As soon as the principle of territorial integrity applies, it necessarily outlaws secession without the consent of the parent state. Such understanding avoids systemic inconsistency under which international law would guarantee territorial integrity yet would not prohibit secession.'

the affected state does not consent to independence of a part of its territory (for example, the Spain/Catalonia scenario).[50]

In the *Kosovo* Advisory Opinion, the ICJ took a different line. The Court recalled that many, if not most, states in the world have emerged without the predecessor state's consent.[51] The United States emerged against the wishes of Great Britain, for example. Unilateral secession is not prohibited under international law. But the absence of an explicit prohibition should not be conflated with the existence of an entitlement to independence. The principle of territorial integrity does not make unilateral secession illegal *per se*.[52] It does mean, however, that the difficult task of altering the territorial status quo lies on the independence-seeking territorial entity. Taking the relationship between Somalia and Somaliland as an example: Somalia has been entirely ineffective for more than two decades, but its statehood status continues to exist.[53] As long as Somalia's statehood is not extinguished under international law, Somalia remains protected by the principle of territorial integrity. Somaliland is a territorial entity within the broader territory of Somalia and it is generally considered that Somaliland meets the statehood criteria.[54] But Somalia is a state under international law, while Somaliland is not.[55]

Unless Somalia's presumption of territorial integrity is overcome, Somaliland's statehood will not be created – regardless of meeting the Montevideo criteria – as there cannot be two overlapping states in a certain territory. Bosnia and Herzegovina in 1992 was in a different legal position. At the time it had become universally accepted that its parent state, the Socialist Federal Republic of Yugoslavia (SFRY), had ceased to exist.[56] There was no competing claim to territorial integrity and Bosnia and Herzegovina emerged as a new state, in spite of having clear deficiencies in meeting the statehood criteria and not being able to control large parts of its territory.[57]

In the process of decolonisation 'the only territorial relationship to be altered was that with the metropolitan power. Achieving independence … did not come at the expense of another sovereign state's territory or that of an adjacent colony.'[58] Now the process of decolonisation is virtually over and the world

[50] Helen Taylor, 'Catalan Independence: An international law perspective' (*Cambridge University Law Society*) www.culs.org.uk/per-incuriam/catalan-independence-an-international-law-perspective, accessed 31 January 2023.

[51] *Kosovo* Advisory Opinion, para 79.

[52] ibid.

[53] Pablo Moscoso de la Cuba, 'The Statehood of "Collapsed" States in Public International Law' (2011) 18(29) *Agenda Internacional* 121.

[54] Janis Grzybowski, 'To Be or Not to Be: The Ontological Predicament of State Creation in International Law' (2017) 28(2) *European Journal of International Law* 416.

[55] ibid.

[56] Jure Vidmar, 'Territorial Integrity and the Law of Statehood' (2013) 44 *George Washington International Law Review* 132.

[57] ibid.

[58] Fox (n 17) 733–81.

is completely divided between states.[59] All permanently populated territories have a parent state which is, in turn, protected by the principle of territorial integrity.[60] It is thus impossible to make a claim for independence in the contemporary world in the absence of a competing claim to territorial integrity.[61]

The principle of territorial integrity of states is one of the cornerstones of the UN Charter system and the post-Second World War international legal order. In this era it appears to be the most challenging hurdle an entity needs to overcome on its path to statehood.[62] In the UN Charter, a reference to territorial integrity appears in Article 2(4) only. This reference is thus contextualised with the prohibition of the use of force. What is discussed here is the territorial integrity of states in the context of claims for independence not involving the use of force in international relations. The UN Charter is silent on this issue.

The Declaration on Principles of International Law,[63] which is reflective of customary international law,[64] makes a reference to the principle of territorial integrity in two instances. In one instance, the Declaration provides: 'Every State shall refrain from any action aimed at the partial or total disruption of the national unity and territorial integrity of any other State or country.'[65] This elaboration obviously understands the territorial integrity of states more broadly than Article 2(4) of the UN Charter and liberates the principle from the context of the use of force. Nevertheless, it remains confined to relations between states.

In another elaboration, however, the principle is invoked as a limitation on the right of self-determination. As the right of self-determination applies to peoples, not states, it follows that the principle of territorial integrity is not applicable in relations between states exclusively.[66] The relevant provision reads:

> Nothing in the foregoing paragraphs [referring to the right of self-determination] shall be construed as authorizing or encouraging any action which would dismember or impair, totally or in part, the territorial integrity or political unity of sovereign and independent States conducting themselves in compliance with the principle of equal rights and self-determination of peoples as described above and thus possessed

[59] 'UN decolonization successes can "inspire us today" UN chief tells Special Committee' (*UN News*, 21 February 2019) news.un.org/en/story/2019/02/1033231, accessed 7 December 2022.

[60] Peters (n 18) 1–14.

[61] Patricia Carley, 'Self-Determination, Sovereignty, Territorial Integrity, and the Right to Secession' (*United States Institute of Peace*, 1996) www.usip.org/sites/default/files/pwks7.pdf, accessed 17 October 2022.

[62] Crawford (n 3) 403.

[63] UNGA Res 2625 (24 October 1970) UN Doc A/RES/2625(XXV), Annex, principle 5, para 7.

[64] *Kosovo* Advisory Opinion, para 80.

[65] ibid.

[66] This elaboration was ignored by the ICJ in the *Kosovo* Advisory Opinion, where the Court, by selective references to the Declaration on Principles of International Law, (wrongly) established that the principle of territorial integrity only applies in relations between states: *Kosovo* Advisory Opinion, para 80. For more see Jure Vidmar, 'The *Kosovo* Advisory Opinion Scrutinized' (2011) 24(2) *Leiden Journal of International Law* 355.

> of a government representing the whole people belonging to the territory without distinction as to race, creed or colour.[67]

The principle of territorial integrity is thus liberated not only from the context of the use of force but also from its applicability in international relations. As it provides for limitations on the peoples' right of self-determination, the elaboration is reflective of the doctrine that outside of colonialism the right of peoples to self-determination will be normally consummated internally, ie within the international borders of the parent state, and will not result in a new state creation.[68]

In one view, the operation of the principle of territorial integrity leads to an absolute prohibition of unilateral secession.[69] This argument has little support in international legal doctrine. The first elaboration of the principle of territorial integrity says that secession is not 'authorised' or 'encouraged', yet nowhere does it say that secession would be prohibited or even illegal. The elaboration is thus evidence of the neutrality of international law in respect of secession.[70] In this vein, the International Court of Justice (ICJ) in the *Kosovo* Advisory Opinion recalled extensive practice of state creation upon an initial issuing of a unilateral declaration of independence and such state creations were not considered to be illegal only because independence was declared against the applicable claim to territorial integrity of the parent state.[71] The position in international law is that secession and emergence of a new state against the applicable claim to territorial integrity is not an entitlement under international law;[72] but neither is it prohibited.[73]

The consequence of the neutrality of international law in respect of unilateral secession is that an entity which issues a unilateral declaration of independence is at the same time not precluded from becoming a state, yet creating statehood is not only a matter of declaring independence. In other words, a declaration of independence does not create the legal fact of the existence of a new state, even if the entity, in principle, functions as an independent jurisdictional unit.[74] In the end, this entity may or may not become a state. But it is not a state if the claim to territorial integrity of the parent state continues to apply and the hurdle is not overcome. The consequence of a competing claim to territorial integrity

[67] UNGA Res 2625 (24 October 1970) UN Doc A/RES/2625(XXV), Annex, principle 5.

[68] *Quebec* case, para 126.

[69] Orakhelashvili (n 8) 1–44. Consider the following argument: 'As soon as the principle of territorial integrity applies, it necessarily outlaws secession without the consent of the parent state. Such understanding avoids systemic inconsistency under which international law would guarantee territorial integrity yet would not prohibit secession.'

[70] Crawford (n 3) 390.

[71] *Kosovo* Advisory Opinion, para 79.

[72] *Quebec* case, para 126.

[73] ibid, para 155.

[74] Jure Vidmar, 'Conceptualizing Declarations of Independence in International Law' (2012) 32(1) *Oxford Journal of Legal Studies* 153–77.

is thus not that emergence of a state would be illegal but rather that states in international law do not emerge automatically and self-evidently on meeting certain criteria.

B. Overcoming the Counterclaim to Territorial Integrity

As states do not emerge automatically as a matter of entitlement, they can only emerge as a matter of 'a grant of legal authority'. As argued above, such a grant is essentially concerned with overcoming the claim to territorial integrity.[75] This will be now clarified with references to the practice of emergence of new states outside of the process of decolonisation. By *consent to secession*, the parent state waives its claim to territorial integrity. Such was the recent example of South Sudan.[76] The parent state's waiver may also be produced by international involvement, especially if this is done collectively, through the actions of the UN organs. A good example is Indonesia's consent to independence of East Timor.[77]

The claim to territorial integrity may be removed by dissolution of the parent state. The international legal effect of dissolution is that the parent state no longer exists and so its claim for territorial integrity becomes inapplicable. Practice shows that dissolution can be either consensual or non-consensual. An example of a consensual dissolution was the Soviet Union, where the extinguishing of the federation's international personality was formalised by an agreement between its republics.[78] The Socialist Federal

[75] Lauterpacht (n 35) 41.

[76] South Sudan's path to independence followed from the legal regime established under the Comprehensive Peace Agreement, signed on 9 January 2005, between the central government of Sudan and the Sudan People's Liberation Movement/Sudan People's Liberation Army. The Comprehensive Peace Agreement resulted from the efforts of the regional peace initiative to end the civil war. See 'The Comprehensive Peace Agreement of 2005' (*United Nations*) www.sd.undp.org/doc/CPA.pdf, accessed 7 December 2022. After the adoption of the Comprehensive Peace Agreement, Sudan promulgated a new interim constitution which granted substantive autonomy to Southern Sudan. See Article 222(1), The Interim National Constitution of the Republic of Sudan of 2005. The Constitution further specified that a referendum on the future status of Southern Sudan was to be held six months before the end of the six-year interim period (ibid); whereby people of Southern Sudan were to either '(a) confirm unity of the Sudan by voting to sustain the system of government established under the Comprehensive Peace Agreement and this Constitution, or (b) vote for secession.' ibid, art 222(2). The option for secession was given an overwhelming support of 98.83 per cent, at a turnout of 97.58 per cent. The central government of Sudan announced it would respect the referendum results. See 'President Omar al-Bashir gives South Sudan his blessing' (*BBC News*, 7 July 2011) www.bbc.co.uk/news/world-africa-14060475, accessed 7 December 2022. South Sudan declared independence on 9 July 2011 and the central government of Sudan announced its formal recognition already one day before the declaration of independence was issued. See 'South Sudan counts down to independence' (*BBC News*, 8 July 2011) www.bbc.co.uk/news/world-africa-14077511, accessed 7 December 2022.

[77] Ralph Wilde, *International Territorial Administration: How Trusteeship and the Civilizing Mission Never Went Away* (OUP 2008) 184.

[78] The Agreement Establishing the Commonwealth of Independent States (entered into force 30 December 1991) 31 ILM 138 (Minsk Agreement). On 8 December 1991, the Agreement on the

Republic of Yugoslavia (SFRY) was dissolved non-consensually, whereby state practice universally adopted the opinions of the Badinter Commission.[79] As soon as the SFRY no longer existed, its former republics emerged as states in the absence of a competing claim to territorial integrity. This is also the reason why, despite being non-recognised, it was never disputed that Macedonia was a state.[80] Indeed, if it were not a state, it is questionable what other legal status Macedonia could even have in the absence of any other territorial title in that spatial area. The dissolution of the SFRY could not turn Macedonia into a *terra nullius* – ie having the legal status of a spatial area that is incompatible with the modern rules of international law.[81]

Establishment of the Commonwealth of Independent States (CIS) was signed which, *inter alia*, includes the following formulation: 'We, the Republic of Belarus, the Russian Federation ... and Ukraine, as founder states of the Union of Soviet Socialist Republics and signatories of the Union Agreement of 1922 ... hereby declare that the Union of Soviet Socialist Republics as a subject of international law and a geopolitical reality no longer exists.' On 21 December 1991, a protocol to the Minsk Agreement was adopted by the remaining Soviet Republics, with the exception of Georgia, by way of which the CIS was extended to these former Republics from the moment of ratification of the Minsk Agreement. The Protocol to the Agreement establishing the Commonwealth of Independent States (entered into force 21 December 1991) 31 ILM 147 (Alma-Ata Declaration), *inter alia*, declared: 'With the establishment of the Commonwealth of Independent States, the Union of Soviet Socialist Republics ceases to exist.' Signed by the Republic of Belarus, the Russian Federation (RSFSR) and Ukraine, and 11 former Soviet Republics (in the absence of Georgia).

[79] 'The Badinter Commission' in Snezana Trifunovska (ed), *Yugoslavia through Documents: From its Creation to its Dissolution* (Nijhof 1994) 415. In its Opinion 1, the Badinter Commission expressed the position 'that the Socialist Federal Republic of Yugoslavia is in the process of dissolution'. The Badinter Commission, Opinion 1 (29 November 1991), para 3, reprinted in Snezana Trifunovska. Trifunovska, *Yugoslavia through Documents: From its Creation to its Dissolution* (Brill 1994) 415. The Badinter Commission's Opinion 1 thus provided for a legal interpretation that the developments in the SFRY could no longer be taken as attempts at unilateral secession but rather amounted to dissolution of the federal state. The position of the Badinter Commission was that most former republics of the SFRY became universally recognised as states and were admitted to membership of the UN. The perception of dissolution being at work in the SFRY was clearly adopted even by the Security Council. In Resolution 757, the Security Council declared that 'the claim by the Federal Republic of Yugoslavia (Serbia and Montenegro) to continue automatically the membership of the former Socialist Federal Republic of Yugoslavia (in the United Nations) has not been generally accepted'. SC Res 757, preamble, 30 May 1992.

[80] Declaration on the former Yugoslav Republic of Macedonia, Guimaraes, May 1–2, 1992. On 1 and 2 May 1992, the European Community and its member states adopted the Declaration on the Former Yugoslav Republic of Macedonia, in which it was held that they were 'willing to recognise that State as a sovereign and independent State, within its existing borders, and under a name that can be accepted by all parties concerned.' Declaration on the Former Yugoslav Republic of Macedonia, Informal Meeting of Ministers of Foreign Affairs, Guimaracs, 1 and 2 May 1992, reprinted in Christopher Hill and Karen E Smith, *European Foreign Policy: Key Documents* (Routledge 2000) 376. The use of the term 'state' rather than, for example, 'entity' clearly implies that Macedonia's attributes of statehood were not a subject of dispute, it was rather that the European Community did not want to enter into relations with Macedonia under its constitutional name. In this context see also Craven (n 12) 207–18. It also needs to be noted that in its Opinion 11, the Badinter Commission held that Macedonia became a state on 17 November 1991, the day when it adopted a new constitution which proclaimed Macedonia a sovereign state. The Badinter Commission, Opinion 11 (16 July 1993), para 5.

[81] Cf *Report of International Arbitral Awards, Island of Palmas case*, UN Rep Intl Arb Awards 829 (4 April 1928) (*Palmas* case), paras 845–46.

Under some circumstances states owe an obligation *erga omnes* to withhold recognition.[82] At the same time, nothing in the doctrine or non-recognition practice suggests that an obligation to withhold recognition applies where independence is declared without the consent of a parent state and that an obligation opposable *erga omnes* would apply because of the unilateral character of a declaration of independence. Indeed, the principle of territorial integrity of states cannot be seen as an absolute right of states or even as a norm of *jus cogens*.[83]

The fact that the obligation to withhold recognition does not apply simply because (an attempt at) secession is unilateral also follows from the *Québec* case where the Supreme Court of Canada held that '[t]he ultimate success of … a [unilateral] secession would be dependent on recognition by the international community, which is likely to consider the legality and legitimacy of secession having regard to, amongst other facts, the conduct of Québec and Canada, in determining whether to grant or withhold recognition'.[84] This reasoning can only be based on the underlying position that the unilateral character of (an attempt at) secession does not trigger an obligation to withhold recognition. Rather, the neutrality of international law with respect of unilateral secession affects even the act of recognition: where an entity tries to emerge as an independent state, international law does not prescribe that recognition needs to be either granted or withheld.[85]

What the reasoning in the *Québec* case also implies is that under some circumstances the emergence of a new state may actually depend on recognition. In other words, recognition may create a new state. This is not to say that recognition needs to be seen as primarily a constitutive act. Indeed, the situation of Macedonia is a good example of how in the absence of a competing claim to territorial integrity a territorial entity can have the statehood status even where non-recognition is virtually universal.[86] This is different where an entity tries to emerge as a state *against* a competing claim for territorial integrity. In such circumstances recognition does not merely acknowledge the new legal fact of the existence of a new state but may, rather, produce such a fact.

This understanding also follows from the doctrine of remedial secession. In international law *de lega lata* it is difficult to see remedial secession as a *right* of

[82] Stefan Talmon, 'The Duty Not to "Recognize as Lawful" a Situation Created by the Illegal Use of Force or Other Serious Breaches of a Jus Cogens Obligation: An Obligation without Real Substance?' in Christian Tomuschat and Jean-Marc Thouvenin (eds), *The Fundamental Rules of the International Legal Order* (Brill/Nijhoff 2006) 99–125.

[83] Peters (n 18) 8.

[84] ibid, 1–14.

[85] Daniel H Meester, 'The International Court of Justice's *Kosovo* Advisory Opinion: Assessing the Current State of International Legal Opinion on Remedial Secession' (2016) 48 *Canadian Yearbook of International Law* 215.

[86] Holly A Osterland, 'National Self-Determination and Secession: The Slovak Model' (1993) 25(3) *Case Western Reserve Journal of International Law* 655.

oppressed peoples.[87] However, as Malcolm Shaw argues, remedial secession may be given effects through recognition, which 'may be more forthcoming where the secession has occurred as a consequence of violations of human rights'.[88] In the *Québec case*, the Supreme Court of Canada held that before deciding on whether or not recognition of (an attempt) at unilateral secession would be granted, states consider the legality and legitimacy of the secessionist claim.[89] It may be said that where such a claim is made by 'oppressed peoples', foreign states are more likely to consider the claim as being legitimate and give it priority over the parent state's claim for territorial integrity.

It is thus doctrinally accepted that where an entity declares independence unilaterally, recognition could have constitutive effects. This leads to the well-known problem of constitutive recognition: how many and whose recognitions are necessary for an entity to become a state? Weller suggests that recognition would need to be 'widespread'.[90] In a somewhat similar manner, Crawford argues that collective recognition could be seen as virtually a mode of collective state creation. In this respect Crawford argues:

> [I]n many cases, and this is true of the nineteenth century as of the twentieth, international action has been determinative [for new state creations]: international organizations or groups of States – especially the so-called 'Great Powers' – have exercised a collective authority to supervise, regulate and condition … new state creations. In some cases the action takes the form of the direct establishment of the new State: a constitution is provided, the State territory is delimited, a head of State is nominated. In others it is rather a form of collective recognition – although the distinction is not a rigid one.[91]

The adjectives 'widespread' and 'collective' are not sufficient answers to the question of how many and whose recognitions are necessary for an entity to be seen as a (collectively created) state.

Kosovo may be a good illustration of this problem. For some it is a state, for others it is not.[92] It depends on the perspective one takes but, objectively, we do not know. Is Kosovo a state because it has been recognised by 115 states?[93] Or is it not a state because it has been recognised by *only* 115 states? Similarly, in 1971, Bangladesh (East Pakistan) declared independence.[94] In 1974, Pakistan granted recognition and Bangladesh was accepted to membership of the UN.[95]

[87] Malcom N Shaw, 'Peoples, Territorialism and Boundaries' (1997) 8(3) *European Journal of International Law* 478.
[88] ibid.
[89] *Québec* case, para 155.
[90] Weller (n 43) 127–47.
[91] Crawford (n 3) 501.
[92] 'List of states that recognize Kosovo's independence' (*Kosovo Thanks You*) www.kosovothanksyou.com, accessed 7 December 2022.
[93] ibid.
[94] Crawford (n 3) 141.
[95] ibid; UNGA Res 3203 (17 September 1974) UN Doc A/RES/3203(XXIX).

The prevailing doctrinal interpretation is that the legal status of Pakistan was clarified over time.[96] While this interpretation holds true from today's perspective, it is based on reading history backwards. Knowing that Bangladesh *is* a state, it is easy to say from today's perspective that its legal status 'only' had to be clarified. In 1972, however, one could only say that the legal status of Bangladesh was ambiguous and unclear. The same applies to contemporary Kosovo. International lawyers should admit the possibility of such ambiguity. It is a consequence of the concept of the state in international law: a state is not a matter of an objective physical fact; it is a matter of legal status. Unlike objective physical facts, legal status can be unclear and ambiguous. It will now be demonstrated that a state can also be only a matter of legal fiction.

C. Statehood without Effective Control

That statehood is a question of legal status is also affirmed in the presumption that a state continues to exist even if it no longer meets the statehood criteria. As Robert McCorquodale argues, statehood is difficult to lose.[97] A good example is Somalia.[98] Despite the collapse of effectiveness of the central government of Somalia, the latter continues to be regarded as a state under international law.[99] The presumption of Somalia's territorial integrity prevents Somaliland from becoming a state, although it may well be that Somaliland exhibits more attributes of statehood than Somalia.[100] Somalia thus continues in existence virtually as a legal fiction.

This understanding is further affirmed with regard to occupied states. After the Iraqi occupation, Kuwait clearly did not meet the Montevideo criteria. The collective response to the situation nevertheless demonstrates that Kuwait was still considered to have had the legal status of a state.[101] Contemporary international law is disinclined toward acceptance of an alteration of the legal status of a territory. If the effective situation suggests otherwise, international law establishes a legal fiction and assumes that the occupied state continues in existence.[102]

[96] Crawford (n 3) 141 and 393.

[97] McCorquodale (n 5) 192.

[98] Terrence Lyons and Ahmed I Samatar, *Somalia: State Collapse, Multilateral Intervention, and Strategies for Political Reconstruction* (Brookings 1995).

[99] Abdulqawi A Yusuf, 'Government Collapse and State Continuity: The Case of Somalia' (2003) 13(1) *Italian Yearbook of International Law Online* 11.

[100] ibid.

[101] Jure Vidmar, 'Dissolution of States' in Jure Vidmar, Sarah McGibbon, and Lea Raible (eds), *Research Handbook on Secession* (Edgar Elgar 2022) 218–36; UNSC Res 661 (6 August 1990) UN Doc S/RES/661.

[102] Marco Longobardo, 'Preliminary but Necessary: The Question of the Applicability of the Notion of Apartheid to Occupied Territory' (*Just Security*, 2 December 2021) www.justsecurity.org/79381/preliminary-but-necessary-the-question-of-the-applicability-of-the-notion-of-apartheid-to-occupied-territory, accessed 17 December 2022.

This doctrine has its origins, albeit with some difficulties, in the developments dating to the time before and during the Second World War. The Baltic States were incorporated within the Soviet Union on the basis of the Molotov-Ribbentrop Pact.[103] It remains controversial whether in 1991 Estonia, Latvia and Lithuania were new state creations or whether their pre-Second World War international personalities were revived.[104] Their incorporation in the Soviet Union seemed to be tacitly accepted in international practice.[105] The incorporation nevertheless remained controversial and not universally accepted.[106]

With regard to the puppet states and annexations of the Axis Powers, these were reversed after the Second World War. Austria was re-established as an independent state[107] and so were, for example, Czechoslovakia[108] and Yugoslavia;[109] while the Japanese puppet state of Manchukuo may represent an early example of collective non-recognition on the basis of territorial illegality.[110] These developments clearly announced a new paradigm in the international law of statehood – a shift of effective control over a territory does not necessarily bring a shift of legal status; and 'factually-extinguished-states' can continue to exist in law even where they appear to be no more than legal fiction. This is because factual developments do not automatically alter the legal status.

IV. TERRITORIAL ILLEGALITY AS A LIMITATION ON LEGAL NEUTRALITY

International law is neutral with regard to the *unilateral character* of a declaration of independence, but this does not mean it is neutral in all circumstances.

[103] Secret Supplementary Protocols of the Molotov-Ribbentrop Non-Aggression Pact of 1939, art 1. Article 1 of the Secret Additional Protocol to the Molotov-Ribbentrop Pact reads: 'In the event of a territorial and political rearrangement in the areas belonging to the Baltic States (Finland, Estonia, Latvia, Lithuania), the northern boundary of Lithuania shall represent the boundary of the spheres of influence of Germany and U.S.S.R. In this connection the interest of Lithuania in the Vilna area is recognised by each party.' The German-Soviet Non-Aggression Pact (the Molotov-Ribbentrop Pact), (International Relations and Security Network, Primary Sources in International Affairs, ETH Zurich) www.files.ethz.ch/isn/125339/1393_Molotov-Ribbentrop_Pact.pdf, accessed 16 July 2023.

[104] Susan Himmer, 'The Achievement of Independence in the Baltic States and Its Justifications' (1992) 6 *Emory International Law Review* 253.

[105] Colin Warbrick, 'Recognition of States' (1992) 41 *International & Comparative Law Quarterly* 473.

[106] Himmer (n 104) 253–91.

[107] State Treaty for the Re-establishment of an Independent and Democratic Austria (adopted 15 May 1955, entered into force 27 July 1955) 217 UNTS 223 (Austrian State Treaty).

[108] Official Gazette of the Republic of Czechoslovakia of 1945, art 1, Vol 15, supplement No 30/1945.

[109] Peter Radan, *The Break-up of Yugoslavia and International Law* (Routledge 2002) 141–46.

[110] Crawford (n 3) 133; Henry Stimson, 'Stimson Note' (Reprinted 1932) 26 *American Journal of International Law* 342.

In the *Kosovo* Advisory Opinion, the ICJ made the following very powerful pronouncement:

> [T]he illegality attached to [some other] declarations of independence … stemmed not from the unilateral character of these declarations as such, but from the fact that they were, or would have been, connected with the unlawful use of force or other egregious violations of norms of general international law, in particular those of a peremptory character *(jus cogens)*.[111]

The ICJ thus established a clear distinction between those declarations of independence that are merely unilateral and those that are illegal due to a breach of a particularly strong norm of international law. Historically, illegal declarations of independence were issued by Southern Rhodesia, the South African Homeland States and Northern Cyprus.[112] These declarations were not only unilateral, but also backed by foreign military force, or issued in pursuance of racial discrimination. This is what made them illegal.

More recently, Crimea also issued one of those declarations of independence where international law was *not* neutral. The declaration was marked by illegality. Not because Ukraine did not agree or because it was against the Constitution of Ukraine. The illegality stems from Russia's unlawful involvement in the situation which amounted to an act of aggression.[113]

In his post-annexation speech, Russia's President Vladimir Putin referred to the case of Kosovo:

> Here is a quote from another official document: the Written Statement of the United States America of April 17, 2009, submitted to the same UN International Court [of Justice] in connection with the hearings on Kosovo. Again, I quote: 'Declarations of independence may, and often do, violate domestic legislation. However, this does not make them violations of international law.' End of quote. They wrote this, disseminated it all over the world, had everyone agree and now they are outraged. Over what? The actions of Crimean people completely fit in with these instructions, as it were.

[111] *Kosovo* Advisory Opinion, para 81.

[112] UNSC Res 541 (18 November 1983) UN Doc S/RES/541; UNGA Res 1747 (27 June 1962) UN Doc A/RES/1747 (XVI); UNSC Res 202 (6 May 1965) UN Doc S/RES/202; UNGA Res 2022 (5 November 1965) UN Doc A/RES/2022 (XX); UNGA Res 2024 (11 November 1965) UN Doc A/RES 2024 (XX); UNSC Res 216 (12 November 1965) UN Doc S/RES 216; UNSC Res 217 (20 November 1965) UN Doc S/RES 217; UNSC Res 277 (18 March 1970) UN Doc S/RES 277; UNGA Res 2671F (8 December 1970) UN Doc A/RES/2671F (XXV); UNGA Res 2775 (29 November 1971) UN Doc A/RES/2775 (XXV); UNGA Res 31/6A (26 October 1976) UN Doc A/RES/31/6A; UNGA Res 402 (22 December 1976) UN Doc A/RES 402; UNGA Res 407 (25 May 1977) UN Doc A/RES/407; UNGA Res 32/105 (14 December 1977) UN Doc A/RES 32/105; UNGA Res 34/93G (12 December 1979) UN Doc A/RES/34/93G; UNGA Res 37/43 (3 December 1982) UN Doc A/RES/37/43; UNGA Res 37/69A (9 December 1982) UN Doc A/RES/37/69A.

[113] Nico Krisch, 'Crimea and the Limits of International Law' (*EJIL:Talk!*, 10 March 2014) www.ejiltalk.org/crimea-and-the-limits-of-international-law, accessed 8 November 2022; Aurel Sari, 'Ukraine Insta-Symposium: When does the Breach of a Status of Forces Agreement amount to an Act of Aggression? The Case of Ukraine and the Black Sea Fleet SOFA' (*Opinio Juris*, 6 March

> For some reason, things that Kosovo Albanians (and we have full respect for them) were permitted to do, Russians, Ukrainians and Crimean Tatars in Crimea are not allowed. Again, one wonders why.[114]

The important difference in law between Kosovo and Crimea was that the declaration of independence of Crimea resulted from Russia's unlawful military involvement in the province, while that of Kosovo was not deemed to have stemmed from an illegal territorial situation.[115] Such a finding is not without controversy. In 1999, a group of North Atlantic Treaty Organization (NATO) member states illegally used force against the then Federal Republic of Yugoslavia, which had certain consequences for the subsequent territorial arrangement of Kosovo.[116] However, this special arrangement was legally put in place by the UN Security Council Resolution 1244 adopted under Chapter VII of the UN Charter.[117] In the *Kosovo* Advisory Opinion, the ICJ at least implicitly confirmed that Resolution 1244 interrupted the link between an egregious violation of a norm of general international law and the declaration of independence.[118] According to this position, Kosovo's declaration of independence thus stemmed from the legal arrangement under Resolution 1244 and not from the 1999 illegal use of force.

When a territorial entity seeks to become a state in violation of 'norms of general international law, in particular those of a peremptory character',[119] all states need to withhold recognition under Article 41 of the International Law Commission (ILC) Articles on Responsibility of States for Internationally Wrongful Acts (ARSIWA).[120] This is an obligation owed *erga omnes*, that is, toward everyone in the international community. Foreign states are under the obligation to withhold recognition of the shift of territorial sovereignty over Crimea. This territory may well be incorporated into Russia in fact, but it is not in law. The legal status, however, does not always overlap with effective control. As far as the legal status is concerned, Crimea remains a part of the territory of Ukraine under international law, but is effectively controlled by Russia.

By way of comparison, the situation of Catalonia is different. The declaration of independence was unilateral, but it did not result from an illegal use of force of any other egregious violation of a peremptory norm. As such, the

2014) www.opiniojuris.org/2014/03/06/ukraine-insta-symposium-breach-status-forces-agreement-amount-act-aggression-case-ukraine-black-sea-fleet-sofa, accessed 18 December 2022.

[114] 'Full Text of Putin's Speech on Crimea' (*Prague Post*, 19 March 2014) www.praguepost.com/eu-news/37854-full-text-of-putin-s-speech-on-crimea, accessed 17 June 2022.

[115] Jure Vidmar, 'The Kosovo Advisory Opinion Scrutinized' (2011) 24(2) *Leiden Journal of International Law* 355.

[116] Dino Kritsiotis, 'The Kosovo Crisis and NATO's Application of Armed Force against the Federal Republic of Yugoslavia' (2000) 49(2) *International and Comparative Law Quarterly* 330.

[117] UNSC Res 1244 (10 June 1999) UN Doc S/RES/1244.

[118] *Kosovo* Advisory Opinion, para 81.

[119] ibid.

[120] ARSIWA, art 41.

2017 declaration of independence does not fall within the ICJ's definition of illegality in the *Kosovo* Advisory Opinion and is not illegal under international law. On 6 September 2017, the regional parliament of Catalonia adopted an act that approved the holding of an independence referendum.[121] The act was struck down by the Spanish Constitutional Court on 7 September 2017.[122] The Constitutional Court decided that such a referendum would not have been compatible with the Spanish constitution, which is based on the unity of the Spanish people.[123] While it may have certain implications under domestic Spanish law, the decision does not have any direct legal implications under international law. Indeed, as the Supreme Court of Canada argued in the *Quebec* case, even an extraconstitutional secession could lead to state creation.[124] Illegality under constitutional law does not make (an attempt at) secession illegal under international law.[125] This was further confirmed by the ICJ in the *Kosovo* Advisory Opinion where the Court recalled that most secessions in international practice have been illegal under domestic law.[126]

The unequivocal decision of the Spanish Constitutional Court does have implications that do affect the legal nature and political likelihood of Catalonia's secession claim. The decision confirms that Catalonia's desired path to independence is unilateral, ie without the approval of the parent state and its constitutional organs. While such a path to independence is not *prima facie* illegal, its success is politically highly unlikely.

V. THE INDEPENDENCE REFERENDUMS

Organising an independence referendum is the most common way establishing the will of the people prior to declaring independence, but international practice shows that it is not indispensable. In recent practice, no independence referendum was held in Kosovo, for example.[127] Catalonia is a slightly different example, however. A referendum was organised, but it was illegal under domestic law. The circumstances in which the referendum took place did not allow

[121] Raymond Ridderhof, 'Catalonia's Referendum for Independence' (*Peace Palace Library*, 29 September 2017) peacepalacelibrary.nl/blog/2017/catalonias-referendum-independence, accessed 25 October 2022.

[122] *On the Self-Determination Referendum* (Judgment) ESP SC Court 4334-2017 (17 October 2017).

[123] Rebeca Carranco, 'Spain's Constitutional Court Strikes Down Catalan Referendum Law' (*El Pais*, 17 October 2017) english.elpais.com/elpais/2017/10/17/inenglish/1508250970_489373.html, accessed 8 December 2022.

[124] *Quebec* case, para 155.

[125] ibid.

[126] *Kosovo* Advisory Opinion, para 79.

[127] Jure Vidmar, 'Remedial Secession in International Law: Theory and (Lack of) Practice' (2010) 6(1) *St Antony's International Review* 37.

for a clear expression of the will of the people.[128] Moreover, the general sentiment is that Catalonia's society is split on the question of independence: around half of the population supports it, while the other half opposes it, often rather strongly.[129]

In the *Western Sahara* Advisory Opinion, the ICJ pronounced that 'the application of the right of self-determination requires a free and genuine expression of the will of the peoples concerned'.[130] Such an expression is usually formalised through referendums on the future legal status of a territory. In the aftermath of the First World War, several referendums on the legal status of European territories took place under the League of Nations auspices.[131] Referendums were also held in the process of decolonisation after the Second World War.[132] The post-Cold War period saw the emergence of a number of new states, and independence referendums were held in the territories of the Soviet Union, the SFRY, Eritrea, East Timor, Montenegro and South Sudan.

There were notable absences of independence referendums in Czechoslovakia[133] and Kosovo.[134] However, as the ICJ remarked in *Western Sahara*, the requirement for consultation may be dispensed with where the will of the people is obvious and unambiguous.[135] This was the case in some instances of decolonisation, where referendums were indeed not held but the will of the people was nevertheless clear.[136] The same cannot be said for the dissolution of Czechoslovakia. No referendum was held and it was unclear whether separation really was the will of the people,[137] yet the Czech Republic and Slovakia nevertheless emerged as new states.[138]

Outside of colonialism, independence is not an entitlement under international law.[139] As a consequence, a referendum is only a necessary but not a

[128] *On the Self-Determination Referendum* (n 122).

[129] '52% of Catalans support independence from Spain, according to a Madrid-based media' (*Catalan News*, 11 September 2013) www.catalannews.com/politics/item/52-of-catalans-support-independence-from-spain-according-to-a-madrid-based-media, accessed 14 November 2022.

[130] *Western Sahara* (Advisory Opinion) General List No 61 (1975) ICJ, para 55.

[131] Henry Brady and Cynthia Kaplan, 'Eastern Europe and the Former Soviet Union' in David Butler and Austin Ranney (eds), *Referendums Around the World: The Growing Use of Direct Democracy* (AEI 1994) 175.

[132] Russell Miller, 'Self-Determination in International Law and the Demise of Democracy' (2003) 41 Columbia Journal of Transnational Law 601, 634–44; Yves Beigbeder, *International Monitoring of Plebiscites, Referenda and National Elections: Self-Determination and Transition to Democracy* (Springer 1994) 91.

[133] Crawford (n 3) 402.

[134] Jure Vidmar, *Democratic Statehood in International Law: The Emergence of New States in post-Cold War Practice* (Hart 2013) 190 and 196.

[135] *Western Sahara* Advisory Opinion, para 55.

[136] ibid.

[137] Vidmar (n 134) 190.

[138] ibid.

[139] Kenneth Uzor Eze and Godwin N Okeke, 'The Right of People to Self-Determination and the Principle of Non-Interference in the Domestic Affairs of States' (2013) 7(1) *National Academy of Legal Studies and Research Law Review* 145.

sufficient requirement for independence. Recent practice indeed saw a number of referendums in favour of independence which, however, did not result in a creation of a new state.[140] Under international law, independence referendums are, therefore, not binding on the central government. This needs to be qualified with the pronouncement of the Supreme Court of Canada in the *Quebec* case. Referring to the principle of democracy entrenched in the Canadian constitutional law the Court established that in a democratic state an expression of the will of the people in favour of independence cannot be ignored.[141] An obligation would be put on both sides to negotiate the future legal status of the independence-seeking territory.[142] The Supreme Court of Canada made it clear, however, that such negotiations would not necessarily lead to independence.[143]

It follows that independence referendums generally do not have direct or self-executing legal effects. At best, they can trigger negotiations but do not create a right to independence. The central government can nevertheless commit itself in advance to respecting the outcome of the vote. Such examples were referendums in East Timor,[144] Montenegro[145] and South Sudan.[146] It seems that binding referendums are more of an exceptional feature used in an internationalised peace process rather than a standard in constitutional democracies.

Moreover, where independence referendums are held, international law does not prescribe how large or strong majorities in favour of independence need to be. In terms of political legitimacy, however, the stronger the majority the stronger the claim for independence. This is indeed a matter of political legitimacy rather than international legal rules. Since no self-executing right to independence exists under international law, this body of law does not prescribe a specific (numeric) majority needed.[147] A claim to independence is assessed politically. Determining a legitimate majority can be state and society specific. While in some societies 50 per cent plus one vote of all votes cast can be seen a legitimate expression of the will of the people, this could be problematic in more complex societies with diverging and even polarising identities. In such cases a vote for independence that does not cut across the identities could lead to tyranny of the majority.

[140] Matthew Psycharis, 'What is the legal status of a referendum, and why bother holding one?' (*Constitutional Law Matters*, 25 July 2022) constitutionallawmatters.org/2022/07/what-is-the-legal-status-of-a-referendum-and-why-bother-holding-one, accessed 3 December 2022.

[141] *Quebec* case, para 87.

[142] ibid, para 91.

[143] ibid, para 91.

[144] Murray Stewart Leith and Duncan Sim, 'A Second Scottish Independence Referendum: Should the Diaspora get a Vote?' (Political Quarterly, 18 March 2023) politicalquarterly.org.uk/blog/a-second-scottish-independence-referendum-should-the-diaspora-get-a-vote, accessed 19 March 2023.

[145] ibid.

[146] ibid.

[147] *Quebec* case, para 385.

Looking at comparative practice, in the *Quebec* case, the Supreme Court of Canada expressed the general threshold for validity of an independence referendum: 'The referendum result, if it is to be taken as an expression of the democratic will, must be free of ambiguity both in terms of the question asked and in terms of the support it achieves.'[148] The definition of the phrase 'free of ambiguity' was further specified by the Canadian Clarity Act, passed in 2000.[149] With regard to the winning majority, the Act specifies that clarity of the decision may be determined by: '(i) the size of the majority of valid votes cast in favour of the secessionist option; (ii) the percentage of eligible voters voting in the referendum; and (iii) any other matters or circumstances … consider[ed] to be relevant.'[150] While the Clarity Act refers to, *inter alia*, 'percentage of eligible votes', the threshold for the success of a referendum is not quantified.

Taking Catalonia as an example, was its vote for independence free of ambiguity? There are two issues to be considered. First, the referendum did not meet the standard of a free and fair vote. But that was due to certain interventions of the organs of the Spanish state.[151] Second, while it is possible that in the circumstances of a free and fair referendum vote the turnout and ultimately the support for independence would have been higher, it cannot be ignored that the share of the population opposing independence remains very high. If democracy is not understood as a simple rule of majority, the political legitimacy of this independence claim remains weak until either a more comfortable pro-independence majority is realised or more current anti-independence voters switch from against to the middle-of-the-road position.

Independence referendums are no panacea. While they are commonly used to determine the will of the people where a change of territorial status is sought, their role has to be seen in the context of political legitimacy rather than legal entitlement. In other words, a successful independence referendum may make a claim for a change of legal status of a territory politically more legitimate, but will not create a legal entitlement to a new status.

VI. TERRITORIAL ILLEGALITY AND STATEHOOD

The move away from effectiveness in the law of statehood was a consequence of developments in general international law that no longer tolerated legal entitlements to be created in violation of certain fundamental norms.[152] Referring to

[148] ibid, para 87.

[149] Clarity Act, 2000 (CAN SC 2000 c 26) (29 June 2000). An Act to give effect to the requirement for clarity as set out in the opinion of the Supreme Court of Canada in the *Reference Re Secession of Quebec*.

[150] Clarity Act, 2000, para 2.

[151] Javier Alcalde and Pablo Aguiar, 'Catalan Sovereignty in Practice' (*PRIO Paper*, 2017) www.prio.org/publications/9319, accessed 15 December 2022.

[152] John Dugard, *Recognition and the United Nations* (CUP 1987) 135–37.

the practice of states and UN organs,[153] some writers argue that the traditional (Montevideo) statehood criteria have been supplemented by a set of additional ones.[154] The criteria described as 'additional' do not originate specifically in the law of statehood but are, rather, concepts developed in other fields of international law which impact the law of statehood. The underlying idea behind the concept is that an illegally created entity cannot become a state.[155]

It is most commonly identified that the legality-based additional statehood criteria require that a state is not created as a result of the illegal use of force, in violation of the right of self-determination, or in pursuance of racist policies.[156] The legal norms underlying the concept of additional statehood criteria are often considered to be of *jus cogens* character[157] and therefore a state creation in violation of *jus cogens* would be illegal.[158] There has been some debate on whether territorial illegality can really be associated with *jus cogens* and whether the effect of territorial illegality really is that an illegally created territorial entity is not a state. In a competing view, the norms which underlie the illegality of a state creation are not statehood criteria but recognition requirements.[159] If a state emerges in violation of these norms, this does not mean that it is not a state. It means, rather, that it is an 'illegal state'.[160] This section considers the association of illegality of a state creation with *jus cogens* and clarifies how illegality of this kind interferes with an entity's legal status.

The association of territorial illegality with the concept of *jus cogens* may be controversial because it is not generally accepted that all of the norms underlying an illegal state creation have a *jus cogens* character and,[161] in any case, only a few norms of this character are relevant in the context of the law of statehood.[162] However, the operation of *jus cogens* in the law of statehood has been acknowledged by the ILC in ARSIWA.[163] Article 41(2) provides that 'no State shall recognise as lawful a situation created by a serious breach [of *jus cogens*] nor render aid or assistance in maintaining that situation'.[164] It further specifies that states owe an obligation *erga omnes* to withhold formal or implied recognition of an effective territorial situation, created in breach of *jus cogens*.[165] In this context, it needs

[153] McCorquodale (n 5) 191.
[154] Francois Finck, 'The State Between Fact and Law: The Role of Recognition and the Conditions Under which it is Granted in the Creation of New States' (2016) 36 *Polish Yearbook of International Law* 51.
[155] Crawford (n 3) 107.
[156] McCorquodale (n 5) 191.
[157] Crawford (n 3) 105.
[158] Crawford (n 3) 105; Dugard (n 152).
[159] Talmon (n 6) 101–181.
[160] ibid.
[161] Talmon (n 82) 99–125.
[162] ibid, 99–125.
[163] ARSIWA, arts 40 and 41; UNGA RES 56/83 (28 January 2002) UN Doc A/RES/56/83.
[164] ARSIWA, art 41.2.
[165] Report of the International Law Commission on the work of its fifty-third session, 23 April – 1 June and 2 July – 10 August 2001, Official Records of the General Assembly, Fifty-sixth session, Supplement No 10, UN Doc A/56/10, 283.

to be noted that according to the Commentary to ARSIWA, the prohibition of illegal use of force, the right of self-determination and the prohibition of racial discrimination are among the norms of *jus cogens* character.[166]

In the *Kosovo* Advisory Opinion, the ICJ stated that:

> [T]he illegality attached to [some other] declarations of independence … stemmed not from the unilateral character of these declarations as such, but from the fact that they were, or would have been, connected with the unlawful use of force or other egregious violations of norms of general international law, in particular those of a peremptory character *(jus cogens)*.[167]

The Court avoided any pronouncements on Kosovo's legal status or the legality of its recognition; but it did associate *jus cogens* and territorial illegality. The Court did so by referring broadly to declarations of independence being *connected with* breaches of certain norms and not being a direct result of such a breach. This means that a breach of *jus cogens* in an attempt at state creation should not be understood narrowly, in the sense of a hypothetical situation where the representatives of an entity are coerced into declaring independence by being subjected to torture. In such a circumstance, the declaration of independence would directly follow from a breach of *jus cogens*. The violation of a peremptory norm should be understood in the sense of a declaration of independence being illegal where it tries to *consolidate* an effective situation created in breach of certain norms of international law, 'in particular those of peremptory character'.

Thus, it is doctrinally accepted that in some circumstances state creation may be illegal and, in such situations, other states have a duty to withhold recognition. The association of illegality of state creations with *jus cogens* remains somewhat controversial, yet it seems to have notable support not only among writers but, *inter alia*, also in the ARSIWA and, although expressed carefully, in the reasoning of the ICJ in the *Kosovo* Advisory Opinion. It remains to be clarified what the effects are of an illegal (attempt at) state creation for the entity's legal status. In other words, is the consequence of an illegal state creation that such an entity is not a state?

When clarifying the effects of an illegal state creation for the entity's legal status, it is of central importance to consider the purpose of the collective withholding of recognition on legal grounds. Namely, the advocates of the additional statehood criteria argue that an illegally created effective entity is not a state. At the same time, the illegality underlying the additional statehood criteria triggers an obligation to withhold recognition under general international law.[168] If an illegally created effective entity is not a state and yet it is subject to collective

[166] ibid, 286–90.
[167] *Kosovo* Advisory Opinion, para 81.
[168] Talmon (n 82) 99–125.

withholding of recognition, the interpretation could follow that the purpose of non-recognition is preventing this entity from becoming a state. This interpretation is not easy to square with the prevailing view in contemporary international law of recognition being a declaratory, not a constitutive act.[169]

Those advocates of the declaratory theory who also adopt the concept of the additional set of legality-based statehood criteria argue that the purpose of collectively withholding recognition to illegally created entities is not that recognition could constitute statehood of such an entity but that it would merely affirm a legally non-existent situation. One such argument is well-captured in the following paragraph:

> [T]he obligation of non-recognition has a declaratory character in the sense that States are considered to be under a legal obligation not to recognize a specific situation which is *already* legally non-existent. Thus, the obligation of withholding recognition is not the cause of the fact that an illegal act does not produce the intended results, that is, legal rights for the wrongdoer. Non-recognition merely declares or confirms that fact and the obligation not to grant recognition prevents the validation or 'curing' of the illegal act or the situation resulting from that act.[170]

Such an argument presupposes that a breach of certain fundamental norms of international law *automatically* results in this entity not being a state. The argument is paradoxical as this school of thought denies the automatic effects of the Montevideo criteria, yet presupposes the automatic effects of the additional statehood criteria.[171] In other words, an entity does not become a state automatically upon meeting the Montevideo criteria, but a violation of the additional statehood criteria automatically results in this entity not being a state. This issue will be further discussed below.[172]

Another problem of the explanation is, as Stefan Talmon argues, that the call for collective non-recognition of an illegally created effective entity implies only that such an entity could become a state through recognition and proponents of the declaratory theory do not adequately prove that this is not so.[173] Indeed, illegality being 'cured' through recognition is just a way of saying that recognition could create a state without saying this directly. The problem here is that an illegal state creation triggers an obligation to withhold recognition; at the same time, it is proposed that the underlying illegality *automatically* results in this entity not being a state. Consequently, the territorial illegality triggers an obligation to withhold recognition of an entity which is not considered to be a state in the first place. But why would that be necessary if recognition could not constitute a state? One then needs to accept either that recognition may

[169] Harris (n 11) 145.
[170] David Raič, *Statehood and the Law of Self-Determination* (Brill 2002) 105.
[171] ibid.
[172] See nn 182–98.
[173] Talmon (n 6) 101–81.

constitute a state or that the illegally created effective entities are, in fact, states and non-recognition does not interfere with an entity's legal status.

A. The Problematic Concept of 'Illegal States'

The approach of treating illegally created effective entities as states and preserving the declaratory nature of recognition is very prominently advocated by Talmon, who argues that '[t]he collectively non-recognised States may be "illegal States" [but] they are nevertheless still "States"'[174] and that 'the additional criteria of legality proposed are not criteria for statehood but merely conditions for recognition, *viz* reasons for not recognizing *existing* States'.[175] This explanation thus introduces the concept of 'illegal states' which employs the word 'states' and thereby accepts that collectively non-recognised 'illegal states' are *prima facie* states. Since they are already states, no constitutive effects are ascribed to the act of recognition. In other words, non-recognition only interferes with the adjective 'illegal' and not with the noun 'state'.

The qualification with the adjective 'illegal', however, makes these states somewhat different from states that are not illegal. This is problematic because the concept suggests that a (non-recognised) 'illegal state' does not have all the rights stemming from statehood, ie it does not have all the attributes of statehood.[176] It is rather difficult to accept that there exist two types of states in international law, those with all and those with only some attributes of statehood. In order to accept this argument, one would also need to accept the idea of some states being more equal than others. This seems to be unacceptable from the perspective of sovereign equality of states.[177]

Moreover, the concept of 'illegal states' does not solve the problem of ascribing recognition with constitutive effects. Indeed, unlike 'states', 'illegal states' in this perception do not have the full attributes of statehood. By holding that non-recognition *only* withholds 'the rights inherent in statehood', it is actually implied that recognition could endow an 'illegal state' with the full attributes of statehood. Constitutive effects of recognition are then admitted through the backdoor and the problem merely pushed to another level: it is not a state itself which could be constituted by recognition; 'only' the attributes of statehood could be constituted if recognition were not withheld.

The concept of 'illegal states' thus falls close to Oppenheim's understanding that a state emerges as a matter of fact, yet it does not acquire an

[174] ibid..
[175] ibid..
[176] ibid..
[177] United Nations Charter (adopted 26 June 1945, entered into force 24 October 1945) 1 UNTS 16 (UN Charter), art 2.1.

international personality by its 'natural birth' but rather by recognition.[178] As Lauterpacht noted, such an explanation adopts the 'confusing distinction between (natural) statehood, which is independent of recognition, and membership of the international community (or full international personality), which alone is a source of rights and which is dependent on recognition'.[179] Lauterpacht continues:

> The distinction seems to be of little value. There is, in law, no substance in the assertion that a community is a State unless we attach to the fact of statehood rights and competencies within the internal or international sphere, which international law is ready to recognize. It seems irrelevant to predicate that a community exists as a State unless such existence is treated as implying legal consequences.[180]

The only plausible explanation of the purpose of the obligation to withhold recognition is thus that under some circumstances recognition could have constitutive effects. Certainly, recognition cannot be seen as a constitutive act if this were to mean that a state can never exist without being recognised. As demonstrated by the examples of the Federal Republic of Yugoslavia (FRY) and Macedonia, non-recognised states can indeed exist.[181] But in these circumstances there was no legal obligation to withhold recognition and no other territorial title existed in the spatial areas concerned.

Yet, where an obligation to withhold recognition applies in the sense of Article 41 ARSIWA, it cannot be denied that such an obligation exists precisely to ensure that territorial illegality does not result in the legal status of statehood and shift of territorial title. This is because universal recognition could indeed be creative of statehood. This position challenges the view that recognition is declaratory. However, the declaratory nature of recognition should not be taken as a dogma and defended in all circumstances. The arguments that a state may exist without being recognised and that recognition may create a state are not mutually exclusive. Indeed, these are two separate issues. Where unilateral secession is at issue, the creation of statehood indeed depends on recognition.[182]

Thus, when adjectives are attached to the noun state, the attributes of statehood cannot depend on this adjective. Statehood is a unitary legal concept and there cannot be varying degrees of it; there cannot be first class and second class statehood. The concept of 'illegal states' therefore needs to be rejected. Does this mean that territorial illegality has a statehood-barring effect?

[178] Oppenheim (n 26) 264.
[179] Lauterpacht (n 35) 38.
[180] ibid, 38–39.
[181] Declaration on the former Yugoslav Republic of Macedonia, Guimaraes, May 1–2, 1992. See also Vidmar (n 101) 228–31.
[182] *Québec* case, para 155.

B. The Legal Effects of the Additional Statehood Criteria

Discussing the episode of Southern Rhodesia,[183] Crawford explains that three interpretations are possible: (i) Southern Rhodesia was a state; (ii) Southern Rhodesia was not a state because recognition was collectively withheld; and (iii) Southern Rhodesia was not a state because 'the principle of self-determination in this situation prevented an otherwise effective entity from being regarded as a State'.[184] Crawford then argues that in the light of international practice, the first possibility needs to be rejected.[185] The second possibility is also rejected with the explanation that recognition is declaratory and Crawford thus accepts the third option – although the effectiveness-based Montevideo criteria were met, Southern Rhodesia was not a state because it would have emerged in breach of the right of self-determination.[186]

This reasoning underlies the concept of the additional statehood criteria.[187] The reasoning is premised on the assumption that certain entities would have been states if the Montevideo criteria were the only applicable statehood criteria. If such entities are not states, this means that a set of additional statehood criteria must exist. This is, however, an equation with too few parameters. The logic of this argument only works if it is accepted that states emerge *automatically* upon meeting the statehood criteria; only that here the statehood criteria are not only those elaborated in the Montevideo Convention but also a set of legality-based criteria in addition. It was shown above that states clearly do not emerge only upon meeting the statehood criteria, whether Montevideo or Montevideo-plus.[188] Statehood in contemporary international law is not created by an effective exercise of jurisdiction in a certain territory.

The concept of the additional statehood criteria is influenced by the zeitgeist of Rhodesia, the South African Homelands and Northern Cyprus;[189] while it does not take into account the subsequent situations in which no territorial illegality was involved. The reasoning behind the concept of the additional statehood criteria, therefore, only works where territorial illegality is indeed attached to the creation of an effective entity. It cannot explain, for example, what prevents Somaliland from becoming a state. A strong argument can be made that this entity meets the Montevideo criteria.[190] Furthermore, it did not become effective as a result of the use of force in the sense of Article 2(4) of the

[183] Southern Rhodesia's Unilateral Declaration of Independence of 1965; UNGA Res 1747 (27 June 1962) UN Doc A/RES/1747 (XVI); UNSC Res 202 (6 May 1965) UN Doc S/RES/202 (XX); UNGA Res 2022 (5 November 1965) UN Doc A/RES/2022 (XX).

[184] Crawford (n 3) 129.

[185] ibid.

[186] ibid.

[187] Devine (n 7) 410–17.

[188] ibid.

[189] Raič (n 170) 151–58.

[190] Montevideo Convention, art 1.

UN Charter.[191] It is thus safe to assume that Somaliland, in principle, meets both the Montevideo and Montevideo-plus criteria. The reason why it is not a state is, however, found in the above-discussed presumption of Somalia's statehood and thus the related territorial integrity of Somalia.

Moreover, the argument in favour of the additional statehood criteria somewhat dogmatically rejects the role which recognition may have in the creation of statehood.[192] As has been argued above, claiming that in some circumstances (universal) recognition could have state-creating effects is not the same as saying that non-recognised states cannot exist.[193] In other words, Kosovo-type situations should not be explained by analogy to Macedonia-type situations. Similarly, when territorial illegality is at issue, universal recognition could create a state. The collective call for non-recognition only affirms this logic – if universal recognition could not constitute a state, there would be no logical reason for the existence of an obligation *erga omnes* to withhold recognition of an illegally created effective entity.[194]

With regard to Southern Rhodesia, the UN Security Council specifically called on the United Kingdom not to decolonise the entity.[195] As a consequence, Southern Rhodesia formally still remained on the list of self-governing territories and collective non-acceptance of its statehood created no legal vacuum with regard to its legal status. However, had Southern Rhodesia been formally decolonised and removed from the list of non-self-governing territories, its statehood would have been much more difficult to deny. What other status could it have before Zimbabwe was created? Under contemporary international law, the territory could not be considered *terra nullius*.[196]

Southern Rhodesia is thus a good example of an internationalised response to territorial illegality that results in international non-acceptance of an entity altering its legal status. Where an entity declares independence unilaterally, without territorial illegality being involved, foreign states freely decide whether or not they would accept such a declaration.[197] This is different where territorial illegality *is* involved. Foreign states then do not have this freedom – they are not allowed to accept the declaration as a matter of an obligation *erga omnes*.[198]

It is, however, erroneous to interpret the additional statehood criteria as having a direct effect on an entity's legal status. Such an explanation has severe flaws: (i) it assumes that territorial illegality is the only reason why an illegally created effective entity does not emerge as a state, but cannot explain why meeting the traditional and additional statehood criteria is not necessarily enough

[191] UN Charter, art 2.4.
[192] Devine (n 7) 410–17.
[193] Talmon (n 6) 101–81.
[194] Talmon (n 82) 99–125.
[195] UNSC Res 202 (6 May 1965) UN Doc S/RES/202, paras 3–5.
[196] *Palmas* case (n 81).
[197] *Quebec* case, para 155.
[198] Talmon (n 82) 99–125.

for becoming a state; and (ii) it assumes that an illegally created effective entity lacks statehood, but cannot logically explain the purpose of the obligation to withhold recognition, and why universal recognition of such an entity could not create its statehood.

The concept of legality requirements in the process of state creation nevertheless does not need to be rejected. The legality-based requirements regulate the political process of state creation and impose constraints on the states' political discretion on granting recognition. These constraints then prevent the shift of legal status where the effective territorial situation is realised illegally.

C. Non-state Jurisdictional Units

Thus far, this chapter has argued against the so-called 'states with adjectives'. There is indeed little benefit in calling a territorial community a state if it does not have the rights and duties of statehood. But this is not to say that non-state jurisdictional units cannot exist and in many respects even function as states. This is because they have the capacity to exercise territorial jurisdiction over a certain spatial area and in practice exercise their legislative, executive and judicial powers. As established in chapter two of this book, the statehood criteria indeed much more accurately describe such non-state jurisdictional units rather than statehood.

A non-state entity is a broad category which can cover several situations that can be, in law, quite different from one another. Examples might include Somaliland, Taiwan, Northern Cyprus, Southern Rhodesia, Palestine, Austria before 1955, Bangladesh before 1974, and – for a number of states – even present-day Kosovo. It is common to all of these entities that the political process of creating a state has or had not been completed at a certain point in time. In some circumstances, the political process had not been completed due to an underlying territorial illegality which prevented state creation. Such examples are Northern Cyprus (Turkey's use of force) and Southern Rhodesia (the unrepresentative racist government), while in others it is a matter of politics rather than international law why a new political status has not been established. While the rules of international law may prevent state creation is some circumstances, this is not always the case. For example, Taiwan does not even claim to be a state, although it probably meets the statehood criteria and its territorial effectiveness is not a result of territorial illegality in the sense of paragraph 81 of the ICJ's *Kosovo* Advisory Opinion.[199]

The term 'illegal state' is inaccurate as it assumes that states emerge automatically and self-evidently upon meeting the Montevideo criteria. International practice shows that this is not the case. Furthermore, as Lauterpacht warned,

[199] *Kosovo* Advisory Opinion, para 81.

there is little sense in calling an entity a state if it does not enjoy the rights and duties inherent in statehood. The term 'non-recognised states' can be accurate, although it is often incorrectly used in international legal parlance. An example of a (largely) unrecognised state was Macedonia in 1992 when it actually was a state, but it remained largely unrecognised due to its dispute with Greece over its name.[200]

In academic literature, Somaliland has sometimes been referred to as a *de facto* state or a *de facto* regime.[201] This is designation presumes that the statehood criteria are in principle met, yet the entity nevertheless does not have the legal status of a state under international law. Scott Pegg defines a *de facto* state as:

> a political entity where there is an organised political leadership which has risen to power through some degree of indigenous capability; receives popular support; and has achieved sufficient capacity to provide governmental services to a given population in a specific territorial area, over which effective control is maintained for a significant period of time. … [This political entity] views itself as capable of entering into relations with other states and it seeks full constitutional independence and widespread international recognition as a sovereign state. It is, however, unable to achieve any degree of substantive recognition and therefore remains illegitimate in the eyes of international society.[202]

This definition captures the territorial entities which fit within the statehood criteria and the influential nineteenth-century definitions of the state coined by Max Weber and Georg Jellinek.[203] As argued in the previous chapter of this book, such definitions more accurately define territorial jurisdictional units rather than states or statehood.[204] Moreover, the definition of a *de facto* state in fact acknowledges that the entity is not a state. It is thus questionable why the term state should then be used in the first place. Indeed, the attempt to qualify certain 'states' with adjectives is a rather paradoxical exercise which labels an entity as a state, yet at the same time acknowledges that the entity is actually not a state. This is because statehood should not be equated with the capacity to demonstrate factual exercise of territorial jurisdiction.

It would also be incorrect to say that Kosovo is a state that remains unrecognised by nearly 80 states. The legal status of Kosovo is objectively unclear at present. For some states it is a state while for others it is not. This ambiguity pertains to Kosovo's legal status and whether the political process has created a state in that territory. Unlike with Macedonia in 1992, where the controversy did not pertain to its legal status, it cannot be assumed that Kosovo is a state, albeit

[200] Craven (n 12) 199–200.
[201] Hoehne (n 13).
[202] Scott Pegg, *International Society and the De Facto State* (Ashgate 1998) 26.
[203] Max Weber, 'Politics as a Vocation' in Tony Waters, and Dagmar Waters (eds), *Weber's Rationalism and Modern Society* (Springer 2015) 129–98; Jellinek (n 14).
[204] Stuart Elden, 'Land, Terrain, Territory' (2010) 34(6) *Progress in Human Geography* 799–817.

not a universally recognised one. Its legal status simply needs to be clarified over time, in the same way Bangladesh's legal status was clarified between 1971 and 1974.

Non-state jurisdictional units are therefore entities that in principle satisfy the Montevideo criteria, but these criteria more accurately describe territorial jurisdiction rather than statehood.[205] State creation is a political process that is governed by law, but cannot be explained by legal rules alone. Hence, there can be a discrepancy between territorial legal status and factual exercise of jurisdictional powers. Non-state jurisdictional units exist in the zone of that discrepancy.

The role of the UN and other international organisations in determining the existence as well as the rights and duties of non-state jurisdictional units can be quite central. It was argued above that statehood means legal status under customary international law. Its components are state practice and *opinio juris*, both of which can be expressed through and shaped by collective actions through certain international institutions. The UN General Assembly and Security Council adopted a set of resolutions on Southern Rhodesia[206] and Northern Cyprus[207] which were instrumental in shaping international practice of their legal status as non-states. UN Security Council Resolution 1244 was instrumental in creating Kosovo as a separate territorial legal entity.[208] And it was also UN Security Council Resolutions 757 and 777 which confirmed that the SFRY was no longer a state which, in turn, removed its claim to territorial integrity.[209] As a result, new states emerged within its territory, including non-recognised Macedonia.[210] In the absence of any other state in that territory, what could Macedonia be if not a state? On the other hand, it is often argued that UN membership or even associate membership can clarify an entity's legal status or even create a state. These claims will be considered in chapter five of this book. This chapter now turns to some recent examples of purported changes of territorial status and contrasts the legal circumstances in which they were held.

VII. ATTEMPTS AT ALTERING THE TERRITORIAL STATUS: CONTRASTING SCOTLAND, CATALONIA, CRIMEA AND EASTERN UKRAINE

In 2014, Scotland held a referendum with approval of the parent state, but the consultation did not favour independence. Catalonia in 2017 held a referendum

[205] ibid, 799–817.
[206] UNGA Res 1747 (27 June 1962) UN Doc A/RES/1747 (XVI).
[207] UNGA Res 3212 (1 November 1974) UN Doc A/RES/3212 (XXIX).
[208] UNSC Res 1244 (10 June 1999) UN Doc S/RES/1244.
[209] UNSC Res 757 (30 May 1992) UN Doc S/RES/757; UNSC Res 777 (19 September 1992) UN Doc S/RES/777.
[210] Craven (n 12) 199–200.

without such an approval of the parent state and declared independence unilaterally, although the legal nature of this declaration remains controversial. A referendum on legal status was also held in Crimea in 2014. Moreover, declarations of independence were purportedly also issues in certain areas of Eastern Ukraine. This section seeks to contrast these situation in order to illustrate how the underlying territorial situation determines a claim to territorial title and an attempted change of territorial status.

A. Scotland

Scotland held a referendum on independence on 18 September 2014.[211] The referendum was formalised by an agreement between the governments of the United Kingdom and Scotland.[212] The United Kingdom government had thus committed itself to accepting the outcome of the referendum. Scotland was thus one of the relatively few examples where independence referendum was held with consent of the parent state and a commitment was politically reached to negotiate secession in the case of an affirmative vote. In the end, 55.05 per cent votes cast at a turnout of 84.1 per cent were against independence.[213] The result of the vote therefore did not trigger the secession procedure. But the procedure had been put in place by domestic legislation and had the result been different, Scotland's statehood would have been created on the basis of a domestic political process.

B. Catalonia

The situation in Catalonia in 2017 was much different than that of Scotland in 2014. On 6 September 2017, the regional parliament of Catalonia adopted an act that approved the holding of an independence referendum.[214] The act was struck down by the Spanish Constitutional Court on 7 September 2017.[215] The Constitutional Court decided that such a referendum would not

[211] 'Scottish Independence Referendum Act 2013' (*Scottish Government*, 14 November 2013) www.scottish.parliament.uk/parliamentarybusiness/Bills/61076.aspx, accessed 30 October 2022.

[212] 'Agreement between the United Kingdom Government and the Scottish Government on a referendum on independence for Scotland' (*Parliament UK*, 15 October 2012) assets.publishing.service.gov.uk/government/uploads/system/uploads/attachment_data/file/313612/scottish_referendum_agreement.pdf, accessed 14 July 2023; Stephen Tierney, 'Legal Issues Surrounding the Referendum on Independence for Scotland' (2013) 9(4) *European Constitutional Law Review* 359.

[213] 'The Scottish Independence Referendum Results 2014' (*Fife Council*) www.fife.gov.uk/kb/docs/articles/council-and-democracy/elections2/election-results/the-scottish-independence-referendum-results-2014, accessed 7 April 2016.

[214] Law on the Referendum on Self-determination of Catalonia 19/2017.

[215] 'Spain Catalonia: Court blocks independence referendum' (*BBC*, 8 September 2017) accessed 9 October 2022.

have been compatible with the Spanish constitution, which is based on the unity of the Spanish people.[216] While this decision may have certain implications under domestic Spanish law, the decision does not have any direct legal implications under international law. Indeed, as the Supreme Court of Canada argued in the *Quebec* case, even an extraconstitutional secession could lead to state creation.[217] Illegality under constitutional law does not make (an attempt at) secession illegal under international law.[218] This was further confirmed by the ICJ in the *Kosovo* Advisory Opinion where the Court recalled that most secessions in international practice have been illegal under domestic law.[219]

The independence referendum in Catalonia was organised unofficially on 1 October 2017 and, reportedly, 92 per cent of all votes cast were in favour of independence – although at a rather low turnout of 43 per cent of all eligible voters.[220] In absolute percentages this means that approximately 38.5 per cent of all those eligible to vote cast their ballots in favour of independence.[221] By comparison, in the United Kingdom, withdrawal from the European Union (Brexit) was supported by 37.4 per cent of all those eligible to vote.[222] In absolute percentages Catalonia's independence thus won a slightly higher approval than the Brexit vote did in the United Kingdom.

Due to the turmoil and certain activities of the Spanish coercive apparatus attempting to prevent or undermine the vote,[223] the referendum was generally not deemed to have taken place in the circumstances required for a free and fair expression of the will of the people.[224] Notwithstanding the referendum results, opinion polls suggest that Catalonia is a split society where the pro-independence and the anti-independence camps each generate around 45 per cent support or slightly more, while fewer than 10 per cent generally remain undecided.[225] It is thus noticeable that the part of the population that holds an indifferent view on

[216] Carranco (n 123).

[217] *Quebec* case, para 155.

[218] ibid.

[219] *Kosovo* Advisory Opinion, para 79.

[220] Angela Dewan, Vasco Cotovio and Hilary Clarke, 'Catalonia independence referendum: What just happened?' (*CNN*, 2 October 2017) edition.cnn.com/2017/10/02/europe/catalonia-independence-referendum-explainer/index.html, accessed 14 August 2022.

[221] ibid.

[222] 'EU referendum: The result in maps and charts' (*BBC*, 8 June 2021) www.bbc.com/news/uk-politics-36616028, accessed 15 October 2021.

[223] Alcalde and Aguiar (n 151).

[224] Jorge Valero, 'Independent observers: No proper referendum took place in Catalonia' (*Euroactiv*, 18 October 2017) www.euractiv.com/section/future-eu/news/independent-observers-no-referendum-took-place-in-catalonia, accessed 19 June 2021.

[225] 'Political Opinion Barometer. 1st wave 2019' (*Centre d'Estudis d' Opinio*, 2019) upceo.ceo.gencat.cat/wsceop/7008/Abstract%20in%20English%20-919.pdf, accessed 8 October 2022. These figures change between different opinion polls and some indicate a slight advantage of the opponents of independence. This poll, for example, detects a reversed situation whereas around 44 per cent support independence while 48 per cent oppose it.

the matter is relatively low. The pro-independence camp can thus at best count on a very narrow majority.

On 10 October 2017, Mr Carles Puigdemont, then the President of the Government of Catalonia, announced that following the referendum, he had the mandate to declare independence and that there would be an immediate suspension.[226] It remained unclear whether this actually even was a declaration of independence. The central government in Madrid asked for clarification, but Mr Puigdemont never gave an answer.[227] It appears, however, that he suspended his (perceived) mandate to declare independence rather than the declaration of independence itself.[228] As Mr Puigdemont never unequivocally issued a declaration of independence, he indeed could not have suspended it. It thus appears that the correct date of Catalonia's declaration of independence is 27 October 2017, when a resolution to this effect was passed *in* the Catalan Parliament with a very narrow majority.[229] It should be noted that the resolution was passed *in* the Catalan parliament, ie in the building of the parliament, but not by the Catalan parliament. It would appear that the resolution was not an act of parliament.

Even the title of the document ('resolution') is very significant, as it usually implies a non-binding instrument. Moreover, pursuant to Article 65 of the Statute of Catalan autonomy, every legislative act of the Catalan Parliament needs to be promulgated in the Official Gazette,[230] and pursuant to Article 67(6), the President of Catalonia has the power of promulgation.[231] In the absence of such a formal procedure, the document has no legal effect.

Mr Puigdemont never promulgated the declaration of independence – it was never published in the Official Gazette – which means it was never a legislative act. As such, it remains merely a political act. This is quite important, as independence was thus not really declared by the president or the parliament, but rather by a group of individuals – otherwise members of the parliament – outside of formal institutional structures. The declaration of independence was therefore not a legal act ultra vires, but merely a political manifesto. This position is in line with the ICJ's pronouncement in the *Kosovo* Advisory Opinion:

> [T]he authors of the declaration of independence of 17 February 2008 did not act as one of the Provisional Institutions of Self-Government within the Constitutional Framework, but rather as persons who acted together in their capacity as representatives of the people of Kosovo outside the framework of the interim administration.[232]

[226] 'Catalonia independence declaration signed and suspended' (*BBC*, 10 October 2017) www.bbc.com/news/world-europe-41574172, accessed 8 October 2022.
[227] ibid..
[228] ibid..
[229] ibid..
[230] 'Organic Act 6/2006 of the 19th July, on the Reform of the Statute of Autonomy of Catalonia, art 65' (*Catalonian Parliament*, 19 July 2006) available at www.parlament.cat/document/cataleg/150259.pdf, accessed 12 October 2022.
[231] ibid..
[232] *Kosovo* Advisory Opinion, para 109.

Kosovo, in this regard, is different than Catalonia in that Kosovo's Constitutional Framework could not be separated from international law. The Constitutional Framework for Kosovo was adopted under the authority of the UN Security Council Resolution 1244, adopted under Chapter VII of the UN Charter.[233] In the case of Kosovo, there was thus a fusion of international and constitutional law: the applicable domestic constitutional law was also an international legal instrument. No such direct link between the declaration of independence and a source of international law exists in the case of Catalonia.

It is highly significant that despite the fact that the applicable constitutional law in the case of Kosovo was in fact also an international legal instrument, the ICJ placed the declaration of independence outside of formal legal structures. The ICJ indeed recalled that most declarations of independence in history have been extraconstitutional.[234] Following the ICJ's logic, as long as the declaration of independence was not adopted within the formal legislative process, it does not make any difference in law whether it was declared by members of the Catalan parliament, president of the government, or by a completely random person. It is true that the first two options make such a declaration politically more serious and potentially more likely to produce legal consequences, but they appear to be no different in law from the one issued by a completely random person. This means that, legally speaking, those members of the Catalan parliament who issued the declaration of independence did not act in their official capacity when they did so, but in their private capacity. The declaration of independence is therefore not a legal act, but merely a political manifesto and political speech. Even if it were adopted as a legislative act domestically, this would not have been an internationally wrongful act.[235]

The fact that the declaration of independence is not a legal act has certain consequences for Spain's counter-secession policy. As demonstrated above, a declaration of independence is only a political manifesto. If it is not acted on, it remains without any legal effect. Certainly, the fact that international law is neutral on the question of secession does not mean that domestic law must also be neutral on this matter. However, the process and legal nature of State creation under international law is nevertheless very important for domestic law. In order for a new State to emerge, such legal status needs to be registered in international law. And if a new State does not emerge, this means that nothing has in fact happened in law. This is precisely the situation in Catalonia today: independence was declared in 2017, but then nothing happened in law and a new State never emerged.

The actions of the then Catalan leaders were political and without legal consequences. The declaration of independence was a political manifesto which

[233] UNSC Res 1244 (10 June 1999) UN Doc S/RES/1244.
[234] *Kosovo* Advisory Opinion, para 79.
[235] *Quebec* case, para 155.

did not break Spain's territorial integrity. One could therefore ask whether Spain's response to certain former political leaders of Catalonia has been proportionate, especially in the light of the European Convention on Human Rights (ECHR). It should be recalled that the European Court of Human Rights (ECtHR) has established a high bar for legitimate limitations on Article 10 ECHR (the freedom of expression). When it comes to political speech in the context of secession, limitations tend to be justified where such activities are associated with agitation to violence, terrorist activities, or take place in armed conflict.[236] As the Court's Guide to Article 10 further explains:

> Generally speaking, the Court considers that it is of the essence of democracy to allow diverse political programmes to be proposed and debated, even those that call into question the way a State is currently organised, provided that they do not harm democracy … In assessing whether an interference was proportionate, the Court distinguishes between so-called peaceful or democratic separatist discourse and separatist discourse that is linked to the commission of offences or acts which perpetuate violence.[237]

The Catalan secession activities have been peaceful. There has been no terrorist movement associated with the cause and there has been no armed conflict. The circumstances in which the ECtHR normally accepts legitimate limitations on Article 10 ECHR therefore appear to be missing. Since the declaration of independence had no legal effects, it remained in the sphere of political speech and it is questionable whether limitations on the freedom of speech are justified in the circumstances and whether Spain's actions have always been proportionate. Certainly, Spain is under no obligation to recognise or otherwise accept Catalonia's independence. Spain is permitted to pursue its counter-secession policy and protect its own territorial integrity. But counter-secession policies are not legally unregulated. In this particular case, the ECHR still applies and Spain's actions need to be exercised within the framework of the Convention.

Moreover, even certain provisions of Spanish domestic law need to be read in line with the international effects of declarations of independence. It is true that international and domestic law do not always converge, and that domestic effects of international law are regulated differently in different jurisdictions. Nevertheless, statehood is an international legal status that can be created irrespective of domestic constitutional provisions.[238] And state creation is a complex political process; it is not only a matter of issuing a declaration of independence. Therefore, a declaration of independence as such does not break the national unity or territorial integrity of a state.

[236] 'Guide on Article 10 of the European Convention on Human Rights' (*European Court of Human Rights*, 31 August 2020) www.echr.coe.int/Documents/Guide_Art_10_ENG.pdf, accessed 12 March 2023.
[237] ibid..
[238] *Quebec* case, para 155.

Article 2 of the Spanish Constitution reads:

> The Constitution is based on the indissoluble unity of the Spanish nation, the common and indivisible country of all Spaniards; it recognises and guarantees the right to autonomy of the nationalities and regions of which it is composed, and the solidarity amongst them all.[239]

While it would be possible to say that this provision was violated had the declaration of independence been adopted as an act of parliament and officially promulgated, it is difficult to see how a resolution without any legal effects could have broken 'the unity of the Spanish nation'.[240] As demonstrated above, the declaration of independence was merely a political manifesto under both Spanish and international law. By way of comparison, in the *Kosovo* Advisory Opinion, the ICJ concluded that the declaration of independence was adopted outside of the constitutional framework, whereby it paid particular attention to the fact that 'the procedure employed in relation to the declaration differed from that employed by the Assembly of Kosovo for the adoption of legislation'.[241] The situation was similar in Catalonia, where the procedure followed was not a legislative one and was thus devoid of any legal effects. Indeed, domestically, the declaration of independence was not adopted or promulgated as an act of Catalonia's parliament.

Internationally, the ICJ's position in the *Kosovo* Advisory Opinion is of relevance again: 'general international law contains no applicable prohibition of declarations of independence'.[242] At the same time, a declaration of independence does not by itself change the territorial status quo. Catalonia's declaration of independence did not break national unity or territorial integrity of Spain. While Spain does not need to accept Catalonia's independence, and has the right to conduct its counter-secession-policy, the exercise of such policy needs to be proportionate. It is particularly important to pay due regard in this context to the status of the declaration of independence: it was a political manifesto and not a legal act, neither under domestic nor under international law.

The legal circumstances of Catalonia's attempted path to statehood remain somewhat confusing. The referendum held in 2017 was extraconstitutional, but that does not make it illegal under international law. It is also debatable whether independence was in fact declared on 10 October 2017, or rather on 27 October 2017. Nevertheless, it does appear that any declaration of manifesto remained in the realm of political proclamation rather than legal act. In this vein, even domestic illegality is debatable, while there certainly was no internationally wrongful act attached to the situation. The unequivocal decision of the Spanish

239 Constitution of the Kingdom of Spain, 31 October 1978, art 2.
240 ibid.
241 *Kosovo* Advisory Opinion, para 107.
242 ibid, para 84.

Constitutional Court[243] nevertheless has strong implications that do affect the legal nature and political likelihood of Catalonia's secession claim. The decision confirms that Catalonia's desired path to independence is unilateral, ie without the approval of the parent State and its constitutional organs. While such a path to independence is not *prima facie* illegal under international law, its success is politically highly unlikely to succeed.

C. Crimea and Developments in Eastern Ukraine

The referendum on the future legal status of Crimea was held on 16 March 2014.[244] Reportedly, the choice to join Russia was supported by an overwhelming 95.5 per cent of all votes cast, at the turnout of 83 per cent.[245] A day earlier, Russia vetoed a draft Security Council resolution which sought to declare the referendum as 'having no legal validity' and urged the international community not to recognise its results.[246] The draft resolution was otherwise supported by 13 members of the Security Council, with China abstaining.[247] On 17 March 2014, the Crimean parliament first declared independence and then applied to join Russia.[248] Russia formally annexed Crimea on 21 March 2014. The international legal validity of this act remains contested.

On 27 March 2014, the UN General Assembly adopted Resolution 68/262, which called on all states 'to desist and refrain from actions aimed at the partial or total disruption of the national unity and territorial integrity of Ukraine, including any attempts to modify Ukraine's borders through the threat or use of force or other unlawful means'.[249] The Resolution was adopted with 100 states voting in favour, but it is notable that 11 states voted against and as many as 58 abstained.[250] While widespread, the condemnation was far from being universal.

The general neutrality of international law means that the people of Crimea, in principle, are not precluded from holding a referendum, and even *declaring* independence and/or willingness to integrate with Russia. But international law does not give them a *right* to secession from Ukraine and/or integration with Russia. Not even the will of the people expressed at the referendum, however democratically and overwhelmingly, changes this position. International law

[243] Carranco (n 123).

[244] 'Crimea referendum: Voters "back Russia union"' (*BBC News*, 16 March 2014), www.bbc.com/news/world-europe-26606097, accessed 10 December 2022.

[245] ibid.

[246] 'UN Security Council Resolution on Ukraine' (*C-Span*, 15 March 2014) www.c-span.org/video/?318324-1/un-security-council-meeting-ukraine, accessed 13 December 2022.

[247] ibid.

[248] 'Crimean parliament formally applies to join Russia' (*BBC News*, 17 March 2014) www.bbc.com/news/world-europe-26609667, accessed 13 December 2022.

[249] UNGA Res 67/262 (27 March 2014) UN Doc A/RES/67/262, para 2.

[250] ibid.

remains neutral on this issue. In the absence of widespread international recognition, the Crimean intention would remain ineffective without Russia's use or threat of force.[251] Even if the actual use of force were still contested, Russian activities constituted at least a threat of force,[252] which is likewise prohibited by Article 2(4) UN Charter.[253]

This is where the neutrality of international law on declarations of independence is over. In the sense of para 81, *Kosovo* Advisory Opinion, we are no longer talking about a *unilateral* declaration of independence but an attempt at secession in violation of *jus cogens*. This circumstance triggers Article 41 ARSIWA. All states, including the wrongdoer (ie Russia), are under obligation to withhold recognition. The obligation does not apply because Ukraine's constitution would not allow secession or because there is no political approval from Kiev. It applies because Russia created an illegal territorial situation by use or threat of force. In other words, Russia created a situation legally comparable to Northern Cyprus,[254] albeit integration rather than independence was sought in this instance. Hence, unilateral secession is not illegal per se. It becomes illegal when another state illegally resorts to force to create a new effective territorial situation, be it in the form of annexation or creation of a puppet state. International law in such circumstances does not accept a shift in territorial status or recognise a transfer of territorial title.

The same conclusion in principle applies to the so-called Donetsk Peoples' Republic and Luhansk Peoples' Republic, although there are some factual and even legal differences in comparison to Crimea. Independence of the putative republics was declared in 2014 during the conflict in Eastern Ukraine.[255] On 21 February 2022, recognition was extended by Russia,[256] followed by Syria and North Korea.[257] Russia thus extended its recognition very shortly before its full scale aggression directed against Ukraine which started on 24 February 2022.[258] Even prior to 24 February 2022, Russia's recognition was

[251] Krisch (n 113).

[252] ibid; Sari (n 113).

[253] UN Charter, art 2.4.

[254] Jure Vidmar, 'Crimea's Referendum and Secession: Why it Resembles Northern Cyprus More than Kosovo' (*EJIL:Talk!*, 20 March 2014) www.ejiltalk.org/crimeas-referendum-and-secession-why-it-resembles-northern-cyprus-more-than-kosovo, accessed 16 April 2022.

[255] 'Ukraine crisis: Protesters declare Donetsk "republic"' (*BBC News*, 7 April 2014) www.bbc.com/news/world-europe-26919928, accessed 16 January 2021.

[256] Lilian Wagdy and Lina Najem, 'Syria recognizes independence, sovereignty of Donetsk, Luhansk -state news agency' (*Reuters*, 29 June 2022) www.reuters.com/world/middle-east/syria-recognizes-independence-sovereignty-donetsk-luhansk-state-news-agency-2022-06-29, accessed 18 September 2022.

[257] 'Ukraine cuts N Korea ties over recognition of separatist regions' (*Al Jazeera*, 13 July 2022) www.aljazeera.com/news/2022/7/13/n-korea-recognises-breakaway-of-russias-proxies-in-east-ukraine, accessed 16 September 2022.

[258] Natalia Zinets and Aleksandar Vasovic, 'Missiles rain down around Ukraine' (*Reuters*, 25 February 2022) www.reuters.com/world/europe/putin-orders-military-operations-ukraine-demands-kyiv-forces-surrender-2022-02-24, accessed 9 October 2022.

illegal under international law and the putative republics subject to the obligation to withhold recognition under Article 41 ARSIWA. This is because the two putative republics were a product of Russia's involvement in the conflict in Eastern Ukraine already prior to 2022 and in reality their quasi-independence appeared to be merely a step toward annexation.[259] The choice of the *pro forma* label – independence or annexation – did not determine the legal situation. What mattered was that the situation has been tainted by territorial illegality which prevents any shift in territorial status or legal title to the territory.[260] Russia's formal annexation of Ukraine's Donetsk, Kherson, Luhansk and Zaporizhzhia oblasts on 30 September 2022 did not change the legal status of these spatial areas under international law.[261]

Although Ukraine does not exercise effective control over extensive parts of the spatial area concerned, the territorial status of the area did not change. The legal status of a territory is not created or altered by a mere unilateral declaration, whether of independence or annexation. And territorial title is not created, altered or transferred by de facto ability to exercise territorial jurisdiction. This was implicitly confirmed even by the ICJ in the order on provisional measures in the *Ukraine v Russia* case:

> [R]ecalling the statement of the Permanent Representative of the Russian Federation to the United Nations that the 'Donetsk People's Republic' and the 'Lugansk People's Republic' had turned to the Russian Federation with a request to grant military support, the Court considers that the Russian Federation must also ensure that any military or irregular armed units which may be directed or supported by it, as well as any organizations and persons which may be subject to its control or direction, take no steps in furtherance of these military operations.[262]

Although this decision was not concerned with the merits of the case and its jurisdictional basis is the compromissory clause in the Genocide Convention,[263] the Court's order is far reaching and at least implicitly confirms the objective situation that the so-called Donetsk People's Republic and Luhansk People's Republic remain a part of Ukraine. Indeed, the Court called on Russia to ensure

[259] Marko Milanovic, 'Recognition' (*EJIL:Talk!*, 21 February 2022) www.ejiltalk.org/recognition/, accessed 3 March 2022; Diane Desierto, 'Non-Recognition' (*EJIL:Talk!*, 22 February 2022) www.ejiltalk.org/non-recognition, accessed 3 March 2022.

[260] Annie Charalambous, 'Political controversy in northern Cyprus over proposed name change of breakaway "state"' (*InCyprus*, 23 February 2023) in-cyprus.philenews.com/news/local/political-controversy-in-northern-cyprus-over-proposed-name-change-of-breakaway-state, accessed 2 January 2022.

[261] Pjotr Sauer and Luke Harding, 'Putin annexes four regions of Ukraine in major escalation of Russia's war' (*The Guardian*, 30 September 2022) www.theguardian.com/world/2022/sep/30/putin-russia-war-annexes-ukraine-regions, accessed 2 October 2022.

[262] *Allegations of Genocide under the Convention on the Prevention and Punishment of the Crime of Genocide (Ukraine v. Russian Federation)*, (Provisional Measures) General List No 182 (2022) ICJ, para 81.

[263] Convention on the Prevention and Punishment of the Crime of Genocide (adopted 9 December 1945, entered into force 9 December 1948) 78 UNTS 277 (Genocide Convention), art 9.

that there is no furtherance of military operations which can only mean that the so-called People's Republics had no valid authority to issue a request for military support. Had they been states under international law, they would have such an authority under the intervention by invitation doctrine. Also highly significant is the use of quotation marks in the Court's order when referring to the so-called People's Republics.

The factual developments in the spatial areas in Eastern Ukraine that are now claimed by Russia were a bit different from those in Crimea, but the legal position on territorial title and status is the same. These areas remain Ukrainian territories and Russia's unilateral legal action and effective control did not produce any legal effects with regard to territorial title. However, the extent of Russia's effective control in the spatial areas concerned in Eastern Ukraine may be different from that of Crimea. This may ultimately have consequences for the application of the law of occupation and applicability of the ECHR, for example.[264]

Russia's involvement in Ukraine can be contrasted with the situation in Catalonia in 2017. Its unilateral character does not make a declaration of independence illegal under international law. Territorial illegality is defined by international practice which has been condensed in Articles 40 and 41 ARSIWA and in para 81 of the *Kosovo* Advisory Opinion.[265] The developments in Catalonia did not create an international legality in this sense.[266] Russia's involvement in Ukraine is different. The rules of international law prohibit a shift of territorial title or creation of a new legal status in the spatial areas now claimed by Russia.

VIII. DETACHING STATEHOOD FROM THE STATEHOOD CRITERIA

A great deal of confusion in contemporary international law of statehood is due to the fact that this area of international law is still looked at through the prism of the statehood criteria. Even those writers who question the relevance of the effective-control-based Montevideo criteria do not completely break with them, and tend to subscribe to certain legality requirements for statehood.[267] The result is that the law of statehood is still analysed through the prism of the statehood criteria rather than focusing on statehood as such. The addition of the legality, or more precisely, *jus cogens* based criteria means that there is a combination of positive and negative statehood criteria. The positive ones under

[264] 'Extra-territorial jurisdiction of States Parties to the European Convention on Human Rights' (ECtHR, July 2018), www.echr.coe.int/documents/fs_extra-territorial_jurisdiction_eng.pdf, accessed 7 January 2023.

[265] ARSIWA, arts 40 and 41; *Kosovo* Advisory Opinion, para 81.

[266] 'Catalonia independence declaration signed and suspended' (n 226).

[267] Crawford (n 3) 415–17.

the Montevideo Convention ought to specify which criteria shall be met and the negative ones derived from the concept of *jus cogens* specify which criteria shall not be met for a territorial entity to be a state. This approach still does not explain why Somaliland is not a state and what the legal status is of Kosovo and Taiwan.[268] The idea of there being certain fact-producing statehood criteria stems from the nineteenth-century perceptions of natural statehood.

Historically, many legal theorists analogised statehood with objects and even people.[269] As noted by Jean d'Aspremont, it is common for international lawyers to equate the attributes of states with those of humans,[270] and Philipp Aust adds it was especially significant of German positivism to see states as natural persons of international law.[271] From this line of thought also comes the understanding that states are 'born' as natural persons.[272] Arguably, international law merely issues a birth certificate to 'naturally born states' – via recognition.[273] In municipal law, the existence of a natural person indeed does not depend on whether or not a birth certificate was issued. The same logic ought to apply in international law with regard to states.[274] The theory of a natural birth of a state again reflects the nineteenth-century positivism and the attempt to see states as the only person of international law, as well as to ascribe states a real personality.[275] Referring to John Westlake, Stephen Neff explains that even in positivist scholarship this view was not unanimously accepted and the counterargument was that states are not themselves natural persons but rather 'associations of natural persons'.[276] Indeed, how exactly are states born the way children are born?

By analogy to municipal law, it may be possible to compare states to corporations rather than individuals: they are legal persons, not natural ones. Corporations also have a visible physical component (for example buildings), employees, management and the capacity to conduct business with other corporations. Although a physical aspect of corporations exists, they are legal entities, not natural creatures. The same logic applies to states. They are entities that exist in law. And in some borderline examples, in the decentralised system of international law, this legal status can be unclear.

[268] Alexandra Rickart, 'Emerging Issues: To Be or Not to Be, That Is the Statehood Question' (2015) 3(2) *University of Baltimore Journal of International Law* 145.

[269] Jellinek (n 14) 137.

[270] Jean d'Aspremont, 'The Doctrine of Fundamental Rights of States and Anthropomorphic Thinking in International Law' (2015) 4 *Cambridge Journal of International and Comparative Law* 501.

[271] Helmut Aust, 'Fundamental Rights of States: Constitutional Law in Disguise?' (2015) 4(3) *Cambridge Journal of International and Comparative Law* 521.

[272] Talmon (n 14) 222.

[273] ibid, 218–20.

[274] ibid, 218–20.

[275] Stephen C Neff, 'Jurisprudential Polyphony: The Three Variations on the Positivist Theme in the 19th Century' in Pierre-Marie Dupuy and Vincent Chetail (eds), *The Roots of International Law: Liber Amicorum Peter Haggenmacher*, (Brill/Nijhoff 2014).

[276] ibid.

As states are not naturally born creatures, it needs to be answered where states are grounded in international law. If one is not prepared to accept the natural or even metaphysic theories of statehood, this status needs to be grounded in the sources of international law, as enumerated in Article 38(1) ICJ Statute. Sometimes, states are created by international treaties (for example Austria).[277] As noted by Crawford, 'a quantity of practice attests to the existence of certain international powers to bring about territorial change and to create new territorial entities (States or entities approximating to States) with effects extending beyond the immediate contracting parties'.[278] Indeed, statehood can be created by international treaties, but does also have effects outside of treaty law and beyond the treaty parties.

By analogy, in the *Reparations* Advisory Opinion, the ICJ pronounced that:

> fifty States, representing the vast majority of the members of the international community, had the power, in conformity with international law, to bring into being an entity possessing objective international personality, and not merely personality recognized by them alone.[279]

In other words, where a group of states creates a person of international law, its legal personality may transcend the treaty law framework and be opposable even to non-parties to that treaty. But this is only possible if such a legal status is created under customary international law, just like treaty provisions in general can lead to the emergence of new customary rules.

In some other examples, statehood is accepted by other states in a less explicit way, but in practice states clearly indicate that they are accepting a certain entity as a separate state. The approach is evidently the same as that on the formation of rules of customary international law which requires a uniform (although not universal) state practice and *opinio juris*.[280] The theoretical similarity between the creation of statehood and the emergence of customary rules of international law is no coincidence. Statehood is thus quite simply customary status under international law. It is not the statehood criteria which is customary, but statehood itself.

Grounding statehood in customary international law also explains the concept and purpose of recognition. In contemporary scholarship, recognition is seen a declaratory legal act and is supposed to have no constitutive effects.[281]

[277] 'Staatsvertrag betreffend die Wiederherstellung eines unabhängigen und demokratischen Österreich' (*Rechtsinformationsystem*), www.ris.bka.gv.at/GeltendeFassung.wxe?Abfrage=Bundesnormen&Gesetzesnummer=10000265, accessed 14 December 2022, declaring Austria a sovereign, independent and democratic state.

[278] Crawford (n 3) 504.

[279] *Reparation for Injuries Suffered in the Service of the United Nations* (Advisory Opinion) General List No 4 (1949) ICJ, para 185.

[280] *Case Concerning Military and Paramilitary Activities in and Against Nicaragua* (Judgment) General List No 70 (1986) ICJ (*Nicaragua* case), para 188.

[281] Martin Dixon, Robert McCorquodale and Sarah Williams, *Cases and Materials in International Law* (OUP 2011) 158.

This position is somewhat dogmatic and not entirely in line with state practice. It is true that the constitutive theory is inadequate, as it does not answer how many and whose recognitions are necessary for an entity to become a state.[282] If recognition were constitutive, an entity could be a state for some states but not for others. However, just because the constitutive theory has its flaws, this does not mean that recognition must always be declaratory.

Where independence is declared unilaterally, a state could be created through widespread recognition. As Crawford acknowledges, collective recognition could have the effects of a creative state creation.[283] In the *Quebec* case, the Supreme Court of Canada made the constitutive possibility even more prominent:

> The ultimate success of … a [unilateral] secession would be dependent on recognition by the international community, which is likely to consider the legality and legitimacy of secession having regard to, amongst other facts, the conduct of Quebec and Canada, in determining whether to grant or withhold recognition.[284]

Taking Kosovo as an example, one can question whether its recognition indeed was merely declaratory. Or is it rather that Kosovo falls within the meaning of the 'constitutive' para 155 of the *Quebec* case? Where an attempt at secession is unilateral, widespread recognition *can* have constitutive effects. Notably, Kosovo is often described as a *sui generis* situation.[285] Describing a situation with the *sui generis* label merely acknowledges that it does not fit into the existing theories. And a valid theory needs to withstand scrutiny in difficult situations. Kosovo thus points to the inadequacy of the declaratory theory.

Applying the constitutive theory, one faces the old problem. If the example is Kosovo, are 115 recognitions enough for it to be a state? Is it enough to be recognised by some influential states, such as the United States, the United Kingdom, France and Germany, but not by other states, such as China, Russia, Spain and South Africa and, in general, recognised by very few Latin American, Asian and African states?[286] In the end, Kosovo's legal status cannot be explained by the Montevideo criteria and recognition theories, whether declaratory or constitutive. It is rather that recognition can be seen as an indication of state practice and *opinio juris* in support of an entity's status of statehood under customary international law.

The making of international customary law requires state practice and *opinio juris* that are *sufficiently* uniform, but do not need to be entirely universal.[287] Recognition that is sufficiently uniform can be indicative of the status of statehood under customary international law. Even those writers who

[282] Brierly (n 40) 138.
[283] Crawford (n 3) 501.
[284] *Quebec case*, para 155.
[285] UN Security Council Official Records, 63rd Session (18 February 2008) UN Doc S/PV.5839, paras 13 and 19.
[286] 'List of states that recognize Kosovo's independence' (n 92).
[287] *Nicaragua* case, paras 183–89.

defend the declaratory theory of recognition indeed admit that universal or *near* universal recognition could have the effects of collective state creation.[288] Recognition is, however, only one mode of expression of state practice and *opinio juris*. Other examples exist where states have refused to recognise but nevertheless treated an entity as a state.[289]

IX. CONCLUSION

Knowing that a certain spatial area physically exists does not mean that this is a territory or that it constitutes a separate state. A territory can only be defined according to the law and the question of whether or not a certain 'defined territory' is a state is a question of legal status. The interpretation that a state emerges 'as a matter of fact'[290] is thus problematic as it tries to interpret the question of legal status as though this were a question of existence of an objective physical fact. In this interpretation it is presumed that an entity which meets the (traditional) statehood criteria automatically and self-evidently becomes a state. Such an interpretation is difficult to accept. The traditional statehood criteria are not a simple checklist which could objectively determine whether or not an entity is a state. If states could emerge automatically and self-evidently on meeting the statehood criteria, Taiwan, for example, would probably need to be a state.[291] This would be rather paradoxical because Taiwan itself does not even claim it is a state.[292]

Contemporary international law also knows of the concept of additional statehood criteria.[293] These criteria are defined in negative terms: a state must not emerge as a result of (illegal) use of force, in violation of the right of self-determination and/or in pursuance of racist policies.[294] This is not to say that an entity becomes a state simply by not breaching these norms. Even under the presumption that the additional and traditional statehood criteria are met, the entity in question will not necessarily become a state. The hurdle that the independence-seeking entity needs to overcome is the territorial integrity of its parent state. All claims for independence outside of colonialism are *prima facie* faced with the principle of territorial integrity, which protects their parent states.[295]

It would be erroneous to interpret the principle of territorial integrity as being creative of an absolute right of states which could prohibit the emergence

[288] Crawford (n 3) 501.
[289] Craven (n 12) 199–200.
[290] Weller (n 43) 127–47.
[291] Crawford (n 3) 206–07.
[292] ibid, 219.
[293] Devine (n 7) 410–17.
[294] ibid.
[295] Shaw (n 18); Peters (n 18) 1–14.

of a new state. The operation of the principle of territorial integrity in the context of new state creations only means that independence is not a right or an entitlement under international law.[296] While the absence of a specific right cannot be interpreted as existence of a prohibition, it means that a new state cannot unequivocally emerge as a legal person if the claim to territorial integrity is not removed in some way. The emergence of a new state is thus not a matter of declaring independence but rather a matter of international acceptance of such a declaration and creation of statehood through the ordinary international law-making procedures.[297]

The international law of statehood is marked by the inadequacy of the statehood criteria and the conceptual problems associated with constitutive recognition. Statehood is not a matter of fact; it is a matter of international creation of territorial status. The concept of 'international creation', however, implies constitutive effects of recognition.[298] This is where doctrine tends to become defensive and, in order to avoid implying that recognition could be constitutive, drifts into illogical explanations of the concept of the state, the nature of its emergence, and the purpose of the obligation to withhold recognition.[299]

The statehood criteria are a description of jurisdictional authority in a certain spatial area. Most states, but only states, meet these criteria. Moreover, there is a problem of causality. States meet these criteria *because* they are states, or as soon as they are states;[300] they do not become states simply on meeting the statehood criteria. Related to this matter, the debate on constitutive versus declaratory recognition is futile. Under some circumstances recognition indeed plays no role in the process of state creation while in other circumstances it can be central for creating the legal status of statehood. Recognition should simply be seen as an expression of *opinio juris* in the process of emergence of a new state.

Statehood is a territorial legal status established in the sources of international law. Some states have been created by international treaties, but in most circumstances statehood is created through state practice and *opinio juris*. Statehood is thus also prone to some conceptual difficulties associated with customary international law: how widespread does support for a particular status need to be? In some difficult situations legal status can be ambiguous. Kosovo today may be a state for some states, but not for others. What consequences such status ambiguities may have will be discussed in subsequent chapters, looking at the examples of treaty-making capacity, standing before international judicial bodies, and the law on the use of force.

[296] Crawford (n 3) 390.
[297] *Kosovo* Advisory Opinion, Public sitting held on Thursday 10 December 2009, CR 2009/32, 47 (6) (argument of James Crawford on behalf of the United Kingdom).
[298] *Quebec case*, para 155.
[299] Kelsen (n 30) 223; Marek (n 42) 137; Talmon (n 14) 103.
[300] Lauterpacht (n 35) 66.

4

International Legal Capacity: States, Non-States and Territories

I. INTRODUCTION

THUS FAR, IT has been established that territory is not a natural element but rather a legal status created over a certain spatial area. Statehood is a form of legal status. States are not natural but rather legal persons of international law and as such possess international legal capacity. This chapter turns to the concept of legal capacity in international law. International legal capacity is defined as the capability of certain actors to create and hold international obligations, and incur responsibility for breaches of those obligations. The chapter argues that such capacity is predominantly vested in states and for some functional purposes in international organisations. The state-centrism in international law leaves a great deal of conduct on the international plane unregulated,[1] and a number of actors operate in a legal grey zone.

Can a non-state mount an armed attack on a state and does the attacked state have the right to self-defence against the non-state? Is Taiwan protected by the prohibition of the use of force? Did the so-called Donetsk and Luhansk Peoples' Republics ever have international legal capacity? What is the legal capacity of Palestine? These are some questions that vex the current theoretical and practical application of the law pertaining on legal status of territories.

The legal problem at stake is twofold. First, non-states, apart from international organisations, do not have very many, if any, international legal obligations. Most rules of international law are thus designed for states which are territorial units. When a degree of international legal capacity is ascribed to non-states, the problem emerges when the consequences of their actions need to be accommodated within the territorial paradigm of international law; and *most* non-states do not have a territorial status. Second, certain *non-state territories* can have a degree of international legal capacity, yet it is not entirely clear how international legal obligations and the law of responsibility apply to territorial jurisdictional units without statehood; and how the territorial status of such entities is created in the first place.

[1] Susan Marks, 'State-Centrism, International Law, and the Anxieties of Influence' (2006) 19(2) *Leiden Journal of International Law* 339.

Several doctrines have been proposed for these purposes, including: human rights obligations for various non-state actors;[2] self-defence against non-state actors;[3] a degree of statehood for certain *de facto* territorial regimes;[4] the use of force in the territories of the so-called unwilling or unable states;[5] and different effective control tests that have been developed across the subfields of international legal regulation.[6] But these doctrines have only added more confusion to the international legal system.

This chapter demonstrates that international legal capacity is closely linked to international responsibility. These are indeed two sides of the same coin. The capacity to create legal obligations and incur responsibility for their breaches is primarily vested in states. It can also be functionally extended to territorial jurisdictional units without statehood, whereas non-territorial actors largely appear to lack the legal capacity to create and/or breach international legal obligations. The chapter argues that the nature and structure of international law cannot accommodate the existence of international legal obligations on actors that do not have the authority to exercise jurisdiction in a certain spatial area and where that area does not have the status of a territory under international law. The only exception are international organisations within their functional mandates. This is because the consequences of a breach of an international legal obligation under the law of responsibility can largely be accommodated only on the assumption that the wrongdoer has the status of a territory under international law.

Most territorial actors on the international plane are states. According to the law of state responsibility, a state can breach its legal obligation directly by conduct of its organs or where a non-state conduct is attributed to the state.[7] In this model, one is always looking for a state in order to find a breach of an international legal obligation. This chapter argues that such state-centrism is a consequence of the fact that only very few non-states have the capacity to breach international law. The chapter than seeks to identify which categories of non-states have a certain territorial status established under international law and the capacity to create, hold and breach international legal obligations.

[2] Jean d'Aspremont, 'Non-State Actors in International Law: Oscillating between Concepts and Dynamics' in Jean d'Aspremont (ed), *Participants in the International Legal System* (Routledge 2011); William Worster, 'Relative International Legal Personality of Non-State Actors' (2016) 42(1) *Brooklyn Journal of International Law* 207.

[3] Kimberley Trapp, 'Can Non-State Actors Mount an Armed Attack?' in Marc Weller (ed), *The Oxford Handbook on the Use of Force* (OUP 2015).

[4] William Worster, 'Functional Statehood in Contemporary International Law' (2020) 46(1) *Brooklyn Journal of International Law* 39.

[5] Elena Chachko and Ashley Deeks, 'Which States Support the "Unwilling and Unable" Test?' (*LawFare*, 10 October 2016) www.lawfareblog.com/which-states-support-unwilling-and-unable-test, accessed 3 October 2022.

[6] Marko Milanovic, 'Special Rules of Attribution of Conduct in International Law' (2020) 96 *International Law Studies* 295.

[7] Marco Sassoli, 'State Responsibility for Violations of International Humanitarian Law' (2002) 84(846) *International Review of the Red Cross* 401.

II. INTERNATIONAL LEGAL CAPACITY AND SUBJECTS IN THE INTERNATIONAL LEGAL SYSTEM

This chapter considers the international legal capacity for law-making and law-breaking. In other words, it asks who creates international legal obligations and who can breach these obligations. It is argued that public international law is primarily conceptualised as an inter-state system of private law. International legal capacity can therefore be established in bilateral or multilateral relations between actors and is generally not subject to an overarching regulation by a public law framework.

A. Law-making Capacity

International law is a legal system derived from states. This is not to say that actors other than states do not exist in this system.[8] But states are those actors that have full international legal capacity. This also follows from the formal sources of law: it is states that conclude international treaties in the sense of the Vienna Convention of the Law of Treaties (VCLT);[9] and it is state practice, combined with *opinio juris* (again derived from states), which forms customary international law.[10]

International treaties can be of various kinds. They can be bilateral, multilateral or indeed so multilateral that they are virtually universal. They can regulate something quite technical and specific, such as construction of a system of locks on a river in the border area between two states,[11] or establish something as complex as the United Nations,[12] or the European Union.[13] Treaties between states can thus create international organisations and other legal creatures with their own organs that can also make autonomous decisions,[14] at least to some extent, and some more than others – depending on what states have agreed to in the underlying treaty. Exercising their treaty powers, states may sometimes even create a 'Frankenstein's monster' over which they lose control.[15]

[8] ibid.

[9] Vienna Convention on the Law of Treaties of 1969 (adopted 23 May 1969, entered into force 27 January 1980) 1155 UNTS 332 (VCLT), art 1.

[10] *Case Concerning Military and Paramilitary Activities in and Against Nicaragua* (Judgment) General List No 70 (1986) ICJ (*Nicaragua* case), para 184.

[11] *Case Concerning the Gabčíkovo-Nagymaros Project (Hungary v Slovakia)* (Judgment) General List No 92 (1997) ICJ (*Gabčíkovo-Nagymaros* case), para 15.

[12] United Nations Charter (adopted 26 June 1945, entered into force 24 October 1945) 1 UNTS 16 (UN Charter).

[13] Consolidated Version of the Treaty on European Union (adopted 13 December 2007, entered into force 1 December 2009) OJ C 115/01 (TEU).

[14] UN Charter, arts 39–42; TEU, arts 13–22.

[15] Andrew Guzman, 'International Organizations and the Frankenstein Problem' (2013) 24 *European Journal of International Law* 999, arguing that 'States sometimes create their own form of artificial life, the international organisation (IO). Dr Frankenstein created his monster in an

When the UN Security Council adopts a legally binding resolution, its binding nature is anchored in Chapter VII of the UN Charter, which is an international treaty. Hence, even the law-making powers of the UN can be traced back to states, or more specifically, to this very specific treaty, which has been ratified by nearly all states in the world.[16] At the same time, it is a selection of states that vote in the Security Council; this is not an autonomous organ devoid of state influence.[17] General Assembly resolutions are not legally binding, but they may be relevant for the identification of customary international law.[18] And it is, again, states that vote in the General Assembly. This body may be, *inter alia*, seen as a provider of secretarial services for the identification of international custom. It is always difficult to identify what states believe for the purposes of *opinio juris*, but the General Assembly is probably the most prominent place where states go on the record, and do so in a collective setting.

In terms of legal capacity, international law-*making* appears to be a prerogative of states, although sometimes this happens indirectly and through international organisations.[19] How about law-*breaking*? Is this also only a prerogative of states? Here, we come to the question of capacity to commit an internationally wrongful act. It appears that in most circumstances only an act of state is capable of being an internationally wrongful act. But how does conduct on the international plane become an act of state?

B. Law-breaking Capacity

In the *Reparations* Advisory Opinion, the International Court of Justice (ICJ) acknowledged that rights and duties under international law were inherent in not only states but also in international organisations.[20] The Court importantly added that this does not mean that the level of these rights and duties is the same as that of states, but that even international organisations have international legal capacity for the purposes of their functioning. The ICJ reasoned: 'The subjects of law in any legal system are not necessarily identical in their nature or in the extent of their rights, and their nature depends upon the needs of the community.'[21] After establishing that the UN had international personality, the Court continued:

attempt to improve on a world populated only by humans. States create IOs with the hope of enhancing international cooperation beyond what can be achieved by states alone. Like Frankenstein's monster, IOs created by states may behave differently from the way they are expected to. There is always a risk that an IO will impact the system in ways that harm, rather than help, the interests of states. An IO can become a monster.'

[16] 'UN Members' (*United Nations*) www.un.org/en/member-states, accessed 7 December 2022.

[17] UN Charter, arts 23–32.

[18] *Nicaragua* case, para 188.

[19] ibid.

[20] *Reparation for Injuries Suffered in the Service of the United Nations* (Advisory Opinion) General List No 4 (1949) ICJ (*Reparations* Advisory Opinion), para 174.

[21] *Reparations* Advisory Opinion, 8.

> That is not the same thing as saying that it is a State, which it certainly is not, or that its legal personality and rights and duties are the same as those of a State. Still less is it the same thing as saying that it is 'a super-State,' whatever that expression may mean. It does not even imply that all its rights and duties must be upon the international plane, any more than all the rights and duties of a State must be upon that plane. What it does mean is that it is a subject of international law and capable of possessing international rights and duties, and that it has capacity to maintain its rights by bringing international claims.[22]

The rise of international human rights law also gives international legal subjectivity to individuals,[23] as does international refugee law,[24] while international criminal law sanctions individuals as perpetrators of war crimes and crimes against humanity.[25] But one should not forget that even in these instances treaties concluded by states still are in the background, as well as customary international law which is shaped and formed by states.[26] Moreover, actors such as international organisations in principle can enter into international treaties and thus create international legal obligations.[27] But their treaty-making capacity is limited by their functional purposes and international organisations are in practice not bound by very many international legal obligations.

Municipal legal systems generally distinguish between human beings and corporations who have legal capacity for different purposes, much in line with what the ICJ pronounced in the *Reparations* Advisory Opinion. But then, there certainly exist other actors that shape and influence human life, such as animals. A range of legal rules protect animals against cruelty and regulate hunting. On the other hand, legal rules also regulate liability when animals cause harm.[28] This, of course, does not mean that a shark would be charged with the crime of murder and go to jail for killing a surfer; or that a bear would be charged with animal cruelty and be liable for damages if it attacks your cattle when looking for food.

[22] *Reparations* Advisory Opinion, 9.

[23] Robert McCorquodale, 'An Inclusive International Legal System' (2004) 17 *Leiden Journal of International Law* 477.

[24] Convention Relation to the Status of Refugees of 1951 (adopted 28 July 1951, entered into force 22 April 1954) 189 UNTS 137, art 1.

[25] *Trial of the Major War Criminals before the International Military Tribunal*, Vol.1 (Nurnberg 1947), para 223, recognising that '[c]rimes against international law are committed by men, not by abstract entities, and only by punishing individuals who commit such crimes can the provision of international law be enforced'.

[26] Rome Statute of the International Criminal Court (adopted 17 June 1998, entered into force 1 July 2002) 2187 UNTS 38544 (Rome Statute). This treaty has been ratified by 123 states. Article 5 of this international treaty defines war crimes, crimes against humanity and genocide as crimes for which the Court can – subject to some other conditions – exercise its jurisdiction over individuals.

[27] Jose Alvarez, *International Organizations as Law-Makers* (OUP 2006); Olivier Corten and Pierre Klein, 'Are Agreements between States and Non-State Entities Rooted in the International Legal Order?' in Enzo Cannizzaro (ed), *The Law of Treaties Beyond the Vienna Convention* (OUP 2011).

[28] Walter van Gerven, Jeremy Lever and Pierre Lauroche, *Tort Law* (Hart 2001), ch 6. In many legal systems, different kinds of animals underlie the distinction between strict liability and negligence.

Although animals enjoy a level of protection in our human legal systems, their legal capacity is not such that they could be held liable for breaching human laws.[29] In some circumstances it may be, however, that humans or even corporations, who do have such capacity, would be liable for the conduct of animals.[30] Factual harm caused by an animal may well be crime or tort in law.[31] Not that of a shark or bear, of course; we will need to *attribute* that conduct to someone with a sufficient level of legal personality to even have the capacity to commit a crime, or be legally liable under tort law.[32] In essence, in every legal system actors exist that are capable of causing *factual* harm and may even be capable of being harmed themselves, but do not have the legal capacity to be legally responsible for their own conduct. In the end, their conduct will be wrongful only if an actor with an adequate level of legal capacity can be made liable for it. In other words, a certain conduct – however grave or damaging – will only be wrongful if it can be *attributed* to a person with the right level of legal capacity to have obligations under the legal system in question.

III. ATTRIBUTION AND THE TERRITORIAL STRUCTURE OF INTERNATIONAL LAW

Thus far, it has been argued that the capacity to hold international legal obligations can be, in principle, stretched beyond states, but in practice very few direct non-state obligations exist under treaty or customary international law. In most circumstances, non-state conduct will need to be attributed to a state. This chapter considers how attribution works in international legal doctrine and seeks to untangle the knot of attribution and responsibility. While the attribution theories have been ascribed to the law of responsibility, notably through the inclusion in the Articles on Responsibility of States for Internationally Wrongful Acts (ARSIWA), the attribution rules can do more than merely determine who is responsible for an internationally wrongful act. Even the question of whether there has been an internationally wrongful act can depend on whether or not a certain conduct is attributable to a certain to state, or to any state. In this sense, the law of state responsibility is not only secondary in nature. It does not merely regulate the consequences of a breach of a primary rule. It can in fact determine whether or not there has been a breach.

For example, if your pet tiger causes harm, you will be held liable no matter how much precaution you took that this would not happen. This could be different if such harm were caused by your horse.

[29] ibid, ch 6.

[30] ibid.

[31] ibid.

[32] John R Spencer, 'Tortious Liability for Criminal Acts' in Matthew Dyson (ed), *Unravelling Tort and Crime* (CUP 2014).

A. State Responsibility and the Primary/Secondary Dichotomy

The law of state responsibility is said to be secondary in nature because it regulates the consequences of a breach of legal obligation, while it does not determine whether there has been a breach of the underlying primary norm. As the ICJ put it in the *Gabčíkovo/Nagymaros* case between Hungary and Slovakia:

> A determination of whether a convention is or is not in force, and whether it has or has not been properly suspended or denounced, is to be made pursuant to the law of treaties. On the other hand, an evaluation of the extent to which the suspension or denunciation of a convention, seen as incompatible with the law of treaties, involves the responsibility of the State which proceeded to it, is to be made under the law of state responsibility.[33]

This is a two-step approach. Wrongfulness is identified under the primary norm – in this case originating in treaty law – and once this has been established, the law of state responsibility is used to determine the consequences of wrongfulness. The problem is that this approach only works when the conduct can – by definition – only be an act of state. This was precisely the case in the factual circumstances of *Gabčíkovo/Nagymaros*.

In order to suspend or denounce a treaty, the state needs to act through its organs.[34] It is inherent in the very concept of the act of treaty suspension that such conduct can only come from a state, otherwise this cannot be a treaty suspension. Not all international conduct is so straightforward. States do not only act through their organs in a sense of Article 4 of ARSIWA which reads: '*The conduct* of *any State organ* shall be considered an *act of that State* under international law, whether the organ exercises legislative, executive, judicial or any other functions.'[35]

In a number of other situations, a certain conduct may or may not be an act of state, depending on the circumstances. Contrast Article 4 with Article 8 of ARSIWA: 'The conduct of a person or group of persons shall be considered an act of a State under international law if the person or group of persons is in fact acting on the instructions of, or under the direction or control of, that State in carrying out the conduct.'[36]

This is much more complicated. Unlike in the *Gabčíkovo/Nagymaros* types of situations, in an Article 8 ARSIWA situation we do not start with the assumption that the conduct at stake even was an act of state. We have conduct which is capable of being internationally wrongful when it can be attributable to a state. There is no internationally wrongful act until it can be proven that the actor

[33] *Gabčíkovo-Nagymaros* case, para 47.

[34] Articles on the Responsibility of States for Internationally Wrongful Acts (entered into force 8 January 2008) A/RES/62/61 (ARSIWA), Commentary to art 2, para 2.

[35] ibid, art 4 (emphasis added).

[36] ibid, art 8.

responsible for it had the legal capacity to violate international law in general, and that it was bound by the particular rule in question.

In the much criticised *Tadić* judgment, the International Criminal Tribunal for the former Yugoslavia (ICTY) used the attribution rules from the law of state responsibility to determine whether the armed conflict in Bosnia-Herzegovina, which was *prima facie* of a non-international nature, had been internationalised by the involvement of a foreign state.[37] This distinction is crucial as quite different rules apply in different types of armed conflict: non-international armed conflict (NIAC) as opposed to international armed conflict (IAC).[38] To put it simply, the identification of the primary legal rules of armed conflict depended on whether or not certain acts of Bosnian Serbs could be attributed to what was then the Federal Republic of Yugoslavia (FRY).

As this was an ICTY case, it was about the international criminal responsibility of an individual. However, it was first necessary to establish what the applicable rules even were in that situation. In order to do so, the ICTY resorted to the attribution rules.[39] Criticism of this approach is based on a dogmatic distinction between the primary and secondary rules. The critics claim that the secondary attribution rules should not have been applied before wrongfulness was determined under the primary rules[40] and also that state responsibility should have had no place in a case concerned with individual criminal responsibility.[41]

As Antonio Cassese subsequently argued: 'The ICTY admittedly had to establish in *Tadić* whether the armed conflict in Bosnia was internal or international. However, as no rules of international humanitarian law were of assistance for such determination, the Tribunal explicitly decided to rely upon international rules on state responsibility.'[42] Indeed, how else could the Tribunal determine whether or not a foreign state was involved to a sufficient extent that an internal conflict had become an international one to which quite different rules apply? One can believe that the attribution rules are secondary in nature, but if one interprets that secondary nature as sequential order, how exactly does one then identify the actors in a certain conduct and thus determine the applicable law – NIAC or IAC?

The second alleged problem in *Tadić* is that state responsibility was conflated with individual criminal responsibility.[43] But a conflation of this kind in reality

[37] *Prosecutor v Duško Tadić* (Judgment) IT-94-1-A (15 July 1999) (*Tadić* case), paras 83–87.

[38] ibid, para 83.

[39] ibid, paras 99–114.

[40] Sassoli (n 7) 324–33.

[41] Marko Milanovic, 'State Responsibility for Genocide' (2006) 17(3) *European Journal of International Law* 553.

[42] Antonio Cassese, 'The Nicaragua and Tadić Tests Revisited in Light of the ICJ Judgment on Genocide in Bosnia' (2007) 18(4) *European Journal of International Law* 649.

[43] *Application of the Convention on the Prevention and Punishment of the Crime of Genocide (Bosnia and Herzegovina v Serbia and Montenegro)* (Judgment) General List No 91 (2007) (*Bosnia* case), para 403. Especially consider the following argument: '(T)he Court observes that the ICTY was not called upon in the *Tadić* case, nor is it in general called upon, to rule on questions of State

did not happen. Even with international criminal responsibility we still have states in the background, as individual crimes are derived from violations of international humanitarian law (IHL) – and in IHL, the identity of the actors determines the applicable law. If we start from the general principle of criminal law *nullum crimen nulla poena sine lege*, we indeed first need to know the applicable law: we need to identify *lex* before we can determine *crimen* and *poena*. How could the ICTY identify *lex* in *Tadić* without resorting to the rules of attribution? The attribution rules helped identify the type of armed conflict and thus the applicable law, and only then did it become clear which international crimes Duško Tadić could have committed. There is no conflation of individual criminal responsibility and state responsibility at stake in this case. It is simply that the attribution rules, which are attached to the law of state responsibility, identify the actors and thus also determine the applicable law. Only once this was clarified under general international law was the ICTY able to proceed with determining individual criminal responsibility.

In international law, we always end up coming back to states. States A and B may be parties to treaty X, states A and C may be parties to treaty Y, and states B and C may be parties to treaty Z. In this system, the scope of legal obligations between states A and B is different than between states A and C, which is again different than that between states B and C. If conduct 1 is contrary to the obligations arising under treaty X, the question of whether or not there actually was a breach of international legal obligation will crucially depend on the identity of the actors involved. If the conduct is attributable to state C, there will be no breach. Even if conduct 1 were in principle attributable to state A, there will still be no breach where relations between states A and C are concerned.

Determining the identity of the actor – which happens via attribution – is thus again of primary importance, as only then does it become clear which rules were applicable – and could be breached – in the first place. It is true, however, that sometimes this first step is already determined by the nature of the act. This happens where an act is by definition legal in nature and it is presupposed that the new legal situation could only be created by an act of state in the sense of Article 4 ARSIWA (eg treaty suspension).[44] This is quite different where legal consequences need to be attached to a factual occurrence.

The distinction between primary and secondary rules of international law should not be taken too far. There is no gap between the two sets. These rules

responsibility, since its jurisdiction is criminal and extends over persons only. Thus, in that Judgment the Tribunal addressed an issue which was not indispensable for the exercise of its jurisdiction. As stated above, the Court attaches the utmost importance to the factual and legal findings made by the ICTY in ruling on the criminal liability of the accused before it and, in the present case, the Court takes fullest account of the ICTY's trial and appellate judgments dealing with the events underlying the dispute. The situation is not the same for positions adopted by the ICTY on issues of general international law which do not lie within the specific purview of its jurisdiction and, moreover, the resolution of which is not always necessary for deciding the criminal cases before it.'

[44] ARSIWA, art 4.

help us determine whether or not there was an internationally wrongful act and who is responsible for it. Importantly, the attribution rules do not attribute responsibility; they attribute conduct. Attribution of conduct can, however, determine whether the conduct in question was an internationally wrongful act in the first place, and is not limited to determining only what the consequences are of the internationally wrongful act.

B. Territorialism between Effective Control and Strict Liability

It has been established that international law can only be breached if the conduct is attributable to a legal person with the right level of international legal capacity to bear legal obligations in a particular situation. But how does the concept of attribution work in international law? In chapter two it was argued that attribution is often conflated with jurisdiction.[45] This is becomes effective control over a spatial area may be in the background of both concepts. This chapter demonstrates that conduct may be attributed to states for their territorial and extraterritorial activities, but the attribution theory remains somewhat underdeveloped, which creates a great deal of ambiguity in the application of the rules of international law.

In the *Nicaragua* case, the ICJ had to consider whether the conduct of the Nicaraguan contras was attributable to the United States.[46] The ICJ established a very demanding threshold by holding that, for the United States to incur responsibility, 'it would in principle have to be proved that that State had effective control of the military or paramilitary operations in the course of which the alleged violations were committed'.[47] Where a state does not have full and generalised territorial control, it does not incur responsibility if it is 'merely' financing, training, supplying and otherwise supporting rebels in a foreign state.[48] It needs to be proven that the foreign state had *effective control* of the operation in which the alleged violations happened. This may be quite difficult to prove. International responsibility effectively becomes a question of evidence which may often be unavailable to anyone other than the state trying to escape responsibility. In the *Nicaragua* case, the ICJ referred to responsibility, but the

[45] Marko Milanovic, 'Palestine Sues the United States in the ICJ re Jerusalem Embassy' (*EJIL:Talk!*, 30 September 2018) www.ejiltalk.org/palestine-sues-the-united-states-in-the-icj-re-jerusalem-embassy, accessed 23 November 2022; Alina Miron, 'Palestine's Application the ICJ, neither Groundless nor Hopeless. A Reply to Marko Milanovic' (*EJIL:Talk!*, 8 October 2018) www.ejiltalk.org/palestines-application-the-icj-neither-groundless-nor-hopeless-a-reply-to-marko-milanovic, accessed 19 October 2022; Jure Vidmar, 'Palestine v United States: Why the ICJ Does not Need to Decide Whether Palestine is a State' (*EJIL:Talk!*, 22 November 2018) www.ejiltalk.org/palestine-v-united-states-why-the-icj-does-not-need-to-decide-whether-palestine-is-a-state, accessed 13 September 2022.

[46] *Nicaragua* case, paras 115 and 116.

[47] ibid, para 115.

[48] ibid, para 292.

high *Nicaragua* threshold creates a gap that is not limited to responsibility. It can also mean that the entire conduct was not internationally wrongful.

On 17 July 2014, the aeroplane MH17 was downed over the territory of Ukraine, in a spatial area over which that state does not exercise effective control.[49] It is believed that it was shot down by insurgents fighting against the government of Ukraine, but those insurgents are not a state.[50] Several reports and even judicial findings have linked the event to Russia,[51] but is there enough evidence to conclude that the rather demanding *Nicaragua* threshold test for attribution to a foreign state has been met?[52]

If the conduct cannot be attributed to either state involved in the situation – Ukraine or Russia – does this mean that they escape *responsibility*, or, indeed, that this was not an internationally wrongful act in the first place? Pursuant to Article 2 of the International Law Commission's (ILC) ARSIWA, the latter is correct. The Article reads: 'There is an internationally wrongful act of a State when conduct consisting of an action or omission: (a) is *attributable* to the State under international law; *and* (b) constitutes a *breach of an international obligation* of the State.'[53] Article 2 of ARSIWA thus refers us to the rules of attribution which are, however, also a part of the secondary rules on state responsibility. Moreover, it follows from this formulation that until the conduct can be attributed to a state, wrongfulness remains purely hypothetical and as such it is not an internationally wrongful act. While the MH17 situation was an arbitrary deprivation of human lives in factual terms, it was not necessarily a violation of the right to life under international human rights law.

The attribution threshold applied in the *Nicaragua case* made the contras analogous to a wild animal in tort law: it can cause harm in fact, but no one will be liable for it in law. The animal itself does not have a sufficient level of legal capacity, and if no humans were involved, no one will be legally liable for the factually harmful act of a wild bear. In tort law, human involvement in the life of an otherwise wild animal could lead to strict liability. For example, if I choose to have a pet tiger, I will be liable for its actions no matter what and regardless of any fault on my part. If my tiger escapes and causes harm, I will be liable even if I built a very strong cage and the animal escaped without any negligence on my part.

In international law, the ICJ came close to applying strict liability in the *Corfu Channel case*. The Court established Albania's responsibility merely because this state knew or ought to have known that there were mines in its

[49] 'MH17 Malaysia plane crash: What we know' (*BBC News*, 14 October 2015) www.bbc.com/news/world-europe-28357880, accessed 26 May 2021.

[50] ibid.

[51] 'Transcript of the MH17 judgment hearing' (*Rechtsafspraak*, 17 November 2022) www.courtmh17.com/en/news/2022/transcript-of-the-mh17-judgment-hearing.html, accessed 20 November 2022.

[52] *Nicaragua* case, paras 170–71.

[53] ARSIWA, art 2 (italics added).

territorial waters.[54] The ICJ did not require any fault on the part of Albania for laying mines but, arguably, applied a rough equivalent of strict liability known in municipal tort law. Applying this doctrine to the case of MH17, is Ukraine responsible for not closing the airspace and if it knew or ought to have known that the rebels had access to advanced missile launchers which they could use from Ukrainian territory? If so, Ukraine could have potentially violated the so-called positive obligations under the right to life.

An imbalance is perceivable: when states act through proxy in a foreign territory, they easily fall below the demanding *Nicaragua* threshold; yet when states fail to prevent another actor from causing harm from their territories, they may incur responsibility via the *Corfu Channel* test. The imbalance could be explained by territorialism: states may be held to a higher standard within their own territories than they are for their extraterritorial actions. But should states be strictly liable for any harmful conduct that occurs in or from their own territories? If strict liability could be applied in some circumstances, there appears to be a lack of theoretical clarity with respect to international legal obligations that come with strict liability.

In the case of MH17, it would be unclear which legal obligation Ukraine actually violated by omission. If it is the right to life, is it the negative obligation not to deprive somebody of life, or the positive obligation to ensure that nobody is put at risk of being deprived of life? It is unclear how attribution by omission relates to the multiplicity of legal obligations that can arise under the same treaty provision, such as Article 6 of the International Covenant on Civil and Political Rights (ICCPR).[55]

The concept of attribution in international law is theoretically unclear and confusing, and operates together with the concept of effective control.[56] As explained in chapter two,[57] effective control can be based either on a personal or a spatial model.[58] Both models are concerned with attribution of conduct which occurred outside of the territory of the state to which the conduct concerned is being attributed.[59] But what happens when state A has largely lost control over a part of its territory and state B meets neither the effective control threshold under the spatial model nor the *Nicaragua* test under the personal model? It may well be that non-state conduct (eg that of the insurgents) would then only lead to international responsibility of the territorial states – by

[54] *The Corfu Channel Case (United Kingdom v Albania)* (Judgment) General List No 1 (1947) ICJ (*Corfu Channel* case), para 22.

[55] The International Covenant on Civil and Political Rights (adopted 16 December 1966, entered into force 23 March 1976) 999 UNTS 171 (ICCPR), art 6.

[56] Scott Pegg, *International Society and the De Facto State* (Ashgate 1998) 26.

[57] See ch 2, section IV.C.

[58] Marko Milanovic, 'Al-Skeini and Al-Jedda in Strasbourg' (2012) 23(1) *European Journal of International Law* 121.

[59] Cedric Ryngaert, 'Attributing Conduct in the Law of State Responsibility: Lessons from Dutch Courts Applying the Control Standard in the Context of International Military Operations' (2021) 36 *Utrecht Journal of International and European Law* 170.

omission. This means that the territorial presumption in international law remains very strong even when a state loses control over a part of its territory. If state A supports, funds and trains the insurgents in the territory of state B and state B loses control over a part of its territory as a result, state A may much more easily than state B escape international responsibility for the conduct of the insurgents in the territory concerned. And this is because attribution to territorial state by omission appears to be less demanding than attribution to extraterritorial state by action.

Territory plays a crucial role in the concept of attribution. It will be easier to attribute conduct to a state territorially than extraterritorially; and territorial states can much more easily incur responsibility for omissions than extraterritorial states for actions. It is questionable, however, whether states should ever be strictly liable for any conduct occurring in or from their territories.

C. International Legal Capacity: Authoring Conduct which Creates or Breaches International Legal Obligations

A great deal of conduct can happen on the international plane that is harmful in fact, but will not necessarily be wrongful in law. If this conduct is not attributed to a state with a corresponding international legal obligation, it will fall outside of the purview of international legal regulation.[60] This does not only mean that state responsibility would not be engaged; it can also mean that there would be no illegality. The conduct in question will not amount to an internationally wrongful act.

The rules of state responsibility are often said to be secondary rules that do not regulate whether or not a certain conduct is lawful.[61] But the primary/secondary rules distinction can be arbitrary. For example, the circumstances precluding wrongfulness in many instances deal exactly with what the title suggests – they regulate whether or not a certain conduct was wrongful, and do not only regulate responsibility for wrongfulness. Similarly, the attribution rules can determine whether or not a certain conduct was wrongful. Several possibilities exist. Certain conduct can be an internationally wrongful act if it is attributable to state A, but not if it is attributable to state B. This is because the conduct may be unlawful under treaty T to which state A is a party, but state B is not. Furthermore, if certain conduct is in principle unlawful under a treaty or customary international law, but was authored by a non-state actor, it will not be an internationally wrongful act if it is not attributed to a state that is either party to the relevant treaty or bound by the relevant customary rule. This means that there would be no internationally wrongful act if the conduct is not attributable to a relevant state.

[60] Robert Kolb, *The International Law of State Responsibility* (Edward Elgar 2017) 70–108.
[61] *Gabčíkovo/Nagymaros* case, para 47.

While the law of international responsibility is broader than state responsibility, other actors do not tend to have very many international legal obligations. International organisations have treaty-making capacity for their functional purposes, but they are not party to very many treaties.[62] The nexus of their international legal obligations is therefore rather limited. Individuals can incur international criminal responsibility, but this is restricted to a rather narrow list of international crimes.[63] Finally, non-state armed groups have certain rights and duties under international humanitarian law pertaining to non-international armed conflict.[64] But again, these rules are rather restricted and functionally limited to situations of non-international armed conflict.

The nexus of international legal obligations for the most part applies to states. Therefore, if conduct is not attributable to a state, it cannot be internationally wrongful. Furthermore, the ICJ has established a very high threshold requirement for attribution of conduct to a state where conduct does not originate directly from a state organ. This threshold was elaborated on in the cases of *Nicaragua* and *Bosnian Genocide* and is reflected in Article 8 ARSIWA.[65] Where states act by proxy, for example in armed conflict, they will escape international responsibility relatively easily as the attribution threshold is high and evidence often in the hands of the implicated state itself. When the attribution threshold in such circumstances is not reached, the conduct in question remains unattributed. This does not mean that nobody was responsible for an unlawful conduct. It actually means that the conduct was not unlawful.

International legal capacity should thus be defined as the capacity to create, hold and breach international legal obligations, and to incur international responsibility as a consequence for such breaches. International legal capacity is predominantly limited to states. It will be considered below what conceptual problems arise when international legal capacity is extended to non-territorial actors. These problems will be illustrated on the example of the rules governing the use of force and the exercise of self-defence against non-state actors. Subsequently, it will be argued that even certain territorial jurisdictional units without statehood can have a degree of international legal capacity.

IV. SELF-DEFENCE AND NON-STATE ACTORS: BACK TO TERRITORIALISM

The broader framework of self-defence is the UN Charter mechanism regulating the use of force. Article 2(4) of the UN Charter contains the general prohibition

[62] Jan Klabbers, 'The EJIL Foreword: The Transformation of International Organizations Law' (2015) 26(1) *European Journal of International Law* 9.

[63] Rome Statute, art 5.

[64] *Tadić* case, paras 83–87.

[65] *Nicaragua* case, paras 170–71; *Bosnia* case, paras 400–09; ARSIWA, art 8.

of the use of force.[66] Articles 42 and 51 regulate departures from this prohibition: Security Council authorisation[67] and self-defence.[68] In other words, Article 2(4) determines that the use of force is *prima facie* wrongful under international law, while Articles 42 and 51 provide for defences. In the *Wall* Advisory Opinion, the ICJ pronounced: 'Article 51 of the Charter … recognises the existence of an inherent right of self-defence in the case of armed attack by one State against another State.'[69] Some writers have nevertheless argued that an armed attack can come even from a non-state actor and thus trigger the right to self-defence.[70] If one is prepared to accept this proposition, it is then doctrinally unclear why some – and only some – non-state actors have legal obligations under general international law, and why such obligations appear to exist for some purposes, but not for others.[71]

Even if an expansive reading of Article 51 and its customary reflection is accepted, another conceptual problem will arise when an attacked state is to exercise self-defence against a non-state actor which is also a non-territorial actor. In other words, where certain non-territorial actors are deemed to enjoy a degree of international legal capacity to author conduct on the international plane, a problem emerges where the consequences of their (unlawful) conduct need to be accommodated in the territorially designed international legal system.

A number of doctrinal writers have here turned to the law of state responsibility and have attempted to stretch the doctrine of self-defence. Some have based their arguments in the distinction between primary and secondary rules of international law to conceptualise primary and secondary self-defence on this basis.[72] Another approach uses the doctrine of self-defence triggered by the unwilling or unable states.[73] The present analysis takes a stance against such propositions. It will be argued that self-defence cannot be divided between the primary and secondary rules; and that the doctrine of unwilling or unable states better reflects political expedience rather than legal determinacy. The operation of the right to self-defence can be appropriately determined only on the basis of the correct assessment of its territorial scope.

[66] UN Charter, art 2.4.

[67] ibid, art 42.

[68] ibid, art 51.

[69] *Legal Consequences of the Construction of a Wall* (Advisory Opinion) General List No 131 (2004) ICJ (*Wall* Advisory Opinion), para 139.

[70] Trapp (n 3) 679–96.

[71] Worster (n 2) 207–74.

[72] Nicholas Tsagourias, 'Self-Defence against Non-state Actors: The Interaction between Self-Defence as a Primary Rule and Self-Defence as a Secondary Rule' (2016) 29(3) *Leiden Journal of International Law* 801; Federica I Paddeu, 'Self-Defence as a Circumstance Precluding Wrongfulness: Understanding Article 21 of the Articles on State Responsibility' (2015) 85(1) *British Yearbook of International Law* 90.

[73] Chachko and Deeks (n 5).

A. Primary and Secondary Self-defence?

In scholarship, an attempt has been made, on the basis of the commentary of Special Rapporteur Crawford to Article 21 ARSIWA, to separate self-defence under the UN Charter and ARSIWA.[74] Federica Paddeu argues that pursuant to Article 51 UN Charter, self-defence can be exercised where an armed attack has occurred.[75] The exercise of self-defence may, however, also require a number of other acts which would otherwise have been illegal under international law, such as intervention and violation of sovereignty.[76] Strictly speaking, Article 51 does not justify such secondary actions as it does not specifically authorise the defending state to enter the territory of the attacking state for defensive purposes. Building on James Crawford's argument, Paddeu argues that Article 21 then exculpates the self-defending state for breaches of such rules.

This argument assumes that the exercise of self-defence requires certain ancillary breaches of international legal obligations (eg violation of territorial sovereignty and of the principle of non-intervention). The defending state did not primarily intend to breach these rules, but had to engage in such conduct in the exercise of self-defence (eg its military forces entered the territory of the attacking state). Such breaches become secondary because they occurred in the exercise of a right that exists under primary rules. Paddeu argues that 'the state is exonerated for the breach of other obligations as long as the breach was related to its defensive action pursuant to Article 51 UN Charter',[77] and acknowledges that the right of self-defence includes the right to enter the territory of the aggressor state if necessary. In this view, Article 51 only serves as an exception to the prohibition of the use of force, but not as an exception to the prohibition of intervention and breach of sovereignty. These are then the ancillary breaches of legal obligations which are precluded by self-defence under Article 21 ARSIWA.

In accordance with this explanation, if state A attacks state B, Article 51 UN Charter authorises state B to use (defensive) force against state A, while Article 21 ARSIWA exculpates state B from intervening in state A and breaching territorial sovereignty of state A. This is, however, an artificial division of the right to self-defence. The understanding further proves that the theoretical distinction between primary and secondary rules is problematic. The secondary nature of the rules on state responsibility is then ascribed with another meaning: the rules governing ancillary (ie secondary) breaches arising from a certain primary conduct.

If it were doctrinally accepted that a lawful exercise of the right of self-defence under Article 51 leads to ancillary or secondary breaches of the

[74] Paddeu (n 72) 90–132.
[75] ibid.
[76] ibid.
[77] ibid, 122.

principle of non-intervention and territorial sovereignty, one could then ask what does Article 51 authorise at all. If the defending state is *prima facie* in breach of the principle of non-intervention and territorial sovereignty of the attacking state, it logically follows that Article 51 UN Charter only authorises self-defence in the *territory* of the defending state, while all other self-defence conduct is covered by Article 21 ARSIWA. Yet, if Article 51 were limited only to own territory, it would be in fact hollow. Resorting to force within own territory cannot be a *prima facie* violation of Article 2(4) UN Charter and does not need to be justified under Article 51 UN Charter.[78] Indeed, if the ancillary self-defence doctrine were accepted, Article 51 UN Charter would then authorise an exception to something which is not unlawful in the first place, that is, using military force within *own territory* in response to an attack coming from a foreign actor.

Another version of separating self-defence under Article 51 UN Charter and Article 21 ARSIWA has been developed by Nicholas Tsagourias who argues that where the Article 51 conditions for self-defence are *not* met, states could invoke Article 21 ARSIWA as an *excuse*.[79] This proposal essentially establishes two regimes of self-defence: the primary regime and the other regime under the secondary rules, where Article 51 UN Charter is used as a justification and Article 21 ARSIWA as an excuse.[80] This argument clearly adopts the conceptual distinction between justifications and excuses. This is not problematic per se. The problem is rather that self-defence in international law is conceptualised as a justification, and its inclusion in ARSIWA is a consequence of undue conflation between justifications and excuses. In other words, the inclusion of self-defence in ARSIWA does not automatically mean that this is an excuse, as Tsagourias silently assumes.

As Vaughan Lowe illustrates, a legal system may wish to provide a defence for emergency drivers who breach the speed limit on the way to the hospital.[81] There are two ways of achieving this goal. One is to give such drivers an explicit authorisation to breach the speed limit. The other option, however, does not authorise speeding, but instead ensures that emergency drivers are not prosecuted for such a breach of traffic rules. The first (justification) relaxes the norm itself and may well result in more widespread disobeying of the speed limit than the second, which merely provides for a carefully weighed excuse of culpability where the norm was doubtlessly breached.[82] In other words, it is better if the general norm is strong and catches more violators, whose excuses are then considered on a case-by-case basis.

[78] UN Charter, arts 2.4 and 51.
[79] Tsagourias (n 72) 801–25.
[80] ibid.
[81] Vaughan Lowe, 'Precluding Wrongfulness or Responsibility: A Plea for Excuses' (1999) 10 *European Journal of International Law* 405.
[82] ibid.

In international law, defences are enumerated in the 'circumstances precluding wrongfulness' in the ILC's ARSIWA.[83] While ARSIWA do not make a systematic distinction between the different types of defences, some concepts adopt the logic of justifications (eg self-defence) and others that of excuses (eg necessity, distress).[84] The distinction between the primary and secondary rules of international law has become a mantra, if not an outright dogma. The systems of rules have now been interpreted as two hermetically closed systems. The distinction between the two sets of rules – primary and secondary – stems from the methodological work of the ILC which was in this case concerned with the rules regulating the consequences of an internationally wrongful act.[85] It was understood from the very beginning, however, that the distinction is in many respects arbitrary and that these are not two separate legal regimes.[86]

The distinction between the primary and secondary rules as two separate regimes has now been reinforced by drawing a strict division of the legal effects of self-defence under Article 51 UN Charter as opposed to Article 21 ARSIWA. These have been presented as two separate concepts, although the theoretical approaches to this matter vary to an extent. Self-defence is listed in Article 21 ARSIWA as one of the circumstances that preclude wrongfulness. As aptly noted by Vaughan Lowe in 1999, the chapter on the 'circumstances precluding wrongfulness', in ARSIWA conflates justifications and excuses, which are two separate concepts of defences in municipal criminal and tort law. It is submitted in this book that self-defence found its way into ARSIWA because of the confusion between justifications and excuses, and some other historical circumstances. As a matter of legal effects, however, Article 21 ARSIWA is merely a reflection of Article 51 UN Charter; it is not a separate right to self-defence.

Certainly, self-defence is not a carte blanche, neither domestically nor internationally. The elements of necessity and proportionality need to be met for a claim of self-defence to be valid,[87] and this book does not try to suggest otherwise. A mistaken or exaggerated self-defence will fall outside of the scope of the justification. If state A launches an armed attack on state B, the right to self-defence authorises state B to respond with military means and even enter the territory of state A. This does not mean, however, that state B can annex state A as a whole or even a part of it, and it does not mean that state B can commit genocide in state A. Likewise, state B will need to comply with international humanitarian law even when its defensive military activities are conducted within its own territory.[88] International law here follows the

[83] ARSIWA, ch V.
[84] ARSIWA, arts 21, 24 and 25.
[85] Jean d'Aspremont, *International Law as a Belief System* (CUP 2017) 75.
[86] ibid.
[87] *Case Concerning Oil Platforms (Islamic Republic of Iran v United States of America)* (Judgment) General List No 91 (2003) ICJ (*Oil Platforms* case), para 43 (arguing 'the criteria of necessity and proportionality must be observed if a measure is to be qualified as self-defence').
[88] Elizabeth Wicks, *The Right to Life and Conflicting Interests* (OUP 2010) 79–101.

logic of self-defence in municipal legal systems where exaggerated or mistaken self-defence also oversteps the boundaries of a legally warranted exception.

Article 21 ARSIWA is a consequence of some doctrinal work in the early years of UN Charter when a group of scholars believed that any use of force in international relations was illegal, even if used pursuant to Article 51 UN Charter. These writers adopted the logic of excuses rather than justifications and advanced the view that UN Charter prohibits the use of force absolutely. According to this early understanding, force could never be used legally, and the UN Charter's Chapter VII mechanisms could only preclude responsibility for it.[89] This led to the idea that there should be a reflection of Article 51 UN Charter in the law of state responsibility.[90] Subsequent developments departed from this understanding. It is now generally accepted that the Chapter VII mechanisms provide for legally warranted exceptions (justifications) to Article 2(4) UN Charter,[91] but self-defence nevertheless stayed in the final version of ARSIWA.[92]

It is thus important to note that self-defence became a part of ARSIWA when some influential writers conceptualised the law governing the use of force quite differently from how we understand it nowadays, and that Article 21 is a relic of subsequently rejected understanding that the prohibition of the use of force ought to have no justifications.[93] The law of state responsibility should not be read as being secondary to and thus separate from the substantive rules of international rules. There is therefore only one concept of self-defence in the law on the use of force. Furthermore, the law of state responsibility regulates not only responsibility for wrongfulness, but also attribution of conduct to those actors with adequate legal capacity to carry international legal obligations.[94] This is also where the regulatory underpinnings of the doctrine of unwilling or unable states lie.

B. Self-defence against Non-state Actors: Attribution by Omission?

Thus far, it has been argued that self-defence in international law works as a justification. Article 21 ARSIWA is a duplication of Article 51 UN Charter and does not have a separate regulatory meaning. It is thus not tenable to conceptualise self-defence against non-state actors as a separate concept that operates within the so-called secondary rules of international law. This section now explores the doctrine of unwilling or unable states.

[89] Paddeu (n 72) 90–132.
[90] ibid.
[91] ibid.
[92] ibid.
[93] ibid.
[94] Vladyslav Lanovoy, 'The Use of Force by Non-State Actors and the Limits of Attribution of Conduct' (2017) 28(2) *European Journal of International Law* 563.

The doctrine of unwilling or unable states first appeared in international legal discourse in the context of humanitarian intervention. It is said that where the Security Council is unwilling or unable to use its Chapter VII powers and authorise force on humanitarian grounds, an *ad hoc* group of states may be at least morally if not legally compelled to intervene.[95] The second instalment of this controversial doctrine pertains to states which are deemed to be unwilling or unable to prevent their territories from being used by non-state actors for mounting an armed attack on a foreign state. The gist of the doctrine is well-captured in the following statement made on behalf of thc Kingdom of Belgium:

> ISIL [the so-called Islamic State] has occupied a certain part of Syrian territory over which the Government of the Syrian Arab Republic does not, at this time, exercise effective control. In the light of this exceptional situation, States that have been subjected to armed attack by ISIL originating in that part of the Syrian territory are therefore justified under Article 51 of the Charter to take necessary measures of self-defence. Exercising the right of collective self-defence, Belgium will support the military measures of those States that have been subjected to attacks by ISIL. Those measures are directed against the so-called 'Islamic State in Iraq and the Levant' and not against the Syrian Arab Republic.[96]

Belgium is here trying to distinguish between the use of force *in the territory* of another state and the use of force *against the state*. It is implicit in Belgium's statement that force used against the government forces of another state could constitute an illegal use of force, while this is not the case if the target is a non-state actor.

This argument is untenable. It is builds on a problematic distinction between states and governments. But governments do not have a separate international legal personality. They only act on behalf of states. Moreover, the doctrine is nothing other than attribution to the territorial state of an armed attack by omission. Finally, unwilling is not quite the same as unable, and the two concepts should be separated. Where a state is unwilling, this may indeed imply complicity in the armed attack. Being unable is a different thing, however. Attribution to the unwilling states is very problematic and requires strict liability. It is unclear whether and under what circumstances international law supports the use of strict liability.[97] In the context of the use of force, it is then dangerous that the choice would be a matter of policy goals and political expediency rather than pre-determined legal certainty.[98] Ultimately, the unwilling or unable doctrine seeks to bypass the fact that self-defence against a non-state actor nevertheless

[95] Thomas Franck and Nigel Rodley, 'After Bangladesh: The Law of Humanitarian Intervention by Military Force' (1973) 67(2) *American Journal of International Law* 275.

[96] Letter dated 7 June 2016 from the Permanent Representative of Belgium to the United Nations addressed to the President of the Security Council (9 June 2016) UN Doc S/2016/523.

[97] Chachko and Deeks (n 5).

[98] Sarah McGibbon, 'The "Unwilling or Unable" Doctrine Unmasked: A Case Study on ISIL and Syria' (2019) 32 *Hague Yearbook of International Law* 69.

has to be exercised in the *territory* of a certain state; and does so by silent attribution of non-state conduct to the territorial state.

The so-called Islamic State in Iraq and Syria (ISIS) could attack Belgium or France, but that is not an armed attack in the sense of Article 51 UN Charter, as ISIS was never a state under international law. Moreover, ISIS was not a puppet authority of a state (such as, for example, Northern Cyprus vis-à-vis Turkey),[99] and there was no state to whose international legal capacity one could attribute the conduct of ISIS. In other words, whatever ISIS did, this was not an act of state – unless one could make the conduct of ISIS an act of Syria. And this is precisely what is in the background of the so-called unwilling or unable doctrine and of Belgium's Article 51 claim:[100] attribution of ISIS's conduct to Syria by omission.

Already the phrase unwilling or unable clearly indicates that this is not about an act but about an omission. The state responsibility and attribution terminology is clearly lingering in the background of this doctrine. But can an armed attack occur by omission? In *Bosnian Genocide*, the ICJ reasoned that 'complicity always requires that some positive action has been taken to furnish aid or assistance to the perpetrators of the genocide, while a violation of the obligation to prevent results from mere failure to adopt and implement suitable measures to prevent genocide from being committed'.[101] The Court summed up: '[W]hile complicity results from commission, violation of the obligation to prevent results from omission.'[102]

More broadly speaking, what the ICJ established here is that an act and an omission do not breach the same legal obligation. Committing genocide is one thing, but failing to prevent genocide or punish those who committed genocide is quite another. The latter may still be a breach of an international obligation, but this is not the same obligation or indeed the same conduct as in the case of the former. Following this logic *mutatis mutandis*, Syria could not have attacked Belgium by omission,[103] it could possibly only violate international law by failing to prevent an attack on Belgium. Even if such positive obligation exists under general international law, this is a different legal obligation than the negative one which requires that Syria refrains from an armed attack on another state.

In *Bosnian Genocide*, the ICJ specifically acknowledged that some international treaties do not only create a negative obligation to abstain from certain conduct, but also to take positive action to prevent such conduct (eg genocide, torture).[104] It is indeed specified in the Genocide Convention

[99] *Loizidou v Turkey* App No 15318/89 (ECtHR, 23 March 1995), para 62.
[100] Marko Milanovic, 'Belgium's Article 51 Letter to the Security Council' (*EJIL:Talk!*, 17 June 2016) www.ejiltalk.org/belgiums-article-51-letter-to-the-security-council, accessed 15 June 2022.
[101] *Bosnia* case, para 432.
[102] ibid.
[103] Milanovic (n 100).
[104] *Bosnia* case, para 432.

that acts and omissions breach different legal obligations.[105] Is it possible to transplant this logic to the Charter and the customary rules on the use of force? Unlike the Genocide Convention, the Charter does not make prevention a separate obligation which individual states could violate, unless a Chapter VII resolution were adopted to this effect as *lex specialis*. In fact, the Charter strongly prohibits the use of force, with two well-known exceptions.

Nevertheless, the unwilling or unable doctrine is different in the sense that an omission would not put a third state in breach of an international legal obligation; it would put in breach the state *from the territory of which* non-state actors cause harm to another state. This is not a conduct of state organs and this not even attribution under the *Nicaragua* doctrine and Article 8 ARSIWA.[106] The territorial state is in breach simply because its territory is being used for authoring harmful conduct, even when the government of that state determinately (militarily) opposes the actions of the renegade non-state actor in question.

This means that, unlike in *Bosnian Genocide*, we do not distinguish between negative and positive obligations when it comes to actions and omissions. The unwilling or unable doctrine requires that an omission actually leads to a violation of the negative obligation. Even if it were possible to stretch international law this far, it will be argued below that the application of strict liability would also be required.

C. Self-defence and Strict Liability

The unwilling or unable doctrine requires that as soon as harmful conduct originates from the territory of a certain state, the conduct is attributable to that state, no matter what. This is analogous to tort law's application of strict liability to those situations where one chooses to keep a pet tiger.[107] If your tiger escapes, you are responsible for any harm it causes, no matter whether or not its escape was your fault.[108] As noted above, in international law, the ICJ came close to applying strict liability in the *Corfu Channel case*.[109] But the application of strict liability in international law is at least ambiguous and it is not entirely clear which obligations came in pair with it and which obligations require an element of fault.[110]

Furthermore, unable is not quite the same as unwilling. Attribution to a state that is – despite its utmost efforts – *unable* to defeat the non-state actor using its territory for harmful purposes certainly requires strict liability, while

[105] ibid.
[106] ARSIWA, art 8; *Nicaragua* case, paras 115–16.
[107] Van Gerven, Lever and Lauroche (n 28), ch 6.
[108] ibid.
[109] *Corfu Channel* case, para 22.
[110] Chachko and Deeks (n 5).

an unwilling state may rather be complicit. An example of an unwilling state may be Afghanistan's complicity in the activities of al-Qaeda,[111] but even so the coalition's use of force was ultimately authorised pursuant to UN Security Council's Chapter VII powers, ie under a treaty mechanism.[112]

The doctrine of unwilling or unable states is thus problematic as it conflates two concepts that are quite different in nature, and at least in the case of unable states it also requires attribution of an armed attack to the state by omission and applies strict liability for this purpose. If this were not the case, it would be unclear how the right to self-defence could authorise the attacked state to pursue the non-state actor into the territory of another state without that state's consent. And this is precisely the scope of the right to self-defence, as the attacked state does not need a *jus ad bellum* justification within its own territory.[113] As Laura Visser explains, 'by invoking (collective) self-defence, states indicate that they consider themselves justified to strike the attacking state's territory or the territory where the non-state actor is located'.[114]

Self-defence in international law is conceptualised as a justification and hinges on territorial status. In order to mount an armed attack in the sense of international law, the author of the attack first needs to have the legal capacity to do so. It is questionable which non-states have such legal capacity. Even if it were accepted that non-states can mount an armed attack on states, self-defence would generally still need to be exercised in the territory of a certain state, as non-states rarely have territorial status under international law. The doctrines of secondary self-defence and of the unwilling or unable states lack persuasiveness. The former is built on the basis of an alleged gap between the primary and secondary rules of international law, while the latter requires attribution of an armed attack by omission and via strict liability. Neither explanation finds support in contemporary international legal doctrine.

D. Necessity as an Excuse rather than Self-defence as a Justification

Self-defence against non-state actors is thus a misnomer. It may be possible, however, for states to invoke a plea of necessity under such circumstances. Notably, this is not the first instance in international legal doctrine where necessity is conflated with self-defence.

[111] Niaz A Shah, 'The "Unwilling" and "Unable" Test in International Law: The Use of Force against Non-State Actors in Pakistan and Afghanistan' in Javaid Rehman, Ayesha Shahid, and Steve Foster (eds), *The Asian Yearbook of Human Rights and Humanitarian Law* (Nijhoff/Brill 2020).

[112] UNSC Res 1378 (14 November 2001) UN Doc S/RES/1378, UNSC Res 1383 (6 December 2001) UN Doc S/RES/1383, UNSC Res 1386 (20 December 2001) UN Doc S/RES/1386.

[113] Laurie Blank, *Self-defense: Law and Practice* (Edward Elgar 2023) 99–120.

[114] Laura Visser, 'Intervention by Invitation and Collective Self-Defence: Two Sides of the Same Coin?' (2020) 7(2) *Journal on the Use of Force and International Law* 292.

Necessity is elaborated in Article 25 ARSIWA. The ILC Commentary to Article 25 provides:

> Unlike consent … self-defence … or countermeasures … [necessity] is not dependent on the prior conduct of the injured State. Unlike force majeure … it does not involve conduct which is involuntary or coerced. Unlike distress … necessity consists not in danger to the lives of individuals in the charge of a State official but in a grave danger either to the essential interests of the State or of the international community as a whole. It arises where there is an irreconcilable conflict between an essential interest on the one hand and an obligation of the State invoking necessity on the other. These special features mean that necessity will only rarely be available to excuse non-performance of an obligation and that it is subject to strict limitations to safeguard against possible abuse.[115]

Under carefully defined circumstances, the plea of necessity therefore *excuses* the non-performance of an obligation where a grave danger exists either to the state or to the international community as a whole. As such, necessity is not a justification, it is an excuse which, under special and carefully defined circumstances, mitigates against responsibility for non-performance of a legal obligation. It will now be argued that some concepts of the law on the use of force fall under the doctrine of necessity, yet have often been categorised as self-defence.

The plea of necessity of this kind has its foundations in the Caroline incident. As the ILC Commentaries to ARSIWA note: 'The 'Caroline' incident of 1837, though frequently referred to as an instance of self-defence, really involved the plea of necessity at a time when the law concerning the use of force had a quite different basis than it has at present.'[116] What is often understood as a precedent for 'anticipatory self-defence' in international legal doctrine was not self-defence at all, but a plea of necessity where one state pursued a non-state actor into the territory of another state, and did so more than one hundred years before the Charter rules even existed. And even if a customary right to anticipatory self-defence existed prior to 1945, the Charter would have modified this rule with its Article 51 requirement that an armed attack must have occurred, in combination with the Article 103 supremacy clause.[117]

There is no right under international law to anticipatory self-defence and no right to self-defence against non-state actors. An anticipatory first strike on another state or pursuit of non-state actors into the territory of an 'unable state' in exceptional circumstances should, rather, be conceptualised as a plea of necessity and thus an excuse rather than a justification. Self-defence against non-state actors in international law is a misnomer. At best, states that have been attacked by a non-state actor may resort to a plea of necessity. While self-defence in international law works as a justification, necessity operates as an excuse and does not make the use of force legal.

[115] ARSIWA, commentary to art 25, para 2.
[116] ARSIWA, commentary to art 25, para 5.
[117] UN Charter, art 103.

The doctrines of secondary self-defence and the unwilling or unable states are problematic in light of their theoretical underpinnings. The secondary self-defence doctrine builds on the alleged separateness of the primary and secondary rules, but effectively leaves Article 51 UN Charter normatively hollow. The doctrine of unwilling or unable states requires attribution of armed conflict by omission via strict liability. This leads to legal uncertainty and political abuse. At the same time, armed response in another state's territory in response to an attack from a non-state actor has been present in international law for a long time. The Caroline incident was precisely about that, but was subsequently wrongly categorised as a form of self-defence. In reality, it was a plea of necessity and as such doctrinally quite similar to Belgium's recent claim vis-à-vis ISIS and Syria. Since necessity works as an excuse, the use of force remains illegal, but responsibility for it may be precluded.

It should also be recalled that in the *Wall* Advisory Opinion, the ICJ took the position that the right of self-defence under Article 51 UN Charter is triggered by an armed attack of a state on another state,[118] while the Court did not dismiss as a matter of principle a possible plea of necessity for an extraterritorial security action against non-state actors. The Court rejected necessity in the context of the specific factual circumstances of the case at hand.[119] It thus appears that it would be possible, as a matter of principle, to invoke necessity for extraterritorial operations as a circumstance precluding wrongfulness.

Any measures undertaken as a plea of necessity would be subjected to a stringent test of last resort. Indeed, in *Gabcykovo/Nagymaros*, the ICJ observed:

> the state of necessity is a ground recognized by customary international law for precluding the wrongfulness of an act not in conformity with an international obligation ... [which] can only be accepted on an exceptional basis ... [T]he state of necessity can only be invoked under certain strictly defined conditions which must be cumulatively satisfied; and the State concerned is not the sole judge of whether those conditions have been met.[120]

This test was later affirmed by the ICJ in the *Wall* Advisory Opinion.[121]

The rules on the use of force are highly territorial in nature. Not only does Article 2(4) UN Charter refer to 'territorial integrity',[122] territorialism also determines how force is applied and how it is justified. A state cannot breach Article 2(4) within its own territory and a state therefore does not need to justify a resort to force within own territory.[123] The right of self-defence is of relevance where the attacked state needs a justification to act against the attacking state

[118] *Wall* Advisory Opinion, para 139.
[119] ibid, paras 140 and 142.
[120] *Gabcikovo/Nagymaros* case, para 51.
[121] *Wall* Advisory Opinion, para 140.
[122] UN Charter, art 2.4.
[123] Albrecht Randelzhofer and Oliver Dörr, 'Article 2(4)' in Bruno Simma and others (eds), *The Charter of the United Nations: A commentary* (OUP 2012) 200, 215.

in the territory of the attacking state, subject to the tests of proportionality and necessity.[124] It is thus only possible to exercise self-defence against an actor which has a territory under international law. Self-defence also appears to be an inter-state affair, while it may be at least theoretically possible to invoke a plea of necessity as a defence against responsibility for wrongfulness where a state takes extraterritorial military measures against a non-state actor.

V. THE INTERNATIONAL LEGAL CAPACITY OF TERRITORIAL JURISDICTIONAL UNITS WITHOUT STATEHOOD

Thus far, this chapter has established that the nature and structure of international law is such that very few non-states can have international legal obligations. Non-state conduct will be in most circumstances regulated by international law only where it is attributable to a state, while the concept of attribution is highly territorial in nature. Where non-states are ascribed with a degree of international legal capacity, the problem emerges in the next step when the consequences of their conduct need to be accommodated within the territorial paradigm of international law.

This section makes a step further and explores those situations where territories can have a degree of international legal capacity even without statehood. There is no shortage of international practice where special territorial status without statehood was established under treaty law.[125] But such practice transcends the framework of international treaties and is also of customary relevance. This chapter now demonstrates that special territorial status with a degree of international legal capacity can be established also under customary international law only; it does not need to be derived from treaty law. In particular, self-determination units enjoy a separate legal status and certain rules of customary international law functionally apply to them.

A. Territorial Status without Statehood

In his Separate Opinion in the *Southwest Africa* Advisory Opinion, Judge McNair observed:

> From time to time it happens that a group of great Powers, or a large number of States both great and small, assume a power to create by a multipartite treaty some new international régime or status, which soon acquires a degree of acceptance and durability extending beyond the limits of the actual contracting parties, and giving

[124] Christopher O'Meara, *Necessity and Proportionality and the Right of Self-defence in International Law* (OUP 2021) 267–76.

[125] William Worster, 'Territorial Status Triggering a Functional Approach to Statehood' (2020) 8(1) *Penn State Journal of Law & International Affairs* 118.

it an objective existence. This power is used when some public interest is involved, and its exercise often occurs in the course of the peace settlement at the end of a great war.[126]

Judge McNair thus aptly summarised the practice in which a territorial status of certain entities is established by international treaties, yet with effects beyond treaty law; and such a status is not necessarily that of statehood. Judge McNair subsequently concluded that even when the League of Nations ceased to exist, 'the international status of the Territory continue[d] to exist'.[127] This suggests that the creation of a certain territorial status is not merely a treaty mechanism. The treaty-created territorial status transcends the treaty law framework.

Such a conclusion is in line with the pronouncement of the ICJ in the *Reparations* Advisory Opinion that 'fifty States, representing the vast majority of the members of the international community, had the power, in conformity with international law, to bring into being an entity possessing objective international personality, and not merely personality recognised by them alone'.[128] And in *Southwest Africa*, Judge McNair further observed in his Separate Opinion that a territorial legal regime created by a treaty has 'more than a purely contractual basis, and the territories subjected to it are impressed with a special legal status'.[129] But to where does the treaty-created legal status extend when it leaves the framework of a treaty?

If one does not subscribe to the problematic doctrinal views of a natural legal personality, a person of international law needs to be understood as a legal person and as such established in the formal sources of international law. Notably, in the *Reparations* Advisory Opinion, the ICJ explicitly mentioned 'the vast majority of the members of the international community'.[130] The approach is strikingly similar to the emergence and identification of customary international law: state practice and *opinio juris* need to be general and widespread, but not necessarily universal, for a customary rule to emerge.[131] It has already been established earlier in this book that such a similarity is no coincidence.[132] States are sometimes also created by treaties, but their legal status transcends the boundaries of treaty law and is established under customary international law. But customary status is not limited to states. James Crawford noted that 'a quantity of practice attests to the existence of certain

[126] *International Status of Southwest Africa* (Advisory Opinion) General List No 10 (1950) ICJ (*Southwest Africa* Advisory Opinion), Separate Opinion by Judge McNair, para 153.
[127] ibid, para 162.
[128] *Reparations* Advisory Opinion, para 185.
[129] *Southwest Africa* Advisory Opinion, para 154.
[130] ibid, para 154.
[131] International Law Commission 'Draft conclusions on identification of customary international law 2018' UN Doc A/73/10, para 65, conclusion 8.
[132] See ch 2.

international powers to bring about territorial change and to create new territorial entities (States or *entities approximating to States*) with effects extending beyond the immediate contracting parties'.[133]

The 'quantity of practice'[134] refers to international territorial administrations,[135] mandates and trust territories,[136] non-self-governing territories,[137] and similar forms of internationalised territorial governance.[138] Such arrangements have ordinarily been established by international treaties, but have had effects also beyond treaty law and the legal status of such entities was opposable also to non-parties of these treaties.[139] In recent practice, there have been examples of territorial status established by legally binding resolutions of the UN Security Council which also draw the authority from an international treaty – the UN Charter.[140] Examples include Kosovo[141] and East Timor.[142]

Significantly less attention has been paid in scholarship and practice to the legal status of those territorial entities whose special territorial statuses is not derived from international treaty law. It is doctrinally accepted that non-statehood territorial status can percolate through treaty law into customary international law.[143] But customary international law can also develop independently from treaty law and is no less authoritative than treaties are.[144] In other words, special territorial status without statehood could at least theoretically develop under customary international law even without prior legal authority granted to this effect by an international treaty.

In sum, it is states, international organisations and certain non-state territorial units that have the legal capacity to act on the international plane. This means that they can create international legal obligations, breach those obligations and incur responsibility for such breaches. It has already been established that certain non-state territorial units have been functionally given a degree of treaty-making capacity (eg separate customs territories).[145] This chapter now further considers how such units may be regulated by customary international law.

[133] James Crawford, *The Creation of States in International Law* (OUP 2006) 504.

[134] ibid.

[135] Ralph Wilde, *International Territorial Administration: How Trusteeship and the Civilizing Mission Never Went Away* (OUP 2008) 192.

[136] Crawford (n 133) 565.

[137] ibid, 602.

[138] Wilde (n 135).

[139] ibid, 153–90.

[140] Marc Weller, *Contested Statehood* (OUP 2009).

[141] UNSC Res 1244 (10 June 1999) UN Doc S/RES/1244.

[142] UNSC Res 1264 (15 September 1999) UN Doc S/RES/1264.

[143] Cf Jure Vidmar, 'Unilateral Declarations of Independence in International Law' in Duncan French (ed), *Statehood and Self-Determination Reconciling Tradition and Modernity in International Law* (CUP 2013) 60–78.

[144] 'Customary Law' (*ICRC*) www.icrc.org/en/war-and-law/treaties-customary-law/customary-law#:~:text=Customary%20international%20law%20consists%20of,the%20protection%20offered%20to%20victims, accessed 14 November 2022.

[145] See Chapter 2, section III.

B. Self-determination Units and Customary International Law

It would certainly be an exaggeration to say that customary international law applies to non-state actors across the board.[146] But certain customary rules may be functionally applicable to certain non-states. A good example is those rules of international humanitarian law which apply even to non-state parties to armed conflict.[147] Although formed on the basis of state practice and *opinio juris*, customary international law can bind non-states for some functional purposes, in a similar way as international treaty law can functionally extend the treaty-making powers to non-states.[148] It is submitted here that the rules of customary international law can functionally apply also to separate non-state jurisdictional units which have acquired a territorial status other than statehood. The yardstick that determines such a legal status is whether the separate jurisdictional territorial unit in question can be identified as a self-determination unit.[149]

i. The Special International Legal Status of Self-determination Units

A self-determination unit may not necessarily be a state under international law, but nevertheless enjoys territorial status in international law by virtue of the standing of the right of self-determination in the UN Charter era international law.[150] It is settled in contemporary international law that the legal status of a territory cannot be altered against the will of the people populating that territory.[151] That is not to say that the will of the people is sufficient for an alteration of territorial status. The relationship is defined negatively: the legal status may not be altered in violation of the will of the people.[152] For example, the United Kingdom's transfer of Hong Kong to China without popular consultation may have well violated the right of self-determination of the people of Hong Kong.[153] The right of self-determination also acknowledges a special nexus about the people and the spatial area they are populating, and is even considered to have acquired the status of *jus cogens*.[154] The right of

[146] Orfeas Chasapis Tassinis, 'Customary International Law: Interpretation from Beginning to End' (2020) 31(1) *European Journal of International Law* 235.
[147] Waseem Ahmad Qureshi, 'Applicability of International Humanitarian Law to Non-State Actors' (2019) 17(1) *Santa Clara Journal of International Law* 1.
[148] Worster (n 2) 207–73.
[149] Wilde (n 135) 153–90.
[150] UN Charter, art 1.2.
[151] Adriana Kalicka-Mikolajczyk, 'The International Legal Status of Western Sahara' (2020) 18(4) *Opole Studies in Administration and Law* 35.
[152] UNGA Res ES-11/4 (13 October 2022) UN Doc A/RES/ES-11/4.
[153] Robert McCorquodale, 'Diversity and Self-determination in International Law' (2003) 74(1) *British Yearbook of International Law* 451; Robert McCorquodale, 'Self-Determination: A Human Rights Approach' (1994) 43(4) *International and Comparative Law Quarterly* 857.
[154] Salvatore Senese, 'External and Internal Self-Determination' (1989) 16(1) *Social Justice* 19.

self-determination also applies directly to peoples, not to states.[155] Since peoples are not party to international treaties, such as the UN Charter, ICCPR and the International Covenant on Economic, Social and Cultural Rights (ICESCR),[156] it may be said that self-determination applies to peoples by virtue of customary and peremptory international law.[157]

While the whole body of customary international law cannot be extended to separate jurisdictional units that have acquired a special non-state territorial status, customary international law at least protects the self-determination units and their territorial status. Otherwise, international law would allow denial of a customary and peremptory right opposable to peoples *directly* rather than via the statehood status of their political unit.

To take Taiwan as an example, Crawford argues that years of governance in separation from China have probably crystallised a separate identity of the people of Taiwan which, in turn, makes Taiwan a self-determination unit.[158] Although Taiwan, as a non-party to UN Charter, is not protected by Article 2(4) UN Charter by virtue of treaty law, as a self-determination unit it is nevertheless protected from forceful conquest under customary international law. As further argued by Crawford, the principle of self-determination protects Taiwan from being transferred to the authority of the Peoples' Republic of China without the consent of Taiwan's, population and 'attempts to solve the problem of Taiwan otherwise than by peaceful means must now constitute a situation "likely to endanger the maintenance of international peace and security" under Article 33 of the [UN] Charter.'[159]

Kosovo is different than Taiwan in that Kosovo's statehood has been recognised by more than half of the states in the world, while Taiwan undoubtedly is not a state.[160] Nevertheless, there is a question of whether the customary reflection of Article 2(4) of the UN Charter applies between Kosovo and those states that do not recognise it as a state, including Serbia. Regardless of Kosovo's status under the law of statehood, it is a separate self-determination unit with a corresponding legal status.[161] As such, Kosovo is protected from forceful conquest.

[155] Natalie Jones, 'Self-Determination and the Right of Peoples to Participate in International Law-Making' (2021) *British Yearbook of International Law* 1.

[156] UN Charter; ICCPR; International Covenant on Economic, Social and Cultural Rights (adopted 16 December 1966, entered into force 3 January 1976) 1993 UNTS 3 (ICESCR).

[157] Robert McCorquodale, 'Self-Determination: A Human Rights Approach' (1994) 43(4) *International and Comparative Law Quarterly* 857; Sardar MA Waqar Khan Arif, 'Legitimacy of Right to Self-Determination Under International Law' (2019) 7(1) *Pakistan Journal of Humanities and Social Sciences* 15.

[158] Crawford (n 133) 220.

[159] ibid, 220.

[160] 'List of states that recognize Kosovo's independence' (*Kosovo Thanks You*) www.kosovothanksyou.com, accessed 7 December 2022.

[161] Gary Wilson, 'Self-determination, Recognition and the Problem of Kosovo Gary Wilson' (2009) 56(3) *Netherlands International Law Review* 455.

A special status of non-state territories, which can be identified as self-determination units,[162] has been established under Chapter XI of the UN Charter under the heading of Non-Self-Governing Territories.[163] General Assembly Resolution 1541 further identified a non-self-governing territory as 'a territory which is geographically separate and is distinct ethnically and/or culturally from the country administering it'.[164] The status of non-self-governing territories in the sense of Chapter XI of the UN Charter pertains to colonial territories and not to the metropolitan spatial areas of states.[165] Today, 17 non-self-governing territories in the sense of Chapter XI continue to exist.[166]

Nevertheless, international practice and some scholarly writings suggest that the definition of a geographically separate and ethnically distinct territory could reach beyond the context of Chapter XI of the UN Charter and more broadly define the territorial status of a self-determination unit.[167] Bangladesh can be mentioned in this context.[168] While not qualifying as a non-self-governing territory in the sense of Chapter XI of the UN Charter, it was instrumental in the process of the state of Bangladesh that East Bengal could be identified as a self-determination unit in 1971, and such an identification could be functionally derived from the customary principle of a geographically separate and ethnically distinct territory, as expressed in Principle IV of Resolution 1541.[169]

The identification of East Bengal as a self-determination unit was instrumental not only for the future statehood of Bangladesh,[170] but also for the assessment of the legal consequences of India's military intervention in the territory.[171] Although India used force in the sense of Article 2(4) UN Charter, this did not taint the situation with territorial illegality in the sense of Article 40 ARSIWA and was not comparable to Turkey's intervention in Northern Cyprus.[172] India's intervention was deemed to have procured self-determination in the territory of East Bengal and thus cured the consequences of India's *prima facie* illegal use of force.[173]

[162] Crawford (n 133) 602–08.
[163] UN Charter, Chapter 11.
[164] UNGA Res 1541 (15 Dec 1960) UN Doc A/RES/1541, Principle IV.
[165] UN Charter, Chapter 11.
[166] 'Non-Self-Governing Territories' (*United Nations*) www.un.org/dppa/decolonization/en/nsgt, accessed 8 July 2022.
[167] Crawford (n 133) 142.
[168] ibid.
[169] ibid.
[170] Peter Custers, 'Maulana Bhashani and the Transition to Secular Politics in East Bengal' (2010) 47(2) *Indian Economic and Social History Review* 231.
[171] Nicholas J Wheeler, *Saving Strangers: Humanitarian Intervention in International Society* (OUP 2002) 55–77.
[172] Crawford (n 133) 142–45.
[173] ibid, 139–47.

The intrinsic connection between self-determination and the use of force is also acknowledged by Erika de Wet who argues that a military intervention on request that violated the right of self-determination would be prohibited.[174] The right of self-determination therefore has direct effect on the law of the use of force and is not contingent on the statehood status of the self-determination unit concerned. East Bengal was not a state, but a self-determination unit, and this had effects on the consequences of India's resort to force. The right of self-determination also prevents an alteration of the legal status without the consent of the population of the territory, regardless of whether or not the self-determination unit concerned has thc status of a state. Finally, states are not allowed to intervene in situations where self-determination would be supressed.

These doctrinal examples attest that self-determination units form a special territorial status under international law, and as such enjoy a certain level of international legal capacity which is not contingent on statehood status. In particular, self-determination units enjoy protection from military intervention and conquest. While an intervention in violation of self-determination is prohibited, an intervention to procure self-determination may be at least excused, if not justified.[175] Indeed, international legal responses to India's intervention in East Bengal suggest that India's use of force may have been considered illegal, but its consequences were nevertheless accepted.[176]

ii. Self-determination and its Territorial Application

As a human right, self-determination applies to peoples.[177] Nevertheless, this right has always been closely linked to territorial units. As Crawford argues, '[m]uch of the emphasis in practice has been on the application of the principle [of self-determination] to territories to which it has come to apply either by a form of recognition or by agreement pursuant to treaty arrangements'.[178] In making this claim, Crawford also acknowledges that the question of the ambit of self-determination and the territories where self-determination applies is 'as much a matter of politics as law'.[179] Indeed, as demonstrated in chapter two, territories are created in a political process to which legal consequences are attached.[180] A self-determination unit is thus a politically created legal status over a spatial area. A certain level of international legal capacity is attached to this status under international law, and the status is not contingent on statehood.

[174] Erika de Wet, 'The Modern Practice of Intervention by Invitation in Africa and Its Implications for the Prohibition of the Use of Force' (2016) 26(4) *European Journal of International Law* 980.
[175] Jure Vidmar, 'The Use of Force and Defences in the Law of State Responsibility' (2015) Jean Monnet Working Paper 08/15, 1–30.
[176] ibid.
[177] Jones (n 155) 1–33.
[178] Crawford (n 133) 115.
[179] ibid.
[180] See ch 2.

The position on the special territorial status of self-determination units even in the absence of statehood is consistent with the ICJ's pronouncement in the *Chagos* Advisory Opinion, where the Court rejected the view that the principle of territorial integrity was applicable only between states.[181] In the Court's view, 'States have consistently emphasised that respect for the territorial integrity of a non-self-governing territory is a key element of the exercise of the right to self-determination under international law'.[182] This pronouncement further confirms that self-determination units enjoy in their own right a degree of international legal capacity and thus have a separate territorial status under international law. It is not statehood that brings them within the ambit of the principle of territorial integrity, but, rather, the right of self-determination and the status of a self-determination unit. The non-state self-determination units therefore cannot be forcefully split and they cannot be forcefully conquered.

It is important to note that a self-determination unit must not be realised in violation of the rules of international law in the sense of the ICJ's pronouncement in the *Kosovo* Advisory Opinion. The Court summarised international practice to hold that territorial illegality could follow from 'the unlawful use of force or other egregious violations of norms of general international law, in particular those of a peremptory character (*jus cogens*)'.[183] For example, Northern Cyprus, Crimea or Donetsk and Luhansk Peoples' Republic cannot attain the status of self-determination units because they were realised illegally by foreign aggression directed against Cyprus and Ukraine, respectively.[184] The jurisdictional unit once known as Southern Rhodesia was a self-determination unit, but territorial illegality was committed when independence was declared by the racist white minority government.[185] No such illegalities were committed when, for example, the separate jurisdictional units of Taiwan[186] and Somaliland emerged, and hence they qualify as self-determination units.[187] Kosovo is a more complex situation due to the illegal military intervention in 1999.[188] Despite this circumstance, the ICJ in its *Kosovo* Advisory Opinion pronounced that Kosovo's declaration of independence was merely unilateral but, unlike some other situations, not connected to 'the unlawful use of force or other egregious violations

[181] *Legal Consequences of the Separation of the Chagos Archipelago from Mauritius in 1965* (Advisory Opinion) General List No 169 (2019) ICJ (*Chagos* Advisory Opinion), para 160.
[182] ibid.
[183] *Accordance with International Law of the Unilateral Declaration of Independence in Respect of Kosovo* (Advisory Opinion) General List No 141 (2010) ICJ (*Kosovo* Advisory Opinion), para 81.
[184] ibid, para 81.
[185] UNGA Res 2151 (17 November 1966) UN Doc A/RES/2151 (XXI).
[186] Janis Grzybowski, 'To Be or Not to Be: The Ontological Predicament of State Creation in International Law' (2017) 28(2) *European Journal of International Law* 416.
[187] ibid.
[188] Dino Kritsiotis, 'The Kosovo Crisis and NATO's Application of Armed Force against the Federal Republic of Yugoslavia' (2000) 49(2) *International and Comparative Law Quarterly* 330.

of norms of general international law, in particular those of a peremptory character (*jus cogens*)'.[189]

It is of utmost importance in the case of Kosovo that following the illegal use of force by a group of the North Atlantic Treaty Organization (NATO) member states,[190] the UN Security Council acted under Chapter VII of the UN Charter and established a regime of international territorial situation.[191] It is at least implicit in the 2010 pronouncement of the ICJ in the *Kosovo* Advisory Opinion that the present-day status of Kosovo is derived from the legal regime of Resolution 1244 which interrupted the legal link between the 1999 intervention and current legal status.[192] This is not to say that Resolution 1244 *ex post facto* legalised the 1999 situation. It means that due to the subsequently created international territorial regime under the legally binding Resolution 1244, the current territorial status of Kosovo is not affected by the illegality of the 1999 intervention.

The legal status of the Occupied Palestinian Territories as a self-determination unit also results in there being a special legal status attached to that spatial area, although statehood has not been created. In the *Wall* Advisory Opinion, the ICJ stated that 'Israel is bound to comply with its obligation to respect the right of the Palestinian people to self-determination and its obligations under international humanitarian law and international human rights law'.[193] This is despite the fact that Palestine has not attained statehood status under international law. This was ultimately confirmed even by the ICJ:

> The Court considers that it has a duty to draw the attention of the General Assembly, to which the present Opinion is addressed, to the need for these efforts to be encouraged with a view to achieving as soon as possible, on the basis of international law, a negotiated solution to the outstanding problems and the establishment of a Palestinian State, existing side by side with Israel and its other neighbours, with peace and security for all in the region.[194]

The ICJ here confirmed that statehood is not created by a factual occurrence, but rather as a result of a political process. However, the Occupied Palestinian Territories nevertheless enjoy the territorial status of a self-determination unit which brings the territory and its population under direct protection of certain customary rules of international law that are not applicable (exclusively) to states. As the ICJ recalled, such rules pertain to the right of self-determination, and, more broadly, to international human rights and international humanitarian

[189] *Kosovo* Advisory Opinion, para 81.
[190] Kritsiotis (n 188) 330–59.
[191] UNSC Res 1244 (10 June 1999) UN Doc S/RES/1244.
[192] Jure Vidmar, 'The *Kosovo* Advisory Opinion Scrutinized' (2011) 24(2) *Leiden Journal of International Law* 355.
[193] *Wall* Advisory Opinion, para 149.
[194] ibid, para 201.

law.[195] It also follows from the practice of UN organs, including the ICJ, that the territory known as Occupied Palestinian Territories, cannot be subject to conquest, despite the lack of statehood status in that spatial area.[196]

International law accepts that certain separate territorial units can have a special legal status even without statehood, and as such enjoy certain level of legal capacity under international law. Such territorial status can be established under treaty law, but can then transcend the treaty law framework and become customary. It is also possible that such a status emerges under customary international law only. The particularly strongly established territorial status without statehood is that of separate self-determination units. The conditions for the creation of such a legal status may be summarised as follows: (i) an organised political authority has established territorial jurisdiction over a certain spatial area: (ii) the jurisdictional authority was not established illegally in the sense of Article 40 ARSIWA and international practice summarised by the ICJ in para 81 *Kosovo* Advisory Opinion; (iii) the spatial area concerned is geographically separate and populated by ethnically distinct people. The levels of international legal capacity of such self-determination units may vary; some may relatively widely participate in international treaty regimes and others may not. Regardless of the levels of their international legal capacity, their status as a self-determination unit protects such units against conquest as this would lead to denial of the right of self-determination, and this would be violation of a *jus cogens* norm.

VI. CONCLUSION

The concept of international legal capacity is closely linked to the concept of international responsibility. Only those actors that have the capacity to create and hold international legal obligations can breach them and thus incur responsibility for breaches. It is thus not a coincidence that the law of international responsibility is most thoroughly reflected in the documents termed ARSIWA and the Articles on Responsibility of International Organizations (ARIO) which regulate the responsibility of states and international organisations, respectively. International legal capacity is thus the capability of an actor to author conduct, either by action or omission, which can create, fulfil or breach international legal obligations, and incur international responsibility as a result of a breach.

This book does not systematically deal with international responsibility of international organisations.[197] It should suffice to say that international organisations have international legal capacity for the purposes of their functional

[195] ibid, paras 89 and 115.
[196] ibid, para 75.
[197] Jan Klabbers, 'Reflections on Role Responsibility: The Responsibility of International Organizations for Failing to Act' (2017) 28(4) *European Journal of International Law* 1133.

mandates and can conclude treaties within the scope of this mandate.[198] In practice, however, international organisations are not parties to very many treaties.[199] As a consequence, there are few international legal obligations which they could even breach.[200] This is different with states. It is mainly states that create and breach international legal obligations, and incur responsibility for breaches. International legal capacity is thus primarily vested in states. But it is not vested in states exclusively.

This chapter demonstrated that certain territorial jurisdictional units other than states also are vested with territorial status and a degree of legal capacity in international law. Historically, many special non-state territorial regimes have been established under international treaties. It is settled in international law that the treaty-created non-state territorial status transcends the treaty law framework and is of general applicability under customary international law. A non-state territorial status can also develop under customary international law exclusively. This chapter has demonstrated that self-determination units can be vested with a separate territorial status under international law even in the absence of statehood. Such units are protected by the principle of territorial integrity and by the prohibition of conquest.

A great deal of doctrinal discussion has been focused on the question of whether Taiwan as a non-state would be entitled to the protection against the use of force as a matter of a customary reflected of Article 2(4) UN Charter.[201] But the focus on the use of force appears to be too narrow, if not excessively theoretical. Taiwan as a self-determination unit is protected from conquest and can avail itself on the principle of territorial integrity. It is difficult to imagine how conquest could be carried out without resorting to force. Hence, it would appear that the prohibition of the use of force against Taiwan would in any case be a part of the parcel of the prohibition of conquest. Kosovo may be in a different position than Taiwan, as it is recognised by more than half of the states in the world.[202] Still, is Kosovo protected by the prohibition of the use of force vis-à-vis Serbia, which continues to oppose Kosovo's statehood? While the applicability of the customary reflection of Article 2(4) UN Charter between Kosovo and Serbia remains controversial, Kosovo constitutes a self-determination unit and cannot be subjected to forceful conquest either by Serbia or any other state.

[198] Edward Chukwuemeke Okeke, 'Legal Status of International Organizations' in *Jurisdictional Immunities of States and International Organizations* (New York 2018).

[199] Klabbers (n 62) 9–82.

[200] Kristina Daugirdas, 'How and Why International Law Binds International Organizations' (2016) 57(2) *Harvard International Law Journal* 325.

[201] Quoc Tan Trung Nguyen, 'Does International Law Protect Taiwan?' (2022) 2(14) *United States Asia Law Institute Perspectives* 2.

[202] 'Taiwan in the Western Balkans: Low on the list of priorities' (*CEIAS Insights*, 7 February 2023) ceias.eu/taiwan-in-the-western-balkans-low-on-the-list-of-priorities/#:~:text=Both%20Kosovo%20and%20Taiwan%20do,just%2014%20countries%20in%20total, accessed 10 February 2023.

The spatial area known as the Occupied Palestinian Territories also enjoys the status of a self-determination unit under international law, albeit without statehood. In the *Wall* Advisory Opinion, the ICJ derived certain rights and obligations pertaining to this territory directly from the right of self-determination and in the absence of a state-derived legal capacity.[203] In doing so, the ICJ even explicitly stated that the Palestinian State would need to be created in a political process.[204] This further confirms the position taken in this book that statehood is not realised by legal rules alone. Statehood is realised in a political process and registered in law; however, territories can also be vested under international law with a certain status other than statehood.

On a purely theoretical level, the legal status of a self-determination unit under international law can develop where the situation is not marked by territorial illegality in the sense of Article 40 ARSIWA, and there is thus no obligation to withhold recognition under Article 41 ARSIWA.[205] This doctrine thus precludes entities such as Northern Cyprus, Donetsk and Luhansk Peoples' Republics and Crimea from altering their territorial statuses and/or acquiring a territorial status in their own right. Conversely, Taiwan, Kosovo and Somaliland are not tainted by this kind of territorial illegality. Their governance in separation from China, Serbia and Somalia, respectively, is not a result of aggression on these states, but rather a result of developments that are not unlawful under international law.[206] Taiwan, Serbia and Somaliland may well have acted against territorial integrity of China, Serbia and Somalia, but in doing so they do not violate any rules of international law, let alone those of *jus cogens* character.[207]

Paramount in these examples is territorialism. An extension of legal capacity and responsibility to non-states is possible because these are territorial units, territorial 'power containers'[208] capable of making and enforcing the laws domestically, and at least theoretically accommodating the consequences of international wrongdoing. This is different where international legal capacity is sought to be extended to non-territorial actors, such as terrorist organisations. If such groups ought to have international legal capacity, for example to mount an armed attack in the sense of Article 51 UN Charter, it then becomes unclear how the consequences of such wrongdoing are to be accommodated within the territorial paradigm of international law. The example of the use of force illustrates that if a non-territorial actor were to mount an armed attack in the sense of international law, it becomes conceptually impossible for the

[203] *Wall* Advisory Opinion, para 149.
[204] ibid, para 162.
[205] ARSIWA, arts 40 and 41.
[206] Kritsiotis (n 188) 330–59.
[207] Crawford (n 133) 390.
[208] Jure Vidmar, 'International Organizations and Non-State Territorial Entities' in Benedikt C Harzl and Roman Petrov (eds), *Unrecognized Entities* (Brill Nijhoff 2022).

attacked state to exercise self-defence. This is simply because the attacker does not have its own territory.

This chapter demonstrated that states and some scholars have then resorted to certain doctrines which effectively attribute the attack to the territorial state by omission. These doctrines are unpersuasive. The chapter rather proposes that under some circumstances a state could make a plea of necessity for acting against a non-state actor in the territory of another state, but this is not a matter of a justification under the law of self-defence. A plea of necessity was also the original meaning of the Caroline doctrine. The logic of necessity as an excuse has been present in international legal doctrine for a long time, but has been often wrongly categorised as an expansion of the right of self-defence, or as a customary justification for the use of force on humanitarian grounds. In fact, 'self-defence' against non-state actors, 'anticipatory self-defence', and humanitarian intervention without the Security Council's authorisation are all pleas of necessity and as such excuses for otherwise illegal use of force.

International law can accommodate international legal capacity of territories without statehood. Where such territories represent separate jurisdictional units and are not marked with territorial illegality, they are capable of creating, holding and breaching international legal obligations, and incurring responsibility for such breaches. The law of state responsibility is functionally extended to such territories, but the status of statehood is not. International legal capacity for non-territorial actors is a different problem. With a partial functional exception of international organisations, actors in contemporary international law cannot create obligations and incur responsibility if they do not possess a 'bordered power container' in which they exercise jurisdiction, and do not have a territorial status established in the sources of international law. Actors in the international arena therefore should not be distinguished along the state/non-state divide. One should rather distinguish between territorial and non-territorial actors.

It is generally the territorial actors that are capable of having international legal capacity and incur international responsibility. Such actors are mostly, but not exclusively, states. International practice shows that international legal capacity of a non-state territory has often been established by international treaties. A special non-state territorial status can thus be grounded in treaty law. Moreover, self-determination units may enjoy special non-state territorial status under customary international law.

5

States Beyond Statehood

I. INTRODUCTION

IT WAS ESTABLISHED in the previous chapters that statehood is a form of territorial legal status established in the sources of international law. Territories can also have an international legal status other than statehood and a degree of international legal capacity stemming from this status. Self-determination units are protected from conquest under customary international law, while their degree of international legal capacity depends on whether, for which purposes, and to what extent, states are willing to enter into treaties with non-state territorial units.

Territorial status under international law can exist even in the absence of statehood. This chapter now turns to the relationship between the state and territorial status from the other direction: does the term 'state' always denote territorial status? It is argued in this chapter that the word 'state' in international legal doctrine has not always been used only in the context of statehood as a form of territorial status, but also in the procedural sense in the context of treaty-making powers and participation in international treaty procedures.

The chapter sets out by exploring the relationship between United Nations (UN) membership and the status of a non-member observer state on the one hand, and the statehood status on the other. In so doing, it demonstrates that the state requirement for UN membership and the non-member observer state status are doctrinally detached from the law of statehood. The fact that entities without statehood have been members and non-member observer states should not be interpreted as anomalies or situations *sui generis*.[1] Nevertheless, the consequences of UN membership, or membership of the UN specialised agencies, have far-reaching effects and can create an entity's international legal capacity to conclude treaties which are generically open to any state. But this is not state creation or creation of any particular territorial status.

Certain procedural technicalities under international treaty law cannot have incidental side-effects under the law of statehood. This chapter thus demonstrates that UN membership does not create a state or confirm an entity's

[1] Jochen A Frowein, 'The United Nations and Non-Member States' (1970) 25(2) *International Journal* 333.

statehood, but it can enable such an entity to enter into certain multilateral treaties. This does give an entity a degree of international legal capacity. The chapter argues in favour of establishing a persistent distinction between international treaty procedures open to states – including those contained in the UN Charter – and the substantive law of statehood. While the distinction is often preserved in international practice, this is not always the case, and conflation is still common. The conflation of legal statehood with procedural mechanisms under treaty law has led to a great deal of doctrinal inconsistency and uncertainty – in the UN system and beyond. Palestine's use of certain international judicial procedures has been conflated with the question of its territorial status,[2] and so has been Kosovo's conclusion of an agreement with the European Union.[3] On the other hand, Western Sahara's separate legal status has been weaponised by the Court of Justice of the European Union (CJEU) to avoid addressing the *de facto* extension of the territorial scope of an agreement between the EU and Morocco.

II. THE MEMBER STATES AND NON-MEMBER OBSERVER STATES WITHOUT STATEHOOD

Article 4(1) of the UN Charter provides: 'Membership in the United Nations is open to all … peace-loving *states* which accept the obligations contained in the present Charter and, in the judgment of the Organisation, are able and willing to carry out these obligations.'[4] There has been some debate over the meaning of the state requirement for UN membership.[5] Is the *state* requirement expressed in Article 4(1) UN Charter a *statehood* requirement?

In its first advisory opinion, *Conditions of Admission of a State to Membership in the United Nations (Article 4 of the Charter)*, the International

[2] See sections III.B and III.C below.

[3] See section IV.

[4] United Nations Charter (adopted 26 June 1945, entered into force 24 October 1945) 1 UNTS 16 (UN Charter), art 4.1 (emphasis added).

[5] Rosalyn Cohen, 'The Concept of Statehood in United Nations Practice' (1961) 109(8) *University of Pennsylvania Law Review* 1127; Frederick Tse-shyang Chen, 'The Meaning of States in the Membership Provisions of the United Nations Charter' (2001) 12(1) *Indiana International and Comparative Law Review* 25; Christian Hillgruber, 'The Admission of New States to the International Community' (1998) 9 *European Journal of International Law* 491; Rosalyn Higgins, *The Development of International Law through the Political Organs of the United Nations* (OUP 1963) 17; Donna K Ginther, 'Article 4' in Bruno Simma (ed), *The Charter of the United Nations* (OUP 2002); John Dugard, *Recognition and the United Nations* (CUP 1987) 78; Thomas Grant, *Admission to the United Nations: Charter Article 4 and the Rise of Universal Organisation* (Martinus Nijhoff 2009); Iliriana Islami and Remzije Istrefi, 'Consolidation of Statehood through Membership in the UN: Some Remarks on Kosovo, Democracy and International Law' (2018) 43 *Review of Central and East European Law* 331; James Crawford, *The Creation of States in International Law* (OUP 2006), ch 4; Hans Kelsen, *The Law of the United Nations: A Critical Analysis of its Fundamental Problems* (London Institute of Word Affairs 2000, reprint of the 1950 original) 59–61.

Court of Justice (ICJ) specified that 'an applicant must (1) be a State; (2) be peace-loving; (3) accept the obligations of the Charter; (4) be able to carry out these obligations; and (5) be willing to do so'.[6] The ICJ did not further define the state requirement or specify whether the requirement is linked to the law of statehood. While writers acknowledge that UN membership is not a prerequisite for statehood, it is often claimed that membership confirms statehood and ends any doubt in relation to the entity's international legal status.[7] In one such view, '[a[fter the decision has been taken to admit a state to the United Nations, its statehood cannot be called into question with the effect of contesting the validity of mutual rights and obligations arising from co-membership'.[8] This ought to be the case because UN membership is only open to *states* and membership thus implicitly confirms that members have statehood.[9] Such causality has not always worked in practice. The number of UN members without statehood has been rather limited, but the fact that such exceptions do exist suggests that membership does not always overlap with statehood status under general international law.

The UN General Assembly has also established the practice of admitting certain entities to the status of 'non-member observer states'.[10] This status is an extra-Charter arrangement and is not based in any formal source of international law. The UN General Assembly uses its resolutions to accord such status; and General Assembly Resolutions are not legally binding instruments. Nevertheless, the UN General Assembly resolutions can be highly significant in that they can be indicative of *opinio juris* and are thus relevant for custom formation.[11] Especially after the 2012 admission of Palestine to the status of a non-member observer state,[12] there has been a great deal of discussion on the consequences of the General Assembly Resolution 67/19 for the legal status of this entity.[13] This discussion follows similar patterns as the debates on the 'state requirement' for UN membership. What is the legal significance of the term

[6] *Admission of a State to the United Nations (Charter, Art 4)* (Advisory Opinion) General List No 3 (1948) ICJ, paras 57 and 62.

[7] Anthony Aust, *Handbook of International Law* (CUP 2005) 18.

[8] Hillgruber (n 5) 491–509.

[9] Aust (n 7) 1095 and 1101.

[10] Alfred G Mower, 'Observer Countries: Quasi Members of the United Nations' (1966) 20(2) *International Organization* 266.

[11] *Military and Paramilitary Activities in and against Nicaragua (Nicaragua v United States of America)*, (Judgment) General List No 70 (1986) ICJ, para 188.

[12] UNGA Res 67/19 (4 December 2012) UN Doc A/RES/67/19.

[13] Joseph Weiler, 'Differentiated Statehood? "Pre-States"? Palestine@the UN' (*EJIL:Talk!*, 3 April 2013) www.ejiltalk.org/differentiated-statehood-pre-states-palestinethe-un, accessed 10 July 2021; Dapo Akande, 'Palestine as a UN Observer State: Does this Make Palestine a State?' (*EJIL:Talk!*, 3 December 2012) www.ejiltalk.org/palestine-as-a-un-observer-state-does-this-make-palestine-a-state, accessed 23 February 2022; Jure Vidmar, 'Does General Assembly Resolution 67/19 Have Any Implications for the Legal Status of Palestine?' (*EJIL:Talk!*, 4 December 2012) www.ejiltalk.org/does-general-assembly-resolution-6719-have-any-implications-for-the-legal-status-of-palestine, accessed 27 March 2023.

'state' in the phrasing 'non-member observer state'? Does the status of a non-member observer state of the UN accorded through a UN General Assembly resolution confirm, acknowledge, or even recognise that the entity in question has statehood under general international law?

Admission of new states to the UN membership is a politically complex procedure as the Charter provides that admission is 'effected by a decision of the General Assembly upon the recommendation of the Security Council'.[14] Due to the veto power of the permanent five members of the Security Council,[15] it is difficult in practice for a contested territorial entity to secure such a recommendation. It can be speculated that UN membership of entities such as Kosovo and Palestine would have been much more realistic had admission of new states been exclusively in the gift of the UN General Assembly. Is it plausible to say that this procedural technicality in the Charter has consequences, for example in relation to Kosovo's or Palestine's statehood?

The extra-Charter non-member state status bypasses the Security Council and thus the veto obstacle, and so do the admission proceedings in certain UN specialised agencies, such as the United Nations Educational, Scientific and Cultural Organisation (UNESCO).[16] The absence of the veto power makes it politically much more likely for a contested entity to be able to join an institutionalised international regime in principle open only to states. The ability to participate in such regimes can have some far-reaching effects in terms of the international legal capacity of such entities. As will be demonstrated below, such participation can enable them to take part in certain institutional arrangements usually reserved for states. But this is procedural capacity under international (institutional) treaties. Such procedural capacity should not be conflated with status under the law of statehood.

This section argues that the instances of UN members without statehood should not be downplayed as *sui generis* situations, but rather taken as evidence that the state requirement in international treaties should not be automatically equated with statehood as territorial legal status. The section also explains why the extra-Charter club of non-member states lacks legal authority and does not have any consequences under the law of statehood.

A. UN Members without Statehood

Belarus (Byelorussia) and Ukraine were members of the UN when they were still Soviet republics.[17] Likewise, India and the Philippine Commonwealth were

[14] UN Charter, art 4.2.

[15] ibid, art 27.

[16] Constitution of the United Nations Educational, Scientific and Cultural Organisation, (UNESCO, 16 November 1945), art 2.

[17] Aust (n 7) 18.

member states before independence.[18] At the drafting conference, the delegate of the Philippines even suggested that the term 'nation' should be used instead of 'state' to make sure that the Philippines could join the UN.[19] In the end, it was agreed that the term 'state' would stay and all entities participating at the drafting conferences would be able to join regardless of their statehood status.[20] As original members of the UN, these entities without statehood at the time avoided the admissions procedure through the Security Council and the General Assembly. Their pre-statehood UN membership is often explained as an anomaly of the foundational period of the UN system.[21]

Writing in 1961, Rosalyn Cohen made an argument in favour of distinguishing between the original UN member states and those member states that have joined later. In this view, some original members were considered to be states for the purposes of the Charter as a result of a political compromise, while the statehood requirement was imposed rather strictly in subsequent membership applications.[22] Hans Kelsen similarly argued that Article 4(1) UN Charter uses a statehood yardstick that is different than the one that was applied to the original members, and this is a consequence of a political compromise at the drafting conference.[23] Such arguments rightly acknowledge that joining the UN in its formative period was an eminently political question, but ignore the fact that not even subsequent admissions procedures are purely law-governed, and are also affected by policy concerns.

While it may well be true that some original UN member states without statehood were able to join the Charter in a political compromise package, the legal significance of this practice should not be downplayed. Labelling a situation as being anomalous or *sui generis* means that the situation does not fit within the underlying theory. One should then ask whether something is wrong with the theory rather than stick the *sui generis* label to the cases that challenge it. Belarus and Ukraine, and also India and the Philippines, prove that entities without statehood under general international law have been states for the purposes of UN membership. This could happen because concluding a treaty is a procedural exercise under treaty law. As a result, due to political concerns, even an entity without statehood can sometimes be given the legal capacity to participate in a treaty regime that was in principle meant to be open

[18] Kelsen (n 5) 60.

[19] ibid.

[20] ibid.

[21] Cohen (n 5) 1133. This argument is 'with regard to the claim of original membership, decisions ere taken for the admission of territorial communities whose accurate description at that time fell short of meeting traditional legal criteria. There never was any pretense of adherence, and to treat this as a sui generis case not truly indicative of United Nations practice – where at least there is a formal effort at adherence to the criteria – would seem to be a more realistic appraisal than to suggest that the word "state" is not to be understood in its usual legal sense.'

[22] Cohen (n 5) 1131; Kelsen (n 5) 59–61.

[23] Kelsen (n 5) 61.

only for states. This also means that participation in such treaty regimes should not be taken as evidence of statehood. Indeed, UN membership of Belarus and Ukraine was certainly no evidence of their statehood. The statehood status of these two UN members was an outcome of a completely different political and legal process culminating in the Minsk Agreement and the Alma Ata Protocol, and the thus related dissolution of the Soviet Union.[24]

Moreover, it is questionable whether the law of statehood really is behind the fact that territorial entities with contested legal statuses do not pass the UN admissions procedures. One can only ask how different this practice would have been had the UN admission procedure stayed an exclusive prerogative of the UN General Assembly, thus avoiding the veto obstacle in the UN Security Council. Membership of some UN specialised agencies is also textually limited to states, but because the admission procedures do not travel through any 'veto powered' organs, membership has been in practice extended even to certain contested territorial entities that were (probably) not states in the moment of admission.[25] The same would likely happen in the UN admissions procedures had the drafters avoided the veto power. Can such procedural technicality have consequences for the substantive legal status under the law of statehood? Would Kosovo or Palestine have 'more statehood' today had drafters of the UN Charter made a different choice back in 1945 when they designed the admissions procedures? It would appear to be wrong to subject the statehood status of these entities to certain treaty procedures that were drafted for quite different purposes.

The procedural or administrative nature of UN membership is also reflected in the institutional practice with respect to the Socialist Federal Republic of Yugoslavia (SFRY). In a sense, it was an inverted situation if compared to Belarus and Ukraine. The SFRY was a founding member of the UN.[26] In 1992, legally binding Security Council resolutions affirmed that this state no longer existed and that none of its former republics was the sole successor of this state.[27] The General Assembly, however, failed to expel the member, which no longer had statehood under international law.[28]

[24] The Agreement Establishing the Commonwealth of Independent States (entered into force 30 December 1991) 31 ILM 138 (Minsk Agreement); The Protocol to the Agreement establishing the Commonwealth of Independent States (entered into force 21 December 1991) 31 ILM 147 (Alma-Ata Declaration).

[25] Arbër Fetahu, 'Kosovo's Accession to UN Specialized Agencies: What's at stake after the moratorium?' (*Group for Legal and Political Studies*, 8 October 2021) www.legalpoliticalstudies.org/kosovos-accession-to-un-specialized-agencies-whats-at-stake-after-the-moratorium, accessed 31 October 2022.

[26] 'UN membership' (*Dag Hammarskjold library*) research.un.org/en/unmembers/founders, accessed 7 February 2023.

[27] UNSC Res 757 (30 May 1992) UN Doc S/RES/757; UNSC Res 777 (19 September 1992) UN Doc S/RES/777.

[28] Roland Rich, 'Recognition of States: The Collapse of Yugoslavia and the Soviet Union' (1993) 4 *European Journal of International Law* 36.

For nearly a decade, the SFRY thus continued its UN membership as a historic state.[29]

To complicate the situation further, the Federal Republic of Yugoslavia (FRY), composed of Serbia and Montenegro, claimed continuity with the international personality of the SFRY and was effectively occupying the seat of the SFRY in the UN.[30] Although the claim for continuity was, as a matter of principle, internationally explicitly rejected *de jure*, in international practice it was often tolerated *de facto*.[31] The situation of the SFRY is often interpreted as another anomaly that ended in 2000 when the FRY was finally admitted to the UN as a new state.[32]

Certainly, the example of the SFRY was rather peculiar and politically loaded. But this is yet further evidence to prove that participation of states in international treaty regimes open to states should not be conflated for statehood as territorial legal status. The continued UN membership of the SFRY even when this state no longer existed, ie when its statehood had been extinguished, was possible due to political voting procedures in UN organs. The fact that the General Assembly could not secure enough votes to expel the member whose statehood no longer existed did not have any consequences under the law of statehood. It was simply an internal procedural matter within the UN system.

B. The 'Non-member Observer State' Status

Another issue to be clarified is the status of a non-member observer state in the UN. Just like membership under Article 4 UN Charter, the status of 'non-member observer state' has sometimes also been equated with statehood.[33] This is problematic and the practice of admission of entities to this status may well prove that there is no strict causality between statehood and the 'non-member observer state' status.

Unlike UN membership, the 'non-member observer state' status is not grounded in the UN Charter or any other treaty. It is grounded in a General Assembly resolution, which is not a legally binding instrument.[34] Such status

[29] UNGA Res 55/12 (1 November 2000) A/RES/55/12; the FRY was admitted to the membership of the UN as a new state on 1 November 2000.

[30] Constitution of the Federal Republic of Yugoslavia of 1992, preamble (invoking 'uninterrupted international personality of Yugoslavia').

[31] Aust (n 7) 400.

[32] See n 29 above.

[33] John Cerone, 'Legal Implications of the UN General Assembly Vote to Accord Palestine the Status of Observer State' (2012) 16 *The American Society of International Law* 7, www.asil.org/insights/volume/16/issue/37/legal-implications-un-general-assembly-vote-accord-palestine-status, accessed 3 December 2022.

[34] Stephen M Schwebel, 'The Effect of Resolutions of the U.N. General Assembly on Customary International Law Proceedings of the Annual Meeting' (1979) 73 *American Society of International Law* 301.

is thus a political rather than legal category and there are no legal rules that would regulate the consequences of it.[35] With the admission of Palestine to this political status in 2012, there has been much discussion on the implicit confirmation of Palestine's statehood status due to the 'non-member observer state' label.[36] Besides this being merely a political rather than legal category, historic practice shows that certain entities have been members of this club despite not being states at the time, or when their territorial legal statuses were unclear and unsettled.

Austria became a non-member observer state in 1952.[37] Under the 1945 Agreement on Control Machinery in Austria and the 1946 Second Control Agreement,[38] Austria was under occupation of the Allied authorities and did not have the full attributes of statehood under general international law.[39] It took a decade to settle its legal status with the 1955 Austrian State Treaty.[40] This is when the Second Austrian Republic was created and Austria regained its full international personality.[41] In the period of its status of a non-member observer state, between 1952 and 1955, Austria's legal status had not been settled and it is plausible to argue that it was not a state. This does not mean that it had no international legal capacity. For example, under the Second Control Agreement, Austrian government had treaty-making competence vis-à-vis the four occupation powers but not vis-à-vis other states.[42] Austria's limited international legal capacity at the time suggests that it was not a state in that period.

[35] 'About Permanent Observers' (*United Nations*) www.un.org/en/members/aboutpermobservers.shtml, accessed 17 October 2022.

[36] Weiler (n 13); Akande (n 13); Cerone (n 33); Kai Ambos, 'Palestine, UN Non-Member Observer Status and ICC Jurisdiction' (*EJIL:Talk!*, 6 May 2014) www.ejiltalk.org/palestine-un-non-member-observer-status-and-icc-jurisdiction, accessed 22 November 2022.

[37] See n 35 above.

[38] First Control Agreement (adopted 4 July 1945) 'Abkommen über die Alliierte Kontrolle in Österreich Abkommen zwischen den Regierungen des Vereinigten Königreiches, der Vereinigten Staaten von Amerika, der Union der Sozialistischen Sowjetrepubliken und der Französischen Republik über den Kontrollapparat in Österreich' (*Verfassungen*) www.verfassungen.at/at45-/kontrollabkommen46.htm, accessed 3 December 2022; 'Abkommen zwischen den Regierungen des Vereinigten Königreiches, der Vereinigten Staaten von Amerika, der Union der Sozialistischen Sowjetrepubliken und der Französischen Republik über den Kontrollapparat in Österreich' (*UIBK*) www.uibk.ac.at/zeitgeschichte/zis/library/eisterer.html#dok2, accessed 3 November 2022.

[39] Second Control Agreement (adopted 28 June 1946), art 2 establishing organs for governing Austria under the Allied auspices, art 6 giving the Austrian government the authority to conclude international treaties only vis-à-vis the four administering powers, while the Allied Council had to agree with international agreements concluded with other states). These provisions clearly demonstrate that Austria at the time was an internationally administered entity rather than an independent state.

[40] 'Staatsvertrag betreffend die Wiederherstellung eines unabhängigen und demokratischen Österreich of May 1955, Austrian State Treaty' (*Rechtsinformationsystem*), www.ris.bka.gv.at/GeltendeFassung.wxe?Abfrage=Bundesnormen&Gesetzesnummer=10000265, accessed 14 December 2022, declaring Austria a sovereign, independent and democratic state.

[41] UNGA Res 995 (14 December 1955) UN Doc A/RES/995 (X).

[42] Second Control Agreement.

Bangladesh was accorded the non-member observer state status in 1973 when its legal status had not been finally settled.[43] Pakistan had by then lost its control over East Pakistan (Bangladesh) and the latter was widely, although not universally, recognised as a state.[44] Nevertheless, the clarification of its legal status came only in 1974 when Pakistan agreed to Bangladesh's independence and the remaining states granted recognition.[45] Only then did Bangladesh become a member of the UN.[46]

Austria and Bangladesh were thus non-member observer states in the period when their legal statuses were at least ambiguous and they probably were not states under the law of statehood. The list of former non-member observer states, *inter alia*, includes North Vietnam,[47] South Vietnam[48] and Vietnam,[49] before the legal status of the territory was finally settled and the Socialist Republic of Vietnam (as a whole) was admitted to the membership of the UN in 1977.[50] In some other instances, however, states may simply choose not to become members of the UN but instead participate as non-member states. Membership of the UN is not obligatory. The choice not to become a full member of the UN may be based on political grounds or, indeed, follow other international legal commitments. Until 2002, Switzerland interpreted its commitments under the laws of neutrality as being incompatible with UN membership, but had the status of a non-member state.[51] The Vatican City currently also has the status of a non-member observer state.[52]

This practice shows that the extra-Charter category of 'non-member observer states' has been rather diverse. Some have been there by choice but for others this has been more of a remedial award because they could not be admitted to the membership of the UN due to the more complex voting procedures and the role of the Security Council in this process.[53] Notably, the statehood status of some former and present non-member observer states has been contested and there have even been some entities that did not have statehood when they were non-member observer states.

Although this is not always the case, the 'non-member observer state' status has sometimes been used as a club, into which a group of states by a vote in

[43] Connie McNeely, *Constructing the Nation-State: International Organization and Prescriptive Action* (Praeger 1995) 45.
[44] Aleksandar Pavkovic and Peter Radan, *Creating New States: Theory and Practice of Secession* (Ashgate 2007) 102–04.
[45] Crawford (n 5) 140.
[46] UNGA Res 3203 (17 September 1974) UN Doc A/RES/3203 (XXIX).
[47] McNeely (n 43) 42, 45.
[48] ibid.
[49] ibid.
[50] UNGA Res 32/2 (20 September 1977) UN Doc A/RES/32/2.
[51] Michael M Gunter, 'Switzerland and the United Nations' (1976) 30(1) *International Organization* 129.
[52] See n 35 above.
[53] Mower (n 10) 266–83.

the General Assembly places certain contested territorial entities, with the aim of this being a step toward the final settlement of their legal status.[54] It would be, of course, much more difficult to opt for UN membership in such situations, as the vote would also need to go through the Security Council where veto obstacles exist.[55] It is thus politically more feasible to place a contested entity in the extra-Charter club of 'non-member observer states' and, by including the word 'states' in the name of this club, imply that these entities, in fact, are states. But the practice of admitting to this club certain contested entities that were in all likelihood non-states at the time proves that merely calling an entity a non-member observer *state* does not accord it with statehood in the sense of territorial status.

Significant in this regard is the 2012 General Assembly vote on the admission of Palestine to the status of non-member observer state. Several states clearly detached this General Assembly vote from the law of statehood. Resolution 67/19 specifically mentions in the preamble that Palestine had been previously recognised by 132 member states of the UN,[56] while the Resolution was supported by 138 member states in the General Assembly vote. Yet, it would be too simplistic to conclude that Palestine thus benefited from six additional recognitions. A number of states had explicitly stated that this was not recognition.[57] Switzerland supported the Resolution but its representative stated that '[b]ilateral recognition … depended on future negotiations'.[58] The representative of Belgium made a similar sentence: 'The resolution was not recognition of a State in full terms.'[59] The representative of Denmark noted that the vote in favour of the Resolution 'was not formal bilateral recognition of a sovereign Palestinian State'.[60] And the representative of New Zealand 'that the question of recognition of a Palestinian State was a separate issue'.[61] The representative of Finland made a slightly broader statement and stressed that 'the Assembly's vote did not entail a formal recognition of a Palestinian State. Finland's national position on the matter would be considered at a later date.'[62]

These statements have consequences not only for Palestine but also broadly for international legal doctrine pertaining to the relationship between the voting procedures in international organisations and substantive questions of the law of statehood. The statements made in the context of Resolution 67/19 suggest

[54] Martin Wählisch, 'Beyond a Seat in the United Nations: Palestine's U.N. Membership and International Law' (2012) 53 *Harvard International Law Journal* 226, arguing that 'throughout the course of U.N. practice … several entities were addressed … [as non-member states] as to disregard their debated legal quality of statehood'.
[55] UN Charter, art 4.2.
[56] UNGA Res 67/19 (4 December 2012) UN Doc A/RES/67/19, preamble.
[57] UNGA Res 11317 (29 November 2012) UN Doc A/RES/11317.
[58] ibid.
[59] ibid.
[60] ibid.
[61] ibid.
[62] ibid.

that the term 'state' in international legal instruments *can* be used for purely procedural purposes and does not necessarily interfere with the substantive question of statehood as territorial legal status.[63] Indeed, several states made it clear that they supported the vote, ie the General Assembly procedure, in which the 'non-member observer state' status was accorded to a certain entity, while making it clear that this was not an act of recognition or confirmation of the international legal status of a state.

This section has shown that the treaty-based status of UN member states has been extended to some non-states in the institutional practice of the organisation. Likewise, the non-treaty-based political status of non-member states has also been extended to non-states through the voting procedures in the UN General Assembly. These examples suggest that the term 'state' in the UN Charter and in the extra-Charter category of 'non-member states' should not be equated with statehood as territorial legal status. Nevertheless, UN membership and some other procedures within the UN system may have far-reaching effects for an entity's treaty-making capacity where treaties are open generically to states. The chapter will now argue that with regard to multilateral treaties generically open to 'any state' or 'all states,' and in the absence of any additional definition of the term 'state' in that treaty, a purely functional or procedural definition has been applied in practice. Such a definition should not be conflated with statehood as territorial legal status. But what are the limits and conceptual problems of this approach?

III. THE STATE REQUIREMENT IN INTERNATIONAL TREATIES: THE PROCEDURAL APPROACH

According to the Vienna Convention on the Law of Treaties (VCLT), a treaty is a written agreement between states.[64] However, customary rules on treaty law allow for some flexibility when it comes to the identity of treaty parties. International organisations have treaty-making capacity for their functional purposes vis-à-vis states and other international organisations.[65] When referring to their (future) parties, some treaty texts adopt more inclusive language and refer to, for example, high contracting parties.[66] An example is the European Convention on Human Rights (ECHR). The 'high contracting

[63] UNGA Res 67/19 (4 December 2012) UN Doc A/RES/67/19.

[64] Vienna Convention on the Law of Treaties of 1969 (adopted 23 May 1969, entered into force 27 January 1980) 1155 UNTS 332 (VCLT), art 2.1.

[65] VCLT, art 2.1; Jose Alvarez, *International Organizations as Law-Makers* (OUP 2006); Corten Olivier and Klein Pierre, 'Are Agreements between States and Non-State Entities Rooted in the International Legal Order?' in Enzo Cannizzaro (ed), *The Law of Treaties Beyond the Vienna Convention* (OUP 2011) 3.

[66] European Convention on Human Rights of 1953 (adopted 4 November 1950, entry into force 3 September 1953) ETS 5 (ECHR).

parties'[67] phrasing is inclusive enough to accommodate the EU should it decide to join the Convention pursuant to Article 6(2) of the Treaty on European Union (TEU).[68]

An interesting example is also Article XII of the World Trade Organization (WTO) Marrakesh Agreement which provides that: 'Any State or separate customs territory possessing full autonomy in the conduct of its external commercial relations … may accede to this Agreement.'[69] As discussed in the preceding chapters of this book, the expansion to separate customs territories is functionally justified given the nature of the WTO and the fact that in some circumstances entities other than states may constitute self-contained customs regimes. The more inclusive phrasing allowed the EU, Chinese Taipei, Hong Kong and Macao to become parties to the Marrakesh Agreement despite not being states.[70]

The question arises of what happens when a treaty only very generically provides that it is open to a 'states party', 'any state', 'all states' or similar. Does it first need to be decided whether an entity is a state under the law of statehood, and if so, who ought to decide that, and how should it be done? Likewise, if an entity becomes party to a treaty open only to states, does this implicitly confirm or even create its statehood?

Sometimes the object and purpose of a treaty would indeed be state creation and in such instances the treaty will have consequences under the law of statehood.[71] In other instances, a General Assembly or Security Council's resolution may seek to prevent an entity from becoming a state.[72] Such resolutions

[67] ECHR, art 1.

[68] Consolidated Version of the Treaty on European Union (adopted 13 December 2007, entered into force 1 December 2009) OJ C 115/01 (TEU), art 6.2.

[69] Agreement Establishing the World Trade Organization (adopted 15 April 1994, entered into force 1 January 1995) 1867 UNTS 154 (Marrakesh Agreement).

[70] Marrakesh Agreement, art 12.

[71] The Lateran Treaty of 1929 (entered into force 7 June 1929) 130 BFSP 791. Statute of the Council of Europe (adopted 5 May 1949, entered into force 2 August 1949) CETS 001, art 3 which *inter alia* provides: 'Italy recognizes the full ownership, exclusive dominion, and sovereign authority and jurisdiction of the Holy See over the Vatican as at present constituted, together with all its appurtenances and endowments, thus creating the Vatican City, for the special purposes and under the conditions hereinafter referred to. The boundaries of the said City are set forth in the map called Annex I of the present Treaty, of which it is forms an integral part'; Austrian State Treaty, art 1, providing, 'Die Alliierten und Assoziierten Mächte anerkennen, daß Österreich als ein souveräner, unabhängiger und demokratischer Staat wiederhergestellt ist' [author's own translation: The Allied and Associated Powers recognise that Austria is reestablished as a sovereign, independent and democratic state].

[72] See the practice of UN organs in response to declarations of independence in Northern Cyprus, Southern Rhodesia and the South African Homelands: UNSC Res 541 (18 November 1983) S/RES/541; UNGA Res 1747 (27 June 1962) UN Doc A/RES/1747 (XVI); UNSC Res 202 (6 May 1965) S/RES/202; UNGA Res 2022 (5 November 1965) UN Doc A/RES/2022 (XX); UNGA Res 2024 (11 November 1965) UN Doc A/RES 2024 (XX); UNSC Res 216 (12 November 1965) UN Doc S/RES 216; UNSC Res 217 (20 November 1965) S/RES/217; UNSC Res 277 (18 March 1970) S/RES/277; UNGA Res 2671F (8 December 1970) UN Doc A/RES/2671F (XXV); UNGA Res 2775 (29 November 1971) UN Doc A/RES/2775 (XXV); UNGA Res 31/6A (26 October 1976) UN Doc A/RES/31/6A; UNGA Res 402 (22 December 1976) UN Doc A/RES 402; UNGA Res 407 (25 May 1977) UN Doc

can also have certain consequences under the law of statehood. But this type of international instrument is specifically aimed at regulating the question of territorial legal status. Where a treaty drafted for quite different purposes generically specifies it is open for ratification by 'all states' or 'any state,' such a treaty does not intend to regulate statehood. The term 'state' indicates the identity of the treaty's (future) parties, but is not there to have either state-creating or state-denying effects.

This section focuses on international practice to determine how the 'all states' or 'any state' formulation in multilateral treaties is defined in practice. In practice, such definitional problems mostly arise where a contested territorial entity seeks to accede to a treaty that is generically open to 'all states'. Of central importance is the practice of UN Secretary-General in his role as Depository of Multilateral Treaties. How should the Secretary-General or other international institutional organ (eg an international court) decide which entity is a state where the underlying treaty allows accession to 'any state' or 'all states'? This section argues that a functional or even procedural approach is taken in practice. In other words, the substantive statehood question is not dealt with incidentally when it is considered whether an entity can accede to a treaty open to 'all states'.

A. The 'Vienna Formula'

While the VCLT is open to states for ratification,[73] Article 81 of the VCLT defines the term 'state' for these purposes. It opens the Convention for signature to 'all States Members of the United Nations or of any of the specialised agencies or of the International Atomic Energy Agency or parties to the Statute of the International Court of Justice, and by any other State invited by the General Assembly of the United Nations to become a party to the Convention'.[74] Notably, Article 81 VCLT, also called the 'Vienna formula', does not open the Convention to any entity that meets the Montevideo criteria or any other so-called objective criteria for statehood or statehood requirements under general international law.[75] It adopts a purely functional approach for the purposes of treaty participation and without any discussion about the entity's legal status under the law of statehood.

Article 81 VCLT applies to the VCLT itself – it is not a general rule of treaty law. However, this Vienna formula has been in practice attached also to many

A/RES/407; UNGA Res 32/105 (14 Dec 1977) UN Doc A/RES 32/105; UNGA Res 34/93G (12 December 1979) UN Doc A/RES/34/93G; UNGA Res 37/43 (3 December 1982) UN Doc A/RES/37/43; UNGA Res 37/69A (9 December 1982) UN Doc A/RES/37/69A.

[73] VCLT, art 83.

[74] VCLT, art 81.

[75] Montevideo Convention on the Rights and Duties of States of 1933 (adopted 26 December 1933, entered into force 26 December 1934) 165 LNTS 19 (Montevideo Convention), art 1.

other treaties to resolve the 'state dilemma' where the treaty participation is limited to states. In effect, whenever an international treaty contains the Vienna formula, membership of a relevant international body makes it a state for the functional or procedural purposes of that particular treaty. Highly instructive is the Summary of Practice of the [UN] Secretary-General as Depository of Multilateral Treaties:

> A difficulty has occurred as to possible participation in treaties when entities which appeared otherwise to be States could not be admitted to the United Nations, nor become Parties to the Statute of the International Court of Justice owing to the opposition, for political reasons, of a permanent member of the Security Council. Since that difficulty did not arise as concerns membership in the specialized agencies where there is no 'veto' procedure, a number of those States became members of specialized agencies, and as such were in essence recognised as States by the international community. Accordingly, and in order to allow for as wide a participation as possible, a number of conventions then provided that they were also open for participation to States members of specialized agencies … This type of entry-into-force clause was called the 'Vienna formula.'[76]

The Summary of Practice then specifies that whenever a treaty contains the Vienna formula or a similar formulation, the UN Secretary-General has no difficulty accepting that an entity can be considered a state for these purposes.[77] The effect of the Vienna formula is precisely that it defines the term 'state' for the procedural purposes of participation in a treaty regime and does so without any prejudice toward the entity's territorial legal status. This is not to say that either Article 81 or even the VCLT as a whole are necessarily applicable. It only means that the Vienna formula is functionally used in other treaties and beyond its Article 81 effects *sensu stricto*.

B. The Vienna Formula Extended

It has been argued that many other treaties have adopted wording similar to Article 81 VCLT and functionally defined a state for the purposes of that treaty by institutional membership.[78] But some treaties are silent on this matter and do not textually contain such a definitional phrasing. Even in such circumstances, the Vienna formula has been applied in practice. The actions of the UN Secretary-General as Depositary of Multilateral Treaties are also instructive in this regard.

If Entity A wishes to accede to a certain treaty open to states, but the treaty text does not define what a state is for these purposes, how should the

[76] Summary of Practice of the Secretary-General as Depositary of Multilateral Treaties (1999) UN Doc ST/LEG/7/Rev.l, (Summary of Practice), para 79.

[77] ibid, para 80.

[78] VCLT, art 81.

Secretary-General decide whether Entity A is a state and can accede to that treaty? Should the Secretary-General examine the Montevideo criteria, or perhaps look at how many treaty parties have recognised that entity as a state? This would appear to be wrong. If the legal status of Entity A is contested, the UN Secretary-General's determination that Entity A was a state for the purposes of joining a multilateral treaty could effectively create *State* A if his decision were based on any analysis under the law of statehood (eg the Montevideo criteria, recognitions). But state creation by the UN Secretary-General would be an act *ultra vires*.

This problem is indeed acknowledged in the Summary of Practice:

> [T]here are certain areas in the world whose status is not clear … [The Secretary General] would not wish to determine, on his own initiative, the highly political and controversial question of whether or not the areas whose status was unclear were States. Such a determination, he believed, would fall outside his competence.[79]

Our premise should thus be that when deciding whether Entity A is a state for the purposes of its treaty-making capacity, the Secretary-General does not make any determinations under the law of statehood, but under the procedural rules that govern treaty accession.

The UN Secretary-General's practice shows that even where a treaty does not explicitly contain the Vienna formula, he would apply either the proclamations of the UN General Assembly or functionally the Vienna formula to determine whether or not an entity is a state for the purposes of becoming a party to that particular treaty:

> when the 'any State' or 'all States' formula was adopted [in an international treaty], he [UN Secretary-General] would be able to implement it only if the General Assembly provided him with the complete list of the States coming within the formula, other than those falling within the 'Vienna formula,' i.e. States that are Members of the United Nations or members of the specialized agencies, or Parties to the Statute of the International Court of Justice.[80]

In this regards, Dapo Akande observes that 'in the past, the … [Secretary General] has been prepared to accept membership of a UN specialised agency as indicating that an entity is a State since the membership of such agencies is similar to membership of the UN General Assembly'.[81] In practice, this means that membership of the UN or any of the UN specialised agencies brings an entity functionally within the Vienna formula for the purpose of participation in multilateral treaties generically open to states. But this is a procedural yardstick. The Vienna formula is not there to create or recognise a state, or confirm an entity's statehood.

[79] Summary of Practice, para 81.
[80] ibid.
[81] Summary of Practice, para 81; Akande (n 13); Cf also n 129 below.

i. The State of Palestine and the ICC

Highly relevant in this context is Palestine's accession to the Statute of the International Criminal Court (ICC Statute) and Palestine's subsequent 'reference of the Situation in the State of Palestine to the Prosecutor pursuant to articles 13(a) and 14 of the Statute'.[82] The ICC Statute is open to states and uses the depository system of the UN Secretary-General.[83] At the same time, Palestine is a contested entity the legal status of which is ambiguous, and is probably not a state.[84] Difficult doctrinal questions were raised in this situation. Can Palestine even join the ICC Statute if it is not necessarily a state? Can it trigger the treaty mechanisms under the ICC Statute? Should the ICC first clarify Palestine's legal status or perhaps refrain from exercising its jurisdiction since it is not within the ICC's functional mandate to rule on the questions of statehood?

On receiving Palestine's accession instruments for the ICC Statute, the UN Secretary-General stated:

> Many reporters have been asking about the documents transmitted by the Permanent Observer of Palestine to the United Nations relating to the accession of Palestine to 16 multilateral treaties in respect of which the Secretary-General is the depository, including the Rome Statute of the International Criminal Court. In conformity with the relevant international rules and his practice as a depositary, the Secretary-General has ascertained that the instruments received were in due and proper form before accepting them for deposit, and has informed all States concerned accordingly through the circulation of depositary notifications … This is an administrative function performed by the Secretariat as part of the Secretary-General's responsibilities as depositary for these treaties. It is important to emphasize that it is for States to make their own determination with respect to any legal issues raised by instruments circulated by the Secretary-General.[85]

This means that Palestine was considered a state party to the ICC Statute, although the UN Secretary-General did not specify whether this was due to the effects of the Vienna formula or General Assembly Resolution 67/19. The UN Secretary-General also clearly detached this *administrative* function from any substantive legal issues governing the legal status of Palestine. It was made clear that this was not a decision on statehood.

[82] *Situation in the State of Palestine* (*Decision on the 'Prosecution request pursuant to article 19(3) for a ruling on the Court's territorial jurisdiction in Palestine'*) ICC-01/18 (5 February 2021) (Situation in Palestine), para 3.

[83] Rome Statute of the International Criminal Court (adopted 17 June 1998, entered into force 1 July 2002) 2187 UNTS 38544 (Rome Statute), art 125.3.

[84] James Crawford, 'The Creation of the State of Palestine: Too Much Too Soon?' (1990) 1 *European Journal of International Law* 307.

[85] 'Note to correspondents – Accession of Palestine to multilateral treaties', United Nations Secretary-General Statement' (*United Nations*, 7 January 2015) www.un.org/sg/en/content/sg/note-correspondents/2015-01-07/note-correspondents-accession-palestine-multilateral, accessed 21 March 2021.

The question of Palestine's participation in the ICC Statute and its mechanisms was also addressed by the ICC pre-Trial Chamber which subscribed itself to the theory of separation of the term 'state party' from the question of statehood. Indeed, the Chamber explicitly stated that determining whether Palestine is a state party for the purposes of the ICC Statute does not 'require a determination as to whether that entity fulfils the prerequisites of statehood under general international law'.[86] In other words, the state requirement to participate in the legal regime established by the ICC Statute is not measured with the yardstick of the law of statehood.

Moreover, the ICC Statute is one of those treaties that do not contain an explicit Vienna formula definition of the term 'state'. In that respect, the pre-Trial Chamber observed:

> With respect to the Rome Statute, article 125(3) of the Statute provides that the 'Statute shall be open to accession by all States' and neither this provision nor any other provision in the Court's legal texts imposes additional criteria on, or otherwise qualifies, the accession to the Statute.[87]

As the ICC Statute follows the depository system through the UN Secretary-General,[88] the Chamber here referred to the Summary of Practice which provides the central importance of 'unequivocal indications from the [United Nations General] Assembly that it considers a particular entity to be a State even though it does not fall within the "Vienna formula" and [s]uch indications are to be found in [United Nations] General Assembly resolutions'.[89] The Chamber then referred to the General Assembly resolution 67/19 from 2012 by which Palestine was granted the non-member observer state status in the United Nations.[90] For the Chamber, this was an indication that Palestine can be considered a state *for the purposes of the ICC Statute.*

The Chamber clearly subscribed to the view that Palestine can be a state for the procedural purposes of the ICC Statute, but this has nothing to do with the substantive law of statehood. There are three problems in the Chamber's reasoning, however: (i) the Chamber may have overstated the relevance of General Assembly Resolution 67/19; (ii) the Chamber was probably wrong when it indicated that Palestine did not fall within the Vienna formula as it was a member of UNESCO, a specialised UN agency, before it was admitted to the informal club of non-member observer states by the General Assembly Resolution 67/19; (iii) despite defining the concept of state party to the ICC Statute in purely procedural treaty law terms, the Chamber subsequently

[86] *Decision on the 'Prosecution request pursuant to article 19(3) for a ruling on the Court's territorial jurisdiction in Palestine'*, Pre-Trial Chamber I, Decision, ICC-01/18-143 (5 February 2021), (*Palestine Jurisdiction*), para 93.

[87] ibid, para 97.

[88] Rome Statute, art 125.3.

[89] Summary of Practice, para 83, referred to by the ICC in *Palestine Jurisdiction*, para 96.

[90] *Palestine Jurisdiction*, para 98.

nevertheless drew some substantive territorial consequences external to the ICC Statute.

ii. The (ir)relevance of Resolution 67/19

The Chamber in its reasoning relied on the Summary of Practice of the UN Secretary-General and on certain pronouncements of the UN General Assembly with regard to the status of Palestine, and found Resolution 67/19 to be highly significant in that regard and indicative of the fact that the UN General Assembly considers Palestine a state.[91] This reasoning is not without difficulty.

As explained above, the 'non-member observer state' status is not a legally grounded category. It is a politically created extra-Charter club whose membership has included entities that were not necessarily states at the time of their membership.[92] Practice thus shows that granting an entity the non-member observer state status does not mean that this entity is a state. The *non-member observer state* status is a phrasing that needs to be read as a whole. It is a term of art as a whole phrasing and the word 'state' in it should not be read in isolation. This also follows from the statements of a number of states that were otherwise supportive of Resolution 67/19, but clarified that the non-member state status of Palestine in the UN General Assembly should not be understood as recognition or confirmation of its state status under general international law.[93]

It is for these reasons at least debatable whether Resolution 67/19 indeed represents an 'unequivocal indication … from the Assembly that it considers a particular entity to be a State',[94] as the ICC pre-Trial Chamber recalled the Summary of Practice. Rather, Resolution 67/19 admitted Palestine to the politically created extra-Charter club of non-member observer states – nothing more and nothing less.

iii. UNESCO Membership as Palestine's Access to the Vienna Formula

Palestine became a member of UNESCO in 2011,[95] ie prior to its admission to the informal club of non-member observer states in the UN. The admission procedure to UNESCO is governed by Article II of the UNESCO Constitution which provides that UN member states have the right to UNESCO membership, while 'states not members of the … [UN] may be admitted to membership

[91] *Palestine Jurisdiction*, para 98.
[92] See section II.B.
[93] UNGA Res 67/19 (4 Dec 2012) UN Doc A/RES/67/19.
[94] Summary of Practice, para 83; *Palestine Jurisdiction*, para 96.
[95] 'UNESCO votes to admit Palestine as full member' (*United Nations*, 31 October 2011), news.un.org/en/story/2011/10/393562, accessed 3 December 2021.

of … [UNESCO], upon recommendation of the Executive Board, by a two-thirds majority vote of the General Conference'.[96] It is also significant that the rules further specify that '[t]erritories or groups of territories which are not responsible for the conduct of their international relations may be admitted as Associate Members'.[97]

The admission rules thus establish a difference between states – which may be members or non-members of the UN – and certain other territories. While the former can be full members, the latter can only be associate members. Palestine joined UNESCO in 2011 as a *state* not member of the UN.[98] As UN members, Belarus and Ukraine became UNESCO members in 1954, nearly 38 years before achieving statehood.[99] Austria became a UNESCO member in 1948 when it was under allied occupation and some six years before the Austrian State Treaty recreated Austria as an independent state.[100]

This practice also suggests that entities without statehood have become members of UNESCO, not as territories but as *states* under Article II of the UNESCO Constitution. Since this application is not subjected to any veto obstacles in the admission procedure, but to a two-thirds majority of the existing UNESCO membership, a contested territorial entity can politically much more easily 'become' a state for the purposes of the UNESCO Constitution than for the purposes of the UN Charter. But this is not about statehood. UNESCO is not an organisation that creates states and the procedural requirement of a two-thirds majority to admit new members should not be seen as the threshold of constitutive recognition.

In the case of Palestine, the two-thirds majority in the UNESCO General Conference gave Palestine access to the Vienna formula which has been used in practice even with respect to those multilateral treaties that do not explicitly contain it.[101] Arguably, the pre-Trial Chamber of the ICC would have a clearer legal argument if it took the UNESCO membership rather than the Resolution 67/19 route to explain the legal status of Palestine as a party to the ICC Statute. The former makes it a state for the purposes of treaty-making capacity where treaties are generically open to states, while the latter is an informal political label that does not affirm any particular international legal status.[102]

While the legal basis for Palestine's legal capacity to accede the ICC Statute remains debatable, the Chamber's reasoning is highly significant in that it detaches the state requirement to join the treaty from the statehood requirements under general international law. It is questionable, however, whether

[96] UNESCO Constitution, art 2.

[97] ibid.

[98] 'UNESCO votes to admit Palestine as full member' (n 95).

[99] 'Member States' (*UNESCO*) en.unesco.org/countries/member-states, accessed 18 October 2022.

[100] ibid.

[101] 'UNESCO votes to admit Palestine as full member' (n 95); VCLT, art 81.

[102] UNGA Res 67/19 (4 December 2012) UN Doc A/RES/67/19; 'UNESCO votes to admit Palestine as full member' (n 95); VCLT, art 81.

the Chamber subscribed to this distinction consistently throughout its reasoning. Statehood is indeed closely linked with territorialism.[103] But when it is decided that an entity is a state for the purposes of treaty participation, can it also be assumed that this *state* party to the relevant treaty also has a territory? Is this not a conflation of treaty procedures with the substantive questions of territorial legal status?

iv. The Territory of the State of Palestine or of the State Party Palestine?

As explained above, Palestine made a reference under Articles 13(a) and 14 of the ICC Statute.[104] Article 13(a) is subjected to certain preconditions for the exercise of the ICC's jurisdiction which are regulated in Article 12. This Article, *inter alia*, provides:

> In the case of article 13, paragraph (a) or (c), the Court may exercise its jurisdiction if one or more of the following States are Parties to this Statute or have accepted the jurisdiction of the Court in accordance with paragraph 3:
>
> (a) The State on the territory of which the conduct in question occurred or, if the crime was committed on board a vessel or aircraft, the State of registration of that vessel or aircraft.[105]

Once accepted that Palestine was a state party to the ICC Statute, the question appeared of whether this *state party* to the ICC necessarily has a territory, and where this territory is spatially located for the purposes of Article 12(a) ICC Statute. The underlying question here was whether the concept of 'state party' to the ICC Statute automatically comes together with a defined spatial area. The question is especially relevant in light of the Chamber's position that the term 'state' in the ICC Statute is explicitly detached from any legal meaning under the law of statehood.[106]

Central for the pre-Trial Chamber's reasoning was the applicability of the right of self-determination to the Palestinian people in the Occupied Palestinian Territory.[107] While the applicability of the right of self-determination of the Palestinian people in these territories is beyond dispute and has indeed been affirmed in a range of international fora,[108] it is at least debatable whether the pre-Trial Chamber sufficiently substantiated the legal link between the

[103] See ch 3, section II.A.

[104] 'Information for victims, State of Palestine' (*ICC*) www.icc-cpi.int/victims/state-palestine, accessed 30 October 2022.

[105] Rome Statute, art 12.

[106] Malcolm N Shaw, 'In the Matter of the Jurisdiction of the International Criminal Court with regard to the Declaration of the Palestinian Authority, Supplementary Opinion' (*ICC*, 18 October 2010) www.icc-cpi.int/sites/default/files/NR/rdonlyres/D3C77FA6-9DEE-45B1-ACC0-B41706BB41E5/282851/OTP2010000035449SupplementaryOpinionMalcolmShaw.pdf, accessed 13 November 2022.

[107] *Palestine Jurisdiction*, paras 119–22.

[108] ibid, para 121.

applicability of the right of self-determination and defining the territory of this *state party to the ICC Statute*. The Chamber reasoned:

> The Chamber considers that, in light of the broad remit of the Appeals Chamber's determination, it must also ensure that its interpretation of article 12(2)(a) of the Statute … is consistent with internationally recognised human rights. More specifically, the Chamber is of the view that the aforementioned territorial parameters of the Prosecutor's investigation pursuant to articles 13(a), 14 and 53(1) of the Statute implicate the right to self-determination. Accordingly, it is the view of the Chamber that the above conclusion – namely that the Court's territorial jurisdiction in the Situation in Palestine extends to the territories occupied by Israel since 1967 on the basis of the relevant indications arising from Palestine's accession to the Statute – is consistent with the right to self-determination.[109]

The pre-Trial Chamber might have taken too far the provisions in the ICC Statute that require interpretation consistent with international human right law. The question to be answered was not whether the right of self-determination applied to the Palestinian people, but whether Palestine – state party to the ICC Statute – had a territory and, if so, within which spatial area; ie what is Palestine's geographic scope? The right of self-determination applies to peoples, not to states or 'states party' to international treaties, as stated in the International Covenant on Civil and Political Rights (ICCPR), and the International Covenant on Economic, Social and Cultural Rights (ICESCR).[110] And the right of self-determination does not automatically lead to a certain status under the law of statehood or create a self-executing territorial entitlement.[111] The pre-Trial Chamber thus effectively said: Palestine is a state party to the ICC Statute, the Occupied Palestinian Territory is a defined territory where self-determination is applicable, but we do not need to decide whether Palestine has statehood. It appears that the pre-Trial Chamber tried to eat the cake and have it too.

This problem was aptly identified by Judge Kovács in his Partly Dissenting Opinion:

> The real and persisting problem in answering the question concerning the geographical scope of the Court's jurisdiction and the Prosecutor's investigation is linked to the fact that, currently, there are no precise settled borders either at the bilateral Israeli-Palestinian level or at any multilateral level. Instead, UN Resolutions merely allude to the necessity of engaging in bilateral negotiations on the issue of borders, using varying formulas of the pre-1967 borders. These formulas are similar but not

[109] ibid, para 123.

[110] The International Covenant on Civil and Political Rights (adopted 16 December 1966, entered into force 23 March 1976) 999 UNTS 171 (ICCPR), art 1; International Covenant on Economic, Social and Cultural Rights (adopted 16 December 1966, entered into force 3 January 1976) 1993 UNTS 3 (ICESCR).

[111] Robert McCorquodale, 'Self-Determination: A Human Rights Approach' (1994) 43(4) *International and Comparative Law Quarterly* 857.

identical as the emphasis placed on the 1967 borders in each of them is far from being the same.[112]

Indeed, the right of self-determination does not automatically translate into the geographical scope of the State of Palestine and thus the ICC's spatial jurisdiction. As argued in the previous chapter, self-determination is applied territorially within territorial units.[113] Such units constitute self-determination units which do have a degree of international legal capacity. It has also been argued earlier in this book that territory is not a natural feature – it is a politically delimited spatial area to which certain legal consequences are attached.[114] The problem of Palestine is that the political process has never confined the spatial area and thus defined the territory. The pre-Trial Chamber did not convincingly explain why Palestine, here understood as state party to the ICC Statute, geographically overlaps with the Occupied Palestinian Territory. The right of self-determination unto itself does not define the territory of a self-determination unit. The creation and delimitation of a territory is a political process with legal consequences, which,[115] in the case of Palestine, has never been completed.[116]

The question of Palestine points to a deeper conceptual problem of whether and/or for which purposes the procedural category of a 'state' in the context of international legal procedures necessarily overlaps with statehood as substantive legal status of a territory, and how does one identify the territory where the treaty law concept of 'state party' does not overlap with the territorial status of statehood under general international law. The status of a 'state party' to a treaty does not necessarily imply a spatial or geographic dimension of that entity and its legal status.

It appears that something is missing in the puzzle where the pre-Trial Chamber establishes that Palestine is a state party to the ICC Statute and that this has nothing to do with the law of statehood, and then concludes that the territory of this *state party* is in the geographic area where the right of self-determination applies to the Palestinians. There is a sense that the attributes of statehood are nevertheless silently in the background where the pre-Trial Chamber refers to the right of self-determination in the territory of this state party to the ICC Statute. While the pre-Trial Chamber avoided the term 'statehood', it appears that it read the attributes of statehood into the term 'self-determination'. While the right of self-determination is applicable

[112] *Situation in Palestine*, Partly Dissenting Opinion of Judge Péter Kovács, ICC-01/18-143-Anx 1, para 245.

[113] Chapter 4, section IV.B.ii.

[114] Chapter 2, section III.

[115] Jure Vidmar, 'Democratic Statehood in International Law' (*EJIL:Talk!*, 6 August 2013) www.ejiltalk.org/democratic-statehood-in-international-law, accessed 5 January 2023.

[116] Yael Ronen, 'Israel, Palestine and the ICC – Territory Uncharted but not Unknown' (2014) 12(1) *Journal of International Criminal Justice* 7.

to the Palestinian people, the problem is that the political process has never determined the spatial area and the territorial status of the State of Palestine. Palestine may be a state in the sense of the Vienna formula, but this is not a statehood formula under general international law.

C. A Further Extension of the Vienna Formula?

It has been argued that the Vienna formula is in practice stretched even to those treaties that do not explicitly contain it.[117] The conclusion thus far is that the state definition for these purposes is not substantive but procedural in nature. The UN Secretary-General in his capacity as depository of multilateral treaties cannot and does not consider the statehood requirements, be this the Montevideo criteria or any additional requirements.[118] The UN Secretary-General would indeed act *ultra vires* if he made pronouncements on whether an entity has statehood. As Summary Practice suggests, the Secretary-General uses the procedural yardstick whereby membership of the UN or its specialised agencies procedurally define a state for these purposes. But how far can one extend this practice? Does the Vienna formula only apply where an entity wishes to become a party to a treaty, or also where it wishes to use certain treaty mechanisms that may be available to *states* non-party? Sometimes treaties indeed make such provisions for non-parties and the question is then what defines a 'state non-party' for the purposes of using those procedures.

A prominent example of such a scenario is the case of *Palestine v United States*, which is currently pending before the ICJ.[119] Unlike with the ICC Statute, the procedural question before the ICJ is not whether Palestine can become party to the ICJ Statute as such, but rather its capacity to bring a case as a state non-party.[120] Indeed, Article 35 of the ICJ Statute allows non-UN members and states non-party to the ICJ Statute to participate in the proceedings. In this regard, Article 35(2) ICJ Statute provides: 'The conditions under which the Court shall be open to other states shall, subject to the special provisions contained in treaties in force, be laid down by the Security Council, but in no case shall such conditions place the parties in a position of inequality before the Court.'[121] The Security Council laid down these conditions in its Resolution 9 which, *inter alia*, provides that the ICJ:

> shall be open to a State which is not a party to the Statute of the International Court of Justice, upon the following condition, namely, that such State shall previously

[117] VCLT, art 81; Summary of Practice, para 81.
[118] Summary of Practice, para 80.
[119] *Relocation of the United States Embassy to Jerusalem (Palestine v United States of America)* (Application) General List No 176 (2018) ICJ (*Palestine* Application).
[120] ibid, para 30.
[121] Statute of the International Court of Justice of 1945 (ICJ Statute), art 35.2.

> have deposited with the Registrar of the Court a declaration by which it accepts the jurisdiction of the Court, in accordance with the Charter of the United Nations and with the terms and subject to the conditions of the Statute and Rules of the Court, and undertakes to comply in good faith with the decision or decisions of the Court and to accept all the obligations of a Member of the United Nations under Article 94 of the Charter.[122]

When bringing the case against the United States, Palestine followed this procedure and specified that the jurisdictional basis is the 'compromissory clause' in the Protocol to the Vienna Convention on Diplomatic Relations (VCDR).[123] It remains to be seen whether the ICJ decides to exercise its jurisdiction in this case. There has also been some discussion on whether the case is admissible under the so-called *Monetary Gold* principle.[124] Admissibility aside, it may be difficult for the Court to avoid the question of whether Palestine has standing before the ICJ in the first place.

Article 34(1) of the ICJ Statute provides that '[o]nly states may be parties in cases before the Court'.[125] For some this means that Palestine cannot be a party in the proceedings because it is not a state under general international law,[126] while others have suggested that Palestine ought to be treated as a state for the purposes of the ICJ Statute on the basis of General Assembly Resolution 67/19.[127] An argument has also been advanced that the ICJ's decision that Palestine is a state, even if based purely on the ICJ Statute rather than substantive law of statehood, 'could still be considered a great "victory" by Palestine even if the case does not proceed further'.[128] In the background of this claim is the understanding that the ICJ would confirm that Palestine is a state even if the Court decided the case was inadmissible. Indeed, such a procedural decision of the ICJ would mean that Palestine had successfully brought a case to a Court that only hears disputes between states.

If the ICJ decides to elaborate on whether Palestine can be considered a state for the purposes of Article 34(1) of the ICJ Statute, it is probably illusory to expect that the Court would discuss whether Palestine meets the Montevideo

[122] UNSC Res 9 (15 October 1946) UN Doc S/RES/9.

[123] *Palestine* Application, paras 30 and 31.

[124] Marko Milanovic, 'Palestine Sues the United States in the ICJ re Jerusalem Embassy' (*EJIL Talk!;* 30 September 2018) www.ejiltalk.org/palestine-sues-the-united-states-in-the-icj-re-jerusalem-embassy, accessed 3 October 2022.

[125] ICJ Statute, art 34.1.

[126] 'Press Briefing by Press Secretary Sarah Sanders, Small Business Administrator Linda McMahon, and National Security Advisor' (*The White House*, 3 October 2018) trumpwhitehouse.archives.gov/briefings-statements/press-briefing-press-secretary-sarah-sanders-small-business-administrator-linda-mcmahon-national-security-advisor-100318, accessed 7 January 2022.

[127] Alina Miron, 'Palestine's Application the ICJ, neither Groundless nor Hopeless. A Reply to Marko Milanovic' (*EJIL:Talk!*, 8 October 2018), www.ejiltalk.org/palestines-application-the-icj-neither-groundless-nor-hopeless-a-reply-to-marko-milanovic, accessed 14 September 2022.

[128] Victor Kattan, 'It's Time to Take Palestine v. United States of America Seriously' (*Opinio Juris*, 16 October 2018) opiniojuris.org/2018/10/16/its-time-to-take-palestine-v-united-states-of-america-seriously, accessed 8 June 2022.

criteria or any other statehood requirements, whatever they may be. It would appear to be wrong for the ICJ to make such a far-reaching substantive argument, and essentially decide on quite a different substantive dispute in the procedural context of a ruling on its own jurisdiction. What the ICJ could do is decide on the purely procedural question of whether Palestine is functionally a state for the purposes of the ICJ Statute and in particular its Article 35(2). In this sense, the ICJ could *mutatis mutandis* repeat the ICC's reasoning on the matter and detach the question of Palestine's capacity to participate in international treaty procedures from the question of statehood under general international law.[129] However, what is the yardstick for determining whether Palestine is a state for the purposes of the procedures created by the ICJ Statute? Is this yardstick the Vienna formula, even though this is not a question of acceding to the treaty in question?

In this particular case it may actually be highly significant that Palestine brought the case on the basis of the 'compromissory clause' contained in the Protocol to the VCDR.[130] The ICJ here acts as the dispute settlement mechanism of the VCDR and the Court's jurisdiction is limited to the scope of this treaty. Palestine is a state party to the VCDR.[131] One plausible argument could be that if Palestine is a state for the purposes of the treaty that contains the 'compromissory clause' on the basis of which the case is brought before the Court, Palestine should also be treated as a state for the purposes of the ICJ Statute.

The ICJ could thus rule on its jurisdiction without discussing Palestine's statehood. As the ICJ has done in some other cases, albeit in different contexts, it could draw the separation line between substantive and procedural law.[132] It could say that Palestine's participation in certain international treaty regimes gives it the procedural capacity to bring this case as a state non-party to the ICJ Statute, while such a determination has no substantive implications for Palestine's legal status under general international law. In this case the Vienna formula would not apply directly, as Palestine indeed would not be joining the ICJ Statute. It would be of central importance, however, that Palestine is a *state* party to the treaty that provides for jurisdictional basis of this case. Palestine's capacity to bring a case to the ICJ would thus be a consequence of its now undisputed procedural treaty-making capacity established in the procedures of UN organs. This capacity allows Palestine to make treaties open to states, but does not interfere with its territorial legal status.

Whatever the ICJ decides to do with this question, the basic premise should be that a procedural ruling on the Court's own jurisdiction cannot incidentally

[129] Michail Vagias, 'The Territorial Jurisdiction of the International Criminal Court: Certain Contested Issues' (PhD dissertation, Universiteit Leiden 25 May 2011).

[130] VCLT, art 81; Summary of Practice, para 81.

[131] *Palestine* Application, para 25.

[132] *Jurisdictional Immunities of the State (Germany v Italy: Greece intervening)* (Judgment) General List No 143, (2012) ICJ, para 93.

settle the substantive legal question on Palestine's territorial legal status. The ICJ's decision to hear this case would not create or confirm Palestine's statehood, and the ICJ's decision not to hear this case would not confirm that Palestine does not have statehood. Whether the ICJ decides to exercise its jurisdiction or not is a procedural question, and such a decision cannot have incidental effects on quite different substantive legal questions.

D. The Vienna Formula Beyond the International Treaty Law Effects

It has been established that the Vienna formula operates beyond its effects under Article 81 VCLT. It is functionally applied in the UN system to determine which entity is a state for the purposes of accession to multilateral treaties even where a treaty does not specifically contain it. It remains to be clarified whether the Vienna formula functionally applies more generally and outside of the treaty accession context.

Important clarification on this matter was provided in the 1974 Legal Opinion of the Secretariat of the United Nations prepared by the Office of Legal Affairs that was published by the UN Secretary-General in the United Nations Juridical Yearbook, pursuant to General Assembly Resolution 1814.[133] A set of UN General Assembly resolutions tasked the UN Secretary-General to discharge certain administrative duties with respect of 'all Member States, as well as all other Governments and States'.[134] The UN Under-Secretary-General for Political and Security Council Affairs asked the Office of Legal Affairs how the notion 'all other states' ought to be interpreted,[135] ie how should the UN Secretary-General decide which entities are states when he discharges his administrative functions on the General Assembly's request.

It was particularly discussed whether the Secretary-General should use the same yardstick to determine 'all other states' that he uses in the context of its treaty depository function, ie the Vienna formula.[136] The answer was affirmative and the Vienna formula was functionally applied even though this particular matter was not concerned with treaty law in general or treaty accession in particular. The Office of Legal Affairs reasoned:

> we wish to confirm your views concerning the current practice of the Secretariat in interpreting an 'all States' formula … While this understanding was adopted in the context of the depositary practice of the Secretary-General, it must also be taken as providing the necessary guidance in other instances where the Secretary-General has to interpret an 'all States' formula.

[133] United Nations Juridical Yearbook (1974) UN Doc ST/LEG/Ser.C/12, paras 157–59.
[134] ibid, para 157.
[135] ibid.
[136] ibid, para 158.

> The 'practice of the General Assembly' [with respect to the 'all states formula'] … is to be found in unequivocal indications from the Assembly that it considers a particular entity to be a State. Such indications, at the last session, are to be found in resolutions 3067 (XXVIII) and 3104 (XXVIII), in which the General Assembly invited to two United Nations Conferences, in addition to States at this present time coming within the long-established 'Vienna formula', the 'Democratic Republic of Viet-Nam,' which is expressly designated in those resolutions as a 'State.'
>
> In view of the foregoing, the reference in resolution 3183 (XXVIII) to 'all States' is to be understood as referring to States Members of the United Nations or members of the specialized agencies or the International Atomic Energy Agency and States parties to the Statute of the International Court of Justice and also to the Democratic Republic of Vietnam.[137]

The Vienna formula was thus functionally applied as the procedural yardstick to decide which entities are states for the purposes of the UN Secretary-General's administrative function. The following observations are made in this regard. First, the Vienna formula was functionally applied not only outside of its strict Article 81 VCLT effects, but also outside of treaty law altogether where it had to be decided which entity will be treated as a state for procedural or administrative purposes in the practice of UN organs. Second, there was no discussion of the Montevideo criteria or any other requirements under the law of statehood to determine which entity is a state for these purposes of the Secretary-General's administrative functions. Third, there are two possible points of entry into the procedural state definition: the Vienna formula and a specific pronouncement of the UN General Assembly that labels an entity a state for a specific administrative purpose. These are clearly two separate and self-standing points of entry and are not cumulative requirements.[138] Highly instructive in this regard is also General Assembly Resolution 3067 which, *inter alia*, tasks:

> the Secretary-General to invite, in full compliance with General Assembly resolution 2758 (XXVI) of 25 October 1971, States Members of the United Nations or members of specialized agencies or the International Atomic Energy Agency and States parties to the Statute of the International Court of Justice *as well as the following States to participate in the Conference*: Republic of Guinea-Bissau and Democratic Republic of Viet-Nam; …[139]

The phrasing very closely follows Article 81 VCLT and then specifically provides that two territorial entities should fall within the 'all states' phrasing

[137] ibid, para 158.

[138] 'Member States' (n 99). This further confirms that the ICC could have taken Palestine's UNESCO membership as a point of entry into the Vienna formula. The Resolution 67/19 route, taken by the ICC, is much more problematic as it does not specify that Palestine would be a state the way this is done by the General Assembly Resolution 3067 with respect of Guinea-Bissau and the Democratic Republic of Vietnam.

[139] UNGA Res 3067 (16 November 1973) UN Doc A/RES/3067 (XXVIII) (emphasis added).

for the purposes of the Secretary-General's invitation. Notably, the Republic of Guinea-Bissau and the Democratic Republic of Vietnam, were contested territorial entities and probably did not have statehood at the time, and neither did they fall within the Vienna formula.[140] Resolution 3067 specifically called these entities 'states' and thus made them states for the procedural purposes of certain UN administrative procedures.[141] But this did not make them states under the law of statehood and nor was the law of statehood used as a yardstick. Resolution 3067 is rather another example of how non-state territorial entities can be given a degree of international legal capacity.

It has been argued above that in the specific case of *Palestine v United States*, the ICJ's could treat Palestine as a state simply because it is a state for the purposes of the VCDR and the Protocol which forms the jurisdictional basis. The unanswered question remained whether the Vienna formula could also operate directly under the ICJ Statute, ie even if the Court's jurisdiction were not based on, and limited to, a particular treaty to which Palestine was a party. In light of the above-explained practice of other UN organs the answer appears to be affirmative: the ICJ could *prima facie* consider Palestine a state for the purposes of the ICJ Statute and particularly its Articles 34(1) and 35(2).[142]

While Palestine is not seeking accession to the ICJ Statute, the practice of UN organs clearly confirms that the Vienna formula is used as the yardstick to define a state for the procedural functions within the UN system. Palestine's UNESCO membership is the point of entry into the Vienna formula and thus related procedures open to states in the UN organs. This means that Palestine *prima facie* has the capacity to bring *a case* before the ICJ under Article 35(2) ICJ Statute and that it is a state for the purposes of Article 34(1) ICJ Statute. Whether the ICJ has jurisdiction in the particular case of *Palestine v United States* is another question, however, and this is not a matter of state definitions under Articles 34(1) and 35(2).[143] In any case, these two articles are not concerned with the law of statehood and the procedural Vienna formula yardstick should apply.

[140] Richard Lobban, 'Guinea-Bissau: September 1973 and Beyond' (1974) 21(1) *Africa Today* 15; Ronald Cima (ed), *North Vietnam: A Country Study* (United States Government 1981).

[141] UNGA Res 67/19 (4 December 2012) UN Doc A/RES/67/19, This resolution granted Palestine the status of a non-member observer state. It did not label Palestine a state in the same way Resolution 3067 did with respect of Guinea-Bissau and the Democratic Republic of Vietnam. Another difference is in that Resolution 3067 attached these two entities to the Vienna formula and specified for which specific purpose the UN Secretary-General may treat them as states. Resolution 67/19 does not say, for example, that Palestine shall be treated as a state for the purposes of ratification of the ICC Statute.

[142] ICJ Statute, arts 34.1, 35.2.

[143] Andrew Tucker, 'Palestine vs USA – the ICJ should not allow itself to be used in lawfare against Israel' (*Thinc*) www.thinc.info/palestine-vs-usa-the-icj-should-not-allow-itself-to-be-used-in-lawfare-against-israel, accessed 14 October 2022.

IV. STATES, COUNTRIES AND TERRITORIAL ENTITIES

Thus far, it has been discussed that the state requirement in multilateral treaties should not be conflated for statehood requirement under general international law. The focus has been on multilateral treaties and the Vienna formula. Bilateral treaties generally do not lead to such definitional problems for purely practical reasons. Indeed, if State A questions the legal status of territorial entity B, State A will either refrain from entering in treaty relations with Entity B altogether or make a treaty with Entity B only if the treaty text does not use the term state (eg peace agreements between states and insurrectional movements).[144] Whether State A would be willing to enter into a Treaty with Entity B would be a purely political decision for State A to make in *foro politico*. As argued in earlier chapters of this book, international legal capacity is relative and not opposable *erga omnes*.[145] There only exist certain negative criteria under which a territorial entity may not be given a degree of international legal capacity where such an entity was realised illegally in the sense of the state practice reflected in Articles 40 and 41 of the Articles on the Responsibility of States for Internationally Wrongful Acts (ARSIWA) and as summarised by the ICJ in para 81 of the *Kosovo* Advisory Opinion.[146] It may be questionable under some circumstances, however, what the international legal status of such an agreement would be and whether this would be a treaty of public international law.[147]

In May 2022, Kosovo applied for membership in the Council of Europe.[148] While the ECHR uses the phrasing 'high contracting parties',[149] the Statute of the Council of Europe opens membership to 'any European State which is deemed to be able and willing to fulfil the provisions of Article 3'.[150] The admission procedure requires a two-thirds majority in the Parliamentary Assembly.[151] It appears that more than two-thirds of the Council of Europe members are from states that do recognise Kosovo and hence it is very likely that Kosovo's membership bid would be successful.[152] Kosovo would then participate in an international treaty regime as a 'state' together with some states that do not

[144] Olivier and Pierre (n 65) 3.

[145] See Chapter 3, section III.B.

[146] Articles on the Responsibility of States for Internationally Wrongful Acts (entered into force 8 January 2008) A/RES/62/61 (ARSIWA), arts 40 and 41; *Accordance with International Law of the Unilateral Declaration of Independence in Respect of Kosovo* (Advisory Opinion) General List No 141 (2010) ICJ, para 81.

[147] *Kosovo* Advisory Opinion, para 81.

[148] 'Council of Europe membership: A good opportunity for improving human rights in Kosovo?' (*European Western Balkans*, 31 May 2022) europeanwesternbalkans.com/2022/05/31/council-of-europe-membership-a-good-opportunity-for-improving-human-rights-in-kosovo, accessed 15 September 2022.

[149] ECHR, preamble.

[150] Statute of the Council of Europe (adopted 5 May 1949, entered into force 2 August 1949) CETS 001, art 4.

[151] ibid, arts 4 and 20.c.

[152] Mustafa Talha Öztürk, 'Serbia must seek a compromise because it cannot prevent Kosovo's entry into NATO and Council of Europe, says Serbian president' (*Vucic*, 24 January 2023)

recognise Kosovo as a state.[153] Yet, as established above, membership procedures in international organisations that are open only to states should not be conflated with the legal status of statehood.[154]

With regard to Kosovo, an interesting conceptual and terminological confusion has arisen in the case of *Spain v Commission* before the General Court of the European Union (GCEU)[155] and subsequently on appeal before the Court of Justice.[156] The underlying problem is a bilateral treaty between the EU and Kosovo.[157] The matter is a complex entanglement of international and EU law; the background is that some EU member states do not recognise or generally consider Kosovo to be a state, and the EU itself has not taken a position on this matter.[158] The case illustrates the conceptual difficulties when the term 'state' under treaty law is conflated with statehood as territorial legal status. Not surprisingly, this usually happens when contested territorial entities (try to) participate in international treaty regimes. Palestine has created conceptual difficulties within the UN system and before the ICC, while Kosovo has done so in its relations with the EU.

The treaty in question is the EU–Kosovo Stabilisation and Association Agreement which explicitly provides that 'none of the terms, wording or definitions used in this Agreement, including the Annexes and Protocols thereto, constitute recognition of Kosovo by the EU as an independent State nor does it constitute recognition by individual Member States of Kosovo in that capacity where they have not taken such a step'.[159] It was on the basis of this Agreement that the Commission acted in pursuance of Article 35(2) of Regulation 2018/1971 which, *inter alia*, provides:

> The Board of Regulators, the working groups and the Management Board shall be open to the participation of regulatory authorities of third countries with primary responsibility in the field of electronic communications, where those third countries have *entered into agreements* with the Union to that effect.[160]

www.aa.com.tr/en/europe/eus-plan-for-kosovo-is-new-condition-for-serbias-integration-vucic/2795521, accessed 23 August 2022.

[153] Relja Radović, 'Kosovo and International Legal Personality' (*Opinio Juris*, 13 March 2023) opiniojuris.org/2023/03/13/kosovo-and-international-legal-personality, accessed 20 March 2023.

[154] Konstantinos Magliveras, 'Membership in International Organizations' in Jan Klabbers and Åsa Wallendahl (eds), *Research Handbook on the Law of International Organizations* (Edward Elgar 2012) 242–60.

[155] *Kingdom of Spain v European Commission* (Judgment) GC T-370/19 (23 September 2020) (*Spain v Commission* GC).

[156] *Kingdom of Spain v European Commission* (Judgment) CJEU C-632/20 P (17 January 2023) (*Spain v Commission* CJEU).

[157] *Spain v Commission* GC, paras 3–5.

[158] ibid, para 33.

[159] Stabilisation and Association Agreement between the European Union and the European Atomic Energy Community of the one part, and Kosovo, of the other part (adopted 22 October 2015) (2016) OJ L 71/3 (Stabilisation and Association Agreement).

[160] Regulation (European Union) 2018/1971, establishing the Body of European Regulators for Electronic Communications (BEREC) and the Agency for Support for BEREC (BEREC Office), amending Regulation (EU) 2015/2120 and repealing Regulation (EC) No 1211/2009.

This is not the place to cover the full extent of this case.[161] For the purposes of this chapter, it is important to recall that Spain brought an annulment action under Article 263 of the Treaty on the Functioning of the European Union (TFEU) and one of its claims was that 'the Commission infringed Article 35(2) of Regulation 2018/1971 in so far as it found in the contested decision that, as regards Kosovo, there was an "agreement with the Union" within the meaning of that provision'.[162] Although Spain's plea was somewhat complicated, in the background of this problem was the question of whether the EU–Kosovo Stabilisation and Association Agreement was an agreement in the sense of international law, ie a treaty, as only such an agreement could, according to Spain, provide for the necessary legal basis to the Commission to act under Article 35(2) of Regulation 2018/1971.

The position of the General Court (GCEU) was that:

> It is apparent from the context in which that wording appears that it refers to an international agreement concluded between two legal persons governed by public international law, namely the European Union and the third country concerned. The Kosovo SAA [Stabilisation and Association Agreement] is, therefore, certainly capable of constituting such an agreement, since it is binding on the parties under public international law.[163]

However, the GCEU struggled to explain why Kosovo has treaty-making capacity vis-à-vis the EU if Kosovo is not necessarily a state. Central in the its reasoning is the distinction between states and countries in the TFEU. The logic followed by the GCEU is that it did not matter that the EU did not consider Kosovo to be a state. Kosovo could conclude international treaties with the EU as a third country. Even if the state/country distinction could be defensible under EU law, and it is not,[164] the problem is that the GCEU imposed it also on public international law, in particular international treaty law, where such a distinction does not exist.

A. Does International Law Regulate Treaties between International Organisations and Countries?

In paragraph 30, the GCEU argued:

> It follows that the provisions of the TFEU relating to 'third countries' are clearly intended to pave the way for the conclusion of international agreements with

[161] Kushtrim Istrefi, 'The Luxembourg Court Rules on the Difference between States and Countries as International Law Actors' (*EJIL:Talk!*, 27 November 2020) www.ejiltalk.org/the-luxembourg-court-rules-on-the-difference-between-states-and-countries-as-international-law-actors, accessed 31 August 2022.

[162] *Spain v Commission* GC, para 40.

[163] ibid, para 47.

[164] See nn 166 and 167 and accompanying text.

> entities 'other than States.' Thus, the European Union may conclude international agreements with territorial entities, covered by the flexible concept of 'country,' *which have the capacity to conclude treaties under international law but which are not necessarily 'States' for the purposes of international law.* To claim the contrary would be to create a legal vacuum in the European Union's external relations.[165]

In terms of EU law, it is true that the TFEU establishes a difference between member *states* and third *countries* in several languages, but not in all of them.[166] The state/country difference exists in some language versions of the TFEU, including French, Spanish, English, German, Croatian, Italian and Dutch. But it does not exist in some other languages, including Polish and Slovene where the single terms *państwo* (Polish) and *država* (Slovene) are used in the relevant TFEU provisions.[167] No difference is established between states and countries in the TFEU in these languages. Even from the point of view of EU law it thus appears odd to suggest that the TFEU intentionally uses the more flexible term 'third countries' in order to be more comprehensive than 'third states' while this difference is actually not reflected in all language versions of the TFEU. In *Spain v Commission*, the Spanish version of the treaty may have allowed the GCEU to say that there was a difference between *estado* and *país*, but how would the GCEU explain in Polish that the use of the word *państwo* was intentionally different from the word *państwo* or in Slovene that the use of the word *država* was intentionally different from the word *država*?

A detailed analysis of EU law in this matter is not the primary objective of this section, however. The argument will now proceed with the problems under international treaty law. The GCEU rightly established that the treaty-making capacity of countries would need to be derived from international law. However, the GCEU failed to explain why Kosovo, if we do not presume it is a state, should have treaty-making capacity vis-à-vis the EU; and whence is such a putative capacity derived. In other words, the GCEU did not tell us which rule of public international law regulates treaties between international organisations and *countries* if 'countries' and 'states' are not synonyms. Instead, it resorted to practice and recalled that the EU has concluded certain agreements with entities, such as Hong Kong, Macao and Taiwan.[168] These are indeed not states, but is the capacity of these entities to conclude *certain* treaties with the EU really comparable to that of Kosovo?

[165] *Spain v Commission* GC, para 30 (emphasis added).

[166] Consolidated Version of the Treaty on the Functioning of the European Union (adopted 25 March 1957, entered into force 1 December 2009) OJ L 326/47–326/390, (TFEU), arts 216 and 217.

[167] ibid.

[168] *Spain v Commission* GC, para 31.

B. The Problematic WTO Analogy

As argued above, WTO membership is extended by the Marrakesh Agreement to separate customs territories that are not states.[169] Given the nature of trade agreements, the participation of separate customs territories indeed seems to serve a functional objective. This allows for participation of non-states, such as the EU, Chinese Taipei, Macao and Hong Kong in the WTO regime. This is not to say that, for example, Hong Kong has a general treaty-making capacity under public international law. But Hong Kong does have such a capacity vis-à-vis the EU for the functional purposes of trade agreements as both entities are party to the WTO Agreement under the 'separate customs territories' clause. Of crucial importance here is the WTO umbrella, which creates a *lex specialis* that gives the treaty-making capacity for certain functional purposes to certain territorial entities that otherwise do not have such capacity under general international law.

No WTO-like umbrella, or special functional treaty-making regime, exists in the context of the EU–Kosovo Stabilisation and Association Agreement. The EU's internal law and the questionable distinction between third states and third countries is for the purposes of public international law not analogous to the WTO Marrakesh Agreement. While Hong Kong, for example, and the EU are both parties to the WTO Marrakesh Agreement under the separate customs territories clause, and can thus conclude trade treaties under the WTO umbrella, neither Kosovo nor the EU itself are parties to the TFEU. Hence, the TFEU does not provide for a WTO-like international *lex specialis* regime under which the EU and Kosovo could conclude international treaties with each other for a particular functional purpose. The TFEU only enables the EU to enter into agreements with third countries, whatever this may mean, as a matter of internal EU law. The TFEU does not, however, create a functional treaty-making capacity of the *country* of Kosovo.

Even the GCEU itself recalled that the treaty-making capacity of the EU and Kosovo needs to be derived from general rules of public international law.[170] In the absence of any WTO-like functional *lex specialis*, these are then the general customary rules that govern international treaties.[171] In this particular case, the applicable rules are those governing treaties between states and international organisations. There are no international rules in existence that would govern treaty relations between countries and international organisations if 'country' means something different than 'state'. As an international organisation, the EU does have such a capacity, while it remains unclear where the treaty-making capacity of Kosovo is derived from, unless it is presumed that Kosovo actually is a state for the purposes of its treaty-making capacity. It thus appears that the

[169] Marrakesh Agreement, art 12.
[170] *Spain v Commission* GC, para 30.
[171] VCLT, art 5.

GCEU silently presumed that Kosovo was a state for the purposes of its treaty-making capacity, but politically labelled it with the less-loaded term 'country', which is not a term of art under international (treaty) law.

C. Legal Vacuum or the EU's Own Political Problem?

In para 30, quoted above, the GCEU argued that the treaty-making capacity of *countries* prevents a legal vacuum in the EU's external relations and enables the Union to enter into international treaties with territorial entities other than states.[172] It is debatable whether this can be rightly called a legal vacuum or is it simply that international law predominantly regulates relations between states, while obligations between two or more non-states generally do not fall within the purview of international legal regulation.[173] Even so, what created this putative legal vacuum?

Had there been consensus among EU member states that Kosovo was a state, there would be no need to impose the term country on international treaty law. As a state, Kosovo would have treaty-making capacity vis-à-vis the EU. Since no such political consensus exists among EU member states, the GCEU took the 'third country' route, which is implausible not only under EU law, but also under public international law. The legal vacuum in EU external relations therefore exists due to internal politics of the EU and because of the rules on Common Foreign and Security Policy, which in this situation prevent the EU from adopting a common position on the legal status of Kosovo.[174]

The GCEU's *jeu de mots* with states and countries in *Spain v Commission* was thus a highly problematic attempt at an *ad hoc* fix of the problem created by the EU's internal politics and the related fear of the word 'state' when it comes to relations with Kosovo. Using the term 'country' as something that does not necessarily overlap with the term 'state' was politically expedient for the Court because the word 'state' generally implies statehood, which is a term of art under international law, while 'countryhood' is not. But the Court here ignored the problem that 'country' likewise does not have a meaning under international treaty law, unless it is used as a synonym for 'state'.

[172] *Spain v Commission* GC, para 30.

[173] Jean d'Aspremont, 'Subjects and Actors in International Lawmaking: The Paradigmatic Divides in the Cognition of International Norm Generating Processes' in Catherine Brölmann and Yannick Radi (eds), *Research Handbook on the Theory and Practice of International Lawmaking* (Edward Elgar 2016) 32.

[174] TEU art 31.1. 'Decisions under this Chapter [external action and common foreign and security policy] shall be taken by the European Council and the Council acting unanimously, except where this Chapter provides otherwise. The adoption of legislative acts shall be excluded.'

D. The Court of Justice's Take on Kosovo's Legal Capacity

The GCEU's decision was – quite rightly – set aside by the Court of Justice.[175] The judgment bluntly rejects the GCEU's problematic distinction between states and countries.[176] In so doing, the Court of Justice acknowledged that the distinction is not used in all language versions of the TFEU, that the terms are used interchangeably, and that 'states' and 'countries' must therefore have the same meaning.[177] But in its decision, the Court of Justice omitted any references to the international law of treaties and grounded Kosovo's legal capacity for concluding the agreement at stake exclusively in EU law. In other words, the Court of Justice did not feel compelled to consider whether the agreement at stake had the status of a treaty under international law.

Central to the Court's reasoning was the status of Kosovo as a *territorial entity* that was not realised illegally under international law. The Court reasoned: '[A] territorial entity situated outside the European Union which the European Union has not recognised as an independent State must be capable of being treated in the same way as a "third country" within the meaning of [Article 35(2) Regulation 2018/1971.'[178] The Court thus ascribed the legal capacity for *agreement*-making to territorial entities without prejudice to their statehood status.

When holding that a territorial entity has agreement-making capacity, the Court omitted any reference to the status of such an agreement under international treaty law. It is clear that this agreement would not be regulated by the VCLT since it is in any case not an agreement between states.[179] But the Court avoided any discussion on the agreement's possible status under customary international law governing international treaties. Does customary international law afford the status of an international treaty to an agreement between an international organisation and a territorial entity if that territorial entity is not presumed to be a state? The Court of Justice did not delve into this and stayed within the ambit of EU law exclusively.

The question of whether the agreement was in line with the applicable rules of international law was not determined on the basis of treaty law, but on the basis of the law governing territorial illegality. The Court of Justice referred to the ICJ's *Kosovo* Advisory Opinion: '[The ICJ] concluded that the adoption of the Kosovo declaration of independence of 17 February 2008 did not violate general international law, United Nations Security Council resolution 1244 (1999) or the applicable constitutional framework.'[180] Clearly,

[175] *Spain v Commission* CJEU, para 140.
[176] ibid.
[177] ibid, paras 41, 42.
[178] ibid, para 50.
[179] VCLT, art 2.1.
[180] *Kosovo* Advisory Opinion, para 81; UNSC Res 1244 (10 June 1999) UN Doc S/RES/1244.

the Court of Justice here adopted the view that international legal capacity can be functionally created in *inter se* relations with territorial entities to the extent that such entities were not realised illegally, whereby illegality is defined in terms Article 40 ARSIWA and state practice referred to by the ICJ in para 81 of the *Kosovo* Advisory Opinion.[181]

This position of the Court of Justice is much in line with what was argued in previous chapters in this book, namely that territorial entities can be given the capacity to create international legal obligations in their relations with other actors and that the rules of international law only provide for a rudimentary framework of limitations on the process of creation of such capacity.[182] Such limitations are closely connected to *jus cogens* norms.[183] To illustrate, under this doctrine, the EU can enter into an agreement with Kosovo, but could not enter into an agreement with the so-called Turkish Republic of Northern Cyprus or the so-called Donetsk Peoples' Republic.[184]

Subsequently, the Court of Justice explicitly detached the question of statehood from agreement-making capacity: 'The treatment of Kosovo as a third country does not affect the individual positions of the Member States as to whether Kosovo has the status of an independent State that is claimed by its authorities.'[185] The Court then continued: 'It follows from the foregoing that, contrary to what is claimed by the Kingdom of Spain, Kosovo may be treated in the same way as a "third country," within the meaning of Article 35(2) of Regulation 2018/1971, without infringing international law.'[186]

In essence, the Court of Justice avoided the question of Kosovo's status under the law of statehood by deriving Kosovo's legal capacity to enter into the agreement in question from Kosovo's status as a territorial entity which did not emerge illegally under international law. This approach is more convincing than the GCEU's *jeu de mots* with states and countries. It remains unclear, however, whether this legal capacity of Kosovo was in fact *international* legal capacity or merely legal capacity under EU law. The approach of the Court would imply it was the latter as the *agreement*-making capacity was grounded in EU law, but not in international treaty law. Under this model, the agreement would then only have legal status under EU law, but would not be an international treaty.

[181] ARSIWA, art 40; *Kosovo* Advisory Opinion, para 81.

[182] See ch 3.

[183] Stefan Talmon, 'The Duty Not to "Recognize as Lawful" a Situation Created by the Illegal Use of Force or Other Serious Breaches of a Jus Cogens Obligation: An Obligation without Real Substance?' in Christian Tomuschat and Jean-Marc Thouvenin (eds), *The Fundamental Rules of the International Legal Order* (Brill/Nijhoff 2006) 99–125.

[184] Katharina Buchholz, 'Kosovo & Beyond: Where the UN Disagrees on Recognition' (Forbes, 17 February 2022) www.forbes.com/sites/katharinabuchholz/2023/02/17/kosovo--beyond-where-the-un-disagrees-on-recognition-infographic/?sh=4f40a55f448c, accessed 22 October 2022.

[185] *Spain v Commission* CJEU, para 52.

[186] ibid, para 53.

While the Court of Justice left this issue unaddressed, international practice does suggest that international organisations and non-state territorial entities may enter into treaty obligations under international law. For example, the WTO Marrakesh Agreement, *inter alia*, creates a set of international legal obligations between the EU on the one hand, and Hong Kong, Macao and Chinese Taipei on the other.[187] While the WTO Marrakesh Agreement is a multilateral treaty, it does create a set of bilateral obligations between an international organisation and non-state territorial entities.

In *Spain v Commission*, the Court of Justice recalled that the EU 'has entered into several agreements with Kosovo, thus recognising its capacity to conclude such agreements',[188] but without clarifying whether these agreements could be treaties under international law if Kosovo was not, at the same time, ascribed the status of a state. It does appear, however, that even if Kosovo is not necessarily a state, these agreements could still be treaties under international law. It has been argued in previous chapters that states can and do create treaty obligations with non-state territorial entities and thus recognise relative international legal capacity of such entities without recognising their statehood.[189] There is no doctrinal obstacle under international law which would prevent international organisations from doing the same thing as states do in their relations with non-state territorial entities. Some international practice indeed suggests that even international organisations and non-state territorial entities do create in their relations treaty obligations governed by international law.

The EU–Kosovo Stabilisation and Association Agreement is a good example of a detachment of the treaty-making procedures from the substantive questions of the law of statehood, and there was no need for the judicial state/country charade adopted by the GCEU. This *jeu de mots* was built on the fact that 'countryhood' is not a term of art under international law, while conveniently forgetting that neither is 'country'. On appeal, the Court of Justice derived Kosovo's agreement-making capacity from Kosovo's status as a territorial entity which was not tainted by international territorial illegality. While the legal authority for making this agreement was grounded in EU law alone, the agreement could also be seen as having the status of an international treaty. Even if Kosovo were not considered a state under international law, it would appear that the customary rules of treaty law do extend to the agreements between international organisations and non-state territorial entities. The EU thus recognises in its bilateral relations that Kosovo has degree of international legal capacity as a non-state territorial entity, yet without recognising Kosovo's statehood.

[187] Lingliang Zeng, *Contemporary International Law and China's Peaceful Development* (Springer 2021) 493–506.

[188] *Spain v Commission* CJEU, para 55.

[189] See ch 3, section VI.A.

V. WEAPONISING LEGAL STATUS IN THE CJEU'S *POLISARIO* CASE

It has been established thus far that a territorial entity has international legal capacity as long as it was not established contrary to the applicable rules of international law. These rules are reflected in para 81 of the *Kosovo* Advisory Opinion and Articles 40 and 41 ARSIWA.[190] This chapter now turns to the problem of non-state territorial entities that do have a separate legal status under international law, but are occupied by a state that does not hold territorial title. It will be argued on the example of Western Sahara that the territorial status of such entities should not detract from addressing the consequences of territorial illegality, in line with the arguments presented in chapter two.[191] This chapter now demonstrates that the CJEU weaponised Western Sahara's territorial status to avoid addressing the consequences of Morocco's territorial control, which is illegal yet effective.

A. The Status of Western Sahara

Western Sahara is on the list of Non-Self-Governing Territories pursuant to Chapter XI of the UN Charter.[192] At the same time, the Sahrawi Arab Democratic Republic (SADR) is a member of the African Union.[193] The spatial area claimed by SADR overlaps with that of Western Sahara, while the SADR authority effectively controls only a fraction of that territory.[194] The self-determination unit of Western Sahara has been illegally occupied by Morocco.[195] The discrepancy between Western Sahara's territorial status and factual situation has led to a number of problems.

As discussed in chapter two, the ICJ concluded in the 1975 *Western Sahara* Advisory Opinion that the territory of Western Sahara was not a *terra nullius* at the time of Spanish colonisation and also that there were no

> legal ties [between Morocco or Mauritania on the one hand and the territory of Western Sahara on the other] of such a nature as might affect the application of resolution 1514 (XV) in the decolonisation of Western Sahara and, in particular, of the principle of self-determination through the free and genuine expression of the will of the peoples of the Territory.[196]

[190] *Kosovo* Advisory Opinion, para 81; ARSIWA, arts 40 and 41.

[191] See ch 2.

[192] 'United Nations Charter, Chapter XI: Declaration Regarding Non-Self-Governing Territories' (*United Nations*) www.un.org/en/about-us/un-charter/chapter-11, accessed 12 October 2022.

[193] 'Saharawi Arab Democratic Republic' (*African Union*) au.int/en/countryprofiles/saharawi-arab-democratic-republic, accessed 19 August 2022.

[194] Janis Grzybowski, 'To Be or Not to Be: The Ontological Predicament of State Creation in International Law' (2017) 28(2) *European Journal of International Law* 416.

[195] 'The Occupation of Western Sahara' (*Western Sahara Resource Watch*) wsrw.org/en/the-occupation-of-western-sahara, accessed 18 December 2022.

[196] *Western Sahara* (Advisory Opinion) General List No 61 (1975) ICJ, para 68.

Hence, Western Sahara needs to be considered a self-determination unit with its own territorial status.

The Constitutive Act of the African Union refers to member states and does not include any provisions for non-state territories.[197] References to member states are also made in Article 27 which governs signature, ratification, and accession to this treaty,[198] and in Article 28 which regulates the entry into force.[199] Further to that, Article 29 provides:

> Any African State may, at any time after the entry into force of this Act, notify the Chairman of the Commission of its intention to accede to this Act and to be admitted as a member of the Union.
>
> The Chairman of the Commission shall, upon receipt of such notification, transmit copies thereof to all Member States. Admission shall be decided by a simple majority of the Member States …

SADR is an original member state of the African Union, while Morocco joined the organisation in 2017.[200] In 1984, Morocco withdrew from the Organisation of African Unity, the African Union's predecessor, precisely because of its admission of SADR to its membership.[201] However, as of 2017, both SADR and Morocco are members of the same organisation which refers in its constitutive treaty to member *states* and makes provisions for admission of African *states*.[202] Nevertheless, it has been established in this chapter that the use of the term 'state' in international treaties does not make parties to those treaties 'states'.[203] The creation of statehood is a political process with legal consequences.[204] While states can be and have been created by international treaties,[205] this cannot be done by virtue of incidental effects of international treaties, but rather where state creation is the object and purpose of a treaty.[206] The object and purpose of the Constitutive Act of the African Union is not creation of SADR's statehood. Despite its membership of the African Union, SADR is therefore not a state. The legal status of the territory claimed by

[197] Constitutive Act of the African Union (entry into force 26 May 2001).

[198] ibid, art 27.

[199] ibid, art 28.

[200] Constitutive Act of the African Union, art 29; Yasmine Hasnaoui, 'Morocco and the African Union: A New Chapter for Western Sahara Resolution?' (2017) Arab Center for Research and Policy Studies, 1.

[201] Youssef Dahmani, '12 November 1984: When Morocco withdrew from the Organization of African Unity' (*Yabiladi*, 13 November 2017) en.yabiladi.com/articles/details/59322/november-1984-when-morocco-withdrew.html, accessed 12 May 2022.

[202] Arpan Banerjee, 'Moroccan Entry to the African Union and the Revival of the Western Sahara Dispute' (*Harvard International Law Journal*) harvardilj.org/2017/12/moroccan-entry-to-the-african-union-and-the-revival-of-the-western-sahara-dispute, accessed 6 January 2022.

[203] See chs 3 and 6.

[204] Ryal Wun, 'Beyond Traditional Statehood Criteria: The Law and Contemporary Politics of State Creation' (2013) 26 *Hague Yearbook of International Law* 316.

[205] See ch 3, section VII.

[206] See n 40 above.

SADR and occupied by Morocco is a separate self-determination unit and a non-self-governing territory in the sense of Chapter XI of the UN Charter. It has been argued in chapter four that self-determination units may not be subject to territorial conquest.[207] The territorial status of Western Sahara and international responses to Morocco's occupation confirm this doctrinal position.[208]

B. The *Polisario* Case

The status of Western Sahara has also been addressed before the CJEU. Although litigation was based in EU law, some difficult questions regarding the territorial status of Western Sahara, and the discrepancy between this status and the effective situation, had to be addressed along the way. In *Polisario*, the Court of Justice took great pains to prove that the EU–Morocco Liberalisation Agreement only applies to Morocco, but not to Western Sahara, although evidence exists that Morocco effectively also applies the agreement to the territory of Western Sahara.[209]

Polisario was an Article 263 TFEU case that was first heard by the General Court, which decided that Front Polisario met the stringent test of direct and individual concern[210] and thus had standing before the CJEU.[211] But Front Polisario could only meet that test if the EU–Morocco Liberalisation Agreement were applicable not only to the internationally recognised territory of Morocco but also to the occupied territory of Western Sahara.[212]

The Liberalisation Agreement itself did not specify that it would apply to Western Sahara, but neither did it specify that it would not.[213] It was argued in the proceedings before the General Court that it was a well-known fact that in practice Morocco also applies its agreements with the EU to Western Sahara,[214] and the General Court took its position based more on this factual reality rather than the territory's formal legal status under international law. The General Court reasoned:

[207] See chapter 4, section IV.b.

[208] 'Petitioners Put Forward Different Views on Western Sahara as Fourth Committee Continues Decolonization Debate' (*United Nations*, 6 October 2022) press.un.org/en/2022/gaspd750.doc.htm, accessed 3 November 2022.

[209] *Council of the European Union v Front Populaire pour la Libération de la Saguia-el-Hamra et du Rio de Oro (Front Polisario)* (Judgment) ECJ C-104/16 P (21 December 2016) (*Polisario* case ECJ).

[210] Eva Kassoti, 'The Front Polisario v. Council Case: The General Court, Völkerrechtsfreundlichkeit and the External Aspect of European Integration' (2017) 2(1) *European Papers* 339.

[211] ibid.

[212] ibid.

[213] ibid.

[214] *Front Populaire pour la Libération de la Saguia-el-Hamra et du Rio de Oro v Council of the European Union* (judgment) ECJ T-512/12 (10 December 2015), para 77.

> It must also be recalled that there is a divergence between the respective views of the European Union and the Kingdom of Morocco as to the international status of Western Sahara. If the European Union's view is [that Western Sahara is not a part of Morocco] it is common ground that the Kingdom of Morocco has a totally different view. In its opinion, Western Sahara is an integral part of its territory.[215]

On appeal, the Court of Justice did not uphold the General Court's 'effective situation approach' and disagreed with the assumption that the Liberalisation Agreement was applicable to Western Sahara, which was the premise on which Polisario's standing was founded:

> In the present case, although the General Court found, in paragraph 3 of the judgment under appeal, that Western Sahara had been included since 1963 on the list of non-self-governing territories within the meaning of Article 73 of the UN Charter, it did not, however, draw the consequences of the status of Western Sahara under international law as regards the inapplicability of the Association Agreement to that territory.[216]

What mattered for the Court of Justice was Western Sahara's status under international law which is *de jure* indeed separate from that of Morocco, although Western Sahara is *de facto* administered by Morocco and factual evidence exists that Morocco is indeed applying the treaty at stake also to Western Sahara.[217]

It was the international legal situation *de jure* that mattered to the Court, and this is that Western Sahara is not a part of Morocco under international law. In making this pronouncement, the Court of Justice attached significant importance to the ICJ's *Western Sahara* Advisory Opinion[218] and did not find it problematic that the ICJ's findings in *Western Sahara* have been completely disregarded and never implemented in practice. The Court of Justice argued:

> It should be recalled that in its Advisory Opinion on Western Sahara … [the ICJ] considered that, on the one hand, Western Sahara 'at the time of colonisation by [the Kingdom of] Spain was not a territory belonging to no-one (terra nullius),' and, on the other, that the elements and information brought to its knowledge '[did] not establish any tie of territorial sovereignty' between that territory and the Kingdom of Morocco.[219]

The Court then concluded that the people of Western Sahara enjoyed the right of self-determination under international law and 'must be regarded as a "third party" [to the Liberalisation Agreement] within the meaning of the principle of the relative effect of treaties [under the customary reflection of the VCLT]'.[220]

[215] ibid, para 100.
[216] *Polisario* case ECJ, para 93.
[217] cf n 195 above.
[218] *Western Sahara* Advisory Opinion, 12.
[219] *Polisario* case ECJ, para 104.
[220] ibid, para 106.

Declaring the people of Western Sahara a third party under the VCLT rules is problematic, as the VCLT and its customary reflections are not concerned with any third parties, but only with third states and treaty parties (which can only be states under the VCLT).[221] While the right of self-determination indeed applies to peoples under international law, there is no sound basis in international legal doctrine to claim that peoples *directly* have a legal capacity under international treaty law. This capacity would need to be derived from a territorial entity created by a people.[222] It would be arguable that Western Sahara does have such a capacity as a territorial entity, but the Court of Justice probably avoided this route because Western Sahara is not a state, while the VCLT refers to states. Be that as it may, the Court of Justice thus moved Western Sahara outside of the scope of the Liberalisation Agreement which meant that Polisario did not have standing in this case.

Although this case was framed in rather technical EU law terms and was reduced to the question of standing before the CJEU under Article 263 TFEU, the difference between the approaches of the GCEU and the CJEU is quite striking from the international law perspective. The GCEU based its reasoning on the effective situation. The EU may have concluded the agreement with Morocco which does not have territorial title to Western Sahara. But Morocco is in effective control of Western Sahara and *de facto* also applies the agreement to this territory. On appeal, the CJEU very formalistically established that the agreement at stake did not apply to Western Sahara because the latter is not a part of Morocco's territory under international law and the people of Western Sahara have never consented to be bound by it as a third party.[223]

The Court of Justice was certainly completely right in claiming that Western Sahara was not a part of Morocco, but it failed to acknowledge the effects of Morocco's effective control over the territory. As explained in chapter two, international legal doctrine does accommodate certain consequences of effective territorial control, regardless of how illegally it may have been established.[224] In the background of the *Polisario* case was not a question of territorial status, but the question of legal consequences of Morocco's illegally realised effective territorial control. In order to find that Front Polisario did not have standing under Article 263 TFEU, the Court of Justice formalistically resorted to Western Sahara's legal status rather than take into account the consequences of Morocco's illegally established effective control. This goes against the doctrine established by some other courts and in state practice that while effective control does not shift territorial title, its consequences still need to be addressed within the legal order.[225]

[221] VCLT, art 1.
[222] See ch 3.
[223] *Polisario* case ECJ, para 106.
[224] See ch 2.
[225] Grzybowski (n 194), 409–32.

The CJEU's dealing with Western Sahara was a rather strange episode. The Court weaponised the fact that the non-state territorial entity had a territorial status separate from that of Morocco, and deprived the authority representing that entity from remedy when Morocco was unlawfully applying the agreement with the EU also in the territory of Western Sahara. In focusing on the legal status of Western Sahara, the Court of Justice failed to take into account the consequences of the illegal territorial situation and address Morocco's abuse of its agreement with the EU.

VI. CONCLUSION

Certain phrasings in multilateral treaties, such as 'state party', 'all states', 'any state' or 'member states', that are used for treaty-accession purposes, should not be read too broadly. The state requirement in this context is not a statehood requirement, and neither should the causality be interpreted as operating in that direction. In practice, it will usually be the case that entities with statehood also are states for the purposes of treaty-making. Conceptual problems arise where contested territorial entities (try to) accede to international treaties or participate in international treaty regimes. In such situations it can happen that the state status under the law of statehood and the status of 'state party' to an international treaty do not overlap. The problem is presently particularly associated with Palestine and Kosovo. But this is not a new problem in international law and has historically also vexed certain other contested territorial entities, especially during the process of decolonisation. If an entity participates in an international treaty regime open only to states, this does not confirm, acknowledge or even constitute its statehood, and neither should such participation be seen as a form of implicit recognition. It simply means that the entity managed to pass the procedural requirements of that particular treaty to become its party – nothing more and nothing less.

Some treaties establish more complex accession procedures than others. The UN Charter requires a vote in the UN General Assembly on recommendation of the UN Security Council. The path to membership through the Security Council subjects an application to a possible exercise of the veto power. In effect, achieving UN membership for contested entities (eg, currently, Kosovo and Palestine) may be politically difficult. It would be wrong, however, to conflate the UN admission procedure with state creation. Would Kosovo and Palestine be closer to being states today had the drafters of the UN Charter made a different choice back in 1945 and subjected a new application only to a simple majority in the UN General Assembly? It is untenable to subject statehood and state creation to such incidental treaty procedures that were drafted for quite different purposes. Moreover, the UN has in the past had members without statehood and one member whose legal personality had been extinguished and was thus no longer a state under general international law. Such practice should not be labelled as being anomalous but rather taken as evidence that the state requirement in international treaties, including in the UN Charter, should not be conflated with the substantive law of statehood.

This chapter showed that where multilateral treaties generically specify that they are open for accession by 'any state' or 'all states', a purely functional approach is taken in practice to determine what entities may be a 'state' for such purposes. Multilateral treaties often attach the so-called Vienna formula, which is a procedural definition of a state analogous to Article 81 VCLT.[226] The practice of the UN Secretary-General in his capacity as the depository of multilateral treaties suggests that the Secretary-General functionally applies the Vienna formula even where a multilateral treaty does not explicitly contain it. Due to the practical importance of the Vienna formula, membership of the UN or its specialised agencies becomes highly significant for an entity's treaty-making capacity. Moreover, within the UN system, the Vienna formula has also been applied outside of the strict context of treaty accession. The Vienna formula, rather than the substantive law of statehood, has been applied also to determine which entities are states for the purposes of the UN Secretary-General's administrative responsibilities that needed to be discharged under certain General Assembly resolutions.

Two conclusions need to be made in this context. First, by deciding that an entity falls within the Vienna formula and thus meets the state requirement for the purposes of a multilateral treaty, the UN Secretary-General does not acknowledge, recognise or even create a state under the law of statehood. If he did, this would have been an act *ultra vires*. This circumstance further suggests that the state requirement in international treaties needs to be detached from the legal status under the law of statehood. Second, UN specialised agencies, such as UNESCO, can have membership procedures that are politically easier to pass than UN membership procedures.[227] It would be untenable, however, to claim that UNESCO membership effectively creates a state because it brings an entity into the Vienna formula. If that were the case, international legal doctrine would therefore have a constitutive theory of recognition by which a two-thirds majority in the UNESCO General Conference would be required. But state creation is not a functional purpose of UNESCO or its General Conference. States cannot be created by procedural side-effects of international (institutional) treaties.

The conflation of the term state in international treaties with the substantive rules of statehood has had far-reaching consequences that have compromised doctrinal clarity. One such consequence is the GCEU's imposition of the term 'country' on international treaty law to avoid any implications for the law of statehood of the EU's agreement with Kosovo. This chapter has thus advanced

[226] VCLT, art 81.
[227] UNESCO Constitution, art 2.

the argument that the law of statehood should be seen as being substantive in nature, while the treaty procedures that refer to 'states party' should be seen as being procedural in nature. If an entity is procedurally a state party for the purposes of a certain treaty, this does not create or confirm its statehood. On appeal, the CJEU did not develop an EU version of the Vienna formula, but rather derived Kosovo's agreement-making capacity from its status of territorial entity. The Court thus took the position that the legal capacity to create international legal obligations does not need to be derived exclusively from statehood status, but may also be derived functionally from other forms of territorial status. It was concluded in this chapter that although the Court's reasoning was grounded in EU law, the agreement could still have the status of an international treaty.

The challenges posed to judicial bodies from Kosovo and Palestine pertain to similar conceptual problems, but approach them from different directions. With regard to Kosovo, the spatial area in question is clearly defined under international law, not least under the UN Security Council Resolution 1244,[228] but there is no unequivocal position on whether the term 'state' can be applied to Kosovo for the purposes of treaty-making. The problem is reversed in the case of Palestine. The Vienna formula undoubtedly makes Palestine a state for the purposes of its treaty-making capacity, but the spatial area of this entity remains unclear under international law.

Can it be assumed that a state party to a treaty also has to have a geographical or spatial dimension or is 'state party' purely a concept of treaty law? After all, the Vienna formula does not create or define a territory. The consequence of detaching the term 'state party to a treaty' from the law of statehood is that in some situations the procedural term 'state' under treaty law does not overlap with the term 'state' under the law of statehood, which in turn leads to problems pertaining to territorial applicability of that treaty.

Despite some theoretical uncertainties and practical difficulties associated with the detachment of the treaty law term 'state party' from the law of statehood, international treaty practice demonstrates that such a detachment exists in legal doctrine, although it may not always be thoroughly preserved. In the absence of any specific definition provided in the treaty text, the procedural term state for the purposes of participation in international treaties generically open to 'all states' is functionally defined by the Vienna formula, not by any requirements under the law of statehood. Membership of the UN or its specialised agencies can thus have far-reaching effects as they give the entity access to the Vienna formula. But the Vienna formula is not a statehood formula and does not have any implications under the substantive law of statehood.

This chapter has thus demonstrated that the term 'state' can be used procedurally for the purposes of treaty-making capacity, but 'state' in this context

[228] UNSC Res 1244 (10 June 1999) UN Doc S/RES/1244.

does not necessarily derive from or denote the territorial status of statehood. At the same time, even non-state territorial entities can have the legal capacity to enter into international treaties, as long as such entities are not tainted by territorial illegality. When territorial illegality does exist, however, its consequences should not be ignored or interpreted away by reference to territorial title and formal territorial status. In line with what was argued in chapter two,[229] territorial status does not shift with effective control. But international law does address the consequences of *de facto* control, even where the effective situation is realised illegally.

[229] See ch 2.

6

Conclusions: Toward a Theory of Territorial Status

I. INTRODUCTION

THIS BOOK SET out to design a new theory of international legal status of territories.[1] In doing so, the book sought to conceptualise the notion of territory, re-theorise statehood and explain the status of non-state territorial entities.[2] Synthesising legal doctrine and international practice, the new theory rests on the following core propositions: (i) territory is a politically created legal status established in the formal sources of international law; (ii) statehood is territorial status under customary international law; (iii) territorial units other than states can have their status, and a level of rights and duties, established under treaty and/or customary international law; (iv) the term 'state' can be used procedurally in the context of treaty-making powers and procedures, and does not always denote statehood; (v) territorial status under international law is not created by a factual ability to exercise territorial jurisdiction.

This concluding chapter substantiates these core propositions and synthesises them into a theory of international legal status of territories. The theory rejects certain common axioms underpinning the nature and structure of international law. In particular, the theory rejects the position that a territory is a natural element and a statehood criterion. It has been argued in this book that the so-called 'statehood criteria' indeed much more accurately describe territorial jurisdiction rather than statehood. It is thus not the statehood criteria that have the status of customary international law, but statehood directly – not via the criteria. The proposed new theory of international legal status of territories therefore 'de-naturalises' the concept of territory, liberates statehood from the straitjacket of the statehood criteria, and explains the status of non-state territorial units in international law. Yet, it does not claim that territorial status is always objective or opposable *erga omnes*. It seeks, rather, to explain why statehood can be subjective and what the consequences are of its subjective nature.

[1] See ch 1, section I.

[2] See ch 1, section III.

II. CREATING A TERRITORY

Geographers have pointed out that the social science falls into the 'territorial trap', whereby territories are seen as natural features rather than what they really are: social, political and legal constructs.[3] Writing in 1975, Jean Gottmann argued:

> [I]t would be illusory to consider territory as a purely physical phenomenon. The natural components of any given territory have been delimited by human action, and they are used by a certain number of people for specific purposes, all such uses and purposes being determined by and belonging to a political process. Territory is a concept generated by people organizing space for their own aims.[4]

Territory is therefore not to be understood as a naturally given or physical phenomenon, but rather as a concept designed by human activity and for social purposes. As Stuart Elden argues:

> [T]erritory is often assumed to be self-evident in meaning, allowing the study of its particular manifestations – territorial disputes, the territory of specific countries, etc – without theoretical reflection on 'territory' itself. Where it is defined, territory is either assumed to be a relation that can be understood as an outcome of territoriality, or simply as a bounded space … the state [has been described] as a 'bordered power container.'[5]

This book sought to theorise territory as an international legal concept; as a 'bordered power container' created under the sources of international law. It was argued that international law indeed is a discipline that prominently falls in the so-called territorial trap.[6] This trap is reflected in Article 1 of the Montevideo Convention which has been interpreted to, *inter alia*, stipulate territory as a criterion for statehood.[7] While legal scholars have argued against the perception of *natural* state boundaries[8] or that *states* are natural persons of law, territory has continued to be seen as the natural component of states and their statehood.[9]

The assumption of territory as being a natural element and a natural component of statehood has led to several problems in theory and application of international law. Is a state a state because it has a territory or is it rather that there is a territory because the spatial area in question is occupied by a state? Why can an organised political community control a spatial area, but

[3] Stuart Elden, *The Birth of a Territory* (Chicago 2013) 800.

[4] Jean Gottmann, *The Significance of Territory* (University of Virginia Press 1975) 29.

[5] Elden (n 3) 800.

[6] Stuart Elden, 'Thinking Territory Historically' (2010) 15 *Geopolitics* 757.

[7] Montevideo Convention on the Rights and Duties of States of 1933 (adopted 26 December 1933, entered into force 26 December 1934) 165 LNTS 19 (Montevideo Convention), art 1.

[8] Hans Kelsen, *General Theory of Law and State* (Routledge 1961) 213.

[9] *Report of International Arbitral Awards, Island of Palmas case*, UN Rep Int'l Arb Awards 829 (4 April 1928), (*Palmas* case), paras 838–39.

in so doing does not create a state? And what happens when a territory does not come with statehood? Some applicative problems that follow from these theoretical uncertainties are whether Serbia could reintegrate Kosovo and China Taiwan,[10] whether Palestine can participate in international treaty regimes that are open only to states,[11] and whether non-state territorial units can enter into international treaties.[12]

Rejecting the assumption of territories as being natural elements, this book followed the proposition made by geographers and political theorist that a territory is a 'bordered power container'[13] 'generated by people organizing space for their own aims'.[14] When a territory is socially created for the purposes of public international law, this status needs to be founded in the sources of international law. Historically, territories have often been created and adjusted by treaties.[15] But such a status can also develop under customary international law.[16] Territory is thus legal status under treaty and/or customary international law, created over a certain spatial area. One form of territorial status is statehood, but it is not the only one.[17] The different forms of legal status will be discussed in more detail below.

It is important to note at this point that in contemporary international law, territorial status is a zero-sum game.[18] All land on Earth has the status of territory under international law, while the rules on the law of the sea regulate the status of water, including *territorial* waters.[19] In a world without *terrae nullius*, a new territorial status can be created only if an existing territorial status is altered.[20] The prohibition of conquest, the right of self-determination and the

[10] Quoc Tan Trung Nguyen, 'Does International Law Protect Taiwan?' (2022) 2(14) *United States Asia Law Institute Perspectives* 2.

[11] Summary of Practice of the Secretary-General as Depositary of Multilateral Treaties (1999) UN Doc ST/LEG/7/Rev.l (Summary of Practice), para 80.

[12] William Thomas Worster, 'Relative International Legal Personality of Non-State Actors' (2016) 42(1) *Brooklyn Journal of International Law* 207.

[13] Elden (n 3) 800.

[14] Gottmann (n 4) 29.

[15] 'Staatsvertrag betreffend die Wiederherstellung eines unabhängigen und demokratischen' (*Rechtsinformationsystem*), www.ris.bka.gv.at/GeltendeFassung.wxe?Abfrage=Bundesnormen&Gesetzesnummer=10000265, accessed 14 December 2022, declaring Austria a sovereign, independent and democratic state.

[16] James Crawford, *The Creation of States in International Law* (OUP 2006) 504; *Reparation for Injuries Suffered in the Service of the United Nations* (Advisory Opinion) General List No 4 (1949) ICJ, para 185.

[17] William Thomas Worster, 'Territorial Status Triggering a Functional Approach to Statehood' (2020) 8(1) *Penn State Journal of Law & International Affairs* 118.

[18] Charles S Spencer, 'Territorial expansion and primary state formation' (2010) 107(16) *Proceedings of the National Academy of Sciences* 119.

[19] Malcom N Shaw, *International Law* (CUP 2018) 198; Anne Peters, 'Statehood after 1989: "Effectivités" between Legality and Virtuality' (2010) 3 *Proceedings of the European Society of International Law* 1.

[20] Convention on the Law of the Sea (adopted 10 December 1982, entered into force, 16 November 1994) 1833 UNTS 3 (UNCLOS).

prohibition of the use of force have also brought changes to the general international legal framework governing the change of territorial status.

In the era of the UN Charter, territorial status is no longer altered by effective control over a spatial area. International law may regulate certain consequences of effective control, for example the law of occupation,[21] but this has no consequences for territorial status. Where effective control over a certain spatial area is established illegally, international law indeed prohibits the territorial status from being altered.[22] Territorial illegality in this context is defined as a violation of a peremptory norm of international law.[23] International practice shows that changes in territorial status have on some occasions been pursued by carrying out acts of aggression,[24] violation of the right of self-determination and/or pursuance of racist policies.[25] In such circumstances, the rules of international law protect the status quo, although the wrongdoer may have certain rights and duties pertaining to the administration of the territory in question and treatment of its inhabitants.[26]

It is also possible that effective territorial control may be established by a political authority without the situation being tainted by international illegality. This happens where a non-state authority establishes effective control over a spatial area without foreign involvement that would amount to aggression (eg Taiwan and Somaliland).[27] In such situations, international law does not preclude an alteration of territorial status, but whether a new legal status is created will depend on the political process. In other words, the absence of international territorial illegality means that a new legal status *could* be created, but it does *not* automatically mean that it *would* be created. Importantly, territories are protected from conquest, regardless of whether they are states. It was established in this book that Taiwan has a separate territorial status as a self-determination unit. As such, it cannot be subject to conquest even though it is not a state.

As 'bordered power containers,' territories are units in which a political authority exercises jurisdiction. As Margaret Moore explains, territory at its

[21] Marko Milanovic, 'Al-Skeini and Al-Jedda in Strasbourg' (2012) 23(1) *European Journal of International Law* 121.

[22] Jonte van Essen, 'De Facto Regimes in International Law' (2012) 28(74) *Merkourios* 31; Eyal Benvenisti, *The International Law of Occupation* (OUP 1993) 43.

[23] *Accordance with International Law of the Unilateral Declaration of Independence in Respect of Kosovo* (Advisory Opinion) General List No 141 (2010) ICJ, para 81; Articles on the Responsibility of States for Internationally Wrongful Acts (entered into force 8 January 2008) A/RES/62/61 (ARSIWA), arts 40 and 41.

[24] Jure Vidmar, 'Crimea's Referendum and Secession: Why it Resembles Northern Cyprus More than Kosovo' (*EJIL:Talk!*, 20 March 2014) www.ejiltalk.org/crimeas-referendum-and-secession-why-it-resembles-northern-cyprus-more-than-kosovo, accessed 16 April 2022.

[25] Robert McCorquodale, 'The Creation and Recognition of States' in S Blay, R Piotrowicz and BM Tsamenyi (eds), *Public International Law: An Australian Perspective* (OUP Australia 2005) 191.

[26] *Legal Consequences of the Construction of a Wall* (Advisory Opinion) General List No 131 (2004) ICJ, para 159.

[27] Vidmar (n 24).

core means 'the right of jurisdictional authority over a territorial or geographical domain'.[28] A certain political authority can, however, also have a *de facto* capacity to exercise jurisdiction in a certain spatial area (geographical domain), even where there is no international legal entitlement to do so. The factual capacity without an explicit international legal right or entitlement to exercise jurisdiction in a certain spatial area does not create territorial status. The latter needs to be established under treaty and/or customary international law. Creating such a status is not a matter of legal automaticity, but of a political process. International law does not dictate the outcome of this political process, it only imposes some limitations on it: a new legal status cannot be created in violation of a peremptory norm of international law. This is also in line with the general rules of international law-making: a treaty cannot be concluded and a new customary rule cannot emerge in violation of a peremptory norm.[29] Yet, in international legal doctrine the evidence of (factual) exercise of jurisdiction in a spatial area has often been wrongly labelled as one of the criteria for statehood.

III. THEORISING STATEHOOD

In his seminal work *Allgemeine Staatslehre*, which precedes the Montevideo Convention,[30] Georg Jellinek conceptualised the state along similar lines: a territory (*Land*), a population (*Volk*) and a ruler (*Herrscher*).[31] Jellinek presumes that once these criteria have been met, a state exists virtually as a natural person.[32] This is a reflection of what Stephen Neff calls in the nineteenth-century positivist perception of 'the real personality of the state'[33] which even found its into the concept of the statehood criteria expressed in Article 1 of the Montevideo Convention.[34] The statehood criteria rest on the notion of effectiveness of a government over a certain *territory* and the population inhabiting that territory. As such, the 'Jellinek/Montevideo understanding' of statehood reflects Max Weber's sociological definition of a state as a 'human community that (successfully) claims the monopoly of the legitimate use of physical force within a given territory'.[35] But these are at best *descriptions* rather than legal definitions of a state, or at least most states.

[28] Margaret Moore, *A Political Theory of Territory* (OUP 2015) 4.

[29] Vienna Convention on the Law of Treaties of 1969 (adopted 23 May 1969, entered into force 27 January 1980) 1155 UNTS 332 (VCLT), art 53.

[30] Montevideo Convention.

[31] Georg Jellinek, *Allgemeine Staatslehre* (Springer 1914) 137.

[32] Helmut Aust, 'Fundamental Rights of States: Constitutional Law in Disguise?' (2015) 4(3) *Cambridge Journal of International and Comparative Law* 521.

[33] Stephen C Neff, 'Jurisprudential Polyphony: The Three Variations on the Positivist Theme in the 19th Century' in Liber Amicorum and Peter Haggenmacher (eds), *The Roots of International Law* (Brill/Nijhoff 2014) 301.

[34] Montevideo Convention, art 1.

[35] Max Weber, 'Politics as a Vocation' in Tony Waters, and Dagmar Waters (eds), Weber's Rationalism and Modern Society (Springer 2015).

In fact, the Weber/Jellinek/Montevideo model much more accurately describes territorial jurisdiction rather than statehood. It is indeed the case that 'bordered power containers'[36] nowadays mostly are states and it may well also be true that 'the right of jurisdictional authority over a territorial or geographical domain'[37] commonly finds itself on the flipside of statehood, but this is not always the case. It was argued in this book that evidence of effective exercise of territorial jurisdiction should not be equated with statehood. Moreover, the law of statehood should be liberated from the concept of statehood criteria.

Hersch Lauterpacht argued that it is often presumed in international legal doctrine that 'fulfilment of the Montevideo criteria is self-evident',[38] which leads to the circular conclusion that 'a State exists in international law as soon as it exists'.[39] There indeed is a great deal of circularity in the statehood criteria, both in the concept as such and in its individual components. The most obvious circularity is the requirement that in order to be a state an entity needs to have relations with *other* states. Obviously, one has to be a state in order to have relations with *other* states.[40] The territory requirement is also circular in the light of the conclusion in this book that territory is not a natural element, but a legal construct. It may well be that the territory was created precisely because a state managed to establish itself in a particular spatial area or geographic domain. As explained by Nisha Shah:

> Both shaping and shaped by the emergence of the modern sovereign state, territory becomes more than a 'portion of the earth's surface' – a physical space onto which meaning is inscribed – but a normative convention about distinct jurisdictions as the basis of legitimate political authority. Through this, territory and state become inseparable not because the state occupies a (pre-given) territory, but because the state 'is a territory.'[41]

In this sense, a territory cannot be a requirement for statehood, but is, rather, a consequence of it.

The idea of there being statehood criteria has been closely associated with the natural theory of statehood and the position advanced in some positivist intellectual circles that states are '*geborene Völkerrechtssubjekte*',[42] while international organisations are '*gekorene Völkerrechtssubjekte*'.[43] This book took a position against the view of states being naturally born

[36] Elden (n 3) 800.
[37] Moore (n 28) 4.
[38] Hersch Lauterpacht, *Recognition in International Law* (first published 1947, CUP 2013) 41.
[39] ibid, 66.
[40] B Sen, *A Diplomat's Handbook of International Law and Practice* (Springer 1965) 8–14.
[41] Nisha Shah, 'The Territorial Trap of the Territorial Trap: Global Transformation and the Problem of the State's Two Territories' (2012) 6(1) *International Political Sociology* 57, 64–65.
[42] Christian Hillgruber, 'The Admission of New States to the International Community' (1998) 9 *European Journal of International Law* 491. See also Christian Hillgruber, *Die Aufnahme neuer Staaten in die Völkerrechtsgemeinschaft* (Peter Lang 1998).
[43] ibid.

subjects of international law.[44] It is simply untenable to argue that on meeting the Montevideo criteria a state is born the way a child is born. As Jean d'Aspremont argues, it is common for international lawyers to equate the attributes of states with those of humans,[45] and the idea of state birth is a consequence of such anthropomorphic thinking. Yet, how exactly is a state born like a child, and who supposedly gave natural birth to a state?

James Crawford argued that '[a] State is not a fact in the sense that a chair is a fact; it is a fact in the sense in which it may be said a treaty is a fact: that is, a legal status attaching to a certain state of affairs by virtue of certain rules or practices'.[46] Although not addressing anthropomorphism but comparisons with of states with objects, Crawford thus indicated that states are not some mysterious natural creatures or tangible physical objects, but rather creations of law. Crawford nevertheless did not entirely reject the concept of the statehood criteria but rather supplemented the four Montevideo criteria with a list of negatively defined additional criteria. These ought to be: a state shall not be created as a result of (i) aggression; (ii) denial of self-determination; or (iii) pursuance of racist policies.[47] These criteria are obviously closely associated with the concept of *jus cogens*.

The problem of Crawford's theory is that it still does not break with the concept of the statehood criteria, although it does look beyond Montevideo. This is also the main deficiency of the subsequent theory of states and state-like entities proposed by Rowan Nicholson.[48] The theory can explain why Northern Cyprus or Southern Rhodesia are not (were not) states, but it cannot explain the legal status of Kosovo and why Somaliland is not a state.

This book thus proposed a complete break with the concept of the statehood criteria. The statehood criteria were never meant to be a checklist that would objectively and self-evidently bring a state into existence, either by 'natural' birth or some other mysterious, even metaphysical process. This book rather asked what statehood is. The response to this question was that statehood is territorial status established under customary international law. It is not the statehood criteria that have customary status, but statehood as such.[49]

Sometimes states are indeed created by international treaties. But as Judge McNair wrote in his Separate Opinion in *South West Africa*, a territorial legal regime created by a treaty has 'more than a purely contractual basis, and the territories subjected to it are impressed with a special legal status.'[50] This also

[44] Crawford (n 16) 21.

[45] Jean d'Aspremont, 'The Doctrine of Fundamental Rights of States and Anthropomorphic Thinking in International Law' (2015) 4 *Cambridge Journal of International and Comparative Law* 501.

[46] Crawford (n 16) 5.

[47] McCorquodale (n 25) 191.

[48] Rowan Nicholson, *Statehood and the State-Like in International Law* (OUP 2019) 127.

[49] See ch 3, section VII.

[50] *International Status of Southwest Africa* (Advisory Opinion) General List No 10 (1950) ICJ, separate opinion by Judge McNair, para 154.

applies to states. When Austria[51] and the Vatican City[52] were created by international treaties, their legal statuses transcended the treaty law context and became opposable *erga omnes*. But to where does the treaty-created territorial status transcend? In line with the theory of sources of international law, treaties can lead to development of new custom.[53] This is not to say that states always need to be first created by treaties and then such legal status transcends to custom. Their territorial status can also develop under custom directly.

The concept of recognition should also be explained in the context of the nature of statehood, which is not a creature or physical fact, but customary legal status. The great debate between constitutive and declaratory recognition is to a large extent unhelpful. Recognition should be seen as an expression of *opinio juris* in support of the emergence of a new statehood status under customary international law. It is not the only mode of expression, and non-recognised *states* can indeed exist (eg Macedonia in 1992),[54] but it is a very common and central mode of such expression.

Under some circumstances, recognition needs to be withheld by virtue of an obligation *erga omnes*.[55] This is where an attempt at state creation is tainted by territorial illegality in the sense of Article 40 of the Articles on the Responsibility of States for Internationally Wrongful Acts (ARSIWA).[56] At the same time, states are never under an obligation to grant recognition or otherwise accept creation of a new state. The obvious problem is that certain territorial entities can be states for some states, but not for others. This problem follows from statehood's customary status. Statehood is thus also prone to customary ambiguities in the law-making process. How general needs to be state practice and *opinio juris*?[57] Is it possible to tell when exactly has a customary rule emerged?[58] In some situations, it may indeed be impossible to tell objectively whether a territorial entity has emerged as a state, just as identifying a rule of customary international law in a certain moment can be fraught with difficulty. Sometimes, territorial status can only be clarified retrospectively. It is now clear that Bangladesh had emerged as a state by 1974, but its legal status in 1972 was ambiguous.[59] The same applies to Kosovo nowadays. It is a state for some states, but not for others.[60]

[51] State Treaty for the Re-establishment of an Independent and Democratic Austria (adopted 15 May 1955, entered into force 227 July 1955) 217 UNTS 223 (Austrian State Treaty).

[52] The Lateran Treaty of 1929 (entered into force 7 June 1929) 130 BFSP 791; Statute of the Council of Europe (adopted 5 May 1949, entered into force 2 August 1949) CETS 001.

[53] *North Sea Continental Shelf Cases* (Judgment) General List No 51 and 52 (1969) ICJ, para 39.

[54] Matthew CR Craven, 'What's in a Name? The Former Yugoslav Republic of Macedonia and Issues of Statehood' (1995) 16 *Australian Yearbook of International Law* 199.

[55] ARSIWA, art 41.

[56] ibid, art 40.

[57] *Military and Paramilitary Activities in and against Nicaragua (Nicaragua v United States of America)* (Judgment) General List No 70 (1986) ICJ (*Nicaragua* case), para 188.

[58] Christoph Engel, 'The Emergence of a New Rule of Customary Law: An Experimental Contribution' (2011) 7(3) *Review of Law & Economics* 767.

[59] Crawford (n 16) 141 and 393.

[60] Relja Radović, 'Kosovo and International Legal Personality' (*Opinio Juris*, 13 March 2023) opiniojuris.org/2023/03/13/kosovo-and-international-legal-personality, accessed 20 March 2023.

International legal capacity, even that of states, is indeed relative in nature.[61] This is a consequence of the nature and structure of international law which in its essence works like a system of private-law obligations created by the actors *inter se*.[62] The public law framework is rather rudimentary and limited to *jus cogens* norms and obligations *erga omnes*. These rules prevent new states emerging in situations tainted by territorial illegality (eg Northern Cyprus and the so-called Donetsk and Luhansk Peoples' Republics), but state creation is not a centrally administered exercise. It depends on the existing states' exercise of the law-making powers. Whether or not such powers will be exercised depends on political decisions, which are limited by the framework of *jus cogens* norms.

State creation is a political process which aims at creation of the territorial status of statehood under the sources of international law, yet the political process itself is governed by international law only to an extent. The statehood status is not always opposable *erga omnes*; it can also be established relatively, ie only in relations between some states. But this does not mean that non-state territorial units are in a lawless situation. Certain rules of international law, including those prohibiting conquest, also apply to self-determination units other than states.

IV. TERRITORIAL UNITS OTHER THAN STATES

While a great deal of focus in international legal scholarship and practice has been on states, territorial units other than states have always existed in the international system and have had territorial status established under international law.[63] Sometimes such units are established by international treaties. Just like with states, the territorial status of such units then transcends the treaty law framework and becomes a part of customary international law. As the International Court of Justice (ICJ) reasoned in the *Reparations Opinion*: '[F]ifty States, representing the vast majority of the members of the international community, had the power, in conformity with international law, to bring into being an entity possessing objective international personality, and not merely personality recognised by them alone.'[64] While the ICJ here referred to international organisations, the doctrine is of broader relevance and pertains to all entities with a degree of international legal capacity. In line with the separate opinion of Judge McNair in *South West Africa*, a treaty that creates a special territorial regime has more than merely contractual value, it creates 'special legal status'.[65] It was argued in this book that such special legal status has to be

[61] See ch 5, section IV.
[62] ARSIWA, art 40; *Kosovo* Advisory Opinion, para 81.
[63] Marc Weller, *Contested Statehood* (OUP 2009).
[64] *Reparations* Advisory Opinion, para 185.
[65] *Southwest Africa* Advisory Opinion, Separate opinion by Judge McNair, para 154.

grounded in the sources of international law. When territorial status transcends treaty law, it becomes a part of customary international law.

This book has consciously avoided an approach through the concept of international legal personality. While references to international legal personality were made primarily when engaging with primary and secondary sources discussing this concept, international legal personality was not thoroughly theorised in this study. Instead, the position taken was that international legal personality is a concept that should be approached pragmatically and descriptively, rather than prescriptively. It was established that it is untenable to speak of states as natural or born persons of international law.[66] Natural persons under international law can only be humans or, increasingly, non-human animals to the extent that international law accords them with a degree of legal capacity for certain purposes.[67] States, non-state territorial units and international organisations are only capable of being legal persons, rather than natural ones.[68] In this sense, the book was concerned with legal persons under international law.

The concept of international legal personality should not be taken too far, however. Contrary to some other assertions,[69] the position taken in this book is that international legal personality is a descriptive term which does not have a strictly defined legal meaning. This was acknowledged by the ICJ in the *Reparations* Advisory Opinion. After establishing that the UN had international personality, the Court continued:

> That is not the same thing as saying that it is a State, which it certainly is not, or that its legal personality and rights and duties are the same as those of a State. Still less is it the same thing as saying that it is 'a super-State,' whatever that expression may mean. It does not even imply that all its rights and duties must be upon the international plane, any more than all the rights and duties of a State must be upon that plane. What it does mean is that it is a subject of international law and capable of possessing international rights and duties, and that it has capacity to maintain its rights by bringing international claims.[70]

International personality therefore operates on a sliding scale. It is of little help to establish than a certain entity, or indeed an individual, has international legal personality, as this still does not specify any rights and duties under international law. The term international legal personality appears to be used as a descriptive shorthand to describe the capability 'of possessing international rights and duties'.[71] It may be of some utility to use the term international legal personality descriptively, but the label as such is not indicative of the

[66] *Palmas* case, para 839.
[67] Walter van Gerven, Jeremy Lever and Pierre Lauroche, *Tort Law* (Hart, 2001), ch 6.
[68] *Reparations* Advisory Opinion, para 174.
[69] Cf ch 4.
[70] *Reparations* Advisory Opinion, para 9.
[71] ibid.

extent of rights and duties under international law. One may also claim, and in principle quite rightly so, that an individual has international legal personality because of the extent of international human rights law and the capacity to bring claims under some circumstances in certain international fora.[72] But this international legal personality was ultimately created by the treaty-making powers of states.

In domestic legal systems, the categories of natural and legal persons, and the extent of their legal rights and duties, are comprehensively regulated by the public law framework.[73] This framework is missing in international law. When different entities enter into their legal relations on the international plane and create their mutual legal obligations, these entities recognise one another's international legal capacity to create, hold and breach legal obligations, and incur responsibility for any breaches of such obligations. The legal capacity can be relative, established in bilateral or multilateral relations, and not necessarily opposable *erga omnes*.[74] In domestic law, an individual's contractual capacity would be opposable to everyone who also has contractual capacity.[75] This is not necessarily true in the decentralised system of international law where the public law framework is only very rudimentary in nature. There still has to be some minimum understanding, however, as to who can create international legal obligations and incur responsibility for breaches of these obligations, and for what purposes they can do so. Indeed, two individuals or two corporations can enter into a contract, but not into a treaty of international law.[76] What prevents them from entering into treaties?

It was established in this book that the law of international legal capacity is closely related to the law of responsibility. It is in principle states and international organisations that have international legal capacity, ie the capacity to create legal obligations and incur responsibility. The law of responsibility is on the flipside and a corollary of legal capacity.[77] It is thus no coincidence that the International Law Commission (ILC) has been able to synthesise from international practice and *opinio juris* comprehensive rules governing responsibility of states and international organisations, but not of any other actors.[78] The answer why this is the case lies in the sources of international law. International legal capacity is purely legal in nature. It is not created or determined by natural

[72] 'International Legal Personality' (*Icelandic Human Rights Centre*) www.humanrights.is/en/human-rights-education-project/human-rights-concepts-ideas-and-fora/human-rights-actors/international-legal-personality, accessed 7 March 2022.

[73] Martin Loughlin, *The Idea of Public Law* (OUP 2004) 114–30.

[74] See ch 5, section IV.

[75] Sorin Calafus, 'The Opposability of the Effects of the Contract on Third Parties' (2019) 19(1) *Ovidius University Annals* 148.

[76] Anne Peters, *Beyond Human Rights* (CUP 2016) 60–114.

[77] ibid, 115–66.

[78] Daphna Shraga, 'The ILC Draft Articles on Responsibility of International Organizations: The Interplay Between the Practice and the Rule' (2011) 105 *Harmony and Dissonance in International Law* 351.

occurrences, such as birth and aging. It therefore needs to be grounded in the formal sources of international law.

States have their statehood status established in customary international law.[79] States can conclude treaties, and by virtue of their treaty-making powers they can create international organisations which are thus also created in the formal sources of international law. States thus have general legal capacity opposable *erga omnes* and international organisations have functional legal capacity – limited by their functional mandates – that is also opposable *erga omnes*. States and international organisations are thus *capable* of having international legal obligations and incurring international responsibility.

Besides international organisations, international law also knows of some other forms of functional legal capacity. A good example is a non-state armed group in non-international armed conflict.[80] This does not mean that the non-state armed group can function on the same level as states, but, rather, that international humanitarian law functionally imposes on them certain rights and duties.[81] As noted above, international legal capacity can also be recognised in *inter se* relations and is not necessarily opposable *erga omnes*.[82] It does appear that territorialism is paramount to such relative creation of international legal capacity. Territorial units other than states can be recognised as having treaty-making capacity and thus resulting international legal obligations.[83] In such situations, the rules of the law of state responsibility are functionally extended also to these territorial units. At the same time, non-state territorial units may also be regulated by customary international law. For example, the customary law of self-determination protects such units from conquest (eg Taiwan).

The rudimentary public law framework imposes some limitations on the freedom to create relative legal capacity in *inter se* relations. Just as with the limitations on the creation of statehood status, these limitations stem from territorial illegality which follows from the breach of *jus cogens* norms.[84] In other words, relative international legal capacity cannot be created vis-à-vis a territorial unit, however effective it may be, which has emerged as a result of aggression, in violation of the right of self-determination or in pursuance of racist policies.[85]

[79] Crawford (n 16) 501.

[80] *Prosecutor v Duško Tadić* (Judgment) IT-94-1-A (15 July 1999), paras 83–87.

[81] ibid.

[82] ARSIWA, art 40; *Kosovo* Advisory Opinion, para 81.

[83] See ch 2, section III.

[84] Stefan Talmon, 'The Duty Not to "Recognize as Lawful" a Situation Created by the Illegal Use of Force or Other Serious Breaches of a Jus Cogens Obligation: An Obligation without Real Substance?' in Christian Tomuschat and Jean-Marc Thouvenin (eds), *The Fundamental Rules of the International Legal Order* (Brill/Nijhoff 2006).

[85] McCorquodale (n 25) 191.

This book also established that it is untenable to speak of 'unrecognised states',[86] 'illegal states',[87] 'de facto states'[88] and other 'states with adjectives'.[89] There is little sense in labelling a territorial unit a state if it is at the same time qualified as a non-state or if it does not have the rights and duties stemming from statehood.[90] And there is, indeed, no need for such labels. International law has always accommodated a certain level of international legal capacity of non-state territorial units provided that they did not emerge on the basis of territorial illegality.[91]

It has already been established that non-state territorial units can be established by treaties and their legal status can percolate through treaty law into customary international law.[92] The extent of their legal capacity will normally be regulated in the founding treaty itself, much like the case with international organisations and their constitutive treaties. Outside of the treaty law framework, the non-state territorial units with separate customary status are self-determination units. States and international organisations may recognise the international legal capacity of Taiwan relatively. In doing so, they create international legal capacity of Taiwan which is relative and applicable only in *inter se* relations between Taiwan and the recognising entity Taiwan can create – and does create – treaty obligations in its relations with certain states and international organisations.[93] The recognition of Taiwan's international legal capacity for these purposes should not be conflated with recognition of Taiwan's statehood.

Kosovo is a state for some states but not for others. Still, Kosovo as a territorial unit with a separate legal status can have its relative international legal capacity recognised even vis-à-vis those states and international organisations that do not recognise or otherwise consider Kosovo to be a state. This was explicitly established by the Court of Justice of the European Union (CJEU) where Kosovo's *agreement*-making capacity vis-à-vis the European Union (EU) was not derived from Kosovo's statehood but from its status as a territorial entity.[94] It was argued in this book that the agreement between the EU and Kosovo could be a treaty under customary law regulating international treaties, even though this was not necessarily a treaty between an international

[86] Nina Caspersen, *Unrecognized States: The Struggle for Sovereignty in the Modern International System* (CUP 2012).

[87] Stefan Talmon, *Kollektive Nichtanerkennung illegaler Staaten* (Mohr 2006).

[88] Adrian Florea, 'De Facto States in International Politics (1945–2011): A New Data Set' (2014) 40 *International Interactions* 788; Thomas De Waal, *Uncertain Ground: Engaging with Europe's De Facto States and Breakaway Territories* (Carnegie 2018).

[89] See ch 1, section II.F.

[90] William Worster, 'Functional Statehood in Contemporary International Law' (2020) 46(1) *Brooklyn Journal of International Law* 39.

[91] Worster (n 12) 207–73.

[92] Crawford (n 16) 504.

[93] 'Separate Customs Territory of Taiwan, Penghu, Kinmen and Matsu (Chinese Taipei) and the WTO' (*WTO*) www.wto.org/english/thewto_e/countries_e/chinese_taipei_e.htm, accessed 5 March 2022.

[94] *Kingdom of Spain v European Commission*, Case C-632/20 P (2023) CJEU, para 24.

organisation and a state,[95] but rather between an international organisation and a territorial entity.[96] The relations between Kosovo and the EU, which has a neutral position on Kosovo's claim for statehood, is thus a good example of an *inter se* creation of relative international legal capacity which should not be conflated with recognition of statehood. Moreover, a degree of relative international legal capacity has been created even in relations between Kosovo and Serbia, yet without Serbia's recognition of Kosovo as a state.[97]

Whether non-state self-determination units are protected by the customary reflection of Article 2(4) UN Charter remains debatable. Textually, Article 2(4) refers to the prohibition of the use of force in 'international relations'.[98] While this places purely domestic situations outside of the scope of Article 2(4), it leaves open the possibility that non-state territorial units with their own legal status under international law would also be covered by this provision. While they are not states, they have a separate territorial status under international law. Hence, using force against them would mean using force in international relations. In any case, the law of self-determination prevents conquest of self-determination units even where these units do not have the statehood status.

The terms *de facto* states and unrecognised states are also imprecise because they tend to lump together certain territorial units that may be in quite different legal positions, such as Taiwan and Northern Cyprus.[99] The former does in fact have the status of a non-state territorial unit (a self-determination unit) established under international law; the latter does not because it is tainted by territorial illegality. The inaccurate classification is based on the fact that both entities are capable of effectively exercising territorial jurisdiction, but it has been demonstrated in this book that such capability should not be mistaken for statehood.[100] The idea of 'illegal states' does take territorial illegality into account,[101] but also conflates with statehood the capability to effectively exercise territorial jurisdiction.

This book has thus concluded that 'states with adjectives' have no place in international legal doctrine. The whole idea is based on conflation of statehood with the factual ability to exercise territorial jurisdiction. There is no need for this kind of quasi-state without statehood. International law does accommodate and regulate non-state territorial units. In principle, there are three categories of such units: (i) territorial status established by international treaties; (ii) self-determination units with territorial status established under treaty or customary international law; and (iii) occupied territories.

[95] See ch 4, section IV.
[96] See ch 4, Section IV.
[97] Radović (n 60).
[98] United Nations Charter (adopted 26 June 1945, entered into force 24 October 1945) 1 UNTS 16 (UN Charter), art 2.4.
[99] Van Essen (n 22) 31–49.
[100] Talmon (n 84) 101–81.
[101] See ch 2, section III.C.

V. THE RELATIONSHIP BETWEEN THE STATE AND STATEHOOD

While it has been established that states should not be qualified with adjectives, the term 'state' in international law is not always used to denote territorial status. International treaties often specify that they are open to 'all states' or that 'any state' may become a party.[102] This has led to the question of how the term 'state' should be interpreted. The question is especially pertinent in difficult examples where the legal status of certain entities is not objectively clear, and it may be a state in its relations with some states, but not with others.[103]

Article 81 of the Vienna Convention on the Law of Treaties (VCLT) opens the Convention for signature to:

> [A]ll States Members of the United Nations or of any of the specialized agencies or of the International Atomic Energy Agency or parties to the Statute of the International Court of Justice, and by any other State invited by the General Assembly of the United Nations to become a party to the Convention.[104]

This functional definition of treaty-making capacity where a treaty is generically open to states has become known as the 'Vienna formula' and has been followed by the UN Secretary-General in his capacity as depository of multilateral treaties.

It was argued above that in the absence of a public law framework that would regulate international legal personality and provide full clarity on territorial status in every situation, international legal capacity can be relative and not always opposable *erga omnes*. The same can be said of the term state. The Vienna formula takes a pragmatic approach and functionally solves the problem of a lack of objective clarity in every situation. If a territorial unit is a member of certain international bodies, or is explicitly invited by the UN General Assembly, it can also be given the legal capacity for the purposes of treaty-making.[105]

By the application of the Vienna formula, the UN Secretary-General in his role of depository of multilateral treaties also avoids the situation where the UN Secretary-General would be the ultimate arbiter of an entity's legal status. It would appear to be wrong if the role of depository of multilateral treaties could have such far-reaching incidental effects. In practice, the Vienna formula has also been applied in other contexts where it needs to be determined whether an entity can become a *state* party.

While the Vienna formula provides for a pragmatic solution which in principle indeed mostly 'catches' states, it can also create treaty-making capacity for contested territorial units which can then participate in international legal regimes open to states. The membership procedures for membership of different

[102] VCLT, art 2.1.
[103] William Worster, 'Relative International Legal Personality of Non-State Actors' (2016) 42(1) *Brooklyn Journal of International Law* 207.
[104] VCLT, art 81.
[105] United Nations Juridical Yearbook (1974) UN Doc ST/LEG/Ser.C/12, paras 157–59.

international fora vary. For the United Nations Educational, Scientific and Cultural Organisation (UNESCO), a two-thirds majority of existing membership is required.[106] A two-thirds majority in UNESCO thus creates a degree of treaty-making capacity for an entity. It would be too far-fetched to claim that UNESCO membership vote could incidentally create a state,[107] but it does create the legal capacity to enter into treaties generically open to states.

There can thus be a discrepancy between an entity's territorial status and its legal status. An entity can have the capacity to enter into international treaties at the same level as states, but still not have the territorial status of statehood. The Vienna formula may create treaty-making powers, but does not create statehood. This can prove to be problematic where a treaty to which such an entity is a party leads to some territorial effects or is predicated on some territorial assumptions.[108] The problem has been particularly exposed in the context of Palestine joining the International Criminal Court (ICC) Statute as a state party and subsequent questions regarding the territorial scope of the ICC jurisdiction in the territory of this state party.

The ICC founded its reasoning in the right of self-determination: '[T]he Court's territorial jurisdiction in the Situation in Palestine extends to the territories occupied by Israel since 1967 on the basis of the relevant indications arising from Palestine's accession to the Statute – is consistent with the right to self-determination.'[109] However, as Judge Kovács noted in his Partly Dissenting Opinion:

> The real and persisting problem in answering the question concerning the geographical scope of the Court's jurisdiction and the Prosecutor's investigation is linked to the fact that, currently, there are no precise settled borders either at the bilateral Israeli-Palestinian level or at any multilateral level. Instead, UN Resolutions merely allude to the necessity of engaging in bilateral negotiations on the issue of borders, using varying formulas of the pre-1967 borders. These formulas are similar but not identical as the emphasis placed on the 1967 borders in each of them is far from being the same.[110]

Indeed, the right of self-determination is applicable to the Palestinian people.[111] It is too far-fetched, however, to assume that the territory of a state party to the ICC is simply the spatial area populated by a people entitled to the right of self-determination. As argued by Crawford, 'the definition of a "people" at large, outside of the context of "generally accepted political units" has proved

[106] UNESCO Constitution, art 2.
[107] UNESCO votes to admit Palestine as full member (*United Nations*, 31 October 2011) news.un.org/en/story/2011/10/393562, accessed 6 June 2022; VCLT, art 81.
[108] *Decision on the 'Prosecution request pursuant to article 19(3) for a ruling on the Court's territorial jurisdiction in Palestine*, ICC-01/18-143 (*Palestine Jurisdiction* case).
[109] *Palestine Jurisdiction* case, para 123.
[110] ibid, Judge Péter Kovács' Partly Dissenting Opinion ICC-01/18-143-Anx, para 245.
[111] *Palestine Jurisdiction* case, para 9.

fraught with difficulty'.[112] But is there a 'generally accepted political unit' of Palestine, state party to the ICC Statute? Political units, ie territories, are created in a political process and not as a matter of legal automaticity by virtue of application of the right of self-determination. In the situation of Palestine, the political process has not been completed. The situation of Palestine's ICC status is a good illustration of the problem where the functional approach under the Vienna formula creates the legal capacity that is generally inherent in states, yet the spatial scope of this particular entity and its territorial status remain undefined.

When such situations occur, international courts and other interpreters of the rules of international law should not read the spatial dimension into the phrasing *state* party where such a dimension has not been determined. In any case, states and territories cannot be created as a matter of incidental effects of proceedings before international courts. In *East Timor* before the ICJ, Portugal tried to get around the so-called *Monetary Gold* principle by arguing:

> the principal matters on which its claims are based, namely the status of East Timor as a non-self-governing territory and its own capacity as the administering Power of the Territory, have already been decided by the General Assembly and the Security Council, acting within their proper spheres of competence; that in order to decide on Portugal's claims, the Court might well need to interpret those decisions but would not have to decide de novo on their content and must accordingly take them as 'givens;' and that consequently the Court is not required in this case to pronounce on the question of the use of force by Indonesia in East Timor or upon the lawfulness of its presence in the Territory.[113]

Importantly, the ICJ did not dismiss Portugal's claim as a matter of principle. The Court did not pronounce that the UN General Assembly and Security Council resolutions on territorial status could not be treated as 'givens' which the Court needs to take into account. The ICJ rather dismissed Portugal's argument on the facts of the case, ie that the resolutions to which Portugal was referring did not establish what Portugal was claiming they did (which was that they settled the territorial status of East Timor). Ultimately, the ICJ concluded on this matter:

> The Court finds that it cannot be inferred from the sole fact that the above-mentioned resolutions of the General Assembly and the Security Council refer to Portugal as the administering Power of East Timor that they intended to establish an obligation on third States to treat exclusively with Portugal as regards the continental shelf of East Timor. The Court notes, furthermore, that several States have concluded with Indonesia treaties capable of application to East Timor but which do not include any reservation in regard to that Territory.
>
> …

[112] Crawford (n 16) 125.

[113] *Case Concerning East Timor (Portugal v. Australia)* (Judgment) General List No 84 (1995) ICJ (*East Timor* case), para 30.

> Without prejudice to the question whether the resolutions under discussion could be binding in nature, the Court considers as a result that they cannot be regarded as 'givens' which constitute a sufficient basis for determining the dispute between the Parties.[114]

Two conclusions can be derived from the ICJ's reasoning that are also relevant for determination of the territorial scope of states party to international treaties in general and for the ICC's dealing with Palestine in specific. First, the territorial status can be taken as a 'given', ie as a legal fact, only to the extent to which this has been unequivocally determined by competent authorities. Secondly, general pronouncements of the UN's political bodies that call for territorial settlement, reaffirm the right of self-determination and/or condemn certain conduct of a state without territorial title in a certain spatial area, do not amount to an unequivocal determination of territorial status. Indeed, East Timor was on the list of non-self-governing territories under Chapter XI of the UN Charter and its administering power was Portugal,[115] yet this did not prevent the ICJ from holding that, had it exercised its jurisdiction, 'Indonesia's rights and obligations would thus constitute the very subject-matter of such a judgment'.[116]

As counterintuitive as this may be, the word 'state' does not always denote statehood. Some *amici curie* who have acted before the ICC's pre-Trial Chamber in the case of Palestine have pointed out that the word 'state' needed to be interpreted in line with its ordinary meaning.[117] But the problem is that 'state' may actually have two ordinary meanings in international law. A state can mean an entity with the legal status of statehood established under customary international law, but it can also mean an entity that falls within the Vienna formula and thus has treaty-making capacity under international law. While the two meanings often overlap, this is not always the case. The reason for this complication lies in the nature and structure of international law.

There is no centralised public authority to determine the legal status of territories and determine the extent of their legal capacity. In some examples, the judicial bodies and other interpreters of the legal rules are faced with the incidental question of whether an entity is indeed a state. They would act *ultra vires* if they made an incidental pronouncement on an entity's territorial status where they are not explicitly tasked to do so. This is why a pragmatic or functional approach via the Vienna formula has been developed. Whether an entity would be ascribed with legal capacity under treaty law which is ordinarily inherent in states then depends on the voting rules and admission procedures

[114] *East Timor* case, para 32.

[115] 'General Assembly Decides to Remove East Timor from List of Non-Self-Governing Territories Upon Independence Set for 20 May' (*United Nations*, 1 May 2002) press.un.org/en/2002/GA10014.doc.htm, accessed 6 November 2021.

[116] *East Timor* case, para 34.

[117] *Palestine Jurisdiction* case, ICC-01/18-12, para 113.

in certain international fora. But the object and purpose of these membership procedures is not state creation or general clarification of territorial status. It therefore has to be accepted that the word state can have one meaning under the substantive law of territorial status and another one under the Vienna formula.

The reason why this differentiation needs to be preserved is captured in the reasoning of the UN Secretary-General when deciding to resort to the Vienna formula in the first place: '[T]here are certain areas in the world whose status is not clear … [The Secretary General] would not wish to determine, on his own initiative, the highly political and controversial question of whether or not the areas whose status was unclear were States. Such a determination, he believed, would fall outside his competence.'[118] It has been argued in this book that statehood is not created automatically by meeting the statehood criteria. The creation of statehood is a law-governed political process,[119] and not an incidental task of the UN Secretary-General in his capacity of depository of multilateral treaties.

Neither the UN Secretary-General nor international courts can determine an entity's territorial status where this is an incidental question and are not explicitly tasked to do so. That would be an act *ultra vires*. International legal doctrine needs to accept that due to the nature and structure of international law, the term state can have two ordinary meanings: (i) territorial status of an entity under the law of statehood; and (ii) international legal capacity of an entity which was created via the Vienna formula. The latter does not necessarily imply the former and it cannot be automatically presumed that a state under the Vienna formula also has a defined spatial dimension or geographic domain. That would depend whether its territory has been created in the sources of international law and can be taken as a 'given'.

VI. UNTANGLING TERRITORIAL STATUS AND TERRITORIAL JURISDICTION

The Montevideo criteria in principle better *describe* the ability to exercise territorial jurisdiction than statehood.[120] The concepts of statehood and jurisdiction often are two sides of the same coin.[121] An authority's capacity to exercise jurisdiction over a certain spatial area is a corollary of the territorial status of that authority. In contemporary social organisation of the international community, territorial jurisdiction is usually derived from the territorial status of statehood, but this is not always the case. Even non-state territorial

[118] Summary of Practice, para 81.
[119] Crawford (n 16) 21.
[120] Montevideo Convention, art 1.
[121] See ch 2, section III.A.

units may have the capacity under international law to exercise territorial jurisdiction. The capacity to exercise jurisdiction in a certain spatial area, therefore, does not imply the territorial status of statehood. While statehood comes with the capacity to exercise territorial jurisdiction, the reverse is not always true.

With regard to non-state exercises of territorial jurisdiction, three types of situations need to be distinguished: (i) where jurisdictional authority stems from a formal source of international law; (ii) where jurisdictional authority is factual and does not stem from a source of international law, but is not tainted by territorial illegality; (iii) where jurisdictional authority is factual and does not stem from a source of international law, and is at the same time tainted by territorial illegality.

In the first scenario, jurisdictional capacity stems from the non-state territorial status created under treaty or customary international law. Where territorial status is based in a treaty, the treaty may explicitly spell out the extent of jurisdictional capacity. For example, the Free Territory of Trieste was established in 1947 by Annex VI to the Peace Treaty with Italy and was confirmed by the UN Security Council Resolution 16.[122] The Permanent Statute of the Free Territory of Trieste, *inter alia*, defined its territory,[123] citizenry,[124] the executive,[125] legislative[126] and judicial organs,[127] and competencies in foreign policy.[128] In other words, the Free Territory of Trieste did meet the Montevideo criteria, but did not have statehood. It was a territorial unit and its organs had jurisdictional powers. These powers were derived from an international treaty which was confirmed by a Security Council resolution. This territorial status was dissolved in 1954 by a subsequent treaty between Italy and Yugoslavia.[129]

Where the exercise of jurisdiction is factual rather than based in a source of international law, yet not tainted by territorial illegality, the jurisdictional authority may well be committing constitutional illegality domestically, but this is not necessarily or even automatically an internationally wrongful act. The authority of Somaliland has established a *de facto* jurisdictional capacity in a part of the territory of Somalia which has otherwise retained its statehood status.[130] The authority of Somaliland did not change the territorial status of the spatial area concerned, but it did establish jurisdictional authority

[122] Treaty of Paris between Italy and the Allied Powers (entered into force 10 February 1947) 49 UNTS 3 (Treaty of Peace with Italy). See also SC Res 16, S/RES/16 (10 January 1947).
[123] ibid, art 1.
[124] ibid, art 6.
[125] ibid, art 9.
[126] ibid, art 12.
[127] ibid, art 16.
[128] ibid, art 24.
[129] Memorandum of understanding between the Governments of Italy, the United Kingdom of Great Britain and Northern Ireland, the United States of America and Yugoslavia regarding the Free Territory of Trieste (entered into force 5 October 1954) 235 UNTS 3297 (Trieste Agreement).
[130] Crawford (n 16) 413.

which has been to an extent accepted in state practice, yet without accepting Somaliland's statehood.[131] Kosovo is a more complicated situation because it is a state for some state, but not for others. Nevertheless, even those states that do not recognise Kosovo as a state, as well as the EU, accept Kosovo's *de facto* jurisdictional authority based in its status of a territorial unit.

This is different where factual exercise of jurisdiction is tainted by territorial illegality, which is understood in terms of Articles 40 ARSIWA and as summarised in para 81 of the ICJ's *Kosovo* Advisory Opinion.[132] A *de facto* jurisdictional authority may well emerge illegally (eg Northern Cyprus or more recently the so-called Donetsk and Luhansk Peoples' Republics),[133] but the international community as a whole has a duty not to accept such jurisdictional authority.[134] The duty of non-recognition and cooperation to bring to an end an unlawful situation created by a serious breach of a peremptory norm is not limited to non-recognition of an attempt at state creation. Indeed, state practice reflected in Article 41 and Commentaries to Article 41 ARSIWA refer to territorial illegality more broadly to include, for example, South Africa's illegal administration of Namibia.[135] States were here not under an obligation to withhold recognition in the sense of the law of statehood, but were obliged to refrain from recognising and giving effect to South Africa's illegal territorial administration of Namibia, which at the time was a non-state territorial unit.[136]

Jurisdictional units tainted by territorial illegality ordinarily have a patron state that caused the territorial illegality in the first place (eg by illegal intervention or denial of self-determination), although this is not always the case. Southern Rhodesia was an example of a jurisdictional unit where territorial illegality was caused by internal developments.[137] Nevertheless, where jurisdictional units have a patron state, that state can incur international responsibility with respect of the territory concerned. The European Court of Human Rights (ECtHR) has developed comprehensive case law to this effect.[138] The effect of international legal doctrine reflected in Article 41 ARSIWA is that although an internationally illegal jurisdictional authority may have the factual capacity to exercise territorial jurisdiction in a certain spatial area, this capacity is

[131] Sarah McGibbon, 'Seceding from failed states: reconsidering the case of Somaliland,' in Jure Vidmar, Sarah McGibbon, Lea Raible (eds), *Research Handbook on Secession* (Edward Elgar 2022) 293–310.

[132] *Kosovo* Advisory Opinion, para 81.

[133] ARSIWA, arts 40 and 41; *Kosovo* Advisory Opinion, para 81.

[134] ARSIWA, art 41.

[135] UNGA Res 42/14 (6 Nov 1987) A/RES/42/14.

[136] *Southwest Africa* (Advisory Opinion); ARSIWA, commentary to art 1, para 8.

[137] Crawford (n 16) 129.

[138] 'Extra-territorial jurisdiction of States Parties to the European Convention on Human Rights' (*ECtHR*, Jul 2018) www.echr.coe.int/documents/fs_extra-territorial_jurisdiction_eng.pdf, accessed 7 January 2023.

not internationally accepted and not accorded with international legal validity. The doctrine is not absolute and the so-called Namibia exception applies, whereby certain acts of an illegal authority are internationally accepted for the benefit of the population inhabiting the territory in question.[139]

Territorial units other than states may have either legally warranted or factual capacity to exercise jurisdiction in a certain spatial area. Such capacity should not be conflated with statehood, which needs to be created separately. While jurisdictional capacity may be a corollary of statehood, it is not only a corollary of statehood but also of other forms of territorial status. Where jurisdictional capacity of a non-state territorial unit is legally warranted, its scope will be ordinarily defined in the underlying sources of international law. Factual jurisdictional capacity without an authorisation from a source of international law may be given international legal effects and accepted in international practice where it is not tainted by international territorial illegality. Where international territorial illegality does taint the effective situation, the international legal capacity of such illegally realised *de facto* jurisdictional authority is limited to the extent of the so-called *Namibia* exception, and predominantly takes effect in the realm of private international law.

VII. FINAL REMARKS: A THEORY OF INTERNATIONAL LEGAL STATUS OF TERRITORIES

The surface of Earth is a natural given; its territorial division is a matter of social organisation. Territory is a socially constructed concept, not a natural fact. The maxim *ubi societas, ibi jus* applied here means that the social organisation of the Earth surface is grounded also in the formal sources of international law. Territories are created by international treaties and/or under customary international law. Nowadays, the status of a separate territory is in most circumstances derived from the status of statehood. But this was not always the case historically and is not necessarily the case today. The history of the international practice of creating a separate non-state territorial status and regulating the extent of international legal capacity of such territories is quite rich under treaty law. A separate non-state territorial status with a certain level of international legal capacity can also develop under customary international law. Particularly relevant in this regard are the non-state self-determination units. Such territorial units are protected from conquest irrespectively of their statehood status.

Statehood is a form of territorial status established under treaty and/or customary international law. The so-called statehood criteria in principle

[139] *Southwest Africa* Advisory Opinion, para 125; ARSIWA, commentary to art 41, para 8.

describe most states, but do not define them. More specifically, the Montevideo criteria more accurately describe the capacity to exercise jurisdiction rather than statehood. It is true that statehood and jurisdictional powers often are two sides of the same coin, but this is not always the case. The jurisdictional powers are a corollary of statehood, but not vice versa. Neither legal entitlement nor factual ability to exercise jurisdiction in a certain spatial area should be taken as a proof or evidence of statehood, let alone conflated with state creation. The sources of international law may indeed give a non-state entity the (legal) capacity to exercise jurisdiction in a spatial area. A certain political authority may also establish a *de facto* capacity to exercise jurisdiction in a spatial area. International law may refuse to accord such authorities a territorial status, but nevertheless accommodate certain consequences of the factual capacity (eg the law of occupation and the so-called Namibia exception). Yet, such accommodations of factual jurisdictional authority do not interfere with legal status.

This book thus developed a theory of international legal status which 'de-naturalises' the concept of territory. Once territory is understood as a social construct, it also follows that a state does not occupy a pre-existing territory, but rather that a certain spatial area is a territory because a state occupies it. Statehood is a form of territorial status established in the sources of international law. This is not to say that other forms of territorial status do not exist; but statehood is the most common form of legal status in contemporary international law and international community. Its grounding in the formal sources of international law also makes territorial status vulnerable to certain ambiguities and uncertainties that especially pertain to (the formation of) customary international law. The theory presented in this book therefore did not claim that territorial status would always be clear and objectively ascertainable. It rather sought to explain why territorial status cannot always be clear and objectivised. This is because international legal capacity of territorial units can be relative and not necessarily opposable *erga omnes*. This is due to the nature and structure of international law and the private law nature of the international law-making procedures.

Territory is a social construct. For the purposes of the international community and its legal system, the status of a separate territory is established under treaty and/or customary international law. Statehood and other forms of territorial status are also creations of the law-making procedures under treaty and customary international law. Territorial status is created neither naturally nor as a result of legal automaticity by meeting certain pre-given criteria. It is a result of political actions and decisions that create a territory with a certain status under the formal sources of international law.

The theory of territorial status developed in this book departs from the position that territories are not products of nature or natural forces. They are created in social relations and for social purposes. The social, rather than natural, origin of territories has consequences for how international law should understand and conceptualise statehood and other forms of territorial status. States and certain non-state units do not occupy a pre-existing territory. It is rather that political decisions create territorial status in a certain spatial area and establish this status in the formal sources of international law.

Bibliography

MONOGRAPHS

Alvarez, Jose, *International Organizations as Law-Makers* (OUP 2006).

D'Aspremont, Jean, *International Law as a Belief System* (CUP 2017).

Aust, Anthony, *Handbook of International Law* (CUP 2005).

Beigbeder, Yves, *International Monitoring of Plebiscites, Referenda and National Elections: Self-Determination and Transition to Democracy* (Springer 1994).

Benvenisti, Eyal, *The International Law of Occupation* (OUP 1993).

Blank, Laurie, *Self-defense: Law and Practice* (Edward Elgar 2023).

Brierly, James Leslie, *The Law of Nations* (OUP 1963).

Caspersen, Nina, *Unrecognized States: The Struggle for Sovereignty in the Modern International System* (CUP 2012).

Coggins, Bridget, *Power Politics and State Formation in the Twentieth Century: The Dynamics of Recognition* (CUP 2014).

Crawford, James, *The Creation of States in International Law* (OUP 2006).

De Waal, Thomas, *Uncertain Ground: Engaging with Europe's De Facto States and Breakaway Territories* (Carnegie 2018).

Dixon, Martin, McCorquodale, Robert, and Williams, Sarah, *Cases and Materials in International Law* (OUP 2011).

Dugard, John, *Recognition and the United Nations* (CUP 1987).

Elden, Stuart, *The Birth of a Territory* (Chicago 2013).

El Ouali, Abdelhamid, *Territorial Integrity in a Globalizing World* (Springer 2012).

Ezrachi, Ariel, *EU Competition Law: An Analytical Guide to the Leading Cases* (Hart 2014).

Fuller, Lon, *The Morality of Law* (YUP 1969).

Grant, Thomas, *Admission to the United Nations: Charter Article 4 and the Rise of Universal Organisation* (Martinus Nijhoff 2009).

Gottmann, Jean, *The Significance of Territory* (University of Virginia 1975).

Harris, David J, *Cases and Materials on International Law* (Sweet & Maxwell 2010).

Higgins. Rosalyn, *The Development of International Law through the Political Organs of the United Nations* (OUP 1963).

Hill, Christopher and Karen E Smith, *European Foreign Policy: Key Documents* (Routledge 2000).

Hillgruber, Christian, *Die Aufnahme neuer Staaten in die Völkerrechtsgemeinschaft* (Peter Lang 1998).

Jellinek, Georg, *Allgemeine Staatslehre* (O Häring 1905; Springer 1914).

Jennings, Robert Y and Watts, Arthur, *Oppenheim's International Law* (OUP 1992).

Kelsen, Hans, *General Theory of Law and State* (Routledge 1961).

Kelsen, Hans, *The Law of the United Nations: A Critical Analysis of its Fundamental Problems* (London Institute of Word Affairs 2000, reprint of the 1950 original).

Kolb, Robert, *The International Law of State Responsibility* (Edward Elgar 2017).

Knoll, Bernhard, *The Legal Status of Territories Subject to Administration by International Organisations* (CUP 2008).

Lauterpacht, Hersch, *Recognition in International Law* (first published 1947, CUP 2013).

Loughlin, Martin, *The Idea of Public Law* (OUP 2004).

Lyons, Terrence and Samatar, Ahmed I, *Somalia: State Collapse, Multilateral Intervention, and Strategies for Political Reconstruction* (Brookings 1995).

Marek, Krystyna, *Identity and Continuity of States in Public International Law* (Droz 1968).
McNeely, Connie, *Constructing the Nation-State: International Organization and Prescriptive Action* (Praeger 1995).
Milano, Enrico, *Unlawful Territorial Situations in International Law, Reconciling Effectiveness, Legality and Legitimacy* (Brill/Nijhoff 2005).
Moore, Margaret, *A Political Theory of Territory* (OUP 2015).
Nicholson, Rowan, *Statehood and the State-Like in International Law* (OUP 2019).
O'Meara, Christopher, *Necessity and Proportionality and the Right of Self-Defence in International Law* (OUP 2021).
Oppenheim, Lassa, *International Law* (Longmans 1905).
Pavkovic, Aleksandar and Radan, Peter, *Creating New States: Theory and Practice of Secession* (Ashgate 2007).
Pegg, Scott, *International Society and the De Facto State* (Ashgate 1998).
Peters, Anne, *Beyond Human Rights* (CUP 2016).
Radan, Peter, *The Break-up of Yugoslavia and International Law* (Routledge 2002).
Raible, Lea, *Human Rights Unbound: A Theory of Extraterritoriality* (OUP 2020).
Raič, David, *Statehood and the Law of Self-Determination* (Brill 2002).
Ryngaert, Cedric, *Jurisdiction in International Law* (OUP 2008).
Sassen, Saskia, *Territory, Authority, Rights: From Medieval to Global Assemblages* (Princeton 2006).
Sen, B, *A Diplomat's Handbook of International Law and Practice* (Springer 1965).
Stilz, Anna, *Territorial Sovereignty: A Philosophical Exploration* (OUP 2019).
Shaw, Malcom N, *International Law* (CUP 2018).
Talmon, Stefan, *Kollektive Nichtanerkennung illegaler Staaten* (Mohr 2006).
Van Gerven, Walter, Lever, Jeremy and Lauroche, Pierre, *Tort Law* (Hart, 2001).
Vidmar, Jure, *Democratic Statehood in International Law: The Emergence of New States in post-Cold War Practice* (Hart 2013).
Waltermann, Antonia, *Reconstructing Sovereignty* (Springer 2019).
Weber, Max, *Basic Concepts in Sociology* (Citadel 1964).
Weller, Marc, *Contested Statehood* (OUP 2009).
Wheeler, Nicholas J, *Saving Strangers: Humanitarian Intervention in International Society* (OUP 2002).
Wicks, Elizabeth, *The Right to Life and Conflicting Interests* (OUP 2010).
Wilde, Ralph, *International Territorial Administration: How Trusteeship and the Civilizing Mission Never Went Away* (OUP 2008).
Zeng, Lingliang, *Contemporary International Law and China's Peaceful Development* (Springer 2021).

CHAPTERS IN EDITED BOOKS

D'Aspremont, Jean, 'Non-State Actors in International Law: Oscillating between Concepts and Dynamics' in Jean d'Aspremont (ed), *Participants in the International Legal System* (Routledge 2011).
D'Aspremont, Jean, 'Subjects and Actors in International Lawmaking: The Paradigmatic Divides in the Cognition of International Norm Generating Processes' in Catherine Brölmann and Yannick Radi (eds), *Research Handbook on the Theory and Practice of International Lawmaking* (Edward Elgar 2016).
Brady, Henry and Kaplan, Cynthia, 'Eastern Europe and the Former Soviet Union' in David Butler and Austin Ranney (eds), *Referendums Around the World: The Growing Use of Direct Democracy* (AEI 1994).
Breuilly, John, 'Modern Territoriality, the Nation-State, and Nationalism' in Matthias Middell and Steffi Marung (eds), *Spatial Formats under the Global Condition* (De Gruyter Oldenbourg 2019).

Chetail, Vincent, 'The Legal Personality of Multinational Corporations, State Responsibility and Due Diligence: The Way Forward Unity and Diversity of International Law' in Denis Alland, Vincent Chetail, Olivier de Frouville and Jorge E Viñuales (eds), *Essays in Honour of Prof. Pierre-Marie Dupuy* (Nijhoff 2014).

Cima, Ronald (ed), *North Vietnam: A Country Study* (United States Government 1981).

Corten, Olivier and Klein, Pierre, 'Are Agreements between States and Non-State Entities Rooted in the International Legal Order?' in Enzo Cannizzaro (ed), *The Law of Treaties Beyond the Vienna Convention* (OUP 2011).

Czubik, Paweł, 'Sovereignty in International Law' in Anikó Raisz (ed), *International Law from a Central European Perspective. Legal Studies on Central Europe* (Central European Academic 2022).

D'Amato, Anthony, 'Purposeful Ambiguity as International Legal Strategy: The Two China Problem' in Jerzy Makarczyk (ed), *Theory of International Law at the Threshold of the 21st Century* (Brill 1997).

Eisterer, Klaus, 'Austria Under Allied Occupation' in Rolf Steininger, Gunter Bischof, and Michael Gehler (eds), *Austria in the Twentieth Century* (Routledge 2002).

Ginther, Donna K, 'Article 4' in Bruno Simma (ed), *The Charter of the United Nations* (OUP 2002).

Jorritsma, Remy, 'Unravelling Attribution, Control and Jurisdiction: Some Reflections on the Case Law of the European Court of Human Rights' in Helene Ruiz Fabri (ed), *International Law and Litigation: A Look into Procedure* (Baden Baden 2019).

Magliveras, Konstantinos, 'Membership in International Organizations' in Jan Klabbers and Åsa Wallendahl (eds), *Research Handbook on the Law of International Organizations* (Edward Elgar 2012).

McCorquodale, Robert, 'The Creation and Recognition of States' in S Blay, R Piotrowicz and BM Tsamenyi (eds), *Public International Law: An Australian Perspective* (OUP Australia 2005).

McGibbon, Sarah, 'Seceding from failed states: reconsidering the case of Somaliland' in Jure Vidmar, Sarah McGibbon and Lea Raible (eds), *Research Handbook on Secession* (Edward Elgar 2022).

Neff, Stephen C, 'Jurisprudential Polyphony: The Three Variations on the Positivist Theme in the 19th Century' in Liber Amicorum and Peter Haggenmacher (eds), *The Roots of International Law* (Brill/Nijhoff 2014).

Okeke, Edward Chukwuemeke, 'Legal Status of International Organizations' in *Jurisdictional Immunities of States and International Organizations* (New York 2018).

Peters, Anne, 'Statehood after 1989: "Effectivités" between Legality and Virtuality' in James Crawford and Sarah Nouwen (eds), *Select Proceedings of the European Society of International Law* (OUP 2012).

Randelzhofer, Albrecht and Oliver Dörr, 'Article 2(4)' in Bruno Simma and others (eds), The Charter of the United Nations: A commentary (OUP 2012).

Ryngaert, Cedric, 'The concept of jurisdiction in international law' in Alexander Orakhelashvili (ed), *Research Handbook on Jurisdiction and Immunities in International Law* (Edward Elgar 2015).

Ryngaert, Cedric, 'Jurisdiction' in Jean d'Aspremont and Sahib Singh (eds), *Concepts for International Law* (Edward Elgar 2019).

Shah, Niaz A, 'The "Unwilling" and "Unable" Test in International Law: The Use of Force against Non-State Actors in Pakistan and Afghanistan' in Javaid Rehman, Ayesha Shahid, and Steve Foster (eds), *The Asian Yearbook of Human Rights and Humanitarian Law* (Nijhoff/Brill 2020).

Spencer, John R, 'Tortious Liability for Criminal Acts' in Matthew Dyson (ed), *Unravelling Tort and Crime* (CUP 2014).

Talmon, Stefan, 'State Jurisdiction and Immunities' in Stefan Talmon (ed. *German Practice in International Law: 2019* (CUP 2019).

Talmon, Stefan, 'The Duty Not to "Recognize as Lawful" a Situation Created by the Illegal Use of Force or Other Serious Breaches of a Jus Cogens Obligation: An Obligation without Real Substance?' in Christian Tomuschat and Jean-Marc Thouvenin (eds), *The Fundamental Rules of the International Legal Order* (Brill/Nijhoff 2006).

Trapp, Kimberley, 'Can Non-State Actors Mount an Armed Attack?' in Marc Weller (ed), *The Oxford Handbook on the Use of Force* (OUP 2015).

Trifunovska, Snezana, 'The Badinter Commission' in Snezana Trifunovska (ed), *Yugoslavia through Documents: From its Creation to its Dissolution* (Nijhof 1994).

Vidmar, Jure, 'Dissolution of States' in Jure Vidmar, Sarah McGibbon, and Lea Raible (eds), *Research Handbook on Secession* (Edgar Elgar 2022).

Vidmar, Jure, 'International Organizations and Non-State Territorial Entities' in Benedikt C. Harzl and Roman Petrov (eds), *Unrecognized Entities* (Brill Nijhoff 2022).

Vidmar, Jure, 'Kosovo: Unilateral Secession and Multilateral State-Making' in Summers (ed), *Kosovo: A Precedent? The Declaration of Independence, the Advisory Opinion and Implications for Statehood, Self-Determination and Minority Rights* (Nijhoff 2011).

Vidmar, Jure, 'Unilateral Declarations of Independence in International Law' in Duncan French (ed), *Statehood and Self-Determination Reconciling Tradition and Modernity in International Law* (CUP 2013).

Weber, Max, 'Politics as a Vocation' in Tony Waters, and Dagmar Waters (eds), *Weber's Rationalism and Modern Society* (Springer 2015).

JOURNAL ARTICLES

Alvarez, José, 'Are Corporations "Subjects" of International Law?' (2011) 11 *Santa Clara Journal of International Law*.

Anghie, Antony, 'The Evolution of International Law: Colonial and Postcolonial Realities' (2006) 27 *Third World Quarterly* 739.

Arif, Sardar M. A. Waqar Khan, 'Legitimacy of Right to Self-Determination Under International Law' (2019) 7(1) *Pakistan Journal of Humanities and Social Sciences* 15.

Aust, Helmut, 'Fundamental Rights of States: Constitutional Law in Disguise?' (2015) 4(3) *Cambridge Journal of International and Comparative Law* 521.

Berman, Paul Schiff, 'The Globalization of Jurisdiction' (2002) 151 *University of Pennsylvania Law Review* 311.

Beyene, Temesgen Sisay, 'Declaration of Statehood by Somaliland and the Effects of Non-Recognition under International Law' (2019) 10(1) *Beijing Law Review* 196.

Blomley, Nicholas, 'The Territorialization of Property in Land: Space, Power and Practice' (2019) 7(2) *Territory, Politics, Governance* 233.

Bodiford, Andrew, 'Cities in International Law: Reclaiming Rights as Global Custom' (2020) 23(1) *City University of New York Law Review* 1.

Brigham, Albert Perry, 'Principles in the Determination of Boundaries' (1919) 7(4) *Geographical Review* 201.

Calafus, Sorin, 'The Opposability of the Effects of the Contract on Third Parties' (2019) 19(1) *Ovidius University Annals* 148.

Cassese, Antonio, 'The Nicaragua and Tadić Tests Revisited in Light of the ICJ Judgment on Genocide in Bosnia' (2007) 18(4) *European Journal of International Law* 649.

Castellino, Joshua, 'The Secession of Bangladesh in International Law: Setting New Standards?' (1997) 7 *Asian Yearbook of International Law* 83.

Cerone, John, 'Legal Implications of the UN General Assembly Vote to Accord Palestine the Status of Observer State' (2012) 16 *American Society of International Law* 7, www.asil.org/insights/volume/16/issue/37/legal-implications-un-general-assembly-vote-ccord-palestine-status, accessed 3 December 2022.

Chan, P.C.W, 'The Legal Status of Taiwan and the Legality of the Use of Force in a Cross-Taiwan Strait Conflict' (2010) 8 *Chinese Journal of International Law* 455.

Chen, Lung-chu, 'Taiwan's Current International Legal Status' (1998) 689 *Articles & Chapters*.

Cohen, Rosalyn, 'The Concept of Statehood in United Nations Practice' (1961) 109(8) *University of Pennsylvania Law Review* 1127.

Coppieters, Bruno, 'Abkhazia, Transnistria and North Cyprus: Recognition and Non-Recognition in Ceasefire and Trade Agreements' (2021) 226 *Post-Soviet Secessionism: Nation Building and State-Failure after Communism* 15.

Craven, Matthew C. R, 'What's in a Name? The Former Yugoslav Republic of Macedonia and Issues of Statehood' (1995) 16 *Australian Yearbook of International Law* 199.

Crawford, James, 'The Creation of the State of Palestine: Too Much Too Soon?' (1990) 1 *European Journal of International Law* 307.

Cullen, Anthony and Wheatley, Steven, 'The Human Rights of Individuals in De Facto Regimes under the European Convention on Human Rights' (2013) 13(4) *Human Rights Law Review* 691.

Custers, Peter, 'Maulana Bhashani and the Transition to Secular Politics in East Bengal' (2010) 47(2) *Indian Economic and Social History Review* 231.

D'Aspremont, Jean, 'The Doctrine of Fundamental Rights of States and Anthropomorphic Thinking in International Law' (2015) 4 *Cambridge Journal of International and Comparative Law* 501.

Daugirdas, Kristina, 'How and Why International Law Binds International Organizations' (2016) 57(2) *Harvard International Law Journal* 325.

De Wet, Erika, 'The Modern Practice of Intervention by Invitation in Africa and Its Implications for the Prohibition of the Use of Force' (2016) 26(4) *European Journal of International Law* 980.

Del Pilar Peña-Huertas, Rocío, Abondano-Romero, Alejandro, Abril-Bonilla, Natalia, Jiménez-Nicholls, María Camila, and Uribe-Larrota, Luisa Fernanda, 'Land Tenure Systems and Property Rights: Socio-legal Studies in the Colombian Case' (2018) 23(1–2) *Tilburg Law Review* 43.

Devine, Dermott J, 'The Requirements of Statehood Re-Examined' (1971) 34(4) *Modern Law Review* 410.

Downer, Joshua, 'Towards a Declaratory School of Government Recognition' (2021) 46 *Vanderbilt Law Review* 581.

Dumberry, Patrick, 'Remarks by Patrick Dumberry' (2013) 107 *Proceedings of Annual Meeting of the American Society of International Law* 213.

Elden, Stuart, 'Land, Terrain, Territory' (2010) 34(6) *Progress in Human Geography* 799.

Elden, Stuart, 'Thinking Territory Historically' (2010) 15 *Geopolitics* 757.

Engel, Christoph, 'The Emergence of a New Rule of Customary Law: An Experimental Contribution' (2011) 7(3) *Review of Law & Economics* 767.

Eze, Kenneth Uzor and Okeke, Godwin N, 'The Right of People to Self-Determination and the Principle of Non-Interference in the Domestic Affairs of States' (2013) 7(1) *National Academy of Legal Studies and Research Law Review* 145.

Ferraro, Tristan, 'Determining the Beginning and End of an Occupation under International Humanitarian Law' (2012) 94(885) *International Review of the Red Cross* 133.

Finck, Francois, 'The State Between Fact and Law: The Role of Recognition and the Conditions Under which it is Granted in the Creation of New States' (2016) 36 *Polish Yearbook of International Law* 51.

Fisher, Ryan, 'Defending Taiwan: Collective Self-Defense of a Contested State' (2020) 32(1) *Journal of International Law* 101.

Florea, Adrian, 'De Facto States in International Politics (1945–2011): A New Data Set' (2014) 40 *International Interactions* 788.

Fox, Gregory H, 'Self-Determination in the Post-Cold War Era: A New Internal Focus' (1995) 16(3) *Michigan Journal of International Law* 733.

Franck, Thomas and Rodley, Nigel, 'After Bangladesh: The Law of Humanitarian Intervention by Military Force' (1973) 67(2) *American Journal of International Law* 275.

Frowein, Jochen A, 'The United Nations and Non-Member States' (1970) 25(2) *International Journal* 333.

Galan, Alexis, 'New Wine, Old Wineskins: On the Geographical Assumptions of International Constitutional Law' (2016) 19(2) *Journal of International Relations and Development* 222.

Geiß, Robin, 'Russia's Annexation of Crimea: The Mills of International Law Grind Slowly but They Do Grind' (2015) 9 *International Law Studies* 425.

Grzybowski, Janis, 'To Be or Not to Be: The Ontological Predicament of State Creation in International Law' (2017) 28(2) *European Journal of International Law* 416.

Gunter, Michael M, 'Switzerland and the United Nations' (1976) 30(1) *International Organization* 129.

Guzman, Andrew, 'International Organizations and the Frankenstein Problem' (2013) 24 *European Journal of International Law* 999.

Hasnaoui, Yasmine, 'Morocco and the African Union: A New Chapter for Western Sahara Resolution?' (2017) *Arab Center for Research and Policy Studies* 1.

Heintze, Hans-Joachim, 'Are De Facto Regimes Bound by Human Rights?' (2009) *Organization for Security and Co-operation in Europe Yearbook* 267.

Hillgruber, Christian, 'The Admission of New States to the International Community' (1998) 9 *European Journal of International Law* 491.

Himmer, Susan, 'The Achievement of Independence in the Baltic States and Its Justifications' (1992) 6 *Emory International Law Review* 253.

Honig, Friedrich, 'International Law and the Transfer of Mandated Territories' (1936) 18(4) *Journal of Comparative Legislation and International Law* 204.

Ijalaye, David, 'Was "Biafra" at Any Time a State in International Law?' (1971) 65 *American Journal of International Law* 551.

Islami, Iliriana and Istrefi, Remzije, 'Consolidation of Statehood through Membership in the UN: Some Remarks on Kosovo, Democracy and International Law' (2018) 43 *Review of Central and East European Law* 331.

Jones, Natalie, 'Self-Determination and the Right of Peoples to Participate in International Law-Making' (2021) *British Yearbook of International Law* 1.

Jorgensen, Feride Asli Ergul and Latif, Dilek, 'Different than us? Reciprocal perceptions of the societies in Turkey and North Cyprus' (2022) 27(3) *Mediterranean Politics* 369.

Juss, Satvinder S, 'Nationality Law, Sovereignty, and the Doctrine of Exclusive Domestic Jurisdiction' (1994) 9(2) *Florida Journal of International Law* 219.

Kalicka-Mikolajczyk, Adriana, 'The International Legal Status of Western Sahara' (2020) 18(4) *Opole Studies in Administration and Law* 35.

Kaushal, Asha, 'The Politics of Jurisdiction' (2015) 78(5) *Modern Law Review* 759.

Kelsen, Hans, 'Recognition in International Law: Theoretical Observations' (1941) 35(1) *American Journal of International Law* 605.

Klabbers, Jan, 'The EJIL Foreword: The Transformation of International Organizations Law' (2015) 26(1) *European Journal of International Law* 9.

Klabbers, Jan, 'Reflections on Role Responsibility: The Responsibility of International Organizations for Failing to Act' (2017) 28(4) *European Journal of International Law* 1133.

Knight, David B, 'The Middle East and the Emerging New World Order' (1992) 28(3) *GeoJournal* 311.

Kochenov, Dimitry, 'Monitoring and Enforcement of the Rule of Law in the EU: Rhetoric and Reality' (2015) 11(3) *European Constitutional Law Review* 512.

Kontorovich, Eugene, 'International Responses to Territorial Conquest' (2008) 102 *Proceedings of the Annual Meeting (American Society of International Law)* 437.

Kritsiotis, Dino, 'Public International Law and Its Territorial Imperative' (2009) 30 *Michigan Journal of International Law* 547.

Kritsiotis, Dino, 'The Kosovo Crisis and NATO's Application of Armed Force against the Federal Republic of Yugoslavia' (2000) 49(2) *International and Comparative Law Quarterly* 330.

Kukathas, Chandran, 'A Definition of the State' (2014) 33(2) *University of Queensland Law Journal* 357.

Lanovoy, Vladyslav, 'The Use of Force by Non-State Actors and the Limits of Attribution of Conduct' (2017) 28(2) *European Journal of International Law* 563.

Linebarger, Paul M.A, 'The Republic of China on Taiwan: A Descriptive Appraisal' (1963) 126(1) *World Affairs* 5.

Lobban, Richard, 'Guinea-Bissau: September 1973 and Beyond' (1974) 21(1) *Africa Today* 15.

Loughlin, Martin, 'The Erosion of Sovereignty' (2016) 45(2) *Netherlands Journal of Legal Philosophy* 57.
Lulic, Mira and Muhvic, Davor, 'International Law and Cyprus Problem' (2009) 2 *Contemporary Legal and Economic Issues* 65.
Marks, Susan, 'State-Centrism, International Law, and the Anxieties of Influence' (2006) 19(2) *Leiden Journal of International Law* 339.
McCorquodale, Robert, 'An Inclusive International Legal System' (2004) 17 *Leiden Journal of International Law* 477.
McCorquodale, Robert, 'Diversity and Self-determination in International Law' (2003) 74(1) *British Yearbook of International Law* 451.
McCorquodale, Robert, 'Self-Determination: A Human Rights Approach' (1994) 43 *International and Comparative Law Quarterly* 857.
McCorquodale, Robert and Pangalangan, Raul, 'Pushing Back the Limitations of Territorial Boundaries' (2001) 12(5) *European Journal of International Law* 867.
McGibbon, Sarah, 'The "Unwilling or Unable" Doctrine Unmasked: A Case Study on ISIL and Syria' (2019) 32 *Hague Yearbook of International Law* 69.
Medeiros, Eduardo, 'Territorial Cohesion: An EU concept' (2016) 60 *European Journal of Spatial Development* 1.
Meester, Daniel H, 'The International Court of Justice's *Kosovo* Advisory Opinion: Assessing the Current State of International Legal Opinion on Remedial Secession' (2016) 48 *Canadian Yearbook of International Law* 215.
Meydan, Vildan, 'A Paradox of International (Non)Recognition: The Relationship Between De Facto States and Patron States' (2018) 1(1) *International Journal of Economics Politics Humanities and Social Sciences* 1.
Milanovic, Marko, 'Al-Skeini and Al-Jedda in Strasbourg' (2012) 23(1) *European Journal of International Law* 121.
Milanovic, Marko, 'Special Rules of Attribution of Conduct in International Law' (2020) 96 *International Law Studies* 295.
Milanovic, Marko, 'State Responsibility for Genocide' (2006) 17(3) *European Journal of International Law* 553.
Miller, John DB, 'Sovereignty as a Source of Vitality for the State' (1986) 12 *Review of International Studies* 57.
Miller, Russell, 'Self-Determination in International Law and the Demise of Democracy' (2003) 41 *Columbia Journal of Transnational Law* 601.
Mitchell, Ryan, 'Manchukuo's Contested Sovereignty: Legal Activism, Rights Consciousness, and Civil Resistance in a Puppet State' (2016) 3 *Asian Journal of Law and Society* 351.
Moscoso de la Cuba, Pablo, 'The Statehood of 'Collapsed' States in Public International Law' (2011) 18(29) *Agenda Internacional* 121.
Mower, Alfred G, 'Observer Countries: Quasi Members of the United Nations' (1966) 20(2) *International Organization* 266.
Mutiti, M. Aaron Benjamin, 'Rhodesia and Her Four Discriminatory Constitutions' (1974) 4(2) *African Review: A Journal of African Politics, Development and International Affairs* 259.
Nagan, Winston P, and Haddad, Alitza M, 'Recognition of Palestinian Statehood: A Clarification of the Interests of the Concerned Parties' (2012) 40 *Georgia Journal of International & Comparative Law* 343.
Neff, Stephen, 'The Dormancy, Rise and Decline of Fundamental Liberties of States' (2016) 4 *Cambridge Journal of International and Comparative Law* 482.
Newman, Edward and Visoka, Gëzim, 'The Foreign Policy of State Recognition: Kosovo's Diplomatic Strategy' (2018) 14 *Foreign Policy Analysis* 387.
Nguyen, Quoc Tan Trung, 'Does International Law Protect Taiwan?' (2022) 2(14) *United States Asia Law Institute Perspectives* 2.
Nyangaga, Joseph Ooko, 'The Doctrine of Occupation through "Terra Nullius" as a Right of Self-Determination of Peoples and the Legal Status of "Liberland" Territory under International Law' (2022) 13(1) *Beijing Law Review* 119.

Okonta, Ike and Meagher, Kate, 'Legacies of Biafra: violence, identity and citizenship in Nigeria – introduction' (2009) 34(1) *Africa Development* 1.
Orakhelashvili, Alexander, 'Statehood, Recognition and the United Nations System: A Unilateral Declaration of Independence in Kosovo' (2008) 12 Max Planck Yearbook of United Nations Law.
Osterland, Holly A, 'National Self-Determination and Secession: The Slovak Model' (1993) 25(3) *Case Western Reserve Journal of International Law* 655.
Paddeu, Federica I, 'Self-Defence as a Circumstance Precluding Wrongfulness: Understanding Article 21 of the Articles on State Responsibility' (2015) 85(1) *British Yearbook of International Law* 90.
Peters, Anne, 'Statehood after 1989: "Effectivités" between Legality and Virtuality' (2010) 3 *Proceedings of the European Society of International Law* 1.
Qureshi, Waseem Ahmad, 'Applicability of International Humanitarian Law to Non-State Actors' (2019) 17(1) *Santa Clara Journal of International Law* 1.
Ratner, Steven, 'Drawing a Better Line: Uti Possidetis and the Borders of New States' (1996) 90 *American Journal of International Law* 590.
Reid-Henry, Simon, 'The Territorial Trap: Fifteen Years On', (2011) 15 *Geopolitics* 752.
Rich, Roland, 'Recognition of States: The Collapse of Yugoslavia and the Soviet Union' (1993) 4 *European Journal of International Law* 36.
Rickart, Alexandra, 'Emerging Issues: To Be or Not to Be, That Is the Statehood Question' (2015) 3(2) *University of Baltimore Journal of International Law* 145.
Ronen, Yael, 'Israel, Palestine and the ICC – Territory Uncharted but not Unknown' (2014) 12(1) *Journal of International Criminal Justice* 7.
Ryngaert, Cedric, 'Attributing Conduct in the Law of State Responsibility: Lessons from Dutch Courts Applying the Control Standard in the Context of International Military Operations' (2021) 36 *Utrecht Journal of International and European Law* 170.
Ryngaert, Cedric, 'Non-State Actors in International Law: A Rejoinder to Professor Thirlway' (2017) 64 *Netherlands International Law Review* 155.
Ryngaert, Cedric, 'The Legal Status of the Holy See' (2011) 3 *Goettingen Journal of International Law* 829.
Ryngaert, Cedric, and Siccama, Duco W Hora, 'Ascertaining Customary International Law: An Inquiry into the Methods Used by Domestic Courts' (2018) 65 *Netherlands International Law Review* 1.
Sassoli, Marco, 'State Responsibility for Violations of International Humanitarian Law' (2002) 84(846) *International Review of the Red Cross* 401.
Schwebel, Stephen M, 'The Effect of Resolutions of the U.N. General Assembly on Customary International Law Proceedings of the Annual Meeting' (1979) 73 *American Society of International Law* 301.
Seiler, John, 'South Africa in Namibia: Persistence, Misperception, and Ultimate Failure' (1982) 20(4) *Journal of Modern African Studies* 689.
Senese, Salvatore, 'External and Internal Self-Determination' (1989) 16(1) *Social Justice* 19.
Shah, Nisha, 'The Territorial Trap of the Territorial Trap: Global Transformation and the Problem of the State's Two Territories' (2012) 6(1) *International Political Sociology* 57.
Shaw, Malcom N, 'Peoples, Territorialism and Boundaries' (1997) 8(3) *European Journal of International Law* 478.
Shraga, Daphna, 'The ILC Draft Articles on Responsibility of International Organizations: The Interplay Between the Practice and the Rule' (2011) 105 *Harmony and Dissonance in International Law* 351.
Simpson, Gerry, 'MABO, International Law, Terra Nullius and the Stories of Settlement: An Unresolved Jurisprudence' (1993) 19 *Melbourne Law Review* 195.
Smith, Mark, 'Sovereignty Over Unoccupied Territories-The Western Sahara Decision' (1977) 9 *Case Western Reserve Journal of International Law* 135.
Soja, Edward, 'The Political Organization of Space' (1971) 8 Commission on College Geography Resource Paper, Washington D.C, Association of American Geographers.

Spencer, Charles S, 'Territorial Expansion and Primary State Formation' (2010) 107(16) *Proceedings of the National Academy of Sciences* 119.

Sterio, Milena, 'The Case of Kosovo: Self-Determination, Secession, and Statehood Under International Law' (2010) 104 *Proceedings of the Annual Meeting* 361.

Stilz, Anna, 'Why Do States Have Territorial Rights?' (2009) 1(2) *International Theory* 185.

Stimson, Henry, 'Stimson Note' (Reprinted 1932) 26 *American Journal of International Law* 342.

Storey, David, 'States, Territory and Sovereignty' (2017) 102(3) Geography 116.

Talmon, Stefan, 'Determining Customary International Law: The ICJ's Methodology between Induction, Deduction and Assertion' (2015) 26 *European Journal of International Law* 417.

Talmon, Stefan, 'The Constitutive Versus the Declaratory Theory of Recognition: Tertium non Datur?' (2005) 75 *British Yearbook of International Law* 1.

Talmon, Stefan, 'The Responsibility of Outside Powers for Acts of Secessionist Entities' (2009) 58(3) *International and Comparative Law Quarterly* 493.

Tassinis, Orfeas Chasapis, 'Customary International Law: Interpretation from Beginning to End' (2020) 31(1) *European Journal of International Law* 235.

Tataryn, Anastasia, Ertürk, Erdem, 'Unrecognised States: The Necessary Affirmation of the Event of International Law' (2021) 32 *Law Critique* 331.

Tierney, Stephen, 'Legal Issues Surrounding the Referendum on Independence for Scotland' (2013) 9(4) *European Constitutional Law Review* 359.

Tsagourias, Nicholas, 'Self-Defence against Non-state Actors: The Interaction between Self-Defence as a Primary Rule and Self-Defence as a Secondary Rule' (2016) 29(3) *Leiden Journal of International Law* 801.

Tse-shyang, Chen Frederick, 'The Meaning of States in the Membership Provisions of the United Nations Charter' (2001) 12(1) *Indiana International and Comparative Law Review* 25.

Van Essen, Jonte, 'De Facto Regimes in International Law' (2012) 28(74) *Merkourios* 31.

Vaughan, Lowe, 'Precluding Wrongfulness or Responsibility: A Plea for Excuses' (1999) 10 *European Journal of International Law* 405.

Vidmar, Jure, 'Conceptualizing Declarations of Independence in International Law' (2012) 32(1) *Oxford Journal of Legal Studies* 153.

Vidmar, Jure, 'Remedial Secession in International Law: Theory and (Lack of) Practice' (2010) 6(1) *St Antony's International Review* 37.

Vidmar, Jure, 'Territorial Integrity and the Law of Statehood' (2013) 44 *George Washington International Law Review* 132.

Vidmar, Jure, 'The Annexation of Crimea and the Boundaries of the Will of the People' (2014) 16 *German Law Journal* 365.

Vidmar, Jure, 'The Kosovo Advisory Opinion Scrutinized' (2011) 24(2) *Leiden Journal of International Law* 355.

Vidmar, Jure, 'The Use of Force and Defences in the Law of State Responsibility' (2015) Jean Monnet Working Paper 08/15.

Visser, Laura, 'Intervention by Invitation and Collective Self-Defence: Two Sides of the Same Coin?' 7(2) *Journal on the Use of Force* 292.

Wählisch, Martin, 'Beyond a Seat in the United Nations: Palestine's U.N. Membership and International Law' (2012) 53 *Harvard International Law Journal* 226.

Wang, Tay-sheng, 'The Legal Development of Taiwan in the 20th Century: Toward a Liberal and Democratic Country' (2002) 11 *Pacific Rim Law & Policy Journal* 531.

Warbrick, Colin, 'Kosovo: The Declaration of Independence' (2008) 57(3) *International and Comparative Law Quarterly* 675.

Warbrick, Colin, 'Recognition of States' (1992) 41 *International and Comparative Law Quarterly* 473.

Weller, Marc, 'Modesty Can Be a Virtue: Judicial Economy in the ICJ *Kosovo* Opinion' (2011) 24(1) *Leiden Journal of International Law* 127.

Wilson, Gary, 'Self-determination, Recognition and the Problem of Kosovo Gary Wilson' (2009) 56(3) *Netherlands International Law Review* 455.

Winkler, Sigrid, 'Mainland China and Taiwan Face to Face in the WTO: A 10-Year Rollercoaster Ride' (2013)(3–4) 41 *Asian Journal of Social Science* 287.

Worster, William, 'Functional Statehood in Contemporary International Law' (2020) 46(1) *Brooklyn Journal of International Law* 39.

Worster, William, 'Relative International Legal Personality of Non-State Actors' (2016) 42(1) *Brooklyn Journal of International Law* 207.

Worster, William, 'Territorial Status Triggering a Functional Approach to Statehood' (2020) 8(1) *Penn State Journal of Law & International Affairs* 118.

Wun, Ryal, 'Beyond Traditional Statehood Criteria: The Law and Contemporary Politics of State Creation' (2013) 26 *Hague Yearbook of International Law* 316.

Yusuf, Abdulqawi A, 'Government Collapse and State Continuity: The Case of Somalia' (2003) 13(1) *Italian Yearbook of International Law Online* 11.

PHD THESES

Jorritsma, Remy, *International Responsibility and Attribution of Conduct: An Analysis of Case Law on Human Rights and Humanitarian Law* (PhD thesis, University of Maastricht, 2021).

Vagias, Michail, *The Territorial Jurisdiction of the International Criminal Court: Certain Contested Issues*, (PhD thesis, Universiteit Leiden, 2011).

ONLINE PUBLICATIONS

Alcalde, Javier and Aguiar, Pablo, 'Catalan Sovereignty in Practice' (*PRIO Paper*, 2017) www.prio.org/publications/9319, accessed 15 December 2022.

Ambos, Kai, 'Palestine, UN Non-Member Observer Status and ICC Jurisdiction' (*EJIL:Talk!*, 6 May 2014) www.ejiltalk.org/palestine-un-non-member-observer-status-and-icc-jurisdiction, accessed 22 November 2022.

Banerjee, Arpan, 'Moroccan Entry to the African Union and the Revival of the Western Sahara Dispute' (*Harvard International Law Journal*) harvardilj.org/2017/12/moroccan-entry-to-the-african-union-and-the-revival-of-the-western-sahara-dispute, accessed 6 January 2022.

Buchholz, Katharina, 'Kosovo & Beyond: Where The UN Disagrees On Recognition' (*Forbes*, 17 February 2022) www.forbes.com/sites/katharinabuchholz/2023/02/17/kosovo--beyond-where-the-un-disagrees-on-recognition-infographic/?sh=4f40a55f448c, accessed 22 October 2022.

Carley, Patricia, 'Self-Determination, Sovereignty, Territorial Integrity, and the Right to Secession' (*United States Institute of Peace*, 1996) www.usip.org/sites/default/files/pwks7.pdf, accessed 17 October 2022.

Carranco, Rebeca, 'Spain's Constitutional Court Strikes Down Catalan Referendum Law' (El Pais, 17 October 2017) english.elpais.com/elpais/2017/10/17/inenglish/1508250970_489373.html, accessed 8 December 2022.

Chachko, Elena and Deeks, Ashley, 'Which States Support the "Unwilling and Unable" Test?' (*LawFare*, 10 October 2016) www.lawfareblog.com/which-states-support-unwilling-and-unable-test, accessed 3 October 2022.

Charalambous, Annie, 'Political controversy in northern Cyprus over proposed name change of breakaway state' (*InCyprus*, 23 February 2023) in-cyprus.philenews.com/news/local/political-controversy-in-northern-cyprus-over-proposed-name-change-of-breakaway-state, accessed 2 January 2022.

Choi, Jieun, 'The Costs of Not Being Recognized as a country: The Case of Kosovo' (*Brookings*, 16 November 2017) www.brookings.edu/blog/future-development/2017/11/16/the-costs-of-not-being-recognized-as-a-country-the-case-of-kosovo, accessed 3 December 2022.

Dahmani, Youssef, '12 November 1984: When Morocco withdrew from the Organization of African Unity' (*Yabiladi*, 13 November 2017) en.yabiladi.com/articles/details/59322/november-1984-when-morocco-withdrew.html, accessed 12 May 2022.

Desierto, Diane, 'Non-Recognition' (*EJIL:Talk!*, 22 February 2022) www.ejiltalk.org/non-recognition, accessed 3 March 2022.

Dewan, Angela, Cotovio, Vasco and Clarke, Hilary, 'Catalonia independence referendum: What just happened?' (*CNN*, 2 October 2017) edition.cnn.com/2017/10/02/europe/catalonia-independence-referendum-explainer/index.html, accessed 14 August 2022.

Fetahu, Arbër, 'Kosovo's Accession to UN Specialized Agencies: What's at stake after the moratorium?' (*Group for Legal and Political Studies*, 8 October 2021) www.legalpoliticalstudies.org/kosovos-accession-to-un-specialized-agencies-whats-at-stake-after-the-moratorium, accessed 31 October 2022.

Hersi, Mohamed Farah, 'Research Guide to the Somaliland Legal System' (*NYU Law*, February 2009) www.nyulawglobal.org/globalex/Somaliland.html, accessed 18 November 2022.

Hoehne, Di Markus Virgil, 'Somaliland: 30 Years of De Facto Statehood, and No End In Sight' (*ISPI*, 7 May 2021) www.ispionline.it/en/publication/somaliland-30-years-de-facto-statehood-and-no-end-sight-30363, accessed 17 November 2022.

Istrefi, Kushtrim, 'The Luxembourg Court Rules on the Difference between States and Countries as International Law Actors' (*EJIL:Talk!*, 27 November 2020), www.ejiltalk.org/the-luxembourg-court-rules-on-the-difference-between-states-and-countries-as-international-law-actors, accessed 31 August 2022.

Kattan, Victor, 'It's Time to Take Palestine v. United States of America Seriously' (*Opinio Juris*, 16 October 2018) opiniojuris.org/2018/10/16/its-time-to-take-palestine-v-united-states-of-america-seriously, accessed 8 June 2022.

Kay, Steven and Kern, Joshua, 'The Statehood of Palestine and Its Effect on the Exercise of ICC Jurisdiction' (*Opinio Juris*, 5 July 2019) opiniojuris.org/2019/07/05/the-statehood-of-palestine-and-its-effect-on-the-exercise-of-icc-jurisdiction%EF%BB%BF, accessed 15 December 2022.

Krisch, Nico, 'Crimea and the Limits of International Law' (*EJIL:Talk!*, 10 March 2014) www.ejiltalk.org/crimea-and-the-limits-of-international-law, accessed 8 November 2022.

Kohen, Marcelo, 'Conquest' (*Max Planck Encyclopedia*) opil.ouplaw.com/display/10.1093/law:epil/9780199231690/law-9780199231690-e275, accessed 3 January 2023.

Lath, Adhiraj and Jena, Abhinav, 'The Lauterpacht Doctrine: An Objective Attempt Towards State Recognition?' (*Berkeley Journal of International Law*, 31 January 2021) www.berkeleyjournalofinternationallaw.com/post/the-lauterpacht-doctrine-an-objective-attempt-towards-state-recognition, accessed 7 October 2022.

Leith, Murray Stewart and Sim, Duncan, 'A Second Scottish Independence Referendum: Should the Diaspora get a Vote?' (*Political Quarterly*, 18 March 2023) https://politicalquarterly.org.uk/blog/a-second-scottish-independence-referendum-should-the-diaspora-get-a-vote/, accessed 19 March 2023.

Longobardo, Marco, 'Preliminary but Necessary: The Question of the Applicability of the Notion of Apartheid to Occupied Territory' (*Just Security*, 2 December 2021) www.justsecurity.org/79381/preliminary-but-necessary-the-question-of-the-applicability-of-the-notion-of-apartheid-to-occupied-territory, accessed 17 December 2022.

Milanovic, Marko, 'Belgium's Article 51 Letter to the Security Council' (*EJIL:Talk!*, 17 June 2016) www.ejiltalk.org/belgiums-article-51-letter-to-the-security-council, accessed 15 June 2022.

Milanovic, Marko, 'Foreign Surveillance and Human Rights, Part 3: Models of Extraterritorial Application' (*EJIL:Talk!*, 27 November 2013) www.ejiltalk.org/foreign-surveillance-and-human-rights-part-3-models-of-extraterritorial-application, accessed 16 December 2022.

Milanovic, Marko, 'Georgia v. Russia No. 2: The European Court's Resurrection of Bankovic in the Contexts of Chaos' (*EJIL:Talk!*, 25 January 2021) www.ejiltalk.org/georgia-v-russia-no-2-the-european-courts-resurrection-of-bankovic-in-the-contexts-of-chaos, accessed 6 October 2022.

Milanovic, Marko, 'Palestine Sues the United States in the ICJ re Jerusalem Embassy' (*EJIL:Talk!*, 30 September 2018) www.ejiltalk.org/palestine-sues-the-united-states-in-the-icj-re-jerusalem-embassy, accessed 23 November 2022.

Milanovic, Marko, 'Recognition' (*EJIL:Talk!*, 21 February 2022) www.ejiltalk.org/recognition, accessed 3 March 2022.

Milanovic, Marko, 'The European Court's Admissibility Decision in Ukraine and the Netherlands v Russia: The Good, the Bad and the Ugly – Part I' (*EJIL:Talk!*, 26 January 2023) www.ejiltalk.org/the-european-courts-admissibility-decision-in-ukraine-and-the-netherlands-v-russia-the-good-the-bad-and-the-ugly-part-i, accessed 29 January 2023.

Millar, Daniel, 'The Kosovan Precedent for the Annexation of Crimea' (*E-International Relations*, 18 March 2019) www.e-ir.info/pdf/77881, accessed 15 October 2022.

Miron, Alina, 'Palestine's Application the ICJ, neither Groundless nor Hopeless. A Reply to Marko Milanovic' (*EJIL:Talk!*, 8 October 2018) www.ejiltalk.org/palestines-application-the-icj-neither-groundless-nor-hopeless-a-reply-to-marko-milanovic, accessed 19 October 2022.

Moore, Margaret, 'Territorial Rights and Territorial Justice' (*The Stanford Encyclopedia of Philosophy*, 2020) plato.stanford.edu/archives/sum2020/entries/territorial-rights, accessed 22 August 2022.

Öztürk, Mustafa Talha, 'Serbia must seek a compromise because it cannot prevent Kosovo's entry into NATO and Council of Europe, says Serbian president' (*Vucic*, 24 January 2023) www.aa.com.tr/en/europe/eus-plan-for-kosovo-is-new-condition-for-serbias-integration-vucic/2795521, accessed 23 August 2022.

Pifer, Steven, 'Crimea: Six years after illegal annexation' (*Brookings*, 17 March 2020) www.brookings.edu/blog/order-from-chaos/2020/03/17/crimea-six-years-after-illegal-annexation, accessed 17 March 2022.

Psycharis, Matthew, 'What is the legal status of a referendum, and why bother holding one?' (*Constitutional Law Matters*, 25 July 2022) constitutionallawmatters.org/2022/07/what-is-the-legal-status-of-a-referendum-and-why-bother-holding-one, accessed 3 December 2022.

Radović, Relja, 'Kosovo and International Legal Personality' (*Opinio Juris*, 13 March 2023), opiniojuris.org/2023/03/13/kosovo-and-international-legal-personality, accessed 20 March 2023.

Ridderhof, Raymond, 'Catalonia's Referendum for Independence' (*Peace Palace Library*, 29 September 2017) peacepalacelibrary.nl/blog/2017/catalonias-referendum-independence, accessed 25 October 2022.

Sari, Aurel, 'Ukraine Insta-Symposium: When does the Breach of a Status of Forces Agreement amount to an Act of Aggression? The Case of Ukraine and the Black Sea Fleet SOFA' (*Opinio Juris*, 6 March 2014) www.opiniojuris.org/2014/03/06/ukraine-insta-symposium-breach-status-forces-agreement-amount-act-aggression-case-ukraine-black-sea-fleet-sofa, accessed 18 December 2022.

Sauer, Pjotr and Harding, Luke 'Putin annexes four regions of Ukraine in major escalation of Russia's war' (*The Guardian*, 30 September 2022) www.theguardian.com/world/2022/sep/30/putin-russia-war-annexes-ukraine-regions, accessed 2 October 2022.

Serhan, Yasmeen, 'Russia's Annexation of Ukrainian Territory Is a Sign of Military Weakness' (*Time*, 29 September 2022) time.com/6217710/russia-annexation-ukraine-donetsk-luhansk-kherson-aporizhzhia, accessed 19 December 2022.

Shaw, Malcolm N, 'In the Matter of the Jurisdiction of the International Criminal Court with regard to the Declaration of the Palestinian Authority, Supplementary Opinion' (ICC, 18 October 2010) www.icc-cpi.int/sites/default/files/NR/rdonlyres/D3C77FA6-9DEE-45B1-ACC0-B41706BB41E5/282851/OTP2010000035449SupplementaryOpinionMalcolmShaw.pdf accessed 13 November 2022.

Taylor, Helen, 'Catalan Independence: An international law perspective' (*Cambridge University Law Society*) www.culs.org.uk/per-incuriam/catalan-independence-an-international-law-perspective, accessed 31 January 2023.

Tucker, Andrew, 'Palestine vs USA – the ICJ should not allow itself to be used in lawfare against Israel' (*Thinc*) www.thinc.info/palestine-vs-usa-the-icj-should-not-allow-itself-to-be-used-in-lawfare-against-israel, accessed 14 October 2022.

Valero, Jorge, 'Independent observers: No proper referendum took place in Catalonia' (*Euroactiv*, 18 October 2017) www.euractiv.com/section/future-eu/news/independent-observers-no-referendum-took-place-in-catalonia, accessed 19 June 2021.

Vidmar, Jure, 'Crimea's Referendum and Secession: Why it Resembles Northern Cyprus More than Kosovo' (*EJIL:Talk!*, 20 March 2014) www.ejiltalk.org/crimeas-referendum-and-secession-why-it-resembles-northern-cyprus-more-than-kosovo, accessed 16 April 2022.

Vidmar, Jure, 'Democratic Statehood in International Law' (*EJIL:Talk!*, 6 August 2013) www.ejiltalk.org/democratic-statehood-in-international-law, accessed 5 January 2023.

Vidmar, Jure, 'Does General Assembly Resolution 67/19 Have Any Implications for the Legal Status of Palestine?' (*EJIL:Talk!*, 4 December 2012) www.ejiltalk.org/does-general-assembly-resolution-6719-have-any-implications-for-the-legal-status-of-palestine, accessed 27 March 2023.

Vidmar, Jure, 'Palestine v United States: Why the ICJ Does not Need to Decide Whether Palestine is a State' (*EJIL:Talk!*, 22 November 2018) www.ejiltalk.org/palestine-v-united-states-why-the-icj-does-not-need-to-decide-whether-palestine-is-a-state, accessed 13 September 2022.

Wagdy, Lilian and Najem, Lina, 'Syria recognizes independence, sovereignty of Donetsk, Luhansk -state news agency' (*Reuters*, 29 June 2022) www.reuters.com/world/middle-east/syria-recognizes-independence-sovereignty-donetsk-luhansk-state-news-agency-2022-06-29, accessed 18 September 2022.

Weiler, Joseph, 'Differentiated Statehood? "Pre-States"? Palestine@the UN' (*EJIL:Talk!*, 3 April 2013) www.ejiltalk.org/differentiated-statehood-pre-states-palestinethe-un, accessed 10 July 2021.

Zinets Natalia and Vasovic Aleksandar, 'Missiles rain down around Ukraine' (*Reuters*, 25 February 2022) www.reuters.com/world/europe/putin-orders-military-operations-ukraine-demands-kyiv-forces-surrender-2022-02-24, accessed 9 October 2022.

OTHER ONLINE SOURCES

'Abkommen zwischen den Regierungen des Vereinigten Königreiches, der Vereinigten Staaten von Amerika, der Union der Sozialistischen Sowjetrepubliken und der Französischen Republik über den Kontrollapparat in Österreich' (*UIBK*) www.uibk.ac.at/zeitgeschichte/zis/library/eisterer.html#dok2, accessed 3 November 2022.

'Abkommen über die Alliierte Kontrolle in Österreich Abkommen zwischen den Regierungen des Vereinigten Königreiches, der Vereinigten Staaten von Amerika, der Union der Sozialistischen Sowjetrepubliken und der Französischen Republik über den Kontrollapparat in Österreich' (*Verfassungen*) www.verfassungen.at/at45-/kontrollabkommen46.htm, accessed 3 December 2022.

'Agreement between the United Kingdom Government and the Scottish Government on a referendum on independence for Scotland' (*Parliament UK*, 15 October 2012) assets.publishing.service.gov.uk/government/uploads/system/uploads/attachment_data/file/313612/scottish_referendum_agreement.pdf, accessed 14 July 2023.

'Catalonia independence declaration signed and suspended' (*BBC*, 10 October 2017) www.bbc.com/news/world-europe-41574172, accessed 8 October 2022.

'Council of Europe membership: A good opportunity for improving human rights in Kosovo?' (*European Western Balkans*, 31 May 2022) europeanwesternbalkans.com/2022/05/31/council-of-europe-membership-a-good-opportunity-for-improving-human-rights-in-kosovo, accessed 15 September 2022.

'Crimea referendum: Voters back Russia union' (*BBC News*, 16 March 2014) www.bbc.com/news/world-europe-26606097, accessed 10 December 2022.

'Crimean parliament formally applies to join Russia' (*BBC News*, 17 March 2014) www.bbc.com/news/world-europe-26609667, accessed 13 December 2022.

'Customary Law' (*ICRC*) www.icrc.org/en/war-and-law/treaties-customary-law/customary-law#:~:text=Customary%20international%20law%20consists%20of,the%20protection%20offered%20to%20victims, accessed 14 November 2022.

'EU referendum: The result in maps and charts' (*BBC*, 8 June 2021) www.bbc.com/news/uk-politics-36616028, accessed 15 October 2021.

'Extra-territorial jurisdiction of States Parties to the European Convention on Human Rights' (*ECtHR*, July 2018) www.echr.coe.int/documents/fs_extra-territorial_jurisdiction_eng.pdf, accessed 7 January 2023.

'Full Text of Putin's Speech on Crimea' (*Prague Post*, 19 March 2014) www.praguepost.com/eu-news/37854-full-text-of-putin-s-speech-on-crimea, accessed 17 June 2022.

'General Assembly Decides to Remove East Timor from List of Non-Self-Governing Territories Upon Independence Set for 20 May' (*United Nations*, 1 May 2002) press.un.org/en/2002/GA10014.doc.htm, accessed 6 November 2021.

'Glossary of Industrial Organisation Economics and Competition Law' (*OECD*) www.concurrences.com/IMG/pdf/oecd_-_glossary_of_industrial_organisation_economics_and_competition_law.pdf?39924/61543ab059ef02f25a5b58d7b8b4636a8fe2232efa57c3b86700b24cdb1da9ca, accessed 23 February 2022.

'Guide on Article 10 of the European Convention on Human Rights' (*European Court of Human Rights*, 31 August 2020) www.echr.coe.int/Documents/Guide_Art_10_ENG.pdf, accessed 12 March 2023.

'Information for victims, State of Palestine' (*ICC*) www.icc-cpi.int/victims/state-palestine, accessed 30 October 2022.

'International Legal Personality' (*Icelandic Human Rights Centre*) www.humanrights.is/en/human-rights-education-project/human-rights-concepts-ideas-and-fora/human-rights-actors/international-legal-personality, accessed 7 March 2022.

'List of states that recognize Kosovo's independence' (*Kosovo Thanks You*) www.kosovothanksyou.com, accessed 7 December 2022.

'Member States' (*UNESCO*) en.unesco.org/countries/member-states, accessed 18 October 2022.

'Member States' (*United Nations*) www.un.org/en/about-us/member-states, accessed 30 October 2022.

'MH17 Malaysia plane crash: What we know' (*BBC News*, 14 October 2015) www.bbc.com/news/world-europe-28357880, accessed 26 May 2021.

'Negotiations and agreements' (*European Commission*) policy.trade.ec.europa.eu/eu-trade-relationships-country-and-region/negotiations-and-agreements_en, accessed 7 November 2022.

'Non-Self-Governing Territories' (*United Nations*) www.un.org/dppa/decolonization/en/nsgt, accessed 8 July 2022.

'Note to correspondents – Accession of Palestine to multilateral treaties' United Nations Secretary-General Statement' (*United Nations*, 7 January 2015) www.un.org/sg/en/content/sg/note-correspondents/2015-01-07/note-correspondents-accession-palestine-multilateral, accessed 21 March 2021.

'Organic Act 6/2006 of the 19th July, on the Reform of the Statute of Autonomy of Catalonia, art 65' (*Catalonian Parliament*, 19 Jul 2006) available at www.parlament.cat/document/cataleg/150259.pdf, accessed 12 October 2022.

'Palestine as a UN Observer State: Does this Make Palestine a State?' (*EJIL:Talk!*, 3 Dec 2012) www.ejiltalk.org/palestine-as-a-un-observer-state-does-this-make-palestine-a-state, accessed 23 February 2022.

'Petitioners Put Forward Different Views on Western Sahara as Fourth Committee Continues Decolonization Debate' (*United Nations*, 6 October 2022) press.un.org/en/2022/gaspd750.doc.htm, accessed 3 November 2022.

'Political Opinion Barometer. 1st wave 2019' (*Centre d'Estudis d' Opinio*, 2019) upceo.ceo.gencat.cat/wsceop/7008/Abstract%20in%20English%20-919.pdf, accessed 8 October 2022.

'President Omar al-Bashir gives South Sudan his blessing' (*BBC News*, 7 July 2011) www.bbc.co.uk/news/world-africa-14060475, accessed 7 December 2022.

'Press Briefing by Press Secretary Sarah Sanders, Small Business Administrator Linda McMahon, and National Security Advisor' (*The White House*, 3 October 2018) trumpwhitehouse.archives.gov/briefings-statements/press-briefing-press-secretary-sarah-sanders-small-business-administrator-linda-mcmahon-national-security-advisor-100318, accessed 7 January 2022.

'Report of the Steering Committee for Human Rights (CDDH) adopted at its 92nd meeting' (*ECHR*, 26 November 2019) www.echr.coe.int/LibraryDocs/COE-2020-The_place_of_the_ECHR_in_the_European_and_international_legal_order.pdf, accessed 13 December 2022.

'Saharawi Arab Democratic Republic' (*African Union*) au.int/en/countryprofiles/saharawi-arab-democratic-republic, accessed 19 August 2022.

'Scottish Independence Referendum Act 2013' (*Scottish Government*, 14 November 2013) www.scottish.parliament.uk/parliamentarybusiness/Bills/61076.aspx, accessed 30 October 2022.

'Separate Customs Territory of Taiwan, Penghu, Kinmen and Matsu (Chinese Taipei) and the WTO' (*WTO*) www.wto.org/english/thewto_e/countries_e/chinese_taipei_e.htm, accessed 5 March 2022.

'South Sudan counts down to independence' (*BBC News*, 8 July 2011) www.bbc.co.uk/news/world-africa-14077511, accessed 7 December 2022.

'Spain Catalonia: Court blocks independence referendum' (*BBC*, 8 September 2017) www.bbc.com/news/world-europe-41196677, accessed 9 October 2022.

'Staatsvertrag betreffend die Wiederherstellung eines unabhängigen und demokratischen Österreich' (*Rechtsinformationsystem*) www.ris.bka.gv.at/GeltendeFassung.wxe?Abfrage=Bundesnormen&Gesetzesnummer=10000265, accessed 14 December 2022.

'Summary of the Geneva Conventions of 1949 and their Additional Protocols' (*Red Cross*) www.redcross.org/content/dam/redcross/atg/PDF_s/International_Services/International_Humanitarian_Law/IHL_SummaryGenevaConv.pdf, accessed 5 January 2022.

'Taiwan in the Western Balkans: Low on the list of priorities' (*CEIAS Insights*, 7 February 2023) ceias.eu/taiwan-in-the-western-balkans-low-on-the-list-of-priorities/#:~:text=Both%20Kosovo%20and%20Taiwan%20do,just%2014%20countries%20in%20total, accessed 10 February 2023.

'The Comprehensive Peace Agreement of 2005' (*United Nations*) www.sd.undp.org/doc/CPA.pdf, accessed 8 December 2022.

'The EU and the WTO' (*European Commission*) policy.trade.ec.europa.eu/eu-trade-relationships-country-and-region/eu-and-wto_en, accessed 3 September 2022.

'The German-Soviet Non-Aggression Pact (The Ribbentrop-Molotov Pact)' (Geocities) www.geocities.com/iturks/html/ribbentrop_molotov_pact.html, accessed 8 December 2021.

'The Occupation of Western Sahara' (*Western Sahara Resource Watch*) wsrw.org/en/the-occupation-of-western-sahara, accessed 18 December 2022.

'The Scottish Independence Referendum Results 2014' (*Fife Council*) www.fife.gov.uk/kb/docs/articles/council-and-democracy/elections2/election-results/the-scottish-independence-referendum-results-2014, accessed 7 April 2016.

'Transcript of the MH17 judgment hearing' (*Rechtsafspraak*, 17 November 2022) www.courtmh17.com/en/news/2022/transcript-of-the-mh17-judgment-hearing.html, accessed 20 November 2022.

'Ukraine crisis: Protesters declare Donetsk republic' (*BBC News*, 7 April 2014) www.bbc.com/news/world-europe-26919928, accessed 16 January 2021.

'Ukraine cuts N Korea ties over recognition of separatist regions' (*AlJazeera*, 13 July 2022) www.aljazeera.com/news/2022/7/13/n-korea-recognises-breakaway-of-russias-proxies-in-east-ukraine, accessed 16 September 2022.

'Ukraine separatists declare independence' (*AlJazeera*, 12 May 2014) www.aljazeera.com/news/2014/5/12/ukraine-separatists-declare-independence, accessed 23 October 2022.

'UN decolonization successes can "inspire us today" UN chief tells Special Committee' (*UN News*, 21 February 2019) news.un.org/en/story/2019/02/1033231, accessed 7 December 2022.

'UN membership' (*Dag Hammarskjold library*) research.un.org/en/unmembers/founders, accessed 7 February 2023.

'UN Security Council Resolution on Ukraine' (*C-Span*, 15 March 2014) www.c-span.org/video/?318324-1/un-security-council-meeting-ukraine, accessed 13 December 2022.

'UNESCO votes to admit Palestine as full member' (*United Nations*, 31 October 2011) news.un.org/en/story/2011/10/393562, accessed 3 December 2021.

'United Nations Charter, Chapter XI: Declaration Regarding Non-Self-Governing Territories' (*United Nations*) www.un.org/en/about-us/un-charter/chapter-11, accessed 12 October 2022.

'Universal Jurisdiction Law and Practice in England and Wales' (*Redress*, May 2022) redress.org/wp-content/uploads/2022/05/UJ-Law-and-Practice-in-England-and-Wales.pdf, accessed 8 December 2022.

'52% of Catalans support independence from Spain, according to a Madrid-based media' (*Catalan News*, 11 September 2013) www.catalannews.com/politics/item/52-of-catalans-support-independence-from-spain-according-to-a-madrid-based-media, accessed 14 November 2022.

Index

www.ingramcontent.com/pod-product-compliance
Ingram Content Group UK Ltd.
Pitfield, Milton Keynes, MK11 3LW, UK
UKHW020257051026
15470UKWH00020B/946

9 781509 959488